OPEN AND

DISTANCE EDUCATION

IN THE

ASIA PACIFIC

REGION

Edited by
Olugbemiro Jegede
Glenn Shive

香港公開大學出版社
OPEN UNIVERSITY
OF HONG KONG PRESS

Editors: Olugbemiro Jegede
           Glenn Shive

Open University of Hong Kong Press
The Open University of Hong Kong
30 Good Shepherd Street
Ho Man Tin, Kowloon
Hong Kong
Fax: (852) 2396 5009
Email: etp@ouhk.edu.hk

ISBN: 962-7707-25-2

Printed in Hong Kong

Foreword

The phenomenal growth which open and distance education has continued to enjoy world-wide within the past few years, especially in Asia and the Pacific Rim, attests to its popularity and the importance attached to its role in nation building. For many developing economies such as we have in the region, open and distance education should meet the national development initiatives as well as adequately and appropriately address issues such as: access and equity, alleviation of capacity constraints, life-long and life-wide learning, and reduction of illiteracy and poverty.

This growing acceptance of open and distance education requires a number of imperatives. The two most important of these are the need for regular information about the status of open and distance education, and the need to base all development, planning and stock-taking on empirical data. Unfortunately, while the development and management of open and distance education appear to continually occupy the day-to-day activities of those in the field, very little attention is paid to research in open and distance education. Yet research is an incredibly important aspect of education, and indeed of all human endeavour, which many now see as the major factor which will dominate the future scene of open and distance education. Such research efforts should constantly be undertaken to inform and guide planning, management and design of open and distance education; at the very least they should provide the most recent and relevant information and data for public consumption.

It is in this regard that we should welcome the publication of this book as an informative source for open and distance education in the Asia Pacific. Apart from a similar joint publication ten years ago by the National Institute of Multimedia Education (NIME), Japan and the United Nations Education Scientific and Cultural Organisation (UNESCO), no other document as comprehensive has been published to inform on the development of open and distance education in Asia and the Pacific Rim. It is based on and arose out of a major regional research project undertaken by the Open University of Hong Kong's Centre for Research in Distance and Adult Learning (CRIDAL) on a comparative analysis of administrative styles, educational outcomes, and educational processes of open and distance education institutions in Asia. CRIDAL is a centre dedicated to research in open and distance education which, although only four years old, has continued to set an enviable pace for quality research in Asia.

I wish to place on record the OUHK's appreciation for the support received from the Fulbright Programme and Hong Kong American Education. I also must congratulate the authors and contributors for extending the NIME/ UNESCO study which was undertaken ten years ago.

This book is a richer, more comprehensive and up-to-date status of open and distance education in 20 countries in the Asia Pacific. I sincerely recommend it to all those who work in, or are interested in, the development of open and distance education in the Asia Pacific. No library can afford to miss this refreshingly rich and very current source of information from its collection. It gives me great pleasure, therefore, to invite you to savour the content of the book, which gives a panoramic view of open and distance education in today's Asia Pacific region.

Professor S W Tam
President, The Open University of Hong Kong
President, The Asian Association of Open Universities (AAOU)
Vice-President, The International Council for Open and Distance Education (ICDE)

March 2001

Preface

In the early 1990s, the National Institute for Multimedia Education (NIME) in Japan, in collaboration with UNESCO, conducted an extensive region-wide study of distance education in Asia and the Pacific. Their findings were published in five volumes, and included a survey of institutional profiles and a series of 20 country papers authored by leading practitioners and analysts in the field.

This prodigious research effort established a useful benchmark description of the nature and status of open and distance education (ODE) in the Asia Pacific region as the decade started. By then, the number of ODE programmes in the region had already grown and were serving millions of students seeking further education and credentials amid a remarkable period of economic and demographic expansion.

ODE has grown even more in the Asia Pacific region in the decade since the study. Demand for learning in Asian societies has outstripped the capacity of traditional delivery methods by universities. New programmes are now on offer in open universities and also as extension or continuing education services of 'dual-mode' and traditional universities. And shifts towards knowledge-based economies, new demand for skilled manpower, and innovations in the technologies of educational delivery have made ODE a highly dynamic area of the tertiary education sector in the Asia Pacific region.

This study, and the book that resulted from it, returns here, a decade later, to take stock of developments in ODE in the 1990s, and also to look ahead at trends and factors likely to shape ODE in the next decade. This project, based at the Centre for Research in Distance and Adult Learning of the Open University of Hong Kong, invited researchers and leading practitioners in the field from 20 Asian and Pacific countries and territories to comment on the status and the direction of ODE as they see them.

We asked them to consider, among other questions, what significant developments occurred in ODE in the Asia Pacific region during the 1990s; what factors will determine the nature and rate of growth for ODE in the next decade; and what policies and strategic initiatives are important to leaders of ODE in the region.

The country papers describe the general student profile and basic demographics for ODE; patterns in demand for learning and trends in labour markets; general course offerings through ODE; teaching staff characteristics; learning support and assessment services; programme management and quality control regimes for ODE; finance, cost controls and affordability of programmes; technologies in use and being developed; and patterns of international collaboration.

This collection of contributions from leading specialists and professionals in ODE in the region offers us an unprecedented range of unique and personal yet highly insightful views of the developments in ODE and the management of ODE programmes in their countries over the past decade, and their visions of ODE in their institutions and countries as well as world-wide in the new century. The book focuses on the implications for ODE programmes of a number of events and general trends over the 1990s. These have been:

- The region-wide economic downturn in the late 1990s;

- Wider diffusion and availability of low-cost communication technologies;

- Changing manpower demands, demographic trends, and credential culture in the Asia Pacific region;

- Greater internationalization in education in the Asia Pacific region.

These trends, as well as other themes to emerge from the individual papers, are discussed in the introductory chapter. This is followed by the country papers, which are clustered by region and by alphabet within region.

Three of the writers of country papers for the NIME project a decade ago have returned to write papers for this volume: Tom Prebble from New Zealand, Chaiyong Brahmawong from Thailand and Wong Suk-Ying, who contributed the Japan paper. All other authors of this volume are new. We appreciate both the voices of continuity and the fresh perspectives of the many new scholars who have entered this field over the past decade. Their brief biographical descriptions are included at the end of the volume. The editors thank the chapter writers for their contributions to this book, and for their patience and good faith over the course of the project.

The editors wish also to express their deep appreciation to the many other people and organizations that have helped to bring this ambitious project to fruition. The Open University of Hong Kong and its Centre for Research in Distance and Adult Education (CRIDAL) have been the core resource in the conception and implementation of this project. In support, the Fulbright Program also made available a grant that helped provide honoraria for the authors for their contributions to this project.

Special thanks go to Linda Chow, Tina Frow and Caroline Leung for their editorial work on this book, Clarence Fong and Jessie Yum for their assistance and Don Brech, Records Management International Limited, for compiling the index.

We conclude by reflecting on the enormous scale of this subject. These 20 countries and regions and the students within them constitute the proof of the success of ODE and its potential to be the future major source of an alternative and effective form of educational provision in the world. The efforts to extend access and assure quality of higher and further education to people on this scale must be commended. There will always be an important role for elite and campus-based higher education for school leavers in Asia. But the real growth in the next decade, and the area worthy of the investment of our collective moral, intellectual and economic resources is the delivery of quality, cost-effective education made accessible on a mass scale far beyond what we know today. While daunting, to be sure, the demographic and ecological trends in the region also make it necessary that we try.

GS and OJ

About the editors

 Prof. Olugbemiro Jegede is Chair Professor and Director of the Centre for Research in Distance & Adult Learning at the Open University of Hong Kong. He has over 170 publications to his name including books, journal articles and conference proceedings. He is Editor-in-Chief of the *Electronic Journal of Instructional Science and Technology* and an editorial board member of several international journals on distance education, educational research and science teaching. Prof. Jegede is Consultant to various international agencies including UNESCO, UNDP, the World Bank, and the Commonwealth of Learning.

Dr Glenn Shive, Fulbright scholar and former Director of the Board of Governors Program of Governor's State University in Illinois in the USA, is Director of the Hong Kong-America Center and is currently based at the Chinese University of Hong Kong. He has written numerous articles and papers for newsletters, journals, books, and proceedings of international conferences and seminars on education, technology, international exchanges, and US-East Asian relations. He was also responsible for editing the *North-South Scholarly Exchange* (London: Mansell, 1988).

Contents

South Asia

Pacific Rim

Introduction

Trends and issues in open and distance education in Asia and the Pacific

Glenn Shive and Olugbemiro Jegede

The focus in this book is on open and distance education (ODE), which has an emphasis on institutions and the pedagogical aspect of this system of education, rather than on open and distance learning (ODL), which emphasizes the learning or cognitive aspects of it.

Almost all the countries in Asia have at least an open university. The most distinctive feature of these universities is their huge student populations. For example, of the 11 mega-universities (universities with an enrolment of at least 100,000) that offer ODE in all parts of the world, seven are located in Asian countries: China, India, Indonesia, South Korea, Thailand, Iran and Turkey (Daniel 1998). The Asian region also has the largest number of adult learners enrolled in open and distance universities compared with other parts of the world. Amid Asia's vast population of three billion people, which is two-thirds of the global population, 500 million are potential students seeking continuing education opportunities. This implies an acute demand for open, distance and adult education in the Asian region (Tam 1999). India now has more than ten open universities, Iran has two, Vietnam has two, mainland China has a national network of 43 RTVU distance education universities and as many regional ones, and in some other countries the number of intakes doubles every year.

Many of these developments have occurred within the past ten years while copious more are taking place. This book, in broad terms, showcases the tremendous number and range of region-wide activities in open and distance learning witnessed in the Asia Pacific region as the 21st century begins. It follows, and attempts to fill, the information vacuum left after the 1991 UNESCO study conducted by the National Institute of Multimedia Education (NIME) of Japan (UNESCO-NIME 1991). In specific terms, this book provides profiles of 20 countries and regions of the Asia Pacific region: in Northeast Asia (Japan, Korea, China, Mongolia, Taiwan, Hong Kong), Southeast Asia (Vietnam, Thailand, Malaysia, Indonesia, Philippines), South Asia (India, Pakistan, Bangladesh, Sri Lanka) and the Pacific Rim (Australia, New Zealand, the United States, Canada and the island states of the South Pacific). An issue of concern to us has been the geographical definition of Asia and particularly the relationship between North American countries and Asia. It is generally known that Asia extends from Turkey to Japan, and the definition of the Pacific, as used in this book, reflects that of the Asia Pacific political groupings, thus including the South Pacific, Australia, New Zealand, Canada and the United States. While the argument as to the inclusion of the North American and Australasian countries in this grouping may continue to be a topic of debate, their presentation in this book vividly illustrates the contrast within and between the geopolitical regions of the world; in this case, with regard to open and distance learning.

As an introduction, this chapter reviews several cross-cutting themes that appear in many of the papers included in this book. Gradually more people are realizing that the new demand for learning that has been stimulated by the region's rapid industrialization over the past decade cannot be met by simply expanding traditional campus-based programmes and facilities. Many countries in Asia are moving quickly from an elite-selection model to a mass-delivery model for higher education. But the campus-based delivery system involves high costs and limited flexibility, especially in reaching older students in the Asian middle classes for whom further education is an increasing imperative.

This phenomenal growth in the number of open universities and distance learners in Asia has created significant opportunities, and threats, in the region. The increasing number of new courses, more diverse groups of distance learners and the utilization of new approaches to open learning has led to a glaring need for better understanding by practitioners, managers and researchers of the administrative styles, educational processes and education outcomes of the distance learning institutes in Asia, particularly from a comparative perspective. The demand for more open learning opportunities together with subtle government involvement in reaching out to the greater majority of those who would not have received their education through the conventional means present situations that demand cost-effective planning and implementation (McNay 1987), appropriate staffing and operational management, and well-designed teaching and support materials. However, there are no data or reliable syntheses post-1991 of these developments region-wide.

This book, while similar in concept and general format to the earlier UNESCO publication (1991) mentioned above, departs significantly from it primarily because it arose out of a felt need that was supported by a major research project sponsored by the Open University of Hong Kong and undertaken by its Centre for Research in Distance and Adult Learning (CRIDAL). The research, which compared the administrative styles, educational processes and educational outcomes of Asian ODE institutions, examined the leadership styles, teaching and delivery model, methods and forms of student assessment, and importance of outcome indicators in selected Asian open universities from a comparative perspective. The study was also to provide a better understanding of the current state of open and distance learning in the Asia Pacific. Hitherto, limited information available about the ODE within the Asian region was evaluative, valuable to the particular institution, but of limited worth to others.

The sum total of the results of the study begged the need for a status report of open and distance learning in the Asia Pacific reflecting emerging developments within and across the region with a focus on in-depth country reports. The content of this book, therefore, is the outcome to meet this need.

In the sober aftermath of the Asian financial crisis of the last decade, governments have realized that while the social demand for expanding higher education is a political reality, the financial and managerial resources of governments to meet this demand are severely limited. Whereas expanding and overseeing national universities has been a major aspect of state-building and centralized manpower planning since the end of the post-war colonial era, new efforts to meet the burgeoning demand have looked towards market forces in higher education.

While ODE institutions in Asia have drawn significant resources from their governments, especially in the start-up phase, they are being increasingly forced to raise their funds through student fees. With the rise of the market, the long-term cost model of campus-free delivery combined with the promise of new information technologies suggest trends that are moving in favour of open universities in the region.

But unless Asia's open universities move quickly to master new technologies and assure quality in their programmes, campus-based dual-mode universities, ever hungry in this new climate, will grasp the new tools of distance learning and move aggressively into the regions of adult and continuing professional education once largely left to open universities and marginal private providers. In ten years' time, will the open universities of Asia have continued to grow exponentially into mega-universities, or will they be overtaken by dual-mode institutions, private and public, separately or in new consortia, which will have used their academic, technological and managerial assets to expand their programmes to serve this growing population of learners?

ODE programmes in the decade ahead will be shaped by the way in which four key relationships within higher education will evolve in the Asian countries:

- Public or government provision and private market-based supply;
- Domestic and transnational providers;
- Cooperation and competition among providers;
- Campus-based and technology-based strategies for delivery.

Reflecting on these four great relationships, and in light of the country studies that form the chapters of this book, this introductory essay is organized under the following headings:

- New demand for further education outstrips campus-based supply
- From nation-building to market forces and human capital growth
- A blend and competition between local and non-local education programmes in Asia
- Technology transfer and information and communication technologies
- Shifting the costs of learning
- Three types of ODE programme
- ODE programmes in global digital commerce
- A tough choice for open universities in Asia.

New demand for further education outstrips campus-based supply

ODE has grown significantly in the past decade in the Asia Pacific region. Rapid industrialization in many Asian economies has created new demand for knowledge and skills in the changing workplace. Strong traditional values with regard to education, reinforced by new social pressures for upward mobility into the middle class, have also strengthened demand for higher and continuing education.

The economic setbacks of the late 1990s have only intensified the drive for more learning, and for credentials to validate that learning in competitive job markets. The diffusion of new technologies in the workplace, both industrial and managerial, has also sharpened the demand for new technical knowledge and organizational skills, which are not necessarily the outcome of current curricula and teaching methods.

It would be a daunting enough task in itself to expand higher education to satisfy the growing age cohorts in Asian countries that wish to enrol in post-secondary programmes after completing their secondary education. But it has also become essential for these countries to address the needs of a growing number of mature learners who need to return to learning to remain qualified in the changing workforce. Table 1 illustrates the demand for non-conventional methods of instruction delivery, and the average percentage growth as gleaned from various sources and databases. If every country in Asia adheres strictly to a national ideology of the right to learn, as occurs in Japan, the colossal numbers and the concomitant phenomenal growth to be experienced by ODE in Asia, beyond the currently huge numbers, can only be imagined. There are many Asians now in mid-life who did not have a chance to go to university out of secondary school, but who now want, and can pay for, further education relevant to career enhancement.

Table 1   Enrolment and growth of ODE in selected Asian institutions

Institution	Total enrolment as at 2000	Average annual % growth
CCRTVU, China	3,042,950	20
STOU, Thailand	94,810	25
OUSL, Sri Lanka	25,000	30
University of the Air, Japan	81,258	15
IGNOU, India	600,000	19
OUHK, Hong Kong	37,000	14

This education, however, must be made available to these students in ways that are relevant to their interests, address their status-conscious concern for credible credentials, and accommodate their work patterns, lifestyles and family commitments. In addition, several Asian countries, such as China after the Cultural Revolution, also have a significant 'backlog' of demand for further education resulting from the breakdown of the tertiary system at an earlier stage. The indication seems to be that while the world average transition rate from secondary to tertiary education is a little over 20%, in India and China, the two most populous countries in Asia and the world, this rate is less than 10% (see Table 2). The implication is that Asia would need to find a system that will accommodate the remaining 90% of the secondary school graduates who need tertiary education.

The existing capacities of the national higher education sector in Asia are far from being able to satisfy this burgeoning social, economic and demographic demand. Substantial national resources for higher education are devoted to the traditional role of selecting elites and organizing youth through the routine campuses and classrooms. In the boom years of the 1980s and early 1990s, many Asian governments built expensive new campuses that required land, buildings, staff salaries, technical networks and service infrastructure. While creating many new opportunities, this approach was an attempt to achieve mass provision through the methods and assumptions of elite higher education. Following the economic downturn of 1996 to 1998, however, governments have had to consider less costly ways to satisfy the ever-rising social demand for tertiary education. ODE in its various forms tends to be viewed by an increasing number of education planners and government policymakers as a potentially cost-effective strategy to fill the gap.

Until recently, there has not been a sense of the existence of an alternative to the expensive campus model of higher education. But with the growth of telecommunications affecting the work and home life of the aspiring Asian middle classes, there is new interest to develop alternatives to the campus-intensive model that use telecommunications, which may over time become lower in cost and more accessible in practical and cultural terms to students already participating in the workforce. In some cases, technology may be an alternative to campuses. In other cases, technology may make campuses more productive in serving more students with more appropriate learning. In any case, pressure is growing on policy choices between directing resources to maintain the traditional higher education infrastructure, and investing in new and also expensive infrastructure for flexible learning systems. How much of the new resources will go into retrofitting dual-mode institutions to teach at a distance, and how much will go to upgrading the technological infrastructure of open universities?

Table 2   World secondary and tertiary education enrolments and percentage transition rate

Countries/ Regions	1990			1997			1997
	Enrolment in secondary education (millions)	Enrolment in tertiary education (millions)	% transition	Enrolment in secondary education (millions)	Enrolment in tertiary education (millions)	% transition	Public Expenditure on education US$ (billions)
World total	315	68.6	21.8	398	88.2	22.2	1386.8
More developed regions	68.9	29.1	42.2	75.8	34.2	45.1	1098.4
China	52.4	3.8	71.9	71.9	6.1	8.5	20.7
India	55.0	5.0	10	69.7	6.4	9.2	12.9

Source: World Education Report 2000, UNESCO.

In the past two decades the more prosperous Asian societies have stressed the need to build new research universities that can advance their high-tech, knowledge-based economies. It was not enough just to copy innovations developed in the West and make money on agile marketing and aggressive distribution. Science parks, graduate programmes, government funding for research, and partnerships with businesses have engaged the university leaders of Asia for a generation. Many of these young research universities in Taiwan, Korea, Thailand and Hong Kong, for example, have lured successful scholars back after they had been abroad for study. Only a decade before they had been given up as casualties of 'brain drain'. Even so, this 'high-end' talent pool centred on the research university cannot be effective without a broad, well-educated mid-level labour force able to shift from routine manufacturing to the self-reinventing service sector of the economy.

The drive to broaden access to tertiary education is driven by several values. One is to promote further economic growth by building a broad, well-skilled, self-developing middle-class workforce. Another is to mitigate the tensions that can arise from the acute disparities of income and life chances in Asian societies. The economic downturn has exacerbated the tensions between rich and poor in Asian societies.

Economic development has created new resources to invest in expanded provision of higher education. New investments in education have also raised the expectations in society, especially employers, of the skill sets of the graduates of these programmes. One finds much discussion in Asian countries about lack of fit between the skill needs of the workplace and the products of the education system. This criticism may be directed to the traditional content taught by aging professors, and/or to former regimes of manpower planning that tried to predict needs of the workforce. More recently the complaints focus on the incongruity between learning habits based on the factory-like routines of the schools on the one hand, and the needs for flexibility and creative problem-solving in the knowledge-intensive workforce. Given the rapid obsolescence of knowledge, the graduate must be able to move from the campus to the workplace having learned mainly how to learn, and to be motivated to do this throughout his or her life.

From nation-building to market forces and human capital growth

The unmet social demand for learning, as shown by the very poor transition rate in Table 2, is attracting new providers of private higher education. In the decades since the Second World War, the expansion of higher education in Asia was closely tied to nation-building. The best and brightest students were recruited through competitive exams into highly selective universities. The cream of this crop often went into careers in government civil service. This path was ideologically attractive and socially rewarding. It fit traditional patterns of talent selection and the role of the state, and built upon norms of education and social hierarchy from colonial times. Meanwhile, new Asian governments such as Indonesia, Pakistan and Vietnam, as covered in subsequent chapters, made strenuous efforts to infuse the curricula and learning culture of schools and colleges with new nationalist ideologies.

Asia's broadening of the idea of providing options for a 'second chance' at higher education for those who did not or could not go on to further study through the pressurized, exam-intensive transition from secondary school to university has come about for many reasons. First, the elite-sorting model may have been functional, or even inevitable, within an agricultural or early industrial stage of development. But it is clearly obsolete in the emerging knowledge-based society. Second, there is a pervasive concept in Asia that a nation's economic competitiveness in the global system rests increasingly on the calibre and resilience of its workforce. This relatively new social ideology, promoted by the state and captains of industry, stresses that continuous education and training will upgrade human capital, which will add greater value to changing production processes, and thus generate wealth. This is typified by the accounts from Japan, Taiwan and Hong Kong. Third, it has come to be recognized that a perpetually learning society may be the only real long-term security, especially for densely populated smaller states that are highly dependent on exports of goods and services in the treacherous cross-currents of the global economy. This is why there has been a resurgence in lifelong learning in Asia, as in most parts of the world.

As economic globalization intensified during the last decade, market forces began to have a greater impact on higher education in many Asian countries. Like many other social goods, higher education is becoming increasingly viewed as a commodity service to be bought and sold among providers and customers. Responding to unmet social demand for further education, local entrepreneurs, with capital earned from commerce and industry, are beginning to open colleges throughout Asia to attract students from the overflow of the national system.

A blend and competition between local and non-local education programmes in Asia

Through the 1980s and into the 1990s, the two systems of national and off-shore higher education systems co-existed as parallel worlds in Asian countries. Hong Kong probably has the highest number of off-shore distance education programmes with 550 non-local programmes mainly from Australia, the UK, Canada and the US offering more than 60,000 places. Malaysia serves as a centre and overseas campus for many institutions, while Vietnam has recently established study centres for a number of overseas universities. Both systems of local and off-shore programmes grew dramatically from both government subsidies and private spending. The balance of advantages and disadvantages of the two systems, and the career paths they offered, appeared differently to various social and economic groups within and between different Asian countries. Over the decade, partnerships arose between the two sectors involving universities based abroad and local private colleges in twinning programmes and the like. Varieties of collaborations appeared between domestic public, domestic private and off-shore public and off-shore private institutions. In the main, however, the character of instruction remained conventional.

With the abrupt drop in currency exchange rates in 1997 and 1998, many Asian middle class families could no longer afford off-shore higher education; Malaysia is a good example of this. At the same time, the cost of those programmes was also rising. Many overseas universities, concerned at the potential loss of revenue from Asian students, began to explore further strategies to collaborate with local, often private institutions to provide a lower-cost, in-country option to the foreign degree. If the Asian student does not go to the campus abroad, perhaps the campus abroad could come to the Asian student. The '2+2' ratio, meaning two years in one's own country leading to two years abroad, yielded to the ratio of '3+0' used to designate a full three-year programme leading to an overseas degree read entirely in-country through a local partner college that has, in effect, franchised the off-shore institution's programme. The term 'distance learning' is frequently used in this context.

It is noteworthy that the downturn among Asian students (especially from the harder-hit countries of Korea, Thailand, Malaysia and Indonesia) in Australia, the US and the UK has been less severe than was feared. Overall rates of Asian student flows to these four countries have remained rather stable. This suggests that these patterns of student flow are to a certain extent invulnerable to short-term buffeting by economic setback.

Just as the lines between public and private higher education are blurring, so are the traditional markers between domestic and transnational higher education beginning to blur in Asia. The emerging patterns of cooperation and competition across both economic sectors and national boundaries have created a dynamic synergy among academic leaders and the public at large. Many of the new hybrid ventures, from branch campuses to sandwich programmes, are naturally attempting to utilize new communication technologies, increasingly based on the World Wide Web. This had led to experimentations with cross-national instruction using the Internet.

Technology transfer and information and communication technologies

While much of the new discussion, in Asia as elsewhere, is focused on potential uses of information and communication technologies, the major delivery methods for most ODE programmes in Asia still rely heavily on print and the postal system, the 'correspondence education' of yesteryear. There may be a correlation between a country's GDP and its stage or scale of transition from print-and-post to electricity-based communication between the student and the instructor.

Throughout Asia, ODE has its roots in efforts by some universities to print and distribute the course materials and lecture notes by the faculty to correspondence students who did not qualify to enter the campus-based programme. This meant a social stigma for these students, and few services were provided to help them actually succeed in their studies.

In the 1970s and 1980s many Asian countries made significant strides in educational broadcasting through radio and television. The University of the Air in Japan, and its associated National Institute for Multimedia Education, has been a leader in educational broadcasting in the region. The National Open University of Korea and the Radio and Television Universities of China (RTVUs) have enrolled many thousands of students and rank among the 'mega-universities' of the world. In countries like

India and Indonesia, many hoped that satellite delivery of educational TV would revolutionize education. Donors such as IDA/Japan gave major hardware grants to other Asian countries, which set up expensive studios and broadcasting equipment. Access was indeed expanded, but changes to the conventional system were little in evidence. Educational TV grew up essentially as a parallel structure alongside the campus-based higher education systems of Asia, neither within nor a part of it. Television is a 'cool' medium, wrote Marshal McLuhan, but is essentially passive, subliminal and non-participatory. Television may be good for teaching general knowledge, but is more limited, or just not cost-effective, when dealing with more in-depth areas of learning that require pro-active engagement by students. Television is also closely related to the mass entertainment culture, which many people find a problematic semiotic context for teaching and learning at the tertiary education level. Educational TV, in Asia as elsewhere, tended too often to be talking heads with low 'television value'.

The traditional lecture hall, often boring in live performance, becomes even more stilted on the screen in contrast to the normally fast and jazzy formats of commercial television. Making substantial leaps in pedagogical quality in television requires a lot of money. Even then, many expensive telecourses can become quickly out of date and be consigned quietly to the shelf. From contributions to this book, one finds little evidence of broad adoption in Asia of the fine telecourses developed by Annenberg/CPB in the US or by the BBC with the UK Open University in the 1970s and 1980s. Costs and rights and intellectual property issues may have been responsible.

The power of video to teach by visualizing concepts also tended to move against the grain of traditional Asian expectations that teaching and learning should be mainly a matter of studying words on a page. Asian cultures retain a reverence for the book and its expertise, solidarity with one's class at school, and an overwhelming focus on the exam. Distant or virtual relationships in education are new. Even so, educational TV grew apace in Asia as televisions, VCRs and dedicated education broadcast channels gradually became less expensive.

Enter the Internet. The global diffusion of the Internet in the late 1990s is creating another occasion for re-thinking ODE in Asia. Begun in US universities in the 1980s, by the end of the 1990s the Internet and especially its World Wide Web had already diffused widely in Asia and the Pacific.

Internet cafés and computer kiosks are growing up on Asian street corners, and some back alleys, to service the vast majority who do not have access in their homes or at their places of work. Given limited personal space in Asia, the computer is likely to be a more social and public appliance than in the private homes of America.

Projections of Internet growth in Asia are guesswork. However we have found the Internet penetrations as shown in Figures 1 and 2 to be very instructive. The radical information openness of the Web conflicts to a greater or lesser extent with the relatively closed or 'guided' political cultures of Asian countries. If the fax and TV satellites made Tiananmen possible in China in 1989, what political consequences may arise from the diffusion of the Web among Asian students, young and old?

The deregulation of the telecommunications industries in Asia has been slower than in the West. This has slowed the development of private online educational services. Even in such free-market enclaves as Hong Kong, Pacific Century CyberWorks tries to staunch the deregulation process. Market openness in China's telecoms sector was a key issue in WTO negotiations. Global free-trade policy has pushed for greater access for transnational communications companies to the vast populations of Asian societies. China's television market is 900 million. The middle classes of China and India, small by proportion to the total population, is the fastest growing emerging market for telecommunications in the world.

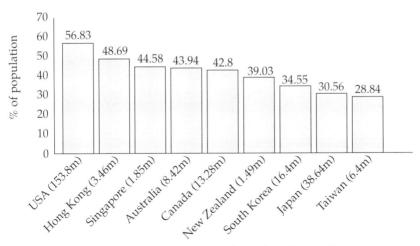

Figure 1   Internet penetration I [over 25% of the population]

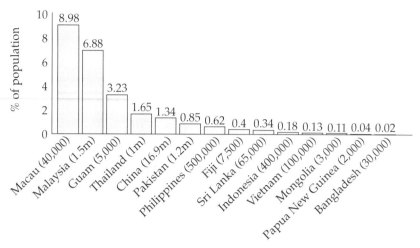

Country (number of people with access)

Figure 2   Internet penetration II [less than 10% of the population]

One of the new Internet-born services to cross national lines is believed to be online university courses and related student services. One finds few concrete and successful examples so far in Asia. But the off-shore marketing of online courses has just begun. The lure of 'first to market' in the e-commerce culture is powerful.

Some online courses for global delivery may lead to degree programmes at institutions or consortia of institutions which students need never visit in person. The lure to actually visit abroad and learn its culture first-hand in a student role will remain powerful — and rightly so. But how feasible will this be for mature learners? Thus mixed-mode programmes (by technology and by provider) will probably be more common. Virtual academic exchanges, such as co-taught Web-based courses within and beyond Asia will likely occur with greater frequency over the next decade. One hopes a whole new round of cross-cultural collaboration in academic course development and delivery will emerge as part of the digital revolution in higher education world-wide.

To date, most of the Internet is in English, which limits its broader dissemination in most Asian societies. But this is changing, as standards and protocols for Chinese, Japanese and other Asian languages will eliminate knowing English as a requirement for accessing the Web. Automatic translation programmes will also promote contact among different language sectors of the Web.

Some important investments in new technologies to support electronic delivery of instruction, such as large inter-campus networks for videoconferencing and servers to support Web-based instruction, have come from national governments. As in most countries, these efforts tend to be 'hardware-first' and 'techno-centric', leaving educators to figure out how to utilize, and maintain, the fast-depreciating tools once they have been installed on their campuses. This has sometimes produced unused capacity and lack of adaptation to the current teaching systems. On the other hand, equipment and connectivity are pre-conditions for most other steps in the process. The traditionally competitive relationships among Asian universities tend to frustrate the utilization of inter-campus networks that require cooperation across institutions.

Some governments, such as Vietnam and Malaysia, have been motivated in part by the expectation of a new round of competition, mediated by new digital technologies, from overseas providers of online higher education. The providers and vendors from abroad have the status sheen of 'high-tech' courseware, combined with a straightforward, often aggressive business orientation. For governments, building their own indigenous technology networks for higher education may serve as a kind of substitute for imports. 'We'd better act or we'll be overrun by outside providers' is sometimes the argument that carries. Given the wide gaps in technology access in Asia (see Figures 1 and 2), some talk of a new 'digital colonialism' or 'digital divide' is an echo of arguments about the new information order of a decade ago.

International and local providers are exploring joint ventures of various kinds. Many higher education leaders in Asia believe it is important to partner with overseas providers to help build new technology-based delivery systems in the indigenous universities. Global technology corporations such as Cisco Systems, Inc. (online networks) and Nortel (videoconferencing) have been marketing their products and setting up training academies in the region. Thus global corporate vendors, sometimes working through local business franchises, are emerging as important new players in distance learning.

Shifting the costs of learning

Throughout Asia one finds greater willingness to shift more of the costs of higher education from government subsidy to students. China, for example, has recently raised tuition fees, and introduced differential fees for students who gain entry outside the national quota and exam system. A sample of the cost of studying some programmes through off-shore offerings in Hong Kong is shown in Table 3 of the Hong Kong chapter. Rates of increase for tuition and fees have outpaced even those in the West. Even as governments cut subsidies, they are reluctant to risk public reaction to severe tuition hikes. Thus budgets have grown very tight for Asian national universities. And there is scarce new money to invest in new delivery for ODE outside the campus structure.

Education at the adult level is generally viewed as an individual benefit for which the direct beneficiary should pay. In contrast, educating young people is generally seen more as a benefit for the larger society, for which governments should bear the major cost through taxation.

Thus we see dual funding regimes in most Asian countries. Government, with a relatively small (but growing) proportion of revenue coming from student fees often funds traditional higher education, focused on the age 18 to 24 cohort. Open universities, which receive relatively modest amounts of government support, must charge a higher proportion of recurrent costs to their (often adult) students. To initiate new single-mode ODE institutions, governments may invest the initial capital costs to build and equip a facility, but mainly it is student fees that finance recurrent costs.

In many Asian countries there is a public higher education system, and there is a shadow system of education for adult learners. In places like China, the 'shadow system' has nearly the same numbers of students as the conventional university sector. Students and teachers literally work in the shadows, at night after work, of the mainstream education system. Sometimes they generate important revenue that helps maintain the conventional campus-based system.

Three types of ODE programme

Peter Dirr (in the US chapter) has discerned that new distance learning programmes tend to be mainly one of three types. *Needs-based* programmes are focused on serving a certain population group. Usually with some government subsidy, they set out to provide educational access to marginal populations, of which there are many in Asia. They have a culture mainly of service and social justice.

The second type emanates from the discovery of a *new technology*. The programme is essentially an adaptation of this new technology to solve a problem. Many new Internet programmes have and will arise with a technology-driven orientation. Many new Internet IPOs begin with a technology innovation that seeks an educational (or other) application.

The third generic type of distance learning programme is *market driven*. They have a culture of competition and a goal of profit. Hopefully their services are of quality and their timeframe is long term. But alas, educational quality and financial profitability are not necessarily directly related.

Most new ODE programmes will actually be a blend of the three motives of addressing a social need, implementing a new technology, and deriving a reasonable profit, however defined, for the investors and stakeholders. Each initiative has one dominant motive: co-existing with some aspects of the other two. As reported in this book, in Asia, the needs-based ODE programme is prevalent.

ODE programmes in global digital commerce

The blast of growth of the Internet world-wide, and the new permeability of national boundaries to electronic discourse, has raised some concerns about 'the digital divide' between the technology haves and have-nots. In a sense, single-mode ODE institutions, the open universities of Asia (members of the Asian Association of Open Universities), have generally represented the educational interests of the less wealthy and socially marginalized groups in society. As they decline in cost, the new digital technologies could have an enormous impact on the systems and services that are designed to reach them with learning services. On the other hand, the target populations for many ODE programmes are likely to be among the last groups in society to have access to, and cultural comfort with, these new technologies.

Technology optimists and free marketers tend to believe that it is just a matter of time for the new online technologies to become so cheap to acquire and so intuitive to operate that the digital divide will gradually take care of itself. The rising tide of telecommunications will raise all boats. More and more people will gain access and their lives will be made better. Granted, the rate of life improvement may be slower than groups who are more wired, but the absolute improvements to their lives will be significant.

By contrast, the technology pessimists tend to see the absolute gap between the technology haves and have-nots growing, leading to greater social tensions, culture conflict and economic inequalities. A plugged-in Indian, for example, will share more in common with a plugged-in American than either of them would have with their respective 'non-plugged-in' countrymen. The synthetic, transnational culture of the Web will define groups in or out, engaged or disengaged, more than other current cultural, economic or regional dividing lines. Some are concerned that Web culture will de-localize people and leave them disconnected from, and apathetic about, their immediate social surroundings. Others say this concern is romantic and overblown. This debate will evolve and be critical for the development of ODE in Asia.

The cost of new digital communication appliances is coming down. Usage of digital media is expanding rapidly among the Asian middle classes. Powerful mass marketing campaigns are making the possession and use of these stylish consumer products essential insignia for success in the new economy. The majority of initial applications relate to business communications and entertainment. Buying a computer for the home to give one's child a boost in Asia's intensely competitive school system is a key motive for parents. To some extent, the future of sales for the new information technologies will depend on finding new mass applications for them.

There is great competition over which companies will provide what kind of channels, such as cable, broadcast, satellite, phone lines, and Internet links to the home. There is also enormous competition over who will sell the user interface units that will blend television, computer and telephone into multi-functional appliances for home, office and on-the-fly. The third element of the digital equation relates to 'content'. Beyond sheer use itself, people will need new reasons to upgrade their systems by wanting what their current appliances cannot do.

Education could become a major part of the new content that will help to justify the perpetual reach for better, faster and cheaper communication appliances. Yet it remains unclear who will want to, and be able to, study and learn through these digital distributive methods. It is also unclear who in the education sector knows how to teach and assess learning this way. And it is far from clear how existing higher education infrastructure needs to be retrofitted in order to recruit, service and credential students who do learn this way.

Much is written about how the younger generation has greater computer literacy than their parents. Younger workers with technical skills make their more senior but technically less capable supervisors nervous. Socially conservative hierarchies are being threatened by new economic imperatives (from this vague and ominous place called 'the global economy') to achieve productivity gains through digital technologies. The more market-vulnerable organizations will push these hierarchies down first. The less market-vulnerable institutions, such as government agencies and most universities, will be able to resist the forces of technology for longer. But not indefinitely.

A tough choice for open universities in Asia

The applications of the Internet to the design, development and deployment of ODE programmes is a major imperative of the age among Asian open universities. Significant work on a broad scale appears to be underway at open universities in Korea, Taiwan, Hong Kong, China, India and Singapore. India is playing a unique role in the global labour pool for the digital technology industry. Increasingly China is as well. Asia's open universities have the potential to open access for their learners to the digital world. But the resources and management talent needed to do this is enormous.

A critical question for the next decade in Asia is whether the single-mode ODE institutions, such as the national open universities in many countries, will be able to use their social position and internal expertise in reaching and serving adult learners at a distance, albeit through still-viable print-and-postal technologies, to 'tool-up' for teaching and learning with technologies that can reach huge numbers of students in lower socio-economic levels of society. If so, they will be critical to the closing of the digital divide.

Or will more aggressive, traditional name-brand universities be able to utilize their faculties, facilities and administrative systems to move beyond their campuses and offer low-cost, high-convenience instruction at comparable quality to the adult learners who might otherwise be drawn to an open university? Unless open universities of Asia absorb and utilize the new digital technologies to upgrade their instructional delivery, there will be other higher education providers from both within and outside their respective countries who will try to compete with them for these markets.

ODE programmes, based at both single- and dual-mode universities, as has been reported for Australia and Canada, have a strategic choice to make in the coming decade. Should they retain the very lowest costs to their students, and also maintain the lowest technology requirements for entry in order to serve the most marginal groups? Is this the meaning of 'open'? Or should the ODE institutions and programmes invest in new technologies, mount extensive staff retraining, and set up high-cost maintenance regimes, in order to convert their instruction to formats in the digital media?

ODE professionals in most Asian countries are themselves stretched across the digital divide, feeling strong pulls from both sides. To stay low-cost and low-tech would risk being overtaken by other institutions and stagnating within. This would be a disservice to their students. To go up the technology scale, however, risks losing the student audience, and in some cases, the core institutional mission. It is not likely that significant increases in either government subsidy or international donor funding for ODE will mitigate this dilemma.

These forces of technological, economic and social change lead to a major question for ODE in Asia. Will mainstream Asian universities use their assets to get into the new distance learning business and overtake the ODE sector, or will the single-mode open universities adapt new technologies to their major assets, especially in their systems for flexible delivery of instructional services, to gain new advantage over their wealthier academic cousins in a new stage of ODE delivery?

Mainstream universities have considerable campus-based resources, the intellectual content of their faculty knowledge (protected by intellectual property rights regimes), the status appeal of their brand name degrees, links to the corporate world through R&D collaborations and human resource recruitment networks, and their continuing education and outreach programme offices. Will governmental funding agencies push them into this new market, and/or will their own academic leaders embrace this broader mission even though it may cut against the cultural grain of their institutions? In the past, the more mainstream universities did not see adult and continuing education to be their market niche or mission.

These outreach and adult-oriented professional programmes were a service function to societies, often lucrative, but not to gain undue prominence in the real core of the academy. For some mainstream universities it may make sense to remain focused on the mission of educating young residential and/or commuter-to-campus students. In addition, the research agenda has become the preferred pathway for many Asian universities to aspire to be recognized as world-class institutions. For them, involvement in ODE must be framed as compatible with these mission imperatives and institutional cultures.

Considerable investments in Asian universities have been made in creating flexible learning centres for English-language instruction using new technologies. Although less honoured in the academy than the teaching of literature and now cultural studies, the language instruction units that can address the massive 'service' needs for English skills by creating and diffusing flexible online teaching and learning strategies will inevitably gain in value to their home institutions. In any case, traditional mainstream universities in Asian countries have considerable assets, but also significant problems and constraints in moving into technology-based distance learning programmes.

On the other hand, will the open, single-mode, mega-universities in the Asia Pacific countries expand into the new delivery systems based on digital technologies for the delivery of flexible learning to adult learners where they already have a strong presence? They need not wean teachers away from the near religious attachments to classrooms and the lecture hall. Their mission is to expand access to higher education to people who cannot avail themselves of the campus-based providers. Their administrative systems are designed to recruit and serve student populations at a distance. Upgrading technologies within a system is less difficult and costly than changing the system fundamentally.

Another major consideration for ODE institutions in Asia is the need to reconsider their mission. When distance education began, it was to meet the needs of learners who were not in the mainstream educational environment. First to use correspondence education was Anna Tickner for teaching remote students shorthand, in North America. There is much talk about ODE now attaining a mainstream status. However, for many countries in Asia and the Pacific Rim, more and more people are in fact becoming marginalized. There are those who are disadvantaged, marginalized, unreached and do not have access to education at all (Dhanarajan 1998). Will these ODE institutions in Asia and the Pacific Rim continue by pursuing so-called mainstream activities or will they review their mission and pursue the principal objectives for which distance education was originally established?

There are in fact three other fundamental issues associated with ODE in the Asia Pacific that ODE institutions must consider. First, as mentioned above and as discussed within this book, there is the increasing use of the globalization of higher education argument to justify the export of programmes to the region. Many of these overseas institutions that export programmes to Asia and the Pacific Rim do not themselves have a tradition and culture in their home institution that supports or is based on ODE. They merely adapt their face-to-face courses or programmes for the world market. In fact, and probably because of globalization, there is a compelling need to develop courses that are relevant to and do not 'injure' the local culture and learning environment contexts. There are concerns in the Asia Pacific for instance (Wah 1997) that globalization (meaning imported off-shore courses and programmes) will destroy local languages and cultures and perpetuate cultural and economic slavery. Second, Evans (1999) has raised the question of the continuing difficulty understanding the contexts for which the term 'distance education' can be and is used. While distance education has become the standard generic term understood by all, the terms derived from it such as 'open learning', 'flexible delivery' and 'flexible learning' that are now in vogue are misconstrued as being synonymous with 'distance education'. The difficulty is, now world-wide, including in Asia and the Pacific Rim, which together host over 60% of the world's ODE practices, to clarify these terms so that they may become standard. Third is the issue of research in ODE. Whereas ODE has been on the educational scene since the 18th century, it has not, for obvious reasons, carried with it, as other segments of education have done, the need to make research a central focus. The ODE field is too busy meeting the teaching and learning needs of students to make room for research activities as well, with detrimental consequences for research. However, it has been posited that research will be the next great development in ODE and will be the future of distance education. Except for IGNOU in India and the OUHK in Hong Kong, research comprises a major part of the operations of no other ODE institution in Asia, and yet it is central to informing practice and providing empirical feedback into the work and the *raison d'être* of these institutions. And only at the OUHK has a dedicated centre for research (CRIDAL) been established. Its achievements within its four years of existence are enviable and can stand as a model for other ODE institutions in Asia and the Pacific to emulate.

But making these upgrades and adaptations within the ODE sector will require considerable leadership skills, new backing and resources from the respective countries' governments, new links to global media and technology corporations, more capital to invest in upgrading their instructional and student service systems, teaching staff who can be trained to transfer their tutorials into Web-based environments, and public validation of their credentials that benchmark the learning outcomes of their students.

The actions of the leaders of Asia's open universities and the heads of continuing and professional studies programmes in the next decade, the first of the 21st century, will determine the future direction of ODE in the region and indeed around the world.

References

Daniel, J (1998) *Mega-Universities and Knowledge Media*, London: Kogan Page Limited.

Dhanarajan, G (1998) 'Access to learning and Asian open universities: in context', Keynote address at the 12th Annual Conference of the Asian Association of Open Universities, Hong Kong SAR, November.

Ding, X F (1999) 'Distance education in China' in Harry, K (ed.) *Higher Education Through Open and Distance Learning*, London: Routledge, 176–89.

Evans, T (1999) 'The strategic importance of institutional research building on reflective practice in open universities', Paper presented at the Specialised Workshop on Institutional Research in Open and Distance Learning, Hong Kong SAR, October.

Gandhe, S K (1998) 'Access and equity: the needs of the disadvantaged', Proceedings of the 12th Annual Conference of the Asian Association of Open Universities, Hong Kong SAR, November, 125–32.

Gibson, C C (1997) 'Teaching/learning at a distance: a paradigm shift in progress', *Open Praxis*, 1:6–8.

Harry, K (1999) *Higher Education Through Open and Distance Learning*, London: Routledge.

Jegede, O J and Shive, G (1999) 'The trend and challenges of open and distance education in Asia with particular reference to research', *Open Education Research*, 19(2–3): 56–58.

Kwok, L, Tsui, C, Zhang, W, Jegede, O and Ng, F (1999) 'Imperative issues on the educational process among Asian open universities', Proceedings of the 13th Annual Conference of the Asian Association of Open Universities', Beijing, October, 131–42.

McNay, I (1987) 'Organisation and staff development' in Thrope, M and Grugeon, D (eds) *Open Learning for Adults*, London: Longman, 13–20.

National Institute of Multimedia Education (1991) Distance education in Asia and the Pacific: Country papers, Tokyo: UNESCO/NIME.

Ng, F, Kwok, L, Tsui, C, Zhang, W and Jegede, O (1999) 'Outcomes in distance education: a comparative study of selected Asian open universities', Proceedings of the 13th Annual Conference of the Asian Association of Open Universities, Beijing, October, 146–53.

Tam, S W (1999) 'The current state of distance education in Asia: challenges and responses', *Open Education Research*, (2/3):8–12 (in Chinese).

Tsui, C, Zhang, W, Jegede, O, Ng, F and Kwok, L (1999) 'Perception of administrative styles of open and distance learning institutions in Asia: a comparative study', Proceedings of the 13th Annual Conference of the Asian Association of Open Universities, Beijing, October, 190–202.

UNESCO/ICDE (1992) *Developments in Distance Education in Asia: An Analysis of Five Case Studies*, UNESCO.

UNESCO (2000) *World Education Report 2000*, UNESCO.

Wah, R (1997) 'Distance education in the South Pacific: issues and contradictions' in Rowan, L O, Bartlett, V L and Evans, T (eds) *Shifting Borders: Globalisation, Localisation and Open and Distance Education*, Geelong: Deakin University Press, 69–82.

Zhang, W, Jegede, O, Ng, F, Kwok, L and Tsui, C (1999) 'A comparative study of the administrative styles, educational processes, and outcomes of selected Asian open universities', Proceedings of the 13th Annual Conference of the Asian Association of Open Universities, Beijing, October, 233–42.

Mongolia

Korea Japan

China

Taiwan

Hong
Kong

Northeast
Asia

China

Ding Xing-fu

Introduction

Since 1978 China has implemented major socio-economic reforms and an international policy of openness, with the result that China is set to play a more active and important role in the international community and particularly the Asia Pacific. In the process of China's modernization, distance education has made a special contribution both to national education and socio-economic development.

Education has been designated a strategic priority area for development since the CPC 14th National Conference in 1992. In 1996, President Jiang Zemin stated that 'Two critical issues in our educational work need to be more effectively addressed; that education has to adapt itself to the task of training personnel as required by modernization; and that educational quality and effectiveness should be improved integrally' (Jiang 1996).

Distance education

The accessibility and flexibility of open and distance learning has made a significant contribution to broadening education opportunities in China, especially higher education, and more broadly to socio-economic development. Distance education in China is focused at secondary and tertiary levels, and more exactly in two areas: distance higher education and distance specialized secondary education. Both areas are within the adult education sector of the national binary system.

Distance higher education has widened opportunities for access to higher education, especially for employed adults, school leavers and some disadvantaged groups. It has also improved the geographical distribution of higher education across China by creating and developing educational provision for advanced study in remote, mountainous, rural and minority nationality areas where the economy, science and technology, education and culture are underdeveloped. In addition it has improved the structure of higher education in particular disciplines and fields of study, and in professional areas of training personnel, as well as providing programmes, curricula and courses in urgent demand from national and local labour markets and various groups. Further, it has achieved economies of scale and a cost effectiveness that has been recognized by governments and the general public (Ding 1998).

China's distance higher education is for in-service adult education and training, though a small percentage of young school leavers are also enrolled. China's distance higher education also provides a variety of non-general qualification education programmes mainly for adults.

China's distance higher education system offers three media of study which provide both normal and short-cycle programmes of undergraduate study and a wide range of study fields (Ding 1994a, 1997). These media are:

- correspondence education;
- radio and TV education;
- the state examination self study (SESS) system.

China's distance secondary education also has this structure:

- correspondence specialized secondary schools;
- radio and TV specialized secondary schools;
- the SESS system (for specialized secondary qualifications).

Distance education within the national system

Table 1 shows how adult education provision for general qualifications was distributed nation-wide for the 1996/97 academic year.

Correspondence higher education

Correspondence and evening education programmes were first provided in China by the People's University of China (PUC) in Beijing in 1953. They have since been representative of the adult higher education programmes offered by RHEIs mainly to provide full-time advanced learning for young school leavers. Except for programmes offered by four independent correspondence colleges, correspondence education in China is dual mode. The main characteristics and models of China's correspondence higher education system at the national, institutional and micro levels follow (Ding 1997).

Table 1   Adult education system (1996/97 academic year)

(Unit: thousands)

Education by level and type	Institutions	Graduates	Entrants	Enrolment
Adult higher education				
Campus-based	1,088	371.3	461.7	1,232.8
Distance teaching	*50+(635)*	*400.2*	*483.5*	*1,422.9*
Subtotal	1,138	771.5	945.2	2,655.7
Adult secondary education				
General education	5,383	457.9	516.1	600.1
Specialized education	5,070	1,020.5	1,271.8	3,097.1
Campus-based	4,816	722.1	853.3	2,070.0
Distance teaching	*254*	*298.4*	*418.5*	*1,027.1*
Technical training	442,768	83,370.2	71,015.5	56,488.7
Subtotal	453,221	84,848.6	72,803.3	60,185.9
TOTAL	617,498	92,258.8	79,695.4	69,573.0

Source: Department of Planning and Construction of the SEdC (1997) *Educational Statistical Yearbook of China 1996*, 3.

At the macro level — the national system

The correspondence higher education offered by China's RHEIs includes programmes in a variety of disciplines and fields of study. These programmes represent a less industrialized form of education in comparison to China's large-scale distance teaching universities. Average enrolment in each institution is around 1,000. Mass telecommunications facilities are not available. Instruction is still print-based and is by correspondence and face-to-face tutorials.

At the median level — institutional structure and function

Most RHEIs providing correspondence education have established a separate administrative body called the Correspondence Division, but teaching and assessment are still conducted by departments. Only a few regular higher education institutions (e.g. the People's University of China in Beijing, Tongji University in Shanghai, etc.) have set up an independent correspondence college or school for both administrative and instructional functions.

Being dual mode, different groups of academic staff teach and assess students on and off campus separately. Correspondence programme curricula, syllabi and course materials are designed specifically for correspondence and are different from full-time study equivalents. This means that assessment, accreditation and awarding systems are also different and separate, and the two types of student are awarded different diplomas and degrees, although the standard of both at the same level is required to be equivalent. Every institution thus runs two parallel subsystems for the operation of full-time and correspondence instruction.

Different providers use one of three kinds of correspondence work station: institutionally, locally and departmentally run. All work stations are responsible for organizing and managing the correspondence classes on behalf of the sponsored RHEIs.

At the micro level — the learning group

The basic structure of correspondence teaching-learning in China is part-time or spare-time independent study under the guidance of correspondence tutors with regular face-to-face tutorials during semesters and intensive face-to-face tutorials before the examinations at the end of each semester. The main course materials are printed correspondence textbooks and study guides with readers and set books. Over the past decade print materials have been supplemented with audio and video materials. This is identified as a consultation model of correspondence teaching.

Group-based learning in the workplace is a common element of China's correspondence education. Students are usually organized into several correspondence classes under the management of a work station. Compulsory pacing is a key feature of correspondence teaching and learning in China.

China's RTVU system

China was one of the first countries to use radio and television for higher education purposes. The first group of urban television universities was set up in the 1960s when television became widespread in urban areas. The Beijing Television University (BTVU) was the first in 1960. Shanghai, Shenyang, Harbin and Guangzhou followed suit. China's RTVU system — national single-mode provision — has been identified as the largest of today's 11 mega-universities (Daniel 1996).

On 6 February 1978, on behalf of the State Council, Deng approved the report jointly submitted by the Ministry of Education and the Central Bureau of Broadcasting on the Founding of a National Radio and Television University System (CRTVU 1989, 1–3). After one year of preparation, the Central Radio and TV University (CRTVU), based in Beijing, and another 28 Provincial Radio and TV Universities (PRTVUs) were set up. On 6 February 1979, CRTVU first transmitted courses via China Central Television's (CCTV) microwave network. From 1979 to 1985, China's radio and TV higher education developed rapidly, and the national system gained international recognition for its performance and achievements. From 1986 onwards China began to transmit TV education programmes via satellite. China Education Television (CETV) was founded in 1986 and given the responsibility of transmitting Satellite TV Education (STVE) programmes. In 1987, the China TV Teacher Training Institute (CTVTTI), responsible for in-service training of primary and secondary school teachers, was set up. Then in 1990, China Liaoyuan Radio and TV School was set up within the CRTVU, aiming to enhance education among the rural population. CTVTTI merged with CRTVU in 1993.

China's RTVU system operates on the principle of unified planning, delivering courses at the top three levels and management by level. The last two decades have seen the creation of a national single-mode system of distance higher education with five levels. In 1997 there were one CRTVU, 44 PRTVUs, 823 city-level branch schools, 1,713 county-level work stations and 13,176 TV sites/classes (ICEM 1998).

SEdC policy states that the main task of China's RTVUs is to offer undergraduate study for short-cycle courses at college level. Statistics show that CRTVU and 44 PRTVUs offered thousands of courses in nine study fields, 53 disciplines and 524 specialities in 1996 (Sun 1997, 178–211). At first, CRTVU courses were transmitted for 1,320 teaching hours (50 minutes each teaching hour) per year nation-wide via the CCTV microwave network. On 1 July 1986, China Education TV (CETV) was founded and began transmitting CRTVU courses as well as other educational programmes via satellite. At present, CCTV has one channel and CETV has three channels for educational programmes. The total number of programmes transmitted via both CCTV and CETV for CRTVU amounts to about 9,000 teaching hours per year. Meanwhile provincial and local radio and TV networks throughout China also transmit CRTVU courses as well as courses delivered by provincial and local RTVUs. In addition to radio and TV programmes, a great number of courses are delivered by audio and video. In the mid-1990s, besides central, provincial and local public TV stations, there were more than 200 specialized TV stations responsible for transmitting educational programmes, 6,100 earth stations for receiving satellite TV programmes, and 53,000 playing sites for audio-visual teaching programmes.

From 1979 to 1996, there were 2.955 million formal registered students in short-cycle courses (Sun 1997, 162). From 1979, when RTVUs were first opened in China, to 1996, higher education institutions recruited 20.54 million undergraduate students, among whom 2.96 million students were educated by RTVUs, which was 14% of total places in all higher education institutions for this period. RTVUs provided 30% of adult higher education. The potential of RTVUs to increase higher education provision is clear.

From 1986 to 1996, nearly 60 non-general qualification education programmes were offered by CRTVU in collaboration with over 40 government organizations, industrial associations, academic bodies and higher education institutions, and completion has reached nearly 4 million. In addition, over 30 million students have completed non-diploma education programmes provided by PRTVUs. Since 1990, the China Liaoyuan Radio and TV School has delivered skills-based training courses for rural areas, and up to now tens of millions of people in rural areas have viewed its programmes.

Most higher education institutions are located in the major cities, but the RTVU system has improved the geographical distribution of higher education. Statistics show the proportion of undergraduates in RTVUs over the total number of undergraduates in other higher education institutions in remote and minority nationality regions (7.0% for Inner Mongolia, 9.8% for Ningxia and 11.5% for Xinjiang and 12.2% for Guizhou) is much higher than in major municipalities (only 1.2% for Beijing and 1.4% for Shanghai) (Sun 1997, 170–5).

For a long time, the level and discipline structures of China's higher education were unbalanced and unsuited to China's changing economy. Before the RTVU system, undergraduate education in short-cycle courses was underdeveloped and the proportion of professional personnel at this academic level was lower than that needed. The RTVU system has been able to improve the level and discipline structures of higher education in China through the provision of short-cycle courses in finance, economics, law and humanities. When China's RTVU system began offering courses in finance and economics, it attracted 0.24 million students. This was eight times new recruitments and 3.3 times the total enrolment in all finance and economics-oriented RHEIs in the same year. Graduates from these courses numbered 7.6 times the graduates from all finance and economics-oriented RHEIs in the same year, or 1.23 times the total number of graduates in finance and economics courses from all RHEIs from 1949 to 1986 (Ding 1991, 166–7).

China's RTVUs have contributed significantly to increasing the total number of qualified professional personnel, especially in the fields mentioned above, through their rapid development of undergraduate programmes. This is particularly true for remote, rural and minority nationality areas where the scale of conventional higher education is extremely small, and the shortage of qualified professional personnel has constituted a severe obstacle to socio-economic development.

In the past two decades, China's RTVU system has also helped make significant improvements in the quality of the national and local labour force by training working people through various non-diploma education programmes (Ding 1998).

The main characteristics and models of the structure and function of the RTVU system at the national, institutional and micro levels follow (Ding 1997).

At the macro level — the national system

China's RTVU system has a unique organizational structure on five levels that parallel the government administration structure.

Central level: the Central Radio and TV University (CRTVU). Based in Beijing, the CRTVU is the heart of the national system. It is currently run by the Ministry of Education.

Provincial level: the Provincial Radio and TV Universities (PRTVUs). There are 31 provincial-level governments. Of these, 23 are provincial, five are autonomous region, and three are municipal. Each (except for Taiwan and Tibet) has a PRTVU. In addition, 15 cities that are listed as independent planning entities also each operate an independent PRTVU, making 44 PRTVUs in total.

Prefecture level: branch schools. There are nearly 330 prefectures and prefecture-level cities in China. Most have established branch schools attached to the national RTVU system and corresponding PRTVUs. There are also hundreds of branch schools run by economic and industrial sector departments and other societal organizations or institutions.

County level: work stations. There are more than 2,200 counties and equivalent administrative units in China. Many of them have set up work stations attached to local branch schools. In addition there are many work stations run by economic and industrial sector departments and other societal organizations and institutions.

Grassroots: TV classes. These classes form the grassroots level of the national RTVU system. The majority are run by grassroots units, i.e. work units such as schools, banks, shops, factories, companies and so on. Most distance learners in China are organized into so-called TV classes by their work units and are group-based as opposed to the individualized style of home-based study offered in other countries. Other classes are run by RTVUs at different levels, by departments and other societal organizations and institutions.

A central authority, the Electronic Education Committee/Office, a department of the SEdC, is responsible for national planning, policy-making, macro-adjustment, control and management of overall electronic education including RTVU education, reporting to the Vice Minister of the SEdC directly.

China's largest national TV networks, CCTV and CETV, offer support services to the RTVUs. CCTV, under the Radio, Film and TV Ministry, provides transmission services through an agreement between the Ministry and the SEdC. CETV, on the other hand, directly under the SEdC, provides support services to educational programmes including those of the RTVUs. In addition, the regional and local radio and TV broadcasting networks at provincial, prefecture and county levels throughout China provide support services to regional and local RTVUs via regional and local governments and relevant departments.

At the median level — the institutional structure and function

Administration subsystem

RTVU education provision is single-mode, i.e. run by a separate national system exclusively for distance learners.

The institutions at the various levels of the RTVU system have different administrative and academic responsibilities.

CRTVU:

- Produces the curricula for RTVUs and ensures that these include all the subjects that are recognized as being of national interest and offers the key courses in each of these subjects;

- Produces syllabi, radio and TV programmes, and writes, edits, publishes and distributes multimedia materials for these courses;

- Sets end-of-semester national unified examinations for these key courses, draws up national examination timetables, and ensures that marking is standardized;

- Trains teachers, technicians and administrative staff;

- Conducts research on higher education through distance learning;

- Directs and supervises the administration of the instruction and teaching of PRTVUs and coordinates academic work shared by more than one PRTVU.

PRTVUs:

- Produce courses in subjects that are of specific regional interest;

- Produce syllabi, TV and radio programmes and write course materials and supplementary materials for the courses they produce;

- Set end-of-semester examinations for their own courses, timetable the examinations set by CRTVU and mark the papers;

- Ensure that teachers follow set administrative and examination procedures. Enrol new students, keep student records and issue diplomas and certificates;

- Train teachers, keep abreast of new teaching methodologies, and promote the interchange of ideas in the running of local RTVU institutions;

- Direct and supervise the teaching and administration work of branch schools and work stations;

- Provide advice, guidance and counselling to students with academic/personal problems.

Branch schools:

- Deal with all aspects of timetabling, including TV programming, tutorials, examinations, tests, laboratory work and field studies as set by CRTVU and the regional PRTVUs;

- Ensure that the teachers follow the set administrative and examination procedures, and that course syllabi are adhered to;

- Set up work stations and TV classes and direct and supervise their work;

- Provide advice, guidance and help to students with academic/ personal problems;

- Award diplomas and certificates;

- Administer established courses in subjects that are of specific interest locally.

Work stations:

- Recruit teachers and tutors;

- Organize TV classes, timetable tutorials, laboratory work and field studies; and distribute teaching materials;

- Provide advice, guidance and help to students with academic/ personal problems.

Operation subsystem

Until early 1996, by the decision of the SEdC, the national RTVU system only provided short-cycle (college level) undergraduate studies but no university level undergraduate and postgraduate studies. A wide range of short-cycle higher education diploma programmes in various study fields, disciplines and specialities have been offered by the CRTVU nation-wide and also by regional PRTVUs and some branch schools to meet local needs. Since 1996 the SEdC has approved the launch of programmes at university level for college graduates by the CRTVU. Since 1999, the Ministry of Education has encouraged CRTVU to launch various programmes at university level in collaboration with conventional campus-based universities such as Tsinghua University, Beijing Foreign Study University, etc. At the end of 2000, CRTVU was providing six such programmes throughout China.

RTVUs mainly provide for in-service adults but also accept some young school leavers. Distance learners in RTVUs can also choose study courses that are structured to suit students' preferred time frames for study; i.e. they can study full-time, part-time or in their spare time.

Institutions at all layers of the RTVU system have their own full-time staff, including academic staff, and employ part-time academic staff recruited from other higher education institutions, research institutes, related business companies and so on.

The course materials in China's RTVUs are mainly developed by individual academic staff. The main textbooks are primarily written by outstanding professors or senior lecturers who are chosen from various RHEIs and work part-time for RTVUs. The TV and radio programmes are also presented by these professors and lecturers. The study guides and other supplementary materials are produced by full-time academics of RTVUs at various levels. There are no professional staff such as educational technologists and instructional designers to support academics in course development.

At the micro level — the learning group

Group-based learning in the workplace is a common element of Chinese RTVU education. Students are usually organized into TV classes. A work station will manage several classes. Compulsory pacing is a key feature of teaching and learning in China's RTVUs, and is organized in the form of regular radio and/or TV programmes, compulsory face-to-face tutorials and compulsory paced assignments. Accordingly, China's RTVUs are run on a two-semester system, which is not as open or flexible.

The basic structure of distance teaching-learning in China's RTVU system is: independent study of print materials; regularly watching TV or video programmes and listening to radio programmes or audio cassettes in groups, usually in fixed classrooms located in their grassroots unit;

regularly attending the face-to-face tutorials in the classrooms; completing and sending homework and regular assignments and receiving feedback (marking and comments) from their face-to-face tutors for every course; doing assessments; and taking end-of-semester examinations. Some courses require laboratory work (or can be completed using experiment kits at home) and other types of practical work such as field exercises, teaching practice, social surveys, course designing and so on. The short-cycle higher education diploma programmes also require students to complete some kind of graduate assignment before a diploma can be awarded.

The administrative and academic responsibilities of TV classes include:

* Drawing up class timetables each semester;

* Organizing the viewing of and listening to course programmes; arranging tutorials, laboratory/experimental work and other practical work;

* Encouraging students to take part in physical education and recreational activities in their spare time;

* Maintaining contact with the work units to which their students are attached.

China's RTVUs offer two basic academic-year systems for short-cycle higher education diploma students: three years of full-time study, or four to five years of part-time and spare-time study and two years of full-time study; or three years or more of part-time and spare-time study. Most young school leavers are registered as full-time students.

RTVUs offer a variety of non-general qualification education programmes ranging from post collegiate continuing education to middle- and lower-level vocational and technical education and training. Non-general qualification education is usually in the form of short-term programmes consisting of certificate courses. Students of these programmes are in-service adults studying to upgrade or update their qualifications. They are organized in groups at their workplaces and study part time or in their spare time. There are no entrance examinations for various non-general qualification education programmes, which are taught using multimedia materials plus face-to-face sessions.

China's RTVU system analysed here is as a hierarchical multi-bodied single mode model. The five-layer structure of the system and the relationships between administration and academia at the various levels are illustrated in Figure 1.

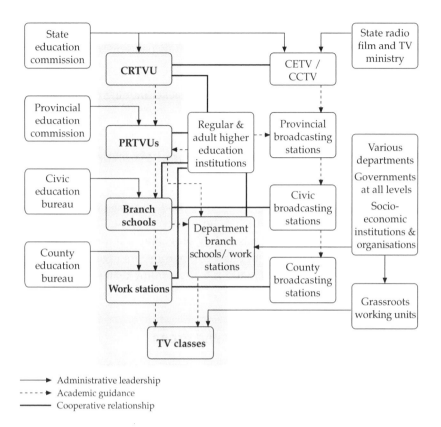

Figure 1   The administrative and organizational structure of China's RTVU
system

China's satellite TV teacher training system

China's satellite TV teacher training system has a structure and functions
that operate according to the course transmission centre model (Ding
1997).

At the macro-level — the national system

The CTVTTI, under the leadership of the SEdC and its department under
the Electronic Education Bureau, is responsible for nation-wide planning,
organizing and managing of in-service training for primary and secondary
school teachers. The CTVTTI has a few administrative staff and no
academic staff. Its main task is to collaborate with China's Higher
Education Publishing House, China's People's Education Publishing House
and various regular higher education institutions in the design, production

and distribution of educational programmes, curricula, syllabi and course materials for teacher training in a variety of study fields by academic staff in RHEIs.

CETV is responsible for the transmission of teacher training programmes via satellite TV education channels.

At the median level — the institutional structure and function

Adult teacher training institutions such as education colleges, teacher training schools and local RTVUs can run schools or classes for teacher training using the course materials and TV programmes transmitted by the CTVTTI and CETV. These institutions are responsible for organizing classes, teaching, assessment and examinations, and awarding their own diplomas or certificates.

At the micro level — the learning group

In-service teachers at primary and secondary schools are organized in groups and use print materials, watch TV programmes and attend face-to-face tutorials organized by registered institutions.

China's state examination self study system

A national examination system called the State Examination Self Study (SESS) system was introduced, first in several cities in 1981, then around the country in 1983. In 1997, the system had nearly 5,000,000 people enrolled and close to 300,000 graduates.

China's SESS system works on three principles: independent study at the base, learning support services provided by various societies, and state-administered examinations at the core of the system. The SESS system offers the usual and short-cycle (specific and fundamental) higher education diplomas (Ding 1997).

The system has been classified as 'quasi-mode' provision because it is a state examination system and not institutionalized education with full teaching, learning support and student management functions (Ding 1995, 1997).

At the macro level — the national system

The SESS has a National Guidance Committee (NGC) approved by the State Council with 13 Professional Committees and an Examination Research Committee under the NGC and a dedicated office in the SEdC. In addition, there are Provincial Guidance Committees (PGC) and SESS offices in each province, autonomous region and municipality. The responsibilities of these Committees and offices are policy-making, planning, coordination and quality control. There are Working Committees or units and offices in prefectures, cities and counties, responsible for organizing the examinations.

At the median level — institutional structure and function

The Examination Holding Institution (EHI) for a certain speciality is chosen and approved by the PGC. It should be a well-known RHEI in that study field, and its academic staff and educational environment and system should have a good reputation. The EHIs are responsible for deciding the standard of the examinations, assigning exam questions, organizing marking and accreditation and practical work (experimental or laboratory work, fieldwork and theses, etc.) for examinees. In addition, the EHIs issue the diplomas jointly with the PGC. The EHIs are by law not permitted to organize tuition for examinees in the courses examined by them. Thus, tuition must be separate from the assigning of examination questions.

At the micro level — the learning group

Examinees can choose to study independently and/or receive learning support services provided by various departments and societal organizations or institutions, including classes by TV or correspondence and face-to-face tutorials.

Funding

Most regular higher education institutions are funded from the national budget at central and provincial levels. However, distance higher education institutions (e.g. the RTVUs) have four sources of funding: government funding (51.6% of total funding at three levels: central — 3.6%, provincial — 20.3% and local — 27.7%); funding from various organizations, mainly work units (40.0%); funding from students themselves or their families through student fees (5.1%); and a mix of other sources (3.3%) (Ding 1991,

1994b). Concerning educational cost, research conducted in the 1980s (Ding 1994b) showed that the average institutional cost of the RTVUs, including all fixed costs consumed by RTVUs and broadcasting organizations at various levels and variable costs consumed by TV classes in both recurrent expenditure and capital depreciation, was only about one-quarter of the average recurrent expenditure of the RHEIs. Excluding capital depreciation, the average recurrent expenditure of RTVUs was only about one-fifth that of the RHEIs. The on-time graduation rate was more than 70% to 80% in RTVUs, so the annual cost per graduate of RTVUs was about one-third to two-fifths that of the RHEIs (about 30% for humanities, 35% for economics and 40% for sciences and engineering courses respectively) (Ding 1991, 1998).

References

Central Committee of the CPC (1993) *The Outline of Innovation and Development for Chinese Education.*

CRTVU (1989) *Selected Documentaries on Radio and TV Universities 1978–1988,* Beijing: The CRTVU Publishing House.

Daniel, J (1996) *Mega-Universities and Knowledge Media: Technology Strategies for Higher Education,* London: Kogan Page.

Ding, X (ed.) (1991) *Evaluating Educational Quality and Effectiveness of China RTVUs,* Muhan Publishing House.

Ding, X (1994a) 'China's higher distance education — its four systems and their structural characteristics at three levels', *Distance Education,* 15(2): 327–46.

Ding, X (1994b) 'Economic analysis of the Radio and Television Universities in China', *Open Praxis,* 2: 14–21.

Ding, X (1995) 'China's higher distance education — its system, structure and administration', in *Conference Papers for the 8th Annual Conference of the AAOU,* New Delhi.

Ding, X (1997) 'A comparative study of higher distance education systems in Australia and China', unpublished PhD thesis, Western Australia: Murdoch University.

Ding, X (1998) 'Evaluation of distance teaching universities: Chinese perspective and experiences', in Keynote Papers and CD-ROM for '98

Shanghai International Symposium on Open and Distance Education, Shanghai: Shanghai TV University.

DPC of SEdC (1984, 1991, 1992, 1993, 1994, 1995, 1996, 1997) *Educational Statistical Yearbook of China*, Beijing: People's Education Press.

Fourth Plenary Meeting of the Eighth National People's Congress (1996) 'The outline of the ninth Five-Year Plan and future goals of national economy and social development in 2010 for the People's Republic of China'.

Huang, Y and Zhao, Y (eds) (1990) 'Report on the first trace study of graduates from China's RTVUs', *China's RTVU Education*, 9: 13–48 and 10: 42–48.

Huang, Y et al. (eds) (1996) *Method and Practice of Comparative Study for Education: A Sino-Japanese Joint Comparative Study Between Radio and TV Higher Education and Conventional Higher Education in China*, Beijing: CRTVU Press.

ICEM of CRTVU (1998) 'The '97 Communique of Basic Statistics of China RTVUs Education', *China RTVU Education*, 3, Beijing: CRTVU.

Jiang, Z (1996) 'Instructions on educational work', *China Education Daily*, 12 March 1998, 1.

Jiang, Z (1997) 'To strive for socialist construction with Chinese characteristics into 21st century integrally by holding high the great banner of Deng Xiaoping theory', 15th National Conference of the CPC, Beijing.

State Council (1994) *The Executive Recommendations for the Outline of Innovation and Development for Chinese Education*.

Sun, L (1997) *1996 Education Statistics Yearbook of Radio & TV Universities in China*, Beijing: CRTVU Press.

World Bank (1997) *The 1997 World Development Report: Governments in a Changing World*, in Chinese, Beijing: Chinese Finance and Economics Press.

Zhu, K (1998) 'The speech at the 1998 educational working meeting by the State Education Commission', *China Education Daily*, 11 February 1998.

Hong Kong

Olugbemiro Jegede

Introduction

Hong Kong has many unique characteristics. Some of these include its small land area and dense population; its position as an international business, commercial and financial centre; its transient and ever-changing population; that it is viewed as being a cultural bridge between the East and the West; and its comparatively small number of institutions of higher learning and correspondingly limited spaces for those willing to study in these institutions. These characteristics have inadvertently created a situation that enables distance education to thrive in the territory. This chapter describes the genesis of distance education in Hong Kong, provides a situational report on contemporary development of distance education in the territory, and documents some of the landmarks in education that make the future of distance education in Hong Kong both appealing and dynamic.

Hong Kong became a Special Administrative Region (HKSAR) of the People's Republic of China (PRC) on 1 July 1997 when it was handed over to China by the British colonial government as set out in the Sino-British Joint Declaration on the Question of Hong Kong (Joint Declaration) signed between the Chinese and the British governments on 19 December 1984. The Joint Declaration laid down the basic policies of the PRC regarding Hong Kong and unequivocally directs that while the socialist policies of the PRC will not be practised in the HKSAR, the capitalist system and lifestyle inherited from its colonial rulers is to remain intact for 50 years. This means that in effect the PRC may not 'interfere' in the affairs of the HKSAR until after 2047. Operating under what is now popularly referred to as the 'one country, two systems' principle, the HKSAR has, as a result, a high degree of autonomy and enjoys autonomous executive and legislative powers and has an independent judiciary.

Located to the southeast of mainland China, the HKSAR adjoins Guangdong province and occupies a land mass of about 1,096 square kilometres with a density of about 6,330 persons per square kilometre. It currently has a population of almost seven million with an average annual growth rate of 1.7%. Hong Kong has enviable population statistics. The death rate is about 4.9 per 1,000 while the live births per 1,000 population are now about 7.9 with the total fertility rate for each woman calculated as 1.0 child compared with 1.4 children 10 years ago. Life expectancy for males is about 77.2 years and 82.6 years for females and infant mortality dropped to about 3.0 per 1,000 in 2000. These figures have a significant impact on education, especially lifelong learning, as will be discussed later in this chapter.

In economic terms, the HKSAR can be described as belonging to the developed world. The statistics for 1998 put its GDP at HK$789 billion (US$101 billion) with a per capita income of HK$192,290 (US$24,652) at today's exchange rate of HK$7.8 to US$1. As one of the world's centres of commerce and business, it enjoys a free market economy and has a labour force participation rate of about 65% of the total population aged 15 and above. In the wake of the Asian financial crisis in 1997, the unemployment rate, which was about 2% on average in the preceding years rose to about 5% in 1998 and has not recovered totally. Hong Kong has excellent communication facilities and a network that is still growing to keep pace with contemporary developments given the emergence of digital technology and gross improvement in telecommunications and computer technology. For instance it has close to four million telephone lines, mobile telephone penetration of seven in every ten persons, over two million personal computers and in excess of 150 Internet service providers. Its media, entertainment and other related technologies are quite advanced with about 50 newspapers, about 700 registered periodicals, four TV stations, one cable TV network and about 13 radio stations. The HKSAR is a bilingual society in which Chinese (Cantonese) and English are freely used both officially and socially although recent developments have seen the emergence of Mandarin (the most widely spoken version of Chinese in mainland China) as a third official language of communication. Indeed, most businesses now increasingly emphasize the ability to speak or have some measure of proficiency in all three languages as an employment advantage.

Education in the HKSAR

Hong Kong has a system of education that reflects its history. Like many countries of the world, it has several levels of schooling made up of kindergarten, primary, secondary, vocational and higher education. Available statistics show that Hong Kong has about 744 kindergartens (175,100 children), 741 public primary schools (431, 600 pupils), and 455,900 students in secondary schools. With regard to higher education, Hong Kong has ten tertiary institutions; eight of these are universities (one of which is self-financing and non-traditional), one is the Hong Kong Institute of Education responsible mainly for teacher training, and the other is the public-funded Hong Kong Academy for Performing Arts. A total of about 60,000 full-time and 20,000 part-time students pursue sub-degree, undergraduate and postgraduate courses in the seven traditional universities while a total of about 26,000 students pursue their education through the distance learning mode at the Open University of Hong Kong (OUHK) — the only recognized distance learning institution in the SAR. The total number of students at school in Hong Kong currently stands at 22% of the population. The government spends about HK$52 billion (about 21.7% of the government's total recurrent expenditure) on education. While the Department of Education provides adult education to the populace at both the primary and secondary levels, almost all institutions of higher learning provide continuing education opportunities to the public. The Vocational Training Council caters for about 21,000 full-time and 42,000 part-time students who need technical education.

Despite its impressive business and commercial success as an international centre and free market economy, and the benefit of the robust educational legacy the colonial government had built in its home country, Hong Kong does not appear to have gained from these educationally. It also has apparently not been able to rise to the challenges of meeting the educational needs of its populace as an avenue to providing the suitable workforce needed to drive its economy. It needs to be recognized that much has been done by the government in terms of provision of education. From only about 10% of the 17 to 20 age group that had the privilege of receiving degree-level education in 1990, that figure has almost doubled to 18%. If the number of students in self-financing, local and non-local programmes and sub-degree courses is anything to go by, the actual number of students in higher education in Hong Kong is by far in excess of this. In money terms, total public spending on tertiary education has increased six-fold from HK$3 billion ten years ago to HK$18 billion (Wong

2000). However, the Hong Kong economy, with only 22% (a total of about 90,000 of its population) in full-time tertiary education, faces a dire shortage of well-trained and qualified human resources. Two other factors could be said to have fuelled the need for education in Hong Kong in recent times. First, the need to be part of an educated workforce to service the ever expanding employment market in Hong Kong motivated many to seek self-improvement opportunities. Second, the unfounded fears of the 1980s regarding the imminent handover of Hong Kong back to China forced people to seek avenues through which to upgrade their educational qualifications in preparation for the massive emigration that occurred during that period. The converse of this was that the emigration created many vacancies needed to be filled by qualified personnel immediately but who were unavailable at that time. An emerging third factor is the post-handover development in Hong Kong created by the digital age. With so much going on in the telecommunications and computing worlds, information technology has become the bride of the employment market. Suddenly, a quiet giant seems to have been awakened, and there is now a shift from the craze for business administration degrees to information technology. The Hong Kong environment that has always been pro-active in updating itself for new job markets could not let this opportunity pass. As a result, the need for opportunities for rapid education or retraining, in their spare time, of those in employment rose sharply. All the above contribute to what may seem to be a greater-than-average demand for education in Hong Kong. Such is the reason that distance education has become a thriving business in Hong Kong, more than anywhere else in the world, when viewed from the perspective of the number of distance education opportunities per member of the population.

Distance education in the HKSAR

As far as I know, no country in the world has been able to meet the educational needs of its people through face-to-face classroom-bound instruction. Put another way, providing all that is needed (physical structures, teachers, resources, etc.) to support on-campus schooling for all the people that need it within a nation, has proved an impossible task no matter how much governments around the world romanticize about it. What seems to be the result of this inadequacy of access to education is the clamour for alternative modes of education. This is especially important for those who wish to upgrade themselves to move ahead or just to remain in employment, or for others such as the unemployed, housewives and the disadvantaged who wish to take a second chance at educating themselves.

The huge unmet demand for education via alternative means has resulted in a flourishing distance education sector in Hong Kong.

The discussion of distance education in Hong Kong will be treated under three headings: 1) off-shore distance education provision; 2) local distance education institutions; and 3) education reform in Hong Kong and its impact on distance education. This break-down is only for the convenience of our discussion in this chapter. The discussion will, however, not be entirely compartmentalized, but will show the relationships among the three areas and also highlight other major issues that have affected the development of distance education in Hong Kong.

Off-shore distance education provision

Hong Kong must have one of the largest concentrations of off-shore distance education provision in the world. As at June 2000, there were 550 non-local programmes in Hong Kong, offering more than 60,000 places: about 270 registered and 242 exempted programmes. Of this total, British courses make up the largest share of 288 programmes (57%), followed by Australia with 157 courses (31%), US programmes (7%), mainland China with 20 programmes (4%), and Canada, Macau and Ireland, which jointly make up the remainder.

Several reasons are attendant to this development, in addition to some issues associated with the surge in the demand for education in Hong Kong already discussed above. Many universities in the developed world have witnessed progressively diminishing funding from their governments and have now sought to augment their budgets from other sources. Marketing education overseas is an attractive option as it gives relatively huge returns for comparatively less work when put side by side with what they offer to their home-based students. This has implications for quality, and I will return to this in a moment.

Given the exceptional or atypical disposable income generally available in Hong Kong, these off-shore distance education courses reap a great financial harvest as shown in the figures contained in Table 1.

Table 1   Fees charged by off-shore distance education providers in Hong Kong

AUSTRALIA

B. Nursing	Monash University (in cooperation with SPEED, Hong Kong Polytechnic University)	HK$48,000
Master of Administrative Leadership	University of New England (in cooperation with School of Continuing Studies, Chinese University of Hong Kong)	HK$75,840
Master of Business in Accounting	Monash University (in cooperation with SPACE, Hong Kong University)	HK$121,344
Master of Business (Information Technology)	Curtin University of Technology (Informatics)	HK$ 79,632
Master of Finance	Curtin University of Technology (in cooperation with the OUHK)	HK$83,424
DBA	University of South Australia	HK$198,000
Master of Technology Management	University of Queensland (in cooperation with Lingnan University, HK)	HK$100,000
Master of Journalism	University of Wollongong (in cooperation with the OUHK)	HK$56,680

CANADA

Executive MBA	University of Ottawa	HK$218,000

USA

Executive MBA	Southern Illinois University (Management Development Institute (HK) Ltd)	HK$100,620
MBA	University of Louisville	HK$109,000

Table 1 cont.

UK

BA (Hons) (Public Administration and Management)	De Montfort University (in cooperation with SCOPE, City University of Hong Kong)	HK$84,000
MSc (Occupational and Environmental Health and Safety Management)	University of Portsmouth (in cooperation with School of Continuing and Professional Education (SCOPE), City University of Hong Kong)	HK$80,000
MBA	University of Strathclyde	HK$133,889

MACAU

MBA	Asia International Open University	HK$152,250

Current exchange rate is HK$7.8 = US$1

Another reason is that some countries such as Australia have made education an explicit part of their international relations or foreign policy. Indeed, about three decades ago, Australia internationalized education and made it a part of its programme to attract the attention of the world. Furthermore, just as trade was used to colonize the world several centuries ago, it is not unlikely that education, given all that it offers now, is also being used as an instrument for cultural imperialism.

Many of the off-shore institutions often seek partnership with local institutions and organizations to run the programme on their behalf. The British Council and IDP Education Australia are the biggest organizations acting as local agents for non-local courses in Hong Kong. The continuing education centres of all the universities in Hong Kong (for example SCOPE of City University of Hong Kong; the School of Professional and Continuing Education (SPACE) of Hong Kong University; Lingnan University; the School of Continuing Studies of Chinese University of Hong Kong; Continuing Education Studies of Hong Kong Baptist University; the School of Professional Education and Executive Development (SPEED) of Hong Kong Polytechnic University; and LiPACE

(Li Ka Shing Institute for Professional and Continuing Education) of the OUHK are involved in this. Apart from acting as agents, the local partners have hardly any input with regard to the content or other academic matters. As a result of this and many other factors, the quality of some of the off-shore distance education programmes is suspect. Many of them offer considerably trimmed curricula that are very different to and of lesser quality than those that they would normally offer to their home students. Others illogically reduce the number of years in which Hong Kong students need to complete the courses to ridiculous periods that even full-time students would normally find it impossible to complete them in.

As mentioned by Evans (2000), one difficulty of a practical nature is that many of the institutions offering distance education off-shore do not have an established distance education or off-shore education culture to draw from or build upon. They also do not have the infrastructure for supporting and teaching students at a distance in their own countries in order to build a successful off-shore offering. For instance, some of the significant services and values itemized by Evans (2000) as attendant to a successful distance education course are often absent in off-shore distance education. They include enabling off-shore students to undertake all of the normal administrative aspects of student life from a distance: obtaining a range of support services and facilities to help cope with study (library services, counselling, book and materials purchases, etc.), obtaining their tuition (course materials and tutoring), assessment (assignments and examinations), and engaging in scholarly interaction (with staff and other students) at a distance. These have both infrastructural and cultural dimensions. All these therefore have implications for quality as mentioned above. As a result of this the Government of Hong Kong decided to put in place a regulatory mechanism primarily to check quality and dissuade the emergence of 'Mickey-Mouse' degrees in Hong Kong. This resulted in the Non-Local Higher and Professional Education (Regulation) Ordinance, which came into effect on 20 June 1997. The Ordinance regulates the operation of non-local courses in Hong Kong and requires that all courses that lead to a higher academic or professional award from a non-local institution in Hong Kong register or apply for exemption from registration with the Non-Local Courses Registry. The procedure for registration is fairly rigorous and involves entering the Register of Registered Courses of the Non-Local Courses Registry at the Education and Manpower Bureau (EMB). Exempted courses are those that operate in partnership with the 11 specified local tertiary institutions. These exempted courses are also entered into the Register of Exempted Courses at the Non-Local Courses Registry.

One important exemption from any form of registration is the group of courses that has neither regulated activities nor examinations. The body responsible for registration and regulation is the Hong Kong Council for Academic Accreditation (HKCAA). The HKCAA is the only independent statutory accreditation authority in Hong Kong and has, in its ten years of existence, done much to uplift the quality of education in Hong Kong through the provision of guidance institutions by way of validations and institutional reviews, seeking the input of local and international experts to ensure that degree programmes offered in Hong Kong will achieve internationally recognized benchmarks (Wong 2000).

Several other initiatives regarding online learning as well as distance education courses with partner institutions or alliances are emerging quite rapidly. One of the online learning programmes is by the Hong Kong University of Science and Technology (HKUST) College of Lifelong Learning established in October 2000. Distance learning courses offered by three mainland Chinese universities —Tsinghua University, Zhongshan University and Zhejiang University — are now offered to Hong Kong students on their website <http://www.ChinaCyberU.net>. The Chinese University of Hong Kong's School of Continuing Studies is partnering the University of Wollongong, Australia, for a new one-year postgraduate certificate programme in Multicultural Journalism and a joint MBA programme with Tsinghua University. Recent developments in the funding of University Grants Commission (UGC) institutions in Hong Kong, which have seen the government reduce the funding for the 2001/04 triennium by an average of 6% for all the universities, seems to be warning the traditional universities to supplement their budgets elsewhere. This might have the result of propelling all of them towards providing many of their courses through the distance mode. This will, of course change the terrain of higher distance education in Hong Kong, and, if these institutions opt to use the online learning avenue, will affect the greater China region and the global village too.

While the various institutions act as local partners in the provision of off-shore distance education, on their own they respond to the needs of society by providing courses that are relevant and meet the demands of the people of Hong Kong. In order to meet the needs of a learning-based society and lifelong education, adult higher education institutions have introduced an increasing number of different programmes at the tertiary level. Currently, for example, there are 102 such programmes offered by the OUHK, 39 by Hong Kong University, 68 by the Chinese University of

Hong Kong, 25 by Hong Kong Polytechnic University, 35 by the City University of Hong Kong and 39 by Hong Kong Baptist University. According to his October 2000 Policy Address, the Chief Executive of the HKSAR pointed out that the quota for new students at the tertiary level would be double current quotas within the next ten years. In order to achieve this goal, the HKSAR government is encouraging higher education institutions to introduce more diploma and sub-degree programmes for school leavers.

Local distance education institutions

Until the mid-1970s, Hong Kong had only two universities, a polytechnic and some tertiary institutions. These were grossly inadequate for the population of about five million people, many of whom for a variety of reasons were tremendously motivated to acquire degrees and other tertiary educational qualifications.

In the past decade three new tertiary institutions, the Open Learning Institute of Hong Kong (OLI), HKUST and the Hong Kong Institute of Education were established. Similarly, five tertiary institutions were transformed into universities. They include Baptist University, City University of Hong Kong, Hong Kong Polytechnic University, the OUHK and Lingnan University.

Although dozens of overseas institutions offer their courses to students in Hong Kong by a variety of avenues, the clear focal point of open learning in the territory is the OUHK. The OLI, which was established in 1989 and was the predecessor to the OUHK, was this focal point until 1997 when it became the OUHK upon being granted university status. The OUHK is the only institution of distance education in the territory that is recognized by the SAR government.

The OUHK typifies the success story of open and distance education (ODE) in Asia. Since its inception, the University has charted a course of activities in providing education to thousands of people in Hong Kong who would not otherwise have had the opportunity to see the inside of a university for reasons associated with employment, time, social and family commitments. As has been aptly stated by Professor Tam Sheung-wai, the President of the University, 'open and distance education has gained increasing recognition, and with continued effort, it may eventually become a mainstream for education and manpower development in Asian countries. We shall play our part by continuing to strive ardently for

Education for All' (OUHK General Information Booklet, 2). This is in keeping with the mission statements of the University, which state that:

- The Open University of Hong Kong dedicates itself to providing sub-degree, degree and postgraduate courses leading to awards and qualifications principally through a system of open and distance education; thereby making higher education available to all those aspiring to it regardless of previous qualifications, gender or race.

- The University commits itself to excellence in teaching, scholarship and public service.

- As a self-financing, non-profit-making organization, the University is further committed to developing and supporting sustainable high-quality courses and programmes that are affordable to its students.

There are six distinctive characteristics of the model of open and distance education practised at the OUHK. These are open access, distance learning as the instructional delivery platform, a credit system, a credit transfer system, assessment and rigorous built-in quality assurance in all its operations. These are elaborated on below.

The OUHK and its history

The conception of the OUHK institution actually began in 1982. As a response to the growing demand for education to learn new skills, enhance existing ones or advance personal development in Hong Kong in the 1980s, the mode of using continuing education, especially for people already in employment but without having had the benefit of tertiary education, was contemplated. Therefore, in 1982, through a report entitled 'A perspective on education in Hong Kong' prepared by a visiting panel from the UK headed by Sir John Llewellyn, a case was made for strengthening continuing education in Hong Kong. The report, now known as the 'Llewellyn Report' argued that, 'with its small geographic size and its high technological standard, Hong Kong would be eminently suitable for a system of education by radio and TV, combined, for example, with weekend study on campus and evening tutorials.... we are thinking in terms of a large-scale, comprehensive alternative to institutionalised education on the school and technical education/vocational training levels as well as higher education' (Section III.6.8, Chapter 6).

This report triggered a chain of events that ended in the establishment of the OUHK. The first of these was the setting up of the Education Commission to advise the government on education matters and discuss the need for open education in Hong Kong. The Commission published its report in 1986 and identified three primary objectives for open education in Hong Kong:

- To provide a second chance for those who had to forgo, or were denied the opportunity of, further education when they left school, or whose requirements for further education develop relatively late in life;

- To provide continuing education to update and enhance the training of those who completed their further education at the beginning of their careers; and

- To provide retraining for those who need to change or extend their career or vocational skills later in life to adapt to technological, economic and social change.

In addition to the above, one key policy recommendation that came out of the Education Commission's discussion on open education for Hong Kong was that a consortium of tertiary education institutions in Hong Kong be set up to offer opportunities for open learning using distance education methods.

The second event was the setting up of an ad hoc working group, including academic members from interested tertiary institutions as well as Government Officers to draw up specific proposals for the government's consideration with regard to the recommendations of the Education Commission on open education.

Based upon the recommendations of the working group, the government of Hong Kong in September 1987 approved the setting up of a Planning Committee to produce implementation plans for the establishment of the OLI. The Governor formally announced this to the Legislative Council on 7 October 1987 when he said: '...the government has now decided to set up a Planning Committee for the establishment of an Open Learning Institute. The provision of an Open Learning Institute, which will be Hong Kong's sixth degree-awarding institution, will considerably increase the opportunity for tertiary education. The institute will offer degree and sub-degree courses. It should admit its first students in 1989.'

The Planning Committee for the OLI appointed by the Governor on 1 January 1988 had six representatives from UPGC-funded institutions in Hong Kong and the UK Open University, three overseas academic members appointed *ad personam*, five local members with experience in commerce and industry, one senior government Officer, and a Principal Assistant Secretary of the Education and Manpower Board as Secretary. Professor Don Swift, then Director of the Open College of the University of East Asia, Macau, who was a member of the Planning Committee was appointed as the Founding Director of the OLI.

With a 39 core staff the OLI began its operations with the first student intake. The exceptional uptake of open learning in Hong Kong took everyone by surprise. As recounted by George Kilo, the first Registrar, 'The government had agreed on an intake of 3,500 for the OLI, with the simplest of entry requirements: a Hong Kong ID card and age of 18 years. The OLI printed 75,000 prospectus and application forms... when the doors opened for prospectuses late in July 1989 the demand was wholly unprecedented. By the end of the application period, the total applications had reached 63,000. The UK Open University had attracted only some 43,000 in a country ten times the size' (pp. 50 and 51).

When the first class opened in October 1989, a total of 4,237 students were enrolled in eight courses. This had a far-reaching effect in endorsing the reasons for providing an alternative route to tertiary education in Hong Kong. Some of these reasons included the following:

- The government's introduction of free and compulsory primary and secondary education in 1971 and 1979 respectively created a tremendous demand for tertiary education among graduates at these levels of education in Hong Kong. As at 1960, only 1% gained entry into first-degree programmes and by the end of the 1970s this figure had increased to 5%. But by this time thousands had graduated from the free education system. The free system actually aggravated the situation and there was a dire need to provide extra places for those seeking tertiary education places.

- During the 1970s and 1980s and indeed the early 1990s the level of emigration from Hong Kong was so great that the human resources needed to sustain the development of Hong Kong as a world business and commercial centre was being sharply depleted. There was therefore an urgent need to seek other avenues to develop the human resources needed.

- Hong Kong's population increased rapidly to six million in the early 1990s and the system needed to educate and train an increasing number of adults who were employed but required further education and training.

All the above provided the fertile ground for the establishment of the then OLI in order to fulfil the primary objectives it was set up to achieve. Some of these objectives included:

- To provide a range of courses and programmes at sub-degree, first-degree and second-degree level;

- To enable students to complete programmes at their own pace, in their own chosen location;

- To provide study facilities and face-to-face tuition to support those students;

- To deliver courses using multimedia to students with widely differing learning preferences and needs;

- To ensure that exit performance standards of degree programmes are equivalent to those of other tertiary institutions in Hong Kong and elsewhere, and to ensure that OLI degrees have equal status to those of other tertiary institutions in Hong Kong and elsewhere;

- To strive to meet the perceived needs of Hong Kong society by developing and maintaining maximum cooperation with a range of interest groups and by offering a suitable range of courses which students wish to take and can afford.

Self-financing plan

One other arrangement for the establishment of the OLI was the entrenchment in the government's memorandum for the institution to be self-financing. This is a departure from the full government financing support other tertiary institutions established by the government in Hong Kong enjoy. It is also a concept foreign to similar institutions in other parts of the world. For example the UK Open University, which served as a model for the OLI, started with and still enjoys 100% government funding. Indeed although the Bill that established the OLI did not specify that the Institute should be self-financing, Report No 2, August 1986 of the Education Commission stated categorically that as a long-term objective the institution should as far as possible be self-financing, i.e. that students should meet the direct costs of the courses they took. An analysis of the literature available revealed that the idea of self-financing came from the Planning Committee. It noted in its section 12.1 that: 'The OLI should as far as possible be self-financing, but in any case students should meet at least the direct costs of producing and delivering courses. The Government should meet the costs of setting up the OLI and, on establishment, the costs of accommodation, equipment, essential administration and core staff, etc. to the extent that these cannot be met through student fees.'

This was translated into operational details that the OLI should break even in three-and-a-half years of academic operation based on subventions of HK\$42.78 million down to HK\$6.82 million. April 1993 was nominated as the time when it would become self-funding. This experiment certainly paid off and has become a model for other institutions of its kind desirous of achieving self-financing within their own environments and situations. The OUHK generates almost all of its revenue from the fees that students pay for their courses. For capital projects such as buildings, laboratories, and specific needs, the government does make a one-off subvention. For example in recent times the government has given HK\$50 million to the OUHK to develop as a regional centre of excellence in open and adult learning, and provided matching funds for its acquisition of the Island Learning Centre in central Hong Kong. It also provided support for the Information Technology Plan of the University. The OUHK also benefits from the generally favourable atmosphere of endowment and charity from sources such as the Hong Kong Jockey Club, The Croucher Foundation and many other charitable and business and commercial organizations in Hong Kong. This self-financing status has helped to focus the University on a market-oriented strategy of providing courses for which there is high and sustained demand. The OUHK applies differential fee-charging criteria, and conducts regular market surveys to determine the needs and relevance of courses directed at the Hong Kong public. All these are undertaken without jeopardizing the quality of its instruction. Indeed a research project commissioned in 1999 by the University Council on employment and student perception of distance learning and studying at the OUHK indicated that employers are quite pleased with the quality of the products and would recommend many more of their employees to embark on distance learning, if they chose to undertake further and continuing education. Financially, the OUHK, although not a profit-making institution, has been able to balance its books and obtain some surplus after expenditure based on all its activities since 1994 when it became self-funding. Indeed it has been able to maintain some funding reserves for a number of activities such as the General Development Fund, Course Material Development, and Research and Development. The University also now provides grants, scholarships and interest-free loans to needy students.

In order to meet with the novel arrangements for open education in Hong Kong, fulfil its unique objectives, become self-financing and exhibit a high degree of quality comparable to that of the traditional universities, the OLI had to adopt strategies, many of which are continued today. Some of these strategies include focusing on appropriate academic programmes in great demand by Hong Kong residents; course development, programme planning and quality assurance; credit transfers, advanced standing, monitoring of courses and tutorials; student support; research; and international outreach and collaboration.

Academic programmes

When the OLI opened its doors to students in October 1989, it admitted 4,237 students in three Schools approved for establishment by the Planning Committee — the School of Arts and Humanities, the School of Commerce and Social Science, and the School of Science and Technology. The Planning Committee in its wisdom recommended in its paragraph 6.20 that 'the appropriateness of the titles and their coverage will be reviewed in the light of experience'. This was prophetic indeed. The OUHK has reviewed the names of the schools, and now has four schools and two centres:

- School of Arts and Social Sciences;
- School of Business and Administration;
- School of Science and Technology;
- School of Education and Languages (added in August 1992);
- Centre for Continuing and Community Education (CCCE) established in June 1992, which changed its name in February 2000 to the Li Ka Shing Institute for Professional and Continuing Education (LiPACE);
- Centre for Research in Distance and Adult Learning (CRIDAL) established in May 1997.

The OUHK provides instruction in programmes and courses leading to a sub-degree, degree or postgraduate degree. With only a core staff of 39, and eight degree and preparatory courses, which signalled the start of open education in Hong Kong in 1989, the OUHK, as at the October 2000 intake, now has 500 full-time staff, 1,000 part-time staff, and a total of 92 programmes, including an MPhil and a Doctorate of Education. While the School of Business and Administration has enjoyed the largest student enrolment, the growing demand globally for IT courses has positively affected demand for such courses and other related courses run mainly by the School of Science and Technology. Each programme consists of a number of required and elective courses. Courses are divided into Pre-foundation, Foundation, Middle, Higher, Honours and Master's levels. More than 148 courses were offered in the October 2000 semester. LiPACE offered 330 courses during the same period while 19 courses were offered in mainland China. The OUHK runs a semester system and has two semesters per year.

Student enrolment has been on an annual continual increase since the inception of the institution as shown in Figure 1 below. If the continuing education programmes and students are counted, the current total number of students stands at 37,000 (see Press Release of 28 February 2001). The University has projected that by 2010, it will have a total student population of 60,000 in response to the government's recent manpower needs study and calculations based upon the OUHK's average growth in enrolment. It is estimated that the number of full-time staff will reach an all-time high of 900 and there will be 1,800 part-time staff. The number of graduates has also been rising year-on-year. The first graduation ceremony was in November 1993. That year 161 students graduated. As at December 2000 when a record number of 4,500 students graduated, the total number of graduates from its degree programmes rose to 14,000. Records indicate that more than 110,000 learners have studied at the OLI/OUHK since 1989.

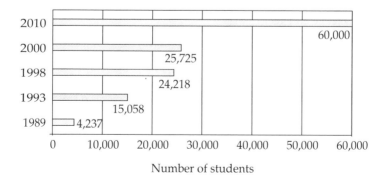

Figure 1   Growth in student population

Other demographic details of students indicate that as of the December 2000 semester, the average age of an OUHK student is 32, with the majority (43.4%) in the 31 to 40 age group and a male-female ratio of about 1:1. Records also show that students who occupy professional managerial positions in their workplace account for about 40% of the OUHK student population. This is an indication that many of the students who undertake open education at the OUHK are gainfully employed, hold responsible positions and need to update their skills and knowledge while in employment.

Course development, programme planning and quality assurance

ODL, unlike the traditional face-to-face teaching and learning environments, is characterized by distinctive course development and delivery features. First, a team must design the courses with members bringing in their expertise in the instructional design process. Second, the courses must be presented in a way that facilitates their study, by students who are removed from their lecturers, study independently and have limited time each day devoted to such self-study. Third, several means, which include an array of appropriate multimedia, must be used to deliver the courses to wherever the students are located. In the unique case of Hong Kong, 'distance' as applied to distance education does not differ by geographical location as most of the students are located within a radius of 50 kilometres of the University. However, the distance referred to here is more of time, than of opportunity, to access the facilities and materials for study. Finally, although distance education relies solely on economies of scale, the overall system for delivery and course presentation must have standardized features appropriate and applicable to the delivery of the courses to mass numbers of students.

As a result of the above and for other pertinent reasons, several programme planning procedures are followed. The long list of programme and course planning items includes the development of an Outline Programme Proposal and a Detailed Programme Proposal. These, at different stages, involve the input or approval of a number of Committees and Bodies including the School Committee, Course Review Committee, Advisory Peer Group, Senate and Council. OUHK courses are developed using the modular model with the singular advantage that it enables learners to choose their own rate of progress by selecting the number of courses they wish to study concurrently. When the University first started as the OLI, to save time and maximize efficiency and cost-effectiveness, it adopted or adapted course materials from a number of overseas sources, which included the UK Open University. While the majority of such courses came from the UK Open University, a few other courses were adopted from Canadian and Australian universities. The OUHK now develops the majority of its courses and the number of bilingual courses (offered both in English and in Chinese) has only grown.

Open and distance education, with so many intricate processes of operation, can easily be subject to a drop in quality if the system does not integrate a quality assurance system within its operations on a step-by-step basis. Wong and Jegede (2000) have provided details of two exemplars (course design, and examination and assessment) of quality assurance in the operations of the OUHK. With regard to course development they affirmed that the process actually begins from an idea of programme development, which results after a market survey. If found to be viable, an Outline Programme Proposal (OPP) is developed followed by a Detailed Programme Proposal (DPP). To become fully developed and acceptable for course development the DPP is quality checked by several groups and statutory bodies which include a Programme Team, Advisory Peer Group, School Board, External Programme Assessor, Programme Review and Validation Committee, and finally the Senate. Once the plan is approved, the course design and development is undertaken through the Course Team Approach model in which a group of academics and experts in content, course design, media and technology, etc., is constituted for the purpose of writing the course materials for students. Some of the quality hurdles to be passed include the external course assessment, internal validation committee, Senate, tutors and external examiners. The final check stage is, of course, the students, who send in feedback and evaluation periodically. The total process of course design and development could take anything between 12 to 24 months before a course is offered to students, providing an extensive period in which all quality assurance mechanisms are put to the test and scrutinized.

The quality assurance in assessment and examinations at the OUHK is extensive and rigorous. Several quality assurance steps are taken to ensure that the examinations and assessment are of a high standard. Essentially, there are about 22 steps involved in the quality procedure, some of which are listed in the following table.

Table 2   Stages of preparation for course examinations

Steps to be taken by Course Coordinator (CC)	Steps to be taken by others
Preparing the examination	
• Design exam paper and marking guide • Application for approval of External Examiner (EE) • Inform registry of exam materials (e.g. calculator) • Nominating and appointing script markers	• Check exam paper and marking guide (External Examiner) • Print exam paper, set exam date, book rooms, etc. (Examinations Office)
After the examination	
• Use Batch X for Coordination Meeting (below) • Mark all Batch T scripts to see how marking guide works • Chair Coordination Meeting (CM) to standardize marking by training the script markers using Batch X • Script monitoring to see script markers' performance • Set the minimum thresholds for each band, etc. • Standardization meeting with the EE • Review borderline cases • Confirm thresholds	• Send two batchs (X and T) of scripts to the CC (Examinations Office) • Collect scripts from the OUHK (script marker) • Send monitoring batch to CC and EE (Examinations Office) • Script monitoring to see script markers' performance (External Examiner) • Compute results, distribution scores (Examinations Office/ ITU) • 2nd computation of results based on confirmed thresholds (Examinations Office/ ITU)

Table 2 cont.

Award Meeting including CC, External Examiner, Dean and others	
• Documentation for the Award Meeting • Comments on performance • Confirmation of standardization results • Confirmation of results status boundaries • Determination of borderline results • Special circumstances? (e.g. illness, occasional misconduct) • Nomination of outstanding students • Recording results	• Oversee all exam results (Course Result Group)
• Prepare and sign minutes of the Award Meeting • Sign the minutes (CC and Dean)	• Send in a report (External Examiner)

Credit transfers, advanced standing, monitoring of courses and tutorials

An open education system must of necessity be open and flexible to accommodate all kinds of student backgrounds and match these with their learning needs. Studying by the distance mode also means a student located anywhere can decide to study with any particular university. In a number of cases there are students who would prefer to study in a system different from the one they are already in or have experienced. While this is exciting for the student it may present all sorts of problems for the university or institution. To meet its mission and objectives, the OUHK decided to institute a comprehensive credit transfer system to enable students to transfer credits accumulated elsewhere to the OUHK so that they could continue a course or programme with the OUHK without losing them.

The OUHK requires students to have gained 160 credits for a Master's degree, 120 for a Bachelor's degree, 160 for a Bachelor's degree with honours, 90 for a Higher Diploma, 60 for a Diploma, and 30 for a Certificate. Students transferring to the OUHK to continue or complete their courses or programmes would therefore make up the total credits needed to earn the qualification they are pursuing from the credits that they transfer from their former institution plus any additional credits to make up the maximum required by the course they enrol in. The OUHK therefore has three types of credit transfer. The General Credit Transfer allows a new student to be exempted from obtaining credits (usually 20 units) that cannot be related to any specific course. These are termed as free-choice or general credits. The OUHK allows exemption from all or some of these in recognition of a student's 'external' studies not directly related to its courses. The Specific Credit Transfer is awarded if it is decided through a process of validation that the student had studied a course or sets of courses in his or her previous institution closely related to an OUHK course. The third transfer is the Block Credit Transfer, which enables a student to transfer in block all or a specified maximum number of credits in exchange for a substantial proportion of undergraduate studies done elsewhere but similar in depth and scope to the course or programme the student is enrolled in at the OUHK.

The decisions about credit transfers are made under the general principle of advanced standing. The Senate's Advanced Standing Committee normally processes all advanced standing applications and makes recommendations for ultimate ratification by the Senate and the Council of all those who meet the requirements and regulations of the University.

The University often monitors course operations. The University uses a large number of tutors, who are qualified academics mainly from the universities and other higher institutions in Hong Kong, to run tutorials at prearranged times, usually weekends, to help students with any cognitive concerns. These tutors, numbering about 1,000 at the beginning of 2001, serve as a significant bridge between the University and its students, and therefore serve a useful monitoring role. Assignments are an important segment of distance learning. They are used as learning tools and as a basis for assessment. All courses contain two types of assignment: Tutor-marked Assignments (TMAs) and Computer-Marked Assignments (CMAs). An extensive system of external examination both for courses, programmes and examinations operates within the ODL environment at the OUHK. This contributes tremendously to the effective and efficient monitoring of courses, programmes and how well students are learning their materials.

Student support

The ODL mode has a number of channels by which students can be reached for contact purposes and to help them accomplish their studies. This synchronizes quite well with the variety of backgrounds, learning styles and specific needs of learners. It also takes cognisance of the teaching styles and preferences of tutors and course development teams. The courses and programmes are offered through study materials, which are in various combinations of print, audio, video, CD-ROMs, and online (electronic courses, etc.). Indeed the OUHK now has over 70 courses running online, and by the year 2010, the Information Technology Plan of the University makes provision for almost all OUHK courses to be online. Other channels for the delivery of instruction include tutorials, assignments, television broadcasts, laboratories, surgeries, and day schools. All these require students to manage learning through several channels, in addition to issues they may have with self-study or what is often called individualized instruction. As a result, the University has in place an extensive student support system. This includes counselling, computer laboratories, science and technology related laboratories, language laboratories, a physical and an electronic library, self-study centres, weekly TV broadcasts of courses, and the provision of audio, video and CD-ROMs in courses where these are found to enhance teaching and learning, and tutors.

Research

One issue the OUHK takes seriously as having an impact on its daily operation as a distance teaching institution, and which sets it apart from similar institutions in Asia and indeed around the world, is research in distance and adult learning. The University saw the need to embark on research activities as a way of supporting, through empirical results and information, how it performs its functions, including teaching and learning, development of courses, technology use in ODL, and student support. As a first step, the institution in 1995 set aside HK$7.5 million for its Research & Development Fund in readiness for setting up a Centre for Research in Distance and Adult Learning (CRIDAL) to, among other objectives:

- Enhance the quality of scholarship and research activities;

- Provide leadership through an approach to ODL research that is responsive to the needs of the community;

- Foster a collaborative research culture within the University and, eventually, with our counterparts around the world.

Since its inception in May 1997, CRIDAL <www.ouhk.edu.hk/cridal> has made significant contributions to the development of research in ODL within the Asia region and indeed with the global ODL environment at the OUHK. Within the University it conducts frequent training and surgeries in research methodology, colloquia, seminars and workshops to help staff acquire or renew their skills and knowledge about ODL research. CRIDAL undertakes three kinds of projects: locally, within the University involving staff from various units as a hands-on skill development and acquisition platform; CRIDAL staff conducting research as part of their normal employment; and consultancy and externally funded research. Within such a relatively short period of existence, CRIDAL and its staff have enhanced the research culture at the OUHK, embarked on capacity-building activities with other staff, undertaken up to two dozen research projects, its staff have won some awards for excellence, conducted a specialized international workshop on institutional research in ODL, and embarked on securing external grants to support research at the OUHK. For three years running, CRIDAL has received support from The Croucher Foundation for support its fellowship programme, which grants academics from mainland China a six-month visiting fellowship at CRIDAL. As a mark of recognition, CRIDAL has become the East Asia regional site for the World Bank Global Distance Education Network, and has recently co-coordinated the International Council for Open and Distance Education (ICDE) Task Force on Research. It successfully held the first Conference on Research in Distance and Adult Learning in Asia in June 2000 (CRIDALA 2000), and due to the role the conference appeared to have played in filling a huge vacuum in ODL research and its dissemination in Asia and beyond, CRIDAL has accepted suggestions to hold the conference every two years.

International outreach and collaboration

The OUHK has many levels of international outreach and collaboration: some are academic, others professional, and others take different forms according to need, requests and affiliations.

On the academic front, it has relationships with several institutions in North America, the UK, Australia and Asia for credit transfer agreements, as for example with the UK Open University, the Open Learning Agency of British Columbia in Canada, Central Radio and TV University in China,

National Open University in Taiwan, and Massey University, New Zealand. An alliance of four key open and distance education universities comprising the UK Open University, the OUHK, Athabasca University, Canada, and Deakin University, Australia, is proposed. The Alliance currently focuses on two major priorities — establishing agreements and arrangements for the granting of credit transfers and establishing protocols to enable members of the alliance to work collaboratively in venturing into new markets, countries or geographical regions and other areas of operation. A new development that the OUHK has embarked upon is the offering of its courses overseas. The bulk of this is concentrated in mainland China (as discussed in a later section and summarized in Table 3, p. 76). It does appear that the growth of the OUHK will in the future be in this direction and should assume larger dimensions in line with global developments and more access to information and communication technology.

Professionally, the OUHK is member of a number of international organizations. It first of all became a professional member of the Asian Association of Open Universities (AAOU) in April 1990, while still the OLI. It has since then assumed some leadership role in the AAOU by hosting its annual conference twice (1993 and 1998), currently serving as the Secretariat for a three-year period. It joined the Association of Commonwealth Universities in 1992, became a member of and hosted the ICDE pre-conference workshop in 1992, and in the same year was the first overseas member of the Open Learning Foundation of the UK.

Future plans of the OUHK

The University has, with its modest achievements, become recognized as a Centre of Excellence in Distance and Adult Learning in the new millennium. The University has operated successfully as a quality higher educational institution on a self-financing basis since 1993. It established and gained public acceptance of ODL in Hong Kong. It incorporated and continues to incorporate in a systematic manner, appropriate technologies into the provision of ODL, enhancing the flexibility and user-friendliness of course delivery and support services, and breaking down the barriers faced by disabled students. These and other achievements have won the University two major international awards in 1999 and one in 2000:

- The *Award of Excellence for Institutional Achievement in Distance Education* conferred by the Commonwealth of Learning in March 1999;

- The *Institutional Prize of Excellence* conferred by the ICDE in June 1999;

- The *Stockholm Challenge Award* for technological achievement for its Electronic Library in June 2000.

These awards demonstrate the high regard in which the OUHK is held by international organizations and the ODL community it is a part of. Given the future plans it has in mind, the OUHK is sure to receive further recognition and many more awards in the years to come.

Education reform in Hong Kong and its impact on distance education

The Education Commission has just promulgated its third consultation document outlining a comprehensive package of reform measures ranging from pre-school to tertiary levels. Within the next decade the changes in the education scene will see the following new developments in Hong Kong: the emergence of community colleges and private universities, more flexible programmes with multiple entry and multiple exit, wider implementation of a credit-unit system and more Web-based programmes.

What culminated in the Education Blueprint for the 21st Century (HKSAR 2000a) began in 1998 and involved wide consultation with all segments of the public in order to review the total education system in line with developments in the 21st century and society's needs for the future. After the third round of consultation from May to July 2000, the Education Commission released the Blueprint in September 2000. The central focus of the whole educational reform is the 'Building of an education system conducive to lifelong learning and all-round development' (HKSAR 2000a, 3). Section 2.6 details the aims of education for the 21st century as follows:

'To enable every person to attain *all-round development* in the domains of ethics, intellect, physique, social skills and aesthetics *according to his/her own attributes* so that he/she is capable of lifelong learning, critical and exploratory thinking, innovating and adapting to change; filled with self-confidence and a team spirit; willing to put forward continuing effort for the prosperity, progress, freedom and democracy of their society, and contribute to the future well-being of the nation and the world at large' (HKSAR 2000a, 4).

The vision of the reform has the following aims:

- To build a lifelong society;

- To raise the overall quality of students;

- To construct a diverse school system;

- To create an inspiring learning environment;

- To acknowledge the importance of moral education;

- To develop an education system that is rich in tradition but cosmopolitan and culturally sensitive.

Although the education reform suggests the use of principles that are student-focused, result in no losers, ensure quality, cater for lifelong learning, and include society-wide mobilization, what seems to run through the whole reform is the need to cater for lifelong learning. This is a major departure from the focus that had previously been given to traditional classroom-bound type education. In effect, it is advocating that the open and distance mode of learning, which had been in the background in the educational scheme in Hong Kong, should move to the mainstream. Indeed the document does allude to this fact by stating that the increasing number of students through the non-traditional mode (in 1999 about 550,000 were enrolled in continuing education courses in Hong Kong) is indicative of the need for education to reflect the variety of the community's needs for continuing education.

The Blueprint recommends that to build on the present strengths of continuing education, education in Hong Kong needs to be flexible and open, assure quality, accredit qualifications obtained through various modes and establish credit transfer mechanisms. These are some of the major tenets which, as mentioned in the preceding section, the OUHK has adhered to and practised since its inception. In a way the Blueprint has not only endorsed this alternative mode of instruction, it has legitimized and put the society's stamp on its efficacy for educating the public and orienting all towards lifelong learning.

The implications of the above are obvious, far-reaching and point to the need for ODL to do more. The Chief Executive of Hong Kong, Mr Tung Chee-hwa, in his Policy Address of October 2000, entitled *Serving the Community Sharing Common Goals*, specifically mentioned the need to double admission into higher education within five years. Among other things, the Chief Executive said that 'a diverse, multi-level, multi-channel system of tertiary education accessible to all must emerge. Education should increasingly become more flexible and diverse... and lifelong learning will increasingly become the norm' (HKSAR 2000b, 19). While calling for diversity and flexibility in tertiary education, he stated that the objective of his government is to double within ten years the number of secondary school leavers who received tertiary education from the current 30% to 60%. This will provide about 28,999 additional places for higher education bringing the total number to about 55,000. As part of the need to address the continuing education of the school leavers within the 17 to 21 age bracket through non-traditional modes, especially for those who cannot go directly to university, some initiatives are already being taken.

The first is the Project Springboard, launched by the Hong Kong Government and run by the Federation for Continuing Education in Tertiary Institutions (FCE) formed by members of the continuing education departments of UGC institutions and the OUHK, Caritas Adult and Higher Education Services and the Vocational Training Council. Project Springboard is a bridging programme for school leavers and adult learners. It is specifically aimed at providing an alternative route and expanding the continuing education opportunities for secondary school leavers and adult learners. The interim assessment report of the project by the HKCAA accepted that the objectives are being realized and that it can suitably prepare its students for further study in these continuing education courses. This should pave the way for the graduates of the scheme to continue with their education via the open and distance education route in the near future.

A second initiative is the establishment of community colleges. A couple of institutions of higher education have already taken steps to establish them while others are preparing to do so. When they are all established the scope of students to learn through the ODL mode will be considerably broadened. It will also mean that the foundation for lifelong learning in Hong Kong will have been solidly laid. To provide a platform for lifelong education, CRIDAL has embarked on a number of research projects, including 'Learning activities, aging and expertise, and metacognitive knowledge of older adults in Hong Kong'. It is hoped that the study when completed will provide Hong Kong with the information and data necessary:

- For an understanding of the factors which determine the preferred learning activities of older adults in Hong Kong;

- In determining what type of learning activities are of particular interest to older adults and how can they can be developed to address changing work and family responsibilities;

- What educational institutions such as the OUHK can do to support informal, self-directed learning of older adults and what role the OUHK can play in fostering and supporting educational programmes for older adults.

Problems and prospects for ODL

Access and credibility

The open access policy of open universities is not yet fully understood by the general public the world over. In Hong Kong this counts as a disadvantage because some segments of the public may perceive it to mean that the University is easy to enter, easy to graduate from, and hence its quality is doubtful. This touches on the fundamental issue about ODL world-wide in which the public perception is that ODL is of lesser quality than full-time on-campus education. As also mentioned by Evans (2000), although distance education is a rapidly expanding form of education internationally, and the world's largest universities are built upon it, its reputation internationally is mixed. Although many high quality courses and programmes are offered from the world's universities (the awards already won by the OUHK are a testimony to the high quality of its offerings), there is a widespread view that, not only is distance education a second-best option to traditional classroom-based teaching, but also there is a view that some 'correspondence courses' are substandard and even not desirable.

In order to obtain empirical information about how ODL is perceived in Hong Kong, the OUHK Council commissioned a study in 1999. This project investigated the perceptions held by employers, OUHK students and OUHK graduates about distance education in general and the OUHK in particular with respect to meeting professional employment requirements in Hong Kong. The summary of the results of the study include the following:

- 70% of the employers agreed that the OUHK's open entry to university education is acceptable;

- More than 90% agreed that the advantages to an organization of the staff studying through the distance learning mode are continuity of staff at work and continuous professional development of staff;

- There were no aspects that employers rated as 'not very helpful'.

From the students' and graduates' questionnaire, several observations can be made:

- More than 70% of the students and graduates rated their education through the OUHK between 'helpful' and 'extremely helpful' in a range of areas including general job skills, motivation to improve work performance, confidence at work, and interest in further education to acquire further work-related skills;

- More than 60% of the students and graduates rated between 'helpful' and 'extremely helpful' the benefits to their specific/technical job skills and ability to relate to professional colleagues;

- 80% said that studying with the OUHK had been beneficial to their professional development, and 90% said it had been beneficial to their personal development. These benefits appeared to be more important for them than career advancement (59%) and job change (53%).

Employer and student groups were both asked to rate, on a scale from 1 to 10, the skills that they regard to be the most important for a graduate employee:

- The skill rated the highest by the employer group was problem-solving, followed by reasoning ability, team skills, self-discipline and presentation and communication skills;

- The students and graduates rated reasoning ability the highest of the skills they consider to be important for a university graduate, followed by problem-solving skills, presentation skills, communication skills and team skills;

- 84% of the students and graduates rated their OUHK courses from 'helpful' to 'extremely helpful' in developing their ability to use problem-solving skills, 73% their ability to engage in creative thinking and 70% their basic communication skills.

The results of this first known study about employers' perceptions of graduates of distance education universities in Asia has helped to dispel the wrong notions held by society about ODL. It is hoped that as the OUHK continues to propagate open access, continuing and lifelong education in Hong Kong, the public will eventually see the erroneous perceptions about ODL as myths rather than realities.

Technology and alliances in Hong Kong higher education

One major global development, which is poised to change the scene of higher education and indeed open and distance education, is technology. Within the past five years developments in telecommunications, computing, and information technology have been phenomenal. The emergence of the Internet and the ability to use the World Wide Web for rapid communication has reduced distances considerably, and time has become immaterial as synchronous communication can now be effected with ease. As a result many open and distance education institutions are venturing into the use of Information and Communications Technology (ICT) for course delivery. This has given rise to a new development for instruction called online education. This also opens up the world as the recruiting ground for students as opposed to the localization of operations that used to be the order of the day. The OUHK has a five-year Information Technology Plan to guide its use of ICT for course delivery. Currently, the OUHK has 70 courses in English and 17 in Chinese on the Web. While the use of ICT is advancing the delivery of instruction by the distance education methods, it is also narrowing the divide between conventional and distance education institutions.

The government of Hong Kong has undertaken an initiative in technology which could be harnessed to the development of ODE in the SAR. The government has set up a HK$5 billion Quality Education Fund to support, among others, IT-related projects in schools and within education generally. In addition the government has also invested over HK$3.2 billion in a five-year IT in Education Plan and set up the Technology Innovative Fund. It has substantial interest in the development of the Cyberport — a project being established to increase development of technology in Hong Kong. Although these are not directly being established to support ODL, given the need and the government's concern for integrated development and lifelong learning, it is possible that many of the projects can be used to address the delivery of instruction at a distance.

With regard to alliances, following the world-wide trend in forming alliances among institutions, businesses and between business and educational institutions, Hong Kong is witnessing some development in this regard. There has emerged a Hong Kong-based Global University Alliance (GUA) — a private company comprising over nine universities from Taiwan, Europe, the USA, Australia and New Zealand, which aims to provide postgraduate education to students in Asia. A second just being floated is the CyberU, which was recently launched by Hong Kong Polytechnic University and the then Cable & Wireless HKT, now Pacific Century Cyberworks. Another is the alliance being formed between the Vocational Training Council and IBM. However, my personal view is that the driving force for global alliances and consortia in education is profit and not education *per se*. The target of these alliances is 'the Asia market which is said to be worth in excess of US$5 billion and growing at more than 25%' (*South China Morning Post* (2000), 9). This is the most fundamental challenge that globalization could pose to the university system as it is traditionally known. The transformation of alliances and consortia in offering educational services began with the emergence of e-learning in 1995 as technology companies sought to develop the use of information and communication technology (ICT) further.

The above will constitute the future challenges for the delivery of instruction through ODL in Hong Kong which must be addressed with urgency if the SAR is to keep up with the current astronomical pace of world-wide development.

Hong Kong–China partnerships

One current development in distance education in Hong Kong, which must be mentioned, is the growing relationship that has emerged between Hong Kong and mainland China. Although some relationship had existed, albeit in an informal way between institutions in Hong Kong and China before reunification in 1997, the confidence engendered by the reunification has given rise to an increased scope and depth of collaboration. While traditional universities in Hong Kong have concentrated their collaborative activities mainly on supporting students and staff from the mainland on scholarship, fellowship and exchange programmes, the OUHK has extended its distance learning activities to the mainland as shown in Table 3. Since 1997, the OUHK has developed academic training programmes in at least 15 major cities in the mainland, mainly in the area of business studies. A total of about 2,000 students in the mainland are currently enrolled in the OUHK's training programmes. An important landmark was the graduation of the first 550 students from the State Statistical Bureau that completed the course in the OUHK's MBA training programmes.

Table 3   Summary of OUHK programmes offered in mainland China*

Programme	Local partner	Commencement date	Location
1. Higher Diploma in Business Studies	Shaanxi Economic Management College	3 Sept 1997	Xi'an
2. Diploma in Business Studies	Sichuan Union College of Vocational Education	27 Sept 1997	Chengdu
3. MBA/PCBA Training Programme	Fuguang Foundation Fuzhou University	18 Oct 1997 15 Nov 1998	Fuzhou
4. MBA/PCBA Training Programme	State Statistics Bureau	15 Nov 1998 Oct 1998	See Note**
5. MBA/PCBA Training Programme	Guangzhou Commission For Foreign Economic Relations & Trade		Guangzhou

* As at 8 February 2001

** Cities where the OUHK provides MBA/PCBA Training Programmes for the State Statistical Bureau: Harbin, Changchun, Dalian, Beijing, Taiyuan, Jinan, Nanjing, Hefei, Zhengzhou, Xi'an, Chengdu, Nanchang, Fuzhou, Xiamen and Guangzhou.

Further exploration for the provision of OUHK training programmes on the mainland has been extended to Inner Mongolia and western China for collaborative ventures. Recent developments have shown prospects for even greater collaboration with the mainland regarding training programmes. The growing need for such training on the mainland has prompted the OUHK to set up a subsidiary of the OUHK (China) Ltd based in Shenzhen. While the programmes mentioned above are to help develop the tremendous amount of human resources that the mainland urgently requires, Hong Kong is also tapping the resources available on the mainland to provide courses that are needed in Hong Kong. LiPACE has begun, from February 2001, to offer professional training programmes in partnership with Xiamen University, to offer courses in Chinese Medicine and Financial Analysis. Training will take place both in Hong Kong and in the mainland, and successful students will be awarded Xiamen University certificates.

Finally, the OUHK has set a standard for other traditional universities in Hong Kong to emulate by opening up its campus to and sponsoring colleagues from the mainland to learn, first-hand, the activities and operations of an open university. The OUHK continues to formulate training programmes for administrators and scholars of the RTVU system. Two such programmes have been organized, the most recent being the training programme organized for 39 administrators and scholars from 23 TV universities. In the area of research in distance and adult learning, the OUHK is collaborating with mainland universities on some research projects, which have potential benefits for both regions. In addition, through fellowship grants received from The Croucher Foundation of Hong Kong, CRIDAL, for three years running, has provided six-month fellowship training opportunities to selected academics from the mainland to learn more about research in ODL in general and research at the OUHK in particular.

Given the sheer size and population of the mainland and the huge demand for education, despite efforts and the desire of the OUHK to contribute to development in mainland China, it appears that such efforts have only scratched the surface. Nevertheless it also appears that future and even more extensive and useful collaborations with the mainland are in the pipeline and moving in the right direction.

References

Carr, R and Fung, Y (1999) 'Internationalisation and distance education: a Hong Kong case study', *International Journal of Education Development*, 18(6): 467–72.

Chan, M S and Kwok, L I (1995) 'Tutor support in distance learning' in Sewart, D (ed.) *One World Many Voices: Quality in Open and Distance Learning*, Proceedings of the 17th World Conference for Distance Education, UK: Birmingham, 237–40.

Educational Resources Information Centre (ERIC) (1999), *ERIC Trends — Finance*, ERIC Clearinghouse on Higher Education.

Evans, T (2000) 'Oz DE OS: building on Australia's distance education background to export education', Paper presented at the IDP Education Australia Conference, Brisbane 9–11 August.

HKSAR (2000a) 'Education Blueprint for the 21st Century', *Learning for Life, Learning Through Life: Reform Proposals for the Education System in Hong Kong*, Education Commission.

HKSAR (2000b) Serving the Community Sharing Common Goals, Address by the Chief Executive The Honourable Tung Chee-hwa at the Legislative Council meeting on 11 October 2000, Hong Kong Special Administrative Region Government.

Jegede, O J (1999) 'The Y2K encounter of a different kind: meeting the challenges of student support in learning and teaching with new technologies', A keynote paper presented at the 8th Cambridge International Conference on Learning and Teaching with New Technologies, The Open University East Anglia Regional Centre, UK: Cambridge, 27 September–1 October 1999.

Jegede, O J (2000) 'A global alliance for OUHK: how would it work?', A lead paper to facilitate discussion at the OUHK 2000 Senior Management Retreat, Shekou, China, 14–15 July 2000.

Jegede, O J (2000) 'The wedlock between technology and open and distance education', in Evans, T D and Nation, D E (eds) *Changing University Teaching: Reflections on Creating Educational Technologies*, London: Kogan Page, 45–55.

Murphy, D and Yuen, K S (1996) Asian Research on Open and Distance Learning, commissioned report for the Open Learning Foundation, UK.

Ng, T C Y and Wong, D S N (2000) 'The Open University of Hong Kong' in V Venugopal Reddy and S Manjiluka (eds) *The World of Open and Distance Learning*.

South China Morning Post (2000), Campus Post, p. 9 columns 6 & 7.

The National Commission on the Cost of Higher Education (1999) *Straight Talk About College Costs and Prices*, USA: ERIC Clearinghouse on Higher Education.

The Open University of Hong Kong (2000), Press Release of 28 February.

The Open University of Hong Kong (2000), *OUHK General Information,* Hong Kong: OUHK.

Wong, D S N (September 1998) 'Resources management in a self-financing university', Presentation at the First National Conference on Open and Distance Learning, UP Dilman, Philippines: Quezon City.

Wong, D S N and Jegede, O J (2000) 'Building a culture of quality in open and distance learning: the practice at the Open University of Hong Kong', Paper presented at the Conference on New Millennium: Quality and Innovations in Higher Education organized by the Hong Kong Council for Academic Accreditation, 4–5 December 2000.

Wong, J (2000) Speech by the Secretary for Education and Manpower, Mr Joseph W P Wong at the Hong Kong Council for Academic Accreditation (HKCAA) 10th Anniversary Dinner, 8 June 2000.

Acknowledgement

I wish to acknowledge the assistance provided by Dr K S Yuen, Head of Educational Technology and Publishing Unit of the OUHK, for locating a number of documents, especially those dealing with the historical details of the OUHK, many of which have become rare and therefore difficult to obtain.

Japan

Wong Suk-ying and Yoshida Aya

Introduction

The right to learn has long been a national ideology firmly institutionalized in Japanese society. Whether as a vehicle for national development, national integration or for economic effectiveness, education frequently commands a central place in the national agenda of policy formation in Japan.

The emphasis on using information technology (IT) as a tool for national progress since the 1980s has had a substantial impact on the reorganization of schooling and, thereby, the basic forms of social life in Japan. The enthusiasm for new technologies reflects a changing demand for educational provision that should also be in line with changes in the wider social environment. Current tendencies of liberalization, marketization, privatization and internationalization have combined to undermine the fundamental functions of schooling and the legitimacy of public education in Japan. Consequently, in recent years, among the most distinct educational reform measures has been to expand and improve the provision of opportunities for learning beyond the formal mode.

The general purpose of these efforts has been to offer a wider range of training programmes as well as to improve the quality of education provided for potential learners. For example, the use of IT in distance education has a distinct appeal not only to the students, but also to those who teach and work in the institutions. Indeed, the sheer confidence that people have in formal schooling is facing an unprecedented challenge in Japan as non-traditional modes of learning are gaining in importance.

This chapter examines the current educational reforms in Japan, focusing on the provision of distance and open learning to promote new education policies that have sparked much discussion among the public as well as the institutions involved.

To do this we will briefly review the development and current status of distance and opening learning in Japan and then consider the changing conditions and prospects for distance and open learning as compared to those existing a decade ago by looking at the expansion of graduate (or postgraduate) programmes in distance learning as one of the major reform measures.

As the notion of 'choice and quality' currently has a central place in open and distance learning, we will also examine the application of IT in distance learning in Japan and the effect that this application has had. To this end, we will also identify obstacles to the use of IT and the challenges and prospects for its further proliferation in the distance higher education sector in Japan.

We will also discuss the dynamics of IT as a popular mode of instruction in current educational reform movements and develop a general perspective as to how global educational cultural influences might shape the educational reform process.

Overview of distance education in Japan

In the history of non-traditional learning in Japan, distance education has made its presence felt mainly in the post-secondary sector. Two types of distance higher education have been established in Japan: 1) correspondence education, which is offered as a formal mode of instruction in private universities; and 2) the University of the Air, an independent distance higher education institution funded by the government that uses broadcasts as its mode of course delivery.

The expansion of distance education took place mainly in the mid-1990s. Prior to the University of the Air, which was established in 1985, Japan had virtually no distance learning institutions. Since 1994, however, almost one institution offering distance education has been established each year. As of 2000, there were 19 four-year private universities and ten private junior colleges, with an enrolment of over 254,000 learners (*Mombusho* Ministry of Education 1998) in correspondence programmes. The University of the Air has also expanded substantially in terms of student enrolments, curricular programmes and the application of instructional devices. Figure 1 shows how dramatically growth in enrolment at the University of the Air has increased.

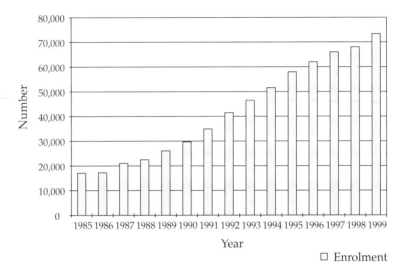

Figure 1   Changes in enrolment in the University of the Air, 1985–1999

Despite this, the number of total enrolments in distance higher education is still low when compared with that for conventional campus-based universities. For example, in 1998, approximately 2.5 million students enrolled in four-year universities, while approximately two hundred thousand students enrolled in distance programmes. Only 8% of all undergraduate students participated in some kind of distance learning.

Distance education as a 'distant' goal of educational attainment

Formal education is key to national development and cohesion. However, distance and open learning programmes also serve to reinforce the belief in educational attainment as a means to social cohesion. We explore this by discussing some of the characteristics of distant learners in Japan. As shown in Table 1a, the late twenties and early thirties age group forms the majority group in terms of age distribution in private correspondence courses. It is noteworthy that 21% of students are aged from 18 to 22, and 12% are aged 23 or 24. This means that around 30% of students in correspondence courses are of the same age cohort as students in conventional universities. This 30% are mainly full-time students who are unemployed and basically perceive some form of continuing education to be an asset in their personal profile. It serves to fill the gap in the otherwise difficult transition from school to work.

Attaining or accumulating educational qualifications as a 'reserve' for mobility is a general belief held as important by most Japanese. The age of University of the Air students is likely to be higher than that of students taking correspondence courses — 30% of students are in their thirties and 20% are in their forties. This reflects the other function of education as a public and general good, and sets the agenda for the kinds of educational pursuits among older Japanese learners, which holds that learning should be viewed not only as an exchangeable form of social capital for material or status attainment, but also as a source of self-enhancement and enrichment. Here, the logic of confidence in education is consistent with the national ideology institutionalized in all sectors and all walks of life in Japan.

Table 1a   Age distribution

	18~22	23~24	25~29	30~39	40~49	50~59	60~	Total (%)
Correspondence universities	20.9	11.6	24.1	24.3	11.7	5.2	2.2	100.0
University of the Air	6.9	5.1	16.3	30.5	20.9	12.5	7.8	100.0

Source: Ministry of Education (1999) *Gakkou Kihon Chosa (Educational Statistics)*

Table 1b   Sex and age distribution of the University of the Air (2000)
(unit: person)

Sex \ Age	18-19	20-24	25-29	30-34	35-39	40-44	45-49	50-54	55-59	Over 60	Total
Male	953	4,398	4,276	4,112	3,501	2,716	2,789	2,247	1,801	6,243	33,036
Female	487	4,570	5,886	6,201	5,410	4,250	4,944	3,758	2,348	2,556	40,410
Total	1,440	8,968	10,162	10,313	8,911	6,966	7,733	6,005	4,149	8,799	73,446

Source: Hoosoo Daigaku Yooran (2000)

The occupational distribution of distant learners in the two major types of distance education institution in Japan may further support our assumptions on how distance education has been perceived by both the providers and consumers. As can be seen in Table 2, in correspondence universities students who are unemployed outnumber students who are employed (36.5%). This is congruent with the largest proportion of enrolment in full-time correspondence education programmes among the

18 to mid-twenties student age cohort shown in Table 1. However, in the University of the Air, one-third of students are office clerks, although, here again, 'unemployed' students also represent a large proportion of student enrolments. Almost all unemployed students in the University of the Air are housewives.

Table 2   Occupational distribution

	Teachers	Civil servants	Office clerks	Self-employed	Unemployed	Others	Total (%)
Correspondence universities	8.8	9.4	22.2	3.6	36.5	19.7	100.0
Univ. of the Air	2.7	14.1	33.3	4.9	23.4	21.7	100.0

Source: Ministry of Education (1999) *Gakkou Kihon Chosa* (*Educational Statistics*)

These differences are also due to programmes of study and the award of a professional licence. Correspondence universities mainly provide programmes of study in social sciences, humanities and education. There are no programmes in natural sciences. Social science programmes are most popular and account for 57% of enrolments. However, the most popular area of study in social sciences is social welfare, in which students can acquire a professional licence to practice. Education courses taught at a distance can also lead to a teaching licence, which also attracts young students. In view of this, young student learners indeed treat distance and correspondence education as an alternative route to attaining an occupation. The government is the main provider of public education to those who might have otherwise been unsuccessful in the rigorous selection processes for advanced formal education.

The University of the Air provides only liberal arts programmes and courses that do not lead to an occupational licence. This may have some bearing on the fact that over 60% of total students are women (Hoso Daigaku Kenkyukai 1997). Our empirical study found that the objective of many of these students is to study for self-fulfilment and improvement.

Given the nature of learning in distance education in which self-motivation, being a self-starter and perseverance are emphasized as factors for success, it is not surprising to see a low graduation rate among students enrolled in this mode of education. Table 3 shows the number of enrolments, entrants, graduates, and graduates who managed to complete their degree in four years as of 1997. The number of entrants in 1998 is just below 10% of total initial enrolments. The graduation percentage is 60% to 70% if we take the ratio of graduates to entrants. Of graduates, the percentage of graduates who manage to complete their degree in four years is 47% in correspondence universities and 24% in the University of the Air. This suggests a high drop-out rate and that over half of the graduates took more than four years to acquire a Bachelor's degree.

Table 3   Enrolments, entrants and graduates

	(A) Enrolments	(B) Entrants	(C) Graduates	(D) Graduates in four years	(%) B/A	(%) C/B	(%) D/C
Correspondence universities	141,280	9,157	6,214	2,947	6.5	67.9	47.4
University of the Air	26,892	2,847	1,686	404	10.6	59.2	24.0

Source: Ministry of Education (1999) *Gakkou Kihon Chosa* (*Educational Statistics*)

Although the number of graduates is small, many remain eager to continue their studies. According to a survey of graduates of the University of the Air, graduates, especially women, expressed a strong desire to enter graduate schools and major preferences were expressed that the University establish graduate programmes of study (Hoso Daigaku Kenkyukai 1997). Another survey has shown that 37% of undergraduate students in correspondence universities want to enter graduate schools in distance mode. This is especially so among students who work as teachers, where the percentage was 67.6% in 1998 (Shiritsu Daigaku Tsusin Kyouiku Kyoukai 1998 — The Association of University Continuing Education). This again reflects the demand for an alternative means of achieving a validated professional status without which upward mobility would be impossible. Attaining a senior teacher licence through distance education is becoming more common among teachers as a means to gain a promotion. These licences require completion of a Master's programme in education. Consequently, teachers have become the largest source of demand for the establishment of graduate programmes of study in distance mode.

However, questions remain as to what extent and under what circumstances educational credentials and licensing validated by distance education authorities will enjoy an equal status with those gained from the conventional education and training sector. If such equity is achieved, then conventional education and training, to which an enormous slice of national resources has been allocated, will surely face a serious challenge in the future. To better understand the development and social dynamics of this new educational movement in distance education, we will examine in greater detail the expansion of postgraduate or graduate training through distance education in Japan.

Changing conditions and social expectations of the school-to-work transition

Graduate students (working adults)

In addition to the demand among in-service teachers for advanced training and licensing, more demand comes from working adults who view training as the best way to upgrade their skills and thereby, make their jobs secure. The past decade has seen Japan in economic recession. Current trends of liberalization, marketization, privatization and internationalization have tended to undermine the traditional functions of schooling and the legitimacy of public education in Japan. In less than two decades from now, the country will have the second largest aging population in the world. With a record for higher education enrolments since the Second World War, Japan has reached a point where the government must take decisive steps to reformulate the country's higher education policies. One reform measure is to relax admission requirements to degree programmes for adult graduate students. Since 1987, adult graduate students have been admitted through a selection process different from the regular entrance examination. Universities are also granted the option of offering graduate programmes of study at night for working adults. This form of graduate education should be structured and managed at the same level and manner as graduate schools in conventional universities, even though the admission system and class hours are different. Graduate students in these schools have to study on campus while working, so the location of graduate schools for working adults is of special relevance. The result is, however, that only universities in big cities can establish such programmes.

The number of students who enrol in this type of night graduate school has been increasing, as can be seen in Table 4. In 1997, working adults at graduate schools, however, accounted for only 4.5% of total graduate students, including conventional graduate schools. Of special admission graduate students, 67.6% enrol in national universities. Of night graduate school students, 70.4% are in private universities. In both types, approximately 70% are in Master's degree courses. Study programmes in social sciences tend mostly to attract working adults.

The number of such graduate students is still small. However, there could be a future for distance education if graduate schools could also target working adults and provide attractive courses and flexible learning in terms of time and place.

Table 4   Working adult graduate students

	1987	1988	1989	1990	1991	1992	1993	1994	1995	1996	1997
Master's courses	815	1,087	1,539	1,647	2,233	2,263	2,752	3,298	3,422	3,742	4,305
Doctorate courses	148	300	288	308	460	931	902	1,343	1,467	1,575	1,807
Night graduate schools	98	98	169	309	422	589	660	925	1,124	1,347	1,564

Source: *Daigaku Singikai Tosin* (*The Final Report of University Council*) (1998)

Government action

The Ministry of Education has recently encouraged universities to enlarge graduate education and plans to increase the number of graduate intakes to 300,000 in the future. The Ministry has, however, also been negatively disposed towards establishing graduate schools in distance mode because the standards and methods of assessment of quality assurance remain debatable, and this is an important issue.

The University Council has recently discussed the possibility of graduate schools by distance, and advised the Ministry to establish graduate schools in distance mode. Based on that advice, the Ministry revised regulations regarding the establishment of graduate schools in 1998 (Standards of Establishment of Correspondence Universities 1998). According to the regulations, only Master's programmes can admit students in distance mode for the purpose of training working adults to attain advanced occupational skills. It is recommended that graduate students be selected through entrance examinations in each university, although this is not expressly stipulated. This requirement that applicants take entrance exams in distance education is unique as it has long been a tradition in both correspondence universities and the University of the Air to employ an open admission policy. In addition to these examinations, the Ministry has stipulated a teacher to student ratio of 1:20, which is the same as in conventional graduate schools. This does show a serious intention on the part of the national authorities to assure and maintain the educational quality of graduate schools in distance mode.

Characteristics of the four distance graduate programmes

Four private universities have been approved to establish distance graduate programmes of study based upon their correspondence undergraduate courses in 1998. Three are located in the Tokyo area, the other is in Kyoto. In 2001, the University of the Air will also establish a Master's degree programme. The characteristics of the four graduate correspondence universities are briefly examined below.

Educational programmes

As shown in Table 5, the educational programmes of the four private universities are humanities, social sciences including child studies, and education. All except Nihon University have the same programmes at undergraduate level. One of the characteristics of these programmes is that professional certificates or occupational licences such as for senior teaching positions, clinical psychologist, or Master of Social Work, are provided in education or social sciences courses. As shown by the survey, the demand for graduate programmes of study among teachers is extremely high. It has become the main attraction for teachers who can thus upgrade their teaching credentials without having to leave the workplace. These programmes also appear competitive by virtue of the small quota allocated based on the regulations on faculty and student ratios as issued by the Ministry of Education.

Admission

All four universities that offered distance graduate programmes conducted entrance examinations in February 1998. As expected, the entrance examinations appeared very competitive, although the pass ratio varied from less than 10% to over 90% among programmes. The average pass ratio was 27%. This is quite low compared with conventional universities. Without doubt, the relatively small quota for each programme accounts for the low pass rate. It also reflects the potential demand for graduate programmes of study in distance education. For the government, controlling the number of intakes is perhaps the most conventional mode of assuring quality, and is thus by no means illegitimate.

Table 5   Educational programmes and quota of new graduate schools in distance mode

Name	Master of Arts	Field	Certificate	Quota
Seitoku Univ.	Child Studies	Child Studies	Senior Teaching Licence/Clinical Psychologist	50
Nihon Univ.	Social and Cultural Studies	International Information		30
		Cultural Information		30
		Human Science	Clinical Psychologist	30
Meisei Univ.	Education	Education	Senior Teaching	30
Bukkyo Univ.	Literature	Japanese Buddhism		10
		Buddhism		10
		Buddhism Culture		10
		Japanese History		10
		Asian History		10
		Chinese Literature		10
		English/ American Literature		10
	Education	Lifelong Learning Licence	Senior Teaching	10
	Sociology	Social Welfare	Master of Social Work	10
TOTAL				260

Source: Survey by Shiritsu Daigaku Tsusin Kyouiku Kyoukai (Association of University Continuing Education) (1998)

The most competitive programmes are likely to be in education and social welfare. As mentioned, this is because such programmes offer occupational certificates or professional licences. The number of enrolments in some programmes is less than the quota, although the number of enrolments overall exceeds the quota. This suggests that the value attached to maintaining the quality of education is more important than the value attached to expanding educational opportunities for the applicants.

Table 6   Applicants and enrolments

Name	Master of Arts	Field	Quota	(A) Applicants	(B) Applicants	(C) Enrolments	(%) B/A	(%) C/A
Seitoku Univ.	Child Studies	Child Studies	50	235		117		49.8
Nihon Univ.	Social and Cultural Studies	International Information Cultural	30	86		47		54.7
		Information	30	22		20		90.9
		Human Science	30	174		57		32.8
Meisei Univ.	Education	Education	30	200		35		17.5
Bukkyo Univ.	Literature	Japanese Buddhism	10	13	8	5	61.5	38.5
		Buddhism	10	31	22	10	71.0	32.3
		Buddhism Culture	10	46	29	11	63.0	23.9
		Japanese History	10	53	22	12	41.5	22.6
		Asian History	10	14	14	12	100.0	85.7
		Chinese Literature	10	21	16	4	76.2	19.0
		English/ American Lit.	10	50	22	15	44.0	30.0
	Education	Lifelong Learning	10	155	21	10	13.5	6.5
	Sociology	Social Welfare	10	270	36	14	13.3	5.2
TOTAL			260	1,370		369		26.9

Source: Survey by Shiritsu Daigaku Tsusin Kyouiku Kyoukai (Association of University Continuing Education) (1998)

Written exams in the field of specialization are exemplified by working experiences. The level of written exams is not necessarily high compared to that of conventional graduate schools, as reported by professors. However, applicants found it difficult to adapt to taking examinations after having been away from academic studies for a long time. Each graduate school requires students to take oral examinations. According to the professors, oral exams are useful in assessing a student's personality and potential to pursue further study.

Student profile

Two universities (Nihon University and Meisei University) offer a student profile. As Table 7 shows, students are mainly in their thirties and forties in both universities. The number of male students is almost twice the number of female students in Nihon University, while there are more female than male students in Meisei University. This difference is probably due to the graduate programmes of study offered. Meisei University offers only education courses, and Nihon University offers a mainly social science curriculum. Those who categorized themselves as unemployed tend to be housewives and a few are retirees.

Table 7   Student profile

	Gender		Age			
	Male	Female	22~30	31~40	41~50	51~
Nihon Univ.	66.1	33.9	11	40.3	37.9	10.5
Meisei Univ.	42.9	57.1	14	37.1	34.3	14.3

Source: *Executive* (July 1999) Daiyamondo-sha, 54

Although Japan has expanded provision of distance education beyond the undergraduate level, the curriculum is still very much confined to social science and humanities disciplines. Many distance education institutions in this geographical region have gained recognition by focusing on the training and retraining of current employees and mature students in practical knowledge and skills (such as IT and computing, management, etc.). Even so, distance learning in Japan seems to have been able to retain a 'cultural' orientation in that the curriculum in distance education has incorporated study areas in humanities and social sciences.

But does open learning in Japan reflect real functional needs of the society, or does it reflect more of a changing conception of a learning society as such is more commonly conceived in the global environment? To respond to these questions we will look more closely at the extent to which IT is being used in Japan's higher education, where the boundaries between on-campus and distance education are becoming increasingly blurred.

IT in Japanese higher education

The world of learning before the end of the last century was channelled towards a uniform vision of educational restructuring. The IT revolution has begun to transform and redefine the meaning of formal schooling as it emerged and became institutionalized in the modern age. The application of IT not only expands the possibilities for distance education, but also presents ample opportunities for campus-based institutions to become dual-mode providers and to offer distance education programmes via IT in addition to on-campus activities. Higher education in Japan is not untouched by these trends.

To what extent has IT been able to penetrate higher education in Japan? Specifically, how far has it been utilized within formal distance education institutions and inside conventional universities as a major form of instructional strategy, gradually replacing the traditional forms such as classroom teaching or face-to-face supervision? These questions will be answered with some of the preliminary research findings in studies we conducted recently (Yoshida 2000). Our study of the use of IT covered all types of media, with a special focus on IT infrastructure, educational applications, internal support systems, the objectives in using IT, and institutional and attitudinal barriers to its utilization.

General trends and status of IT application

IT has been applied in Japanese universities in two principal situations: inside classrooms where face-to-face instruction is still the dominant mode of instruction, and in distance education as a main mode of delivery. As far as classroom use is concerned, video and audio recordings remain the mainstream in Japanese higher education. The most effective use of IT is in educational materials enriched by combining text, sound and image. Contrary to our expectations, around only 5% of respondents said that they made either frequent or constant use of CD-ROMs or other multimedia materials (Yoshida 2000). This figure rose to 40% for occasional use. Compared with other items, CD-ROM and other multimedia use in educational materials is still relatively rare. As far as Internet usage categorized by faculties or by university departments is concerned, national universities are slightly ahead of other universities in databasing library collections, in administrative use of email and electronic bulletin boards, and in the open posting of syllabi on the Internet. With these exceptions, there is little significant difference across either faculties or departments; IT penetration is relatively uniform across the whole spectrum of Japanese higher education.

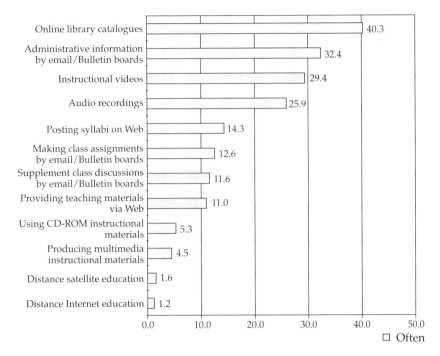

Figure 2   Utilization of multimedia/IT in Japanese universities

To what extent then is IT being applied in distance education? The most common uses include both classroom instruction open to the public on the World Wide Web and instruction via satellite. The result shows the number of institutions implementing such applications remains, however, extremely small. The combined score for both frequent and occasional use is only 10%.

University education by correspondence (one form of distance learning) and university education for students who are physically present on the university campus (commuting students) are regarded as separate categories in Japan, each with its own rules and systems. In the 1998 revision of the Standards for Establishment of a University, however, rules governing correspondence courses were revised to allow the giving of credits for distance education courses that allow dialogue and that are offered at the same time as courses for commuting students. While it was thus possible to fulfil these requirements with interactive TV conferencing systems using communication satellites, this approach was rarely implemented. The

Internet, on the other hand, is the most widely used form of IT that touches almost everybody's social life. We find that Internet utilization is mostly confined to information delivery, being the method most preferred and used by administrative staff. Although the Internet is increasingly being used for database and library materials, email and the use of electronic bulletin boards for providing administrative information, very few schools make frequent use of the Internet to provide teaching materials, pose questions via email, and use email to receive and discuss course-related questions with students. Use of the Internet for actual teaching at a distance is extremely rare. However, the use of email for instruction-related purposes is significant. Despite the apparently small use of the Internet overall in Japanese higher education, an Internet environment is now almost fully in place in Japanese higher education institutions with 99% of universities 'wired' in some form.

What, then, are the prospects for the use of IT in distance education? Table 8 presents some data on current and planned uses of three major IT forms or strategies: satellite networks, terrestrial networks, and the Internet.

To further support our findings on the unpopularity of IT in distance education, Table 9 displays a finer break-down of the possible frequency of IT utilization over the course of one year among higher education institutions in Japan that claim to have adopted the distance mode of teaching or to offer courses by distance.

What are the common objectives of those who make such provision possible? Identifying the purposes for which IT has been adopted will not only clarify areas in which IT has a future in distance education but also the directions in which this new instructional strategy can progress. It will also shed some light on the barriers to the utilization of IT in this field of education. Figure 3 displays the results of responses given by institutions surveyed on the goals they have in mind to achieve through the application of IT.

Table 8 Current state of IT utilization for distance education

Types of higher education institutions		Currently use	Plan to use	No plan to use [%]
Satellite networks	Conventional universities			
	Sub-total	16.2	16.0	67.9
	National	40.8	23.4	35.8
	Public	0.0	12.8	87.2
	Private	7.6	13.2	79.3
	Junior colleges	2.3	5.2	92.5
	Vocational & technical	25.0	35.7	39.3
Terrestrial networks (e.g. ISDN, etc.)	Conventional universities			
	Sub-total	30.1	17.4	52.5
	National	33.2	19.4	47.4
	Public	24.7	14.1	61.2
	Private	29.6	17.0	53.4
	Junior colleges	26.1	11.6	62.3
	Vocational & technical	25.0	17.3	57.7
Online instruction via Internet	Conventional universities			
	Sub-total	17.1	12.7	70.2
	National	20.4	11.4	68.2
	Public	14.0	10.5	75.6
	Private	16.1	13.5	70.4
	Junior colleges	14.1	10.1	75.9
	Vocational & technical	17.2	12.1	70.7

Source: Survey of Multimedia Use in Institutions of Higher Education (January 2000), Japan.

Table 9   Frequencies of IT utilization in one year

Satellite networks	Conventional universities				Junior colleges	Vocational & technical [%]
	Sub-total	National	Public	Private		
Less than 5 times	13.2	29.8	4.6	7.3	4.4	15.5
6–15 times	6.4	15.2	2.3	3.1	0.5	17.2
16–25 times	2.7	4.5	0.0	2.2	0.7	5.2
26–35 times	1.8	4.2	0.0	1.0	0.2	1.7
More than 36 times	3.2	5.5	1.1	2.5	0.2	10.3

Terrestrial networks	Conventional universities				Junior colleges	Vocational & technical [%]
	Sub-total	National	Public	Private		
Less than 5 times	9.5	13.5	6.9	8.1	9.1	13.8
6–15 times	9.1	11.1	8.0	8.1	3.9	10.3
16–25 times	4.9	5.5	4.6	4.7	2.5	8.6
26–35 times	1.6	1.4	2.3	1.6	0.7	0.0
More than 36 times	16.7	13.8	13.8	18.2	17.2	5.2

Source: Survey of Multimedia Use in Institutions of Higher Education (2000) NIME, Japan

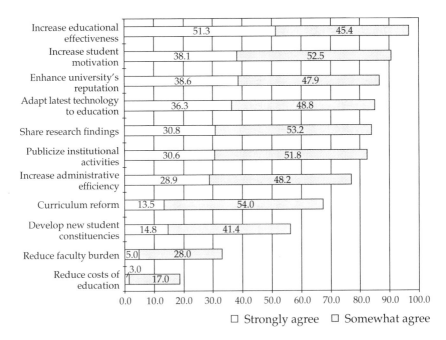

□ Strongly agree   □ Somewhat agree

Figure 3   Goals of IT utilization

The objective of 'to increase educational effectiveness' is shared by virtually all institutions surveyed (combining 'agree' and 'strongly agree' responses). Many institutions also perceive that 'to increase student motivation' and 'to use new technology in education' are equally important, which suggests the cycle in which IT use is driven by the desire to use new technology to increase student motivation and to improve the effectiveness of education. However, it is interesting to note that institutions also regard 'to enhance the university's reputation' as well as 'to adapt the latest technology to education' as important goals, and that they even score slightly higher than the objective of increasing student motivation in the 'strongly agree' category. This implies that institutions regard IT as an essential source of their own legitimacy in the new educational reform movement that can help them gain support and resources from the public. It is a collective vision adhered to by many institutions and has been quickly organized and standardized into norms in the new age of schooling in society. If we examine the findings even more closely, fewer than 15%, however, strongly agree that they use the new technology 'for curriculum reform' or 'to cultivate students from new segments of society'. Also, fewer than 5% strongly agree that their objective in using IT is 'to reduce the burden on faculty' or 'to reduce the cost of education'. It is clear that lowering costs is not a major concern, which suggests that most institutions are operating under the optimistic assumption that use of new technology will increase the effectiveness of education rather than looking to IT for solutions to educational or cost issues with which they are now grappling. Such optimism is crucial to maintain the legitimacy of education as a public project that has to be progressive and rational.

Table 10 shows the postgraduate and graduate programmes of study that the four universities have recently established for working and mature adults. Here, we expected to find more widespread and more popular use of IT in their instructional strategies given the nature of the student profile, i.e. mainly day-time employees, as access to computers or other multimedia equipment would be thought to pose less of a problem to them than to regular full-time students.

Table 10   Credit requirements and teaching methods

Name	Year	Credits	Face-to-face sessions		Internet	Master's thesis
Seitoku Univ.	2	30	3 days/ course	summer/ spring	-	•
Nihon Univ.	2	30	8 credits		•	•
Meisei Univ.	2	30	1 week/ year	summer/ winter	-	•
Bukkyo Univ.	2	30	4~8 credits*	summer/ weekend	-	•

* (4~6 days/ 4 credits)

Source: Survey by Shiritsu Daigaku Tsusin Kyouiku Kyoukai
(Survey by the Association of University Continuing Education) (1998)

As shown in Table 10, two years of learning, or 30 credits, are generally required to obtain Master's degrees. All four distance graduate programmes in each of the universities require students to attend face-to-face sessions, although the Ministry regulations do not stipulate that such sessions are obligatory. It only recommends strongly that every graduate school be concerned about the quality of education. There are two types of face-to-face instruction: 1) a mix of correspondence education and face-to-face instruction; 2) separate correspondence education and face-to-face instruction as distinct courses. Face-to-face instruction is held on campus during summer, winter or spring vacation or weekends. On average, one week per year satisfies this requirement. Regarding IT use, only Nihon University uses the Internet and provides videoconferencing in its teaching. Nihon also loans a personal computer to each student during enrolment. Other universities that offer distance graduate programmes have also expressed an interest in introducing IT as a principal teaching tool. Doing this, however, is not an easy task, due to the cost involved in building an IT infrastructure and helping professors to use IT for their classes. It would also pose difficulties for adult students (except those using computers in their jobs), as they would have to become familiar with IT and its applications in order to do a course. Therefore face-to-face instruction remains the principal means of enabling two-way communication between professors and students and among students. It is quite evident that face-to-face instruction is still the most widely used mode of instruction in the graduate distance learning system in Japan.

Other than face-to-face instruction for regular classes, students can approach professors for individual, one-on-one advice about writing their Master's thesis. Students are required to produce a thesis as part of a Master's programme in all graduate programmes. In Japan, however, as postgraduate programmes via distance mode are now available for the first time, there is no prior experience among institutions as to how to supervise a Master's thesis through this mode. Thus the continuing role of face-to-face contact is a major concern among professors and of the *Mombusho* (Ministry of Education) in Japan because it is important that the quality of theses can be maintained even if the one-on-one supervision mode is largely replaced by some form of distance or IT mode such as using the Internet.

Barriers to the use of IT

Major barriers to the use of IT include 'cost of installing equipment', 'maintaining costs', and 'lack of equipment' as shown in Figure 4. An equally high proportion of responses, more than 90%, identifies human resources issues such as 'lack of support staff', 'burden on designated individuals', and 'time required for preparation' as additional barriers to its use. The primary human resources issue is the lack of a scheme in Japanese higher education for the development of the network of media specialists needed as support staff. Moreover, the personnel structure in faculties and departments in Japanese universities allocates no legitimate position to full-time support specialists. To promote IT as a major form of instructional strategy in Japanese higher education requires a reworking of the personnel structure, which is by no means an easy task given the long tradition of the hiring system.

Another human resources issue is 'the lack of usable materials'. Since instructors must create their own materials to accompany the use of IT in instruction, the need for expert, technical knowledge and for time to develop materials over and above that spent on instruction becomes a serious and ongoing burden. Media literacy, as reported, is primarily a faculty member problem, while only 3% of institutions strongly agree that students have problems with the new technology.

While cost has been identified as the least of the concerns in the use of IT in many institutions, it has nonetheless become a real barrier to IT utilization in the educational process. The lack of human resources as a main support system is also identified as an obstacle to making the use of

IT efficient and effective. These findings might suggest a decoupling nature of educational organizations where many of the day-to-day academic activities when implemented are not congruent with the original educational objectives and plans that the organizations have targeted. The strong tendency in Japan for IT to be used in the classroom as an aid to face-to-face instruction mostly represented by audio cassettes and video does suggest that the traditional applications of IT are still very much the case in teaching and learning in Japan currently. Promotion of computer-based applications such as teaching materials on CD-ROM or creation of multimedia presentations have not really touched the core of learning activities in this new technological age. Even in the University of the Air where distance education is the formal mode of instruction, face-to-face instruction, satellite and radio broadcasting and video cassettes are still the three most dominant methods of delivery. The role of IT in general is restricted and has only a supplementary function.

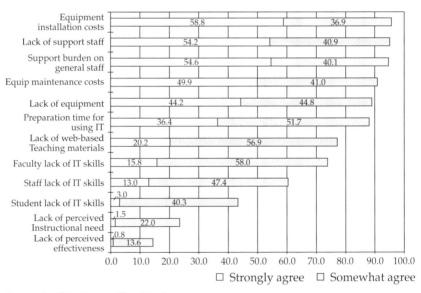

Figure 4   Barriers to IT utilization

Challenges and prospects of ODE in Japan

Social demand for training, retraining and upgrading of skills and knowledge is prevalent in Japan especially among working adults. In Japan, where higher education is a form of mass education, distance education has not had much difficulty consolidating a position for itself. Demand is certain to continue, especially if taking into consideration the challenges currently facing the Japanese government, such as demographic changes, the demand for choice and quality in public education, and the changing expectations and behaviour of consumers of education, etc. As the birth rate falls, the proportion of the population receiving higher education will increase, but it is difficult to envisage the system of higher education continuing to expand. As the system shrinks, rather, it will have to address the increasingly diversifying needs of increasingly diverse groups of students. Whether or not the government can develop a delivery system that accommodates the needs and interests of potential learners will be a crucial factor in determining whether or not distance education will thrive in Japan.

Widespread use of IT in education requires more than just a knowledge of how to operate the equipment. What is necessary is knowledge of how to effectively apply the technology and equipment to create new teaching materials or to shift from lecture-style teaching to a style that emphasizes student self-study and practice. The most important support, then, is organizational support for the creation of teaching materials. The absence of IT will create a major obstacle to the further advancement of distance education as an effective and efficient mode of provision of learning opportunities. On the one hand, IT applications in education are perceived as the most legitimate mode of delivery in terms of the potential it has to enhance educational effectiveness and the reputation of the institutions. On the other, however, the high cost and lack of organizational support are cited as the major barriers to its adoption. The adoption of IT only as a collective norm or educational 'rhetoric' will not benefit those who actually experience the process of learning. In Japan, where online education is not yet widespread, awareness of it is growing, but little serious thought is being given to how to apply it effectively. It is therefore important to foster an IT culture of learning and teaching also at the organizational level to ensure a link from the top down. It is important to attend to real educational needs rather than to educational cosmetic labelling, for example, in which parts of the higher education system the use of IT is possible.

While distance education as an alternative mode of learning has been a world-wide activity since the 1960s (Wong 1992 and 1994; Harry 1994), the internal dynamics of this form of educational provision remain very much a knowledge gap that needs to be filled in research studies. Comprehensive studies on how distance education has contributed to national development, what aspects of development, in which types of countries, and under what educational model are scarce. The triumph of 'every learner's society' is a collective vision held by many national societies. But very often these visions are being organized and standardized into rules, norms and ideologies in the wider society because they are essential for the legitimacy of the educational organizations concerned for the purpose of gaining support and resources from the public. More empirical evidence or comparable data materials that can enable further examination of the effectiveness of distance learning with regard to which national policies on distance education have been implemented effectively at the local level would be useful.

References

Daigaku Singikai Tosin (The Final Report of the University Council) (1999) The University Council Executive, Daiyamondo-sha, 54.

Gakkou Kihon Chosa (Educational Statistics) (1999) Japan: Ministry of Education.

Harry, K (1992) *Africa: A Survey of Distance Education*, New Papers on Higher Education Studies and Research, Paris: UNESCO.

Harry, K (1992) *Latin America: A Survey of Distance Education*, New Papers on Higher Education Studies and Research, Paris: UNESCO.

Hoso Daigaku Kenkyukai (1997) The Study Group of the Open University, *The Study Report of Women Graduates of the University of the Air*, private press, Japan: Chiba.

Shiritsu Daigaku Tsusin Kyouiku Kyoukai (1998) Survey by the Association of University Continuing Education.

Wong, S-Y (1992) *Asia and the Pacific: A Survey of Distance Education*, vol. 1 and vol. 2, New Papers on Higher Education Studies and Research, Paris: UNESCO.

Wong, S-Y (ed.) (1994) *Distance Education in Asia and the Pacific: Country Papers*, New Papers on Higher Education Studies and Research, Paris: UNESCO.

Yoshida, A (2000) *Survey Report of Status and Conditions of IT Utilization in Japanese Higher Education*, National Institute of Multimedia Education, Japan: Chiba.

Korea

Jung In-sung

Introduction

The 1960s and 1970s saw a substantial expansion in education in Korea, resulting in universal primary and secondary education which, in turn, gave rise to remarkable economic progress and changes in politics, society and culture.

This period also saw major reforms in and new approaches to student and teacher education, which the Korea Education Development Institute (KEDI) was established to lead.

During the 1970s and 1980s, the number of students in secondary education had increased sharply, which gave rise to overkeen competition for places in the higher education institutions. Solutions to this explosion at the middle and high school levels included an expansion of vocational educational programmes and the establishment of the Air and Correspondence High School (ACHS) and the Korea Air and Correspondence University (later renamed the Korea National Open University: KNOU) to give young people from underprivileged families and adults seeking further education access to secondary and higher education. Distance education was initially conceived in Korea as a new educational avenue for the growing population of secondary school graduates and also, in part, a way of introducing lifelong education to working adults. As seen in many other countries, distance education institutions in Korea, when they were first introduced into the formal education system, were largely considered second choice or lower grade institutions after the campus-based institutions.

TV and radio in ODE

In the 1980s, the Korean government introduced national policies to improve the quality of education. The formation of a sound personality through education and the reform of civil education, with an emphasis on science and lifelong education, were articulated as the nation's top priorities. As such, the government launched the exclusive Educational Broadcasting System (EBS) to improve the quality of primary and secondary education, founded a national computer education centre, and initiated a new education tax policy to secure financial resources for school investment. Successes included reforms aimed at developing high-level human resources in science and technology, a dramatic increase in investment in education, quality improvement in schools using broadcast programmes, and the pursuit of excellence in higher education.

EBS opened in 1990 as an affiliated organization of the KEDI. EBS now has one broadcast TV channel, two satellite TV channels, and one FM radio frequency. About 50% of EBS's budget is subsidized by the government; the remainder comes from other sources. EBS has played a role of providing formal and non-formal ODE programmes through its TV and radio channels to students at all levels. EBS has provided programmes related to school curricula, foreign language conversation, vocational education, environmental education, and other study fields. It has also provided programmes in supplement to lifelong education for adults. Foreign languages, computer and Internet training, culture, history, teacher training and arts are major areas of these lifelong educational programmes.

Building the foundation of an 'Edutopia'

In the 1990s, Korea focused on the fulfilment of the public need for higher education and lifelong learning and the effective use of advanced technologies in schools. It also developed and implemented the concept of an 'Edutopia', which aims to create an open and lifelong learning society. Education at all levels has been prepared to meet the challenges of globalization and the information era, and the reforms have emphasized the establishment of an educational welfare system.

The government's plans and action strategies for open lifelong education and technology have been developed according to the suggestions made by the Presidential Commission on Education Reform (Presidential Commission on Education Reform 1997). The Commission, established in February 1994 and effective until February 1998, defined the goal of the Korean Education System in the 21st century as an 'Edutopia', meaning 'an education welfare state — a society of open and lifelong education to allow each and every individual equal and easy access to education at any time and place'.

To build the foundation for an open and lifelong learning society, several strategies have been implemented. The national credit system, allowing course credits to be earned in the open education system towards qualifications recognized as equivalent to a formal degree, was established in 1997. Provision of university extension programmes has been encouraged in order to make university education universally available to non-collegiates and to open school facilities to the community as a centre of education and culture. The foundation of a virtual university and private distance teaching universities have also been suggested as a possible means of realizing an Edutopia. In addition, support organizations have been created to provide an administrative and technical foundation for the ODE system.

Technology and research

The independent Bureau of Educational Information and Technology was established in 1996 to promote the active implementation of the national policy that focuses on the use of information and communication technologies in education and research. The Korea Research and Information Centre (KRIC) and the Korea Multimedia Education Centre (KMEC) were founded in 1997. Using government funds, KRIC provides information services for professionals in higher education with its own server and network system. Online journal articles, research papers, academic databases and other academic materials are provided to professors and researchers in Korea. Membership is required, but no individual payment is required for the use of KRIC's services.

KMEC supports the implementation of virtual education in primary and secondary schools and provides online teacher training. Using government funds, KMEC conducts various activities such as research into the current use of technology in schools, implementing technology initiatives in schools, developing online learning materials for teachers, students and parents, supporting schools in creating their homepages, and providing a comprehensive educational Internet service called EduNet.

Since its establishment, KMEC has developed 14 electronic textbooks with supportive information databases, educational programmes that integrate multimedia materials, CAI (Computer-Assisted Instruction) programmes for primary and secondary schools, training materials and research databases for teachers, an educational multimedia programming tool, lifelong education programmes for the public and parents, and a cyber education counselling system (KMEC 1998a). In April 1999, KRIC and KMEC were united to become the Korea Education and Research Information Service.

Promoting ODE using advanced technologies

With the government's support and funding, all formal higher education institutions are now connected to the education and research network and have computer laboratories. Many digital libraries have been established and linked. In 1998, the government initiated the Virtual University Trial Project (VUTP) under which 25% of higher education institutions in Korea and several private companies have used advanced technologies to deliver ODE to university students and working adults.

The VUTP has aimed to explore ways to: 1) create a cost-effective virtual education system without diminishing the quality; 2) develop and implement Web-based or other types of distance education courses; 3) identify appropriate policies and standards for running a virtual university; and 4) share experiences during the trial period to February 2000.

Sixty-five universities and five companies have participated in the VUTP; eight conventional universities participated independently without forming a consortium, and 57 universities and five companies have formed seven consortia. Each of the eight campus-based universities has established a virtual campus within its own university system, and each of the seven consortia has established a virtual institution outside of its member organizations. The government encouraged both partnerships among universities and the private sector and the sharing of existing resources in providing ODE to university students and adults. The VUTP has inspired about 25% of formal higher education institutions and five private companies in Korea to collaborate in providing virtual courses using advanced technologies, to explore the possibility of incorporating distance education into the campus-based system and even to establish a distance teaching university using new modes of technology in the near future.

All the institutions involved in the VUTP have taken on the task of expanding ODE throughout the country using interactive technologies. The VUTP has stimulated new experiments with various advanced technologies such as satellite broadcasting, videoconferencing, video-on-demand, the Internet and the intranet in delivering ODE. Issues of quality with ODE have been raised and explored. It is expected that the VUTP will help integrate ODE more firmly into the formal higher education system and upgrade the status of ODE.

As outcomes of the VUTP, it is reported that the project has increased collaboration among colleges, universities and companies (Jung 2000). Despite their lack of prior experience in such collaboration, many of these institutions have developed highly successful virtual programmes and have entered into formal relationships with foreign virtual universities. In addition, evaluation studies conducted by VUTP participants showed that, overall, students were satisfied with the flexibility offered by virtual courses.

This chapter will now take a closer look at ODE practices at KNOU and online professional training in the fields of in-service teacher education and corporate training.

Developments in ODE through KNOU

By 2000 there were 156 universities, 160 junior colleges, 11 teachers colleges, 18 polytechnics, one distance teaching university — KNOU — and 90 other types of higher education institution in Korea.

Of the 436 formal higher education institutions, 86% are private and 14% are public. The Ministry of Education (MOE) supports between 60% and 70% of the public conventional institutions' budgets and less than 30% of the budgets of private colleges and universities. KNOU receives about 35% of its budget from the government. As indicated in a World Bank programme (Global Links Television 1997), both the private sector and parents have played a major role in financing formal higher education in Korea.

KNOU, which offers four-year university degrees, is supervised by the Bureau of Lifelong Education (along with 160 junior colleges). Other four-year universities and teachers colleges are supervised by the Bureau of Higher Education and Research Support. Different criteria from those of other four-year universities have been applied to the assessment of KNOU's educational services and quality. This has contributed to the failure to establish high social recognition of KNOU and weakened KNOU's competitive power in providing high quality education.

Since the mid-1990s, many campus colleges and universities have begun to use advanced technologies mainly as supplementary modes of instruction.

Some use videoconferencing to connect students in two or more campuses; others use Web-based conferencing systems to promote non-real-time collaboration among students. In particular, quite a number of universities have developed Web-based virtual courses which can be taken by on- and off-campus students. Developments in ODE in more than 25% of other campus universities have challenged KNOU and led the university to address the challenges by implementing various development strategies and creating major initiatives to improve the educational quality of its services and greater use of advanced technologies.

Student profiles

The KNOU <http://www.knou.ac.kr> was founded in 1972 as a branch of Seoul National University (SNU). It began by offering a two-year junior college programme to 12,000 students. Initially, the primary purpose of the university was to raise the public's overall educational level by providing two-year college education to those high school graduates who, for various reasons, could not receive or continue their higher education. In response to the growth in demand for higher education, which conventional colleges and university were unable to accommodate, a more cost-effective way of education and training was sought by the government. As a result, the first national distance teaching college using a TV and radio broadcasting system was created to increase access to higher education at a much lower cost than conventional education.

In 1981, the university became independent from SNU. By 1986 it was providing a five-year university programme serving approximately 150,000 students. In 1992, it added a four-year programme — the standard university system — serving more than 300,000 students. This amounted to roughly 11% of Korea's higher education enrolments (see Table 1). The change in KNOU's institutional identity from a two-year college to a four-year university and the growth of its student body reflected the overall increase in Koreans' education level. In the 1970s, about 25% of all high school graduates advanced to a higher education institution. In the 1980s this number increased to approximately 35% and in the 1990s to over 60%.

Table 1   Number of KNOU students by year (MOE 1998a)

Year	No. of students
1972	12,000
1980	32,053
1985	153,215
1990	148,650
1995	314,977
1998	314,438

KNOU now has full-time, degree-seeking students for four-year university programmes and part-time students for non-degree, lifelong education programmes. The policy of restricting students to registering only as full-time students and to taking six to seven courses in a semester has been indicated as a major reason for high drop-out rates, especially in the first year of study. Considering that more than 95% of KNOU students work, this policy needs to change. Fortunately, with the introduction of a new curriculum, policies accepting course-based registration and part-time attendance will be implemented by 2001.

Table 2 shows new student profiles between 1994 and 1998. As seen in many distance education institutions, more and more female students are entering ODE. In 1983, 68% of KNOU students were male (Harward and Kim 1985). This dropped to 43% in 1998. The average age of KNOU students has increased each year and reached 29.7 in 1998. Enrolment of housewives has increased and now accounts for around 15% of students. More married people with jobs are also entering KNOU. The changes in student profile indicate that KNOU is becoming a lifelong education institution for working adults rather than for the young who enter KNOU just after high school graduation. In the future, the number of female students who are married and/or housewives is likely to steadily increase.

Each year about 10,000 to 15,000 students graduate from KNOU (see Table 3). The graduation rate, compared with the number of students admitted to KNOU each year, is less than 10%. This low rate may principally be explained by a lack of individualized learning support services, rigid policies to force students to take six to seven courses a semester, and implementation of an absolute grade system. By 1998,

192,661 students had graduated from KNOU; among those, 25,571, or one in 7.5, went on to a conventional graduate school for further education.

Table 2   KNOU new student profiles for 1994 to 1998 (KNOU 1998a)

Year		1994	1995	1996	1997	1998
Gender (%)	Male	42	43	43	41	43
	Female	58	57	57	59	57
Average age (years)		26.2	27.2	27.1	28.1	29.7
Profession (%)	Office workers	24.2	24.5	24.0	22.4	20.4
	Public officers	10.2	8.4	7.9	7.7	7.0
	Technical workers	8.3	8.5	7.0	6.7	5.8
	Housewives	7.5	9.4	11.3	13.4	14.8
	Financial workers	7.0	5.2	4.9	4.4	3.7
	Self-employed	7.0	7.4	8.0	7.6	7.7
	Not working	7.9	4.4	3.8	3.2	3.9
Marital status (%)	Married	26.3	30.4	34.2	39.9	41.7
	Single	73.7	69.6	65.8	60.1	58.3

Table 3   Number of graduates between 1994 and 1998 (KNOU 1998a)

Year	No. of students
1994	10,604
1995	10,036
1996	13,517
1997	13,810
1998	15,463

KNOU students come from 12 different regions all over Korea. Figure 1 shows student distribution by region; 43.1% of the registered students in 1998 came from Seoul, which partly reflects the fact that more than one-quarter of the Korean population lives in Seoul. There are two regional study centres in Seoul. The other 11 regions have one study centre each.

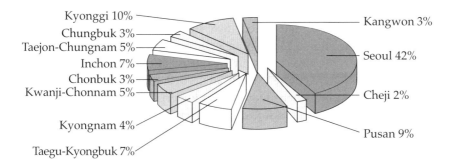

Figure 1   Student distribution by region (KNOU 1999)

KNOU has upheld its mission to serve the advanced educational needs of Korean adults and to award bachelor's degrees upon completion of the degree requirements. As the overall educational level in Korea has risen, KNOU's role in Korean society has also expanded. The university is now seeking to improve the academic and professional proficiency of working people by offering programmes to graduates from two-year colleges and four-year universities. Recent student profiles show that the number of KNOU students who attended other higher education institutions prior to KNOU increased each year. In 1999, more than 40% of new KNOU students already had either a college certificate or a bachelor's degree (KNOU 1999) and transferred to the second or third year of education. The changing nature of KNOU's student body and the increased need of adults to continue their education and training is challenging the university to develop new curricula and a more flexible system.

About 25% of higher education institutions in Korea also offer ODE. It is reported that in the second semester of 1998, about 45,000 students (about 3% of university students) registered in one or more of 536 virtual courses offered by the institutions participating in the VUTP. More than 80% of these students had already entered campus-based higher education institutions; fewer than 20% were adults who took the virtual courses on a part-time basis.

Academic programmes

KNOU offers four-year bachelor's degree programmes and lifelong education courses as non-degree programmes. KNOU is not permitted to offer graduate-level courses. Major reasons for this seem to include:

1) general suspicion of the quality of distance education at graduate level; 2) resistance among campus-based universities to allow KNOU to offer graduate programmes to a large number of students at low cost; and 3) lack of confidence in the government in the quality of the distance education provided by KNOU. As more working adults seek more flexible modes of education to continue their study beyond undergraduate degree level, there has been growing social pressure on the government to allow KNOU to have graduate level programmes. Recognizing this, KNOU has attempted to promote confidence through its proposal to integrate a quality assurance system into the curriculum and its management.

KNOU's curriculum consists of general education courses and majors in liberal arts and social and natural sciences for which 140 or more credits (42 credits in general education and 66 or more credits in one's major) and a satisfactory pass in a graduation test are required for a student to graduate with an undergraduate degree. Table 4 shows the fields of the 18 majors and the number of courses offered (KNOU 1999). These major areas are similar to those of campus-based universities. Unfortunately, there is no formal mechanism to consider the specific learning needs of adult students in developing the courses and to create new courses based on those needs.

Students have only limited choices. For example, the first year students in a certain department are given the same seven courses to take in their first semester. Starting in the second semester, students can choose one or two courses out of six that they have to take each semester. Even though KNOU defers the degrees of those who fail to apply for three consecutive semesters, course choices and part-time registration opportunities are limited. However, with a new computerized management system and a new curriculum, KNOU plans to adopt a more flexible curriculum policy that will permit students to register on a part-time basis and to have more choice in course selection from 2001 onwards.

While the degree programmes are operated in a rather closed way, the non-degree programmes delivered by the Centre for Lifelong Education, affiliated with KNOU, are more flexible. The Centre aims to provide distance education to the public, especially to professionals who want practical education without pursuing a degree programme. The Centre's programmes are based on learner needs assessment. Since 1997, KNOU has provided in-service teacher training courses to teach open education, logical thinking and writing skills; courses for small and medium-sized industry management; and courses for Korean language instructors. All have received positive feedback from participants.

Table 4   Major areas of study and courses at KNOU (KNOU 1999)

Schools	Majors	Number of courses offered in a semester
School of Liberal Arts	Korean Language and Literature	30
	English Language and Literature	30
	Chinese Language and Literature	31
	French Language and Literature	31
	Japanese Studies	32
School of Social Science	Law	31
	Public Administration	29
	Economics	30
	Management	30
	International Trade	29
	Media Arts and Sciences	25
School of Natural Science	Agricultural Science	31
	Home Economics	28
	Computer Science	30
	Applied Statistics	30
	Environmental Health/Nursing	29/17
School of Education	Education	30
	Early Childhood Education	30
School of General Education		36

Table 5   Staff (KNOU 1998b, 1999)

Full-time academics (242)	President	1
	Professors	58
	Associate professors	38
	Assistant professors	15
	Guest professors	3
	Research workers	9
	Teaching assistants	62
Part-time academics (5,779)	Part-time lecturers	5,651
	Tutors	128
Administrative/technical staff (511)	Educational officials	14
	General administrators	145
	Special govt. personnel	12
	Support associates	242
Technicians		98

Teaching methods and technologies

The main teaching and learning methods at KNOU are printed textbooks, satellite TV, radio or audio cassettes. Videoconferencing systems, the Internet and PC networks are supplementary, as are face-to-face schooling and tutoring. Thirteen regional study centres in major provinces and 31 local study centres in small cities provide instruction sessions, individualized tutoring, and other support services such as assistance with completion and submission of application forms.

A typical three-credit course at KNOU consists of a basic textbook, a series of 20 half-hour TV, radio or audiocassette programmes, eight hours of face-to-face instruction or lectures via videoconferencing, one assignment and a final examination. KNOU's major strategies to incorporate technology into this system include:

- To become a cutting-edge open university in an effort to differentiate itself from other conventional universities and was the first university in Korea to invest in a videoconferencing network system, a satellite TV channel, a multimedia digital library and a computerized administration system.

- Its development of a substantial database of online learning materials and a multimedia digital library so that students and others may obtain online information at a distance. These online multimedia materials are electronic forms of printed materials and broadcast programmes produced by KNOU.

- Increased interactivity between its instructors and students and among students using telecommunications technologies such as the Internet, the commercial PC network and the videoconferencing system. The computer-mediated communication system will help KNOU improve the quality of its student support by providing interactivity at low cost.

- Its investment in an integrated management system of administration and student services. Handling more than 300,000 students with a small staff and the implementation of decentralized policies require extensive use of computer network technology in the management of the university.

In the 1990s KNOU launched projects or initiatives to implement these strategies. In 1992, it began to develop and implement text-based database services for its students and to provide for two-way interaction through three nation-wide PC network systems. As a result, a database with supplementary learning materials for more than 300 courses (60% of all courses offered by KNOU) was developed. Using the database services, students can obtain supplementary learning materials, keep up-to-date with their departments and receive other news in the KNOU Weekly News. A PC network was also added as a formal channel for students to ask their instructors questions and to interact with other students.

As the Internet has become increasingly popular in higher education since the mid-1990s, KNOU established a multimedia digital library system on the Web in 1997. With technical and financial help from IBM, this initiative digitized KNOU's TV and radio programmes and integrated those digitized programmes in a teaching and learning platform so that students can study their courses in a multimedia format on the Web. All KNOU TV, radio and recorded programmes — 760 hours of video and 4,730 hours of audio materials — were digitized in 1998 and stored in the digital library system. KNOU added lifelong educational CATV (cable TV) programmes to the digital library system in 1999, thus allowing the public to access its digital library system and take Web-based lifelong educational courses.

In February 1998, KNOU joined the VUTP. Through it KNOU began to provide Web-based courses to students. About 80 Web-based courses were developed in 1998 in cooperation with eight other campus-based universities.

In autumn 1995, KNOU launched a project to study the educational uses of the Internet with funds from the Ministry of Information and Communication (MIC). As a result, an interactive videoconferencing network was introduced for educational programmes in the geographically scattered regional and local study centres. Using this network, the project connected 14 study centres, introduced interactive tutorial sessions, held meetings among university members in different places, encouraged open discussions among students, faculty members and general citizens, and created non-degree programmes such as teacher training programmes.

A CATV channel for distance education, called the Open University Network (OUN), was founded in September 1996 to promote open and lifelong education at the higher education level. With modern digital broadcasting facilities and about 80 staff members, OUN has been providing regular degree course programmes to KNOU students and lifelong education courses to the general public in higher education and retraining. About 40% of OUN's broadcasting time is allocated to lifelong education programmes for adults. This cable TV channel was augmented by a satellite TV channel in March 1999 to extend distance education services to people living in remote areas where cable has not yet been installed.

What have been the results of using these technologies? Most notable is the increase in online interaction, although this has been lower than expected. Factors such as a lack of computers in regional study centres, slow access by home computer using standard telephone lines, and high phone fees are cited as the major reasons. The slow speed feedback system also appears to be behind low interaction between instructors and students (Shin 1999). In addition to limited access to the network and the lack of facilitating skills among instructors, passive involvement of students in discussions was also indicated in a study (Shin 1999) to be central to inactivity in online group discussions. The study indicated that most students used the PC network to download materials and exchange study information but not as a communication tool.

Secondly, there is a question of the cost-effectiveness of KNOU's technology strategies to improve the quality of its educational services. Daniel (1996) expressed a doubt as to the ability of KNOU's technology strategies to improve the quality of distance education without providing extensive tutoring services. As recognized in several papers (Kim 1991; Hong 1992; Han 1995), it is clear that KNOU's efforts to change current views of distance education in Korea by providing interactivity through advanced technologies must be combined with more investment in the development of high quality learning materials, extensive individualized learning support from tutors, and a more flexible learner-centred system.

Learning support services

Thirteen regional and 31 local study centres provide learning support services such as face-to-face schooling, private tutoring and learning materials services. A typical centre is a building with numerous lecture and seminar rooms, a large classroom equipped with an interactive videoconferencing system connected to the other regional centres and a KNOU head office, a multimedia lab with 20 to 30 computers with Internet connections, a library with books and KNOU learning materials, a few administration offices and one or two professors' offices. University management recognizes that technology facilities and learning materials alone are not adequate to serve the 20,000 students in each region. Each year the university invests in hardware and network facilities in regional study centres.

Since each regional study centre has only 10 to 15 tutors, not much private tutoring is provided. Even though tutors are encouraged to provide one-to-one interaction with students, a lack of tutors has led tutors in the regional centres to provide large-classroom lectures and learning support to only limited numbers. This has been indicated as the main reason for the high drop-out rates in the first and second years (Park 1995).

Interactive technology seems to enable students to receive learning support from the university. PC networks and the Internet along with telephone and fax have been used as formal channels by which students can contact their instructors and interact with other students. Even though interaction has been lower than anticipated, it is now growing rapidly. More than 30% of KNOU students now use the computer network to communicate with KNOU faculties and staff and other students.

However, introducing advanced technologies does not seem to provide sufficient learning support services to enable KNOU students to successfully complete their study. To make up the shortfall in intensive learning support, KNOU students have formed voluntary study groups within their major fields. One study found about 500 groups in the Seoul region and more than 700 throughout Korea (Jung et al. 1995). Each study group had between 100 and 3,000 KNOU student members. More than 40% of all KNOU students participated in one of the study groups. A typical study group met once or twice a week, for two to three hours in the evenings, and studied various learning materials prepared by the group members. Learning materials included summaries of KNOU textbooks, supplementary materials provided through the KNOU computer network, explanation of test items and a summary of broadcast programmes. External experts or KNOU graduates were sometimes invited to deliver special lectures to group members. Involvement in study group activities were positively related to course completion rates and GPA (grade point average).

The results of the study showed that the voluntary study groups played a significant role in providing learning support. Recognizing the importance of the study groups in improving student learning at KNOU, the university has provided various learning materials and study places within the regional study centres to motivate and enable further study group activities.

Student assessment and evaluation

Students at KNOU are assessed and given an absolute grade on the basis of their performance in a final test with multiple-choice questions consisting of 70% of the grade. This is augmented by an assignment or an essay-type mid-term examination. For some courses, practicals and demonstration of certain skills are required. Internet courses involve a variety of assessment methods: multiple choice tests, participation in online discussions, essays, assignments and quizzes. About 40% of KNOU courses require eight hours of schooling sessions in regional study centres; attendance is taken into account.

A need to revise KNOU's assessment methods has been recognized by educators and students. Several policy papers (KNOU 1994; Kwak 1997; Lee 1997) have suggested alternatives. Introducing a relative grade scheme rather than the current absolute grade scheme, requiring more essay-type assignments, providing tutor feedback on assignments, implementing different assessment methods for different courses, and introducing computer-assisted assessment have all been suggested. With the introduction of a new curriculum and related policies in 2001, assessment methods are expected to change.

Programme management and quality assurance

A textbook development committee at KNOU consists of faculty members and a chief administrative officer responsible for approving development and revision of all textbooks. Once approved by the committee, the content is written by a team of experts made up of KNOU professors and external academics. Since the early 1990s, KNOU has encouraged its professors to develop textbooks with more than one other external content expert. A completed draft goes to an external instructional designer with expertise in the design of distance education materials. Revisions are based on this designer's comments before publication. The publishing department is in charge of textbook publishing. A student evaluation sheet is attached for feedback from the learner's point of view on the last page of each textbook. Since this evaluation is not compulsory, the return rate is very low.

Broadcasting programmes, including satellite TV, radio and audio cassettes, are produced by the Education Media Development Centre at KNOU. The education media management committee decides programme areas and time schedules for broadcasting. A typical TV production team consists of a professor, a director, a graphic designer and other technical staff. Once the programmes are produced, they are reviewed by the production team before broadcasting and only a few changes can be made during this review process. There is no formative evaluation before broadcasting, but after a programme is delivered, a group of students and media specialists review and make suggestions to the production team for improvements for subsequent programmes. Related studies have shown that this monitoring system is effective (Hong et al. 1998).

The activities of external examiners or monitoring teams are not, however, fully integrated into the programme management system. It is each individual professor's choice whether or not to implement reviewers' recommendations. No rigorous system has been set up to evaluate academic faculties' activities at KNOU. As KNOU faces challenges to improve education quality and provide more flexibility, the university is to introduce a course evaluation system requiring every course to be evaluated by students and external experts. The results will be publicized and be reflected in course revisions.

Financing

About 35% of KNOU's budget comes from the government and another 65% from student fees. In 1997 KNOU's total budget was about US$50 million. Tuition per student has been between US$120 and US$150 since 1993. Campus-based institutions receive 60% to 70% of their budget from the government but must compete for a portion of that based on evaluation results. KNOU is not required to compete.

For new technologies such as videoconferencing, satellite TV and the multimedia digital library, KNOU has solicited outside financial support, either from the government or the private sector. For example, for the development of the PC network database in 1992, KNOU received US$150,000 from a commercial PC network company and matched this amount in the first year. To generate the funds needed for database maintenance and revision, KNOU reduced the amount of printed materials provided to students, instead requiring students to print their own copies from the online database.

Videoconferencing systems were established in 1995 with funds from the MIC, as a part of the national information superhighway project. A total of US$1.6 million (US$1.2 million from the MIC and US$0.4 million from KNOU) was invested in equipment for videoconferencing systems connecting 13 study centres and the KNOU headquarters. During the three-year experimental phase, no telecommunications fees were charged for the use of the videoconferencing systems. Since 1998, however, KNOU has paid about US$15,000 a month for these fees and other operational costs. Most of this amount has been recovered from costs saved by substituting face-to-face sessions with videoconferencing.

Developments in professional open and distance training

As a result of the exponential growth in information and communication technology, many new forms of educational media have been made available over the years. ODE media mitigate the spatial limitations and time constraints of education, removing the need for the learner to be present at an instructional site at a designated time. This has made ODE more affordable, flexible and effective. Many training institutions have adopted such new technologies. The following are examples of how ODE has been used in in-service teacher education and corporate training.

In-service teacher training

Although ODE is not yet widespread in in-service teacher education for the 340,000 teachers in Korea, several teacher training centres in the provinces and other teacher education institutions have been using the PC network as a supplementary tool to distribute learning materials and encourage interaction between trainees and trainers for several years. In addition, with government support, major initiatives in developing Internet-based distance teacher education programmes have been launched.

The 16 provincial Offices of Education are responsible for providing in-service teacher training programmes within their respective provinces. To meet these responsibilities, each Office has operated a Teacher Training Centre (TTC) in cooperation with colleges and universities in nearby provinces. Several teacher training institutions have adopted the PC network and eventually the Internet as a teaching and communication tool alongside conventional training methods.

Nine of the provincial TTCs have used the PC network in all 79 general and specialized training courses to distribute course materials, announce important messages, allow participants to interact with others on specific issues and to encourage interaction between trainers and learners. The network has been used as a supplementary medium to conventional teacher training in most of these online programmes. For some courses, the network has been adopted as the main training medium. Teachers can study course materials at home with individualized interaction with instructors.

Distance or online training courses for teachers were not credited by the provincial office until KNOU offered a distance teacher training programme in 1997. KNOU, with the support of the MOE, created a 60-hour nation-wide distance training programme entitled 'Introducing Open Education in Primary Schools: Why and How?' for primary school teachers using a self-study textbook, CATV and a two-way videoconferencing system. Up to winter 1998, the programme was delivered four times, and each time about 1,000 primary school teachers, including some administrators and school principals, took this virtual training course at home. Their performance was assessed by assignments, participation in the videoconferencing and a final examination.

The course evaluation report of the first term (KNOU 1998c) indicated that more than 70% of participants were in their forties and fifties, 62% were from big cities, 60% were male teachers, 69% of the teachers said that the course was satisfactory overall and 90% indicated that the content was useful for understanding basic concepts and applying open education to classroom activities. In 1999, another distance programme with similar topics was delivered to secondary school teachers nation-wide.

KNOU also created a winter vacation distance training programme for teachers at all levels with the support of the Korea Philosophy Association. The aim was to improve the teaching of logical and technical writing. This 60-hour programme using a self-study textbook and videoconferencing in 12 study centres was delivered three times to about 1,000 teachers at primary and secondary school levels each time. Assessment was based on attendance at the videoconferencing sessions, a mid-term report and a final examination. The completion rate was 90%.

The course evaluation report of the first term indicated that 39% of participants were in their forties, 29% in their fifties, and 23% in their thirties. 70% were male teachers. More than 65% of participants came from big cities. 89% indicated the course was useful in improving their teaching. 78% enjoyed active interaction with instructors via videoconferencing. Integration of the Internet or PC network as a communication medium was suggested by the teachers.

In summer 1997, the MOE and the MIC funded a project to create a Cyber Teacher Training Centre (CTTC) <http://edunet.kmec.net> within the KMEC. A software platform for managing virtual teacher training and 11 training courses in the field of general education were developed as a result. With an additional six courses developed in 1998, these virtual courses are now available through the EduNet, an integrated educational service on the Web. The CTTC is managed by the KMEC with assistance from the provincial TTCs and the Korea University of Teacher Education (KUTE).

The TTC in each provincial Office of Education is encouraged to use the virtual teacher training programmes developed by the KMEC, to revise them to meet their own purposes and to offer them to teachers in its province along with conventional face-to-face training. In 1998, one provincial Office and the KUTE used these virtual programmes for teacher training.

Campus-based universities or consortia of the universities participating in the VUTP also offer some online teacher training courses. For example, the Open Cyber University (OCU), Sookmyung Cyber Education Centre, SNU and Ewha Women's University offer Web-based training courses for teachers. It is expected that more universities in the VUTP will offer Internet courses for teachers this year.

In winter 1998, teacher training materials were digitized by the KMEC. As a result, teachers in each province could access these training materials via the EduNet or commercial PC network, search the materials according to training institution, content, instructor, year of publication and type of training and download them for home study. These online materials can be used for individual study in conjunction with face-to-face courses, or as learning resources for online teacher training courses offered by educational institutions. Since all teachers are encouraged to have an EduNet ID, online materials on the EduNet will be actively used by individual teachers as well as by teacher training institutions.

Beginning in 1998, individual teachers' autonomy in selecting their own training courses based on personal need has increased. It is anticipated that more teachers will choose online courses over traditional, face-to-face group-based courses. To meet demand for online training of teachers, many teacher training institutions including the TTCs in 16 provinces, KMEC, KUTE and other universities are preparing Web-based in-service teacher training courses.

Corporate training

Since the mid-1990s, many companies in Korea have begun to explore the use of networked training strategies such as Web-based training as an alternative to regular training classes. According to the report by the Korea Society for Corporate Education, more than 70% of 500 big companies have adopted ICT for training. About 20% have used computer networks such as PC networks, the Internet or intranets as a main delivery mode or as a supplementary communication tool for training.

The Human Resources Development Centre (HRDC) in Samsung Group formed a Distance Education Team (DET) and, after establishing a HRDC Web server in 1994, started developing virtual courses. In 1998, Samsung's Cybercampus provided virtual training courses in a more integrated form through a total of 28 online courses. In 1999, it became the Samsung Cyber University (SCU) and over 100 online courses were provided to employees of all Group companies. The courses provided by the SCU cover the areas of basic and advanced job-related skills acquisition, management, English and Samsung induction programmes for foreigners. These Web-based virtual training courses are planned, designed, managed and evaluated by the DET within the HRDC. Courses are produced externally using the Samsung Network-ISD model. Distance Learning Support System software is used to manage the SCU and follow each student's progress.

In July 1998, the LG Group, one of the largest enterprises in Korea, opened the LG Cyber Academy within the LG HRDC. This Cyber Academy aims to provide just-in-time, on-demand, Web-based training programmes within its intranet system to LG employees who, for whatever reason, cannot attend face-to-face training sessions. A total 757 employees enrolled in one of the five Web-based training courses during 1998. Five steps in a conventional ISD model are applied in course development: needs assessment, design, development, implementation and evaluation.

A typical virtual training course consists of learning content on the Web, small group interaction among learners, Q&A between learners and online instructors and a relevant information library. Each employee's learning progress is managed and monitored by the Cyber Academy platform system.

Unlike big *chaebol* companies, most small and medium-sized enterprises (SME) do not have in-house training centres. To meet their employees' training needs, they have to use outside training institutes, both private and government-supported. Since the mid-1990s, many such institutes have begun introducing distance education including online training. The recent financial crisis increased the need for virtual training because of cutbacks in training budgets and increased responsibilities of employees.

Sungjin Information Technology Systems, a training institute providing training courses to SMEs in Korea, has begun to provide intranet-based training courses to respond to new training needs in the market. In September 1998, Sungjin ITS developed two virtual programmes, each consisting of three modules: one for teaching skills to use IT for performance improvement and the others for teaching strategies to economize production and management systems. Two thousand employees from different companies are now taking these virtual training programmes.

Sungjin ITS is now preparing an Internet broadcasting training programme, which teaches Korean to Koreans who live outside the country. They collaborate with the Arirang International TV Broadcasting System. A Web-based training course on the use of IT has been developed for public officers in the Seoul City Hall. Sungjin ITS has also been asked to develop intranet-based training courses for the Ministry of Defence.

Based on feedback, Sungjin ITS will revise existing virtual programmes by applying instructional and motivational design strategies and adding face-to-face components to its learning environments.

Besides these organizations, the Korea Banking Association has set up a Cyber Banking School to provide virtual training courses for its member institutions. Korea Telecom and Posco Company have used the Web and desktop videoconferencing to deliver training courses. Samsung Data System has been implementing virtual training programmes for its employees since the mid-1990s. It is expected that more companies will adopt distance education methods in training to reduce training costs in the long run.

Implications for policy and future directions

Recent developments in ODE in Korea show that more and more higher education institutions, including colleges, universities and professional training centres, will adopt IT and communication technology in education and training to implement ODE programmes. With the expansion of ODE programmes nation-wide, issues of quality will be more seriously discussed and pedagogical models for ODE will be sought. In addition, ways of reducing the cost of ODE using advanced technologies without a decline in quality will be explored. Allowing more flexibility and openness in distance education will be key issues for distance educators and policy-makers. The Korean experience suggests several major implications for policy and future directions in the successful implementation of ODE for higher education and training.

It is being said that distance education, through IT and communication technologies, has changed the nature of learning. Greater and more timely access to information has been achieved and wider cooperation in knowledge-building among people has become possible. We see a paradigm shift from distance teaching to distributed learning. Distance teaching organizations using broadcasting media and print materials cannot afford to ignore the tremendous potential of interactive technologies such as the Internet.

More and more distance teaching institutions are now integrating interactive technology into their activities. But it has to be emphasized that interactive technologies such as the Internet can provide a real and timely service to distance learners only if quality and effectiveness outweigh the costs.

Adopting systems approach in instruction design

The experience of KNOU confirms that introducing advanced technologies or hiring famous content experts to deliver virtual courses does not necessarily guarantee the quality of educational services. Rather, the need and the means must be analysed, an optimal solution must be sought, the solution must be implemented, and the results must be evaluated and fed back into the design.

Adoption of an Instructional Systems Design (ISD) model helps distance educators to take a step-by-step approach in developing and implementing effective open and distance courses. In applying the ISD model, pedagogical features of advanced technologies are identified, and teaching strategies are carefully selected based on these features. Content experts or famous scholars in certain subjects may provide professional support to instructional designers to develop and implement high-quality courses that satisfy learner needs and employ optimal open and distance teaching strategies.

Establishing a regular quality management system

A regular system to monitor and evaluate the development and implementation of ODE will be required to ensure the quality of the educational services. This requires major investments in building research capacity in ODE institutions. Quality management systems through continuous monitoring and evaluation will help identify problems in academic programmes and support services and suggest possible solutions. In particular, feedback from students must be sought and used to revise programmes and improve services. Also, regular examination by external experts needs to be conducted to identify problems in organization, policies and operations. This external evaluation will help ODE institutions compare their performance with campus-based institutions.

Providing training programmes

KNOU's experience tells us that the successful completion of a distance education programme requires each learner to have good self-directing learning skills and well-organized learning support from the institution. Organized sessions to facilitate self-directed learning are necessary to help learners develop and strengthen competencies in managing the independent learning process at the very beginning of their study.

Staff development is very important to successfully implement ODE. Continuous staff development programmes that emphasize educational effectiveness, design and interaction strategies of courses, and technical skills need to be integrated into the ODE system in order to improve the educational quality. Online technologies have important promise in providing staff development programmes.

Implementing cost reduction policies

Institutional partnerships are important for ODE providers because they reduce the cost of introducing new technologies and also improve the quality of developing programmes. By forming appropriate partnerships with campus-based universities, open and distance teaching universities can secure external content experts and teaching support. Partnerships with business sectors may help reduce investment costs in hardware systems such as a computer network, recruit students and obtain advanced technical skills. Open and distance teaching universities that wish to commercialize their educational programmes and research must, from the outset, consider forming partnerships with business. Finding creative ways to share resources will be the key issue in forming partnerships with other organizations.

Open and distance teaching universities also need to find ways of reducing the cost per graduate by improving the graduation rate. Several cases show that per student costs in distance teaching universities were lower than in campus-based universities (Perraton 1994). Yet per graduate costs were not necessarily lower because of the lower graduation rate in distance teaching universities. The experience of the UK Open University shows that individualized tutoring services help increase graduation or completion rates. Unfortunately, tutoring costs are too high for many distance teaching universities with large numbers of students. Therefore, other ways of helping students complete their study need to be sought. Combining tutor support with computer-mediated support, encouraging voluntary study activities among students by providing incentives and using outside volunteers as tutors can be considered as alternatives to current fully human-based tutoring services.

Implementing open policies

A distance teaching organization is not necessarily an open system. KNOU shows that even if it does accept working adults as students once they have high school graduation certificates, regardless of their age, KNOU has not been open in its curriculum. Open policies towards access, curriculum, methods and learning processes have to be institutionalized in order that institutions aspiring to be ODE institutions are successful in this goal.

In addition, providing the appropriate legal foundation is necessary for the promotion of virtual education in various fields such as in-service teacher training and corporate training. Learning from its prior experiences in in-service virtual teacher training, the government should provide legal incentives and policies for teacher training institutions to restructure their programmes to include open and distance teaching as future initiatives.

References

Daniel, J S (1996) *Mega-Universities and Knowledge Media*, London: Kogan Page.

Global Links (1997) *Education For All: The South Korean Experience*, The World Bank, Washington, DC.

Han, W (1995) 'Korea National Open University: towards open and distance learning in a telecomputing age', in Sewart D (ed.) *One World*

Harwood, R F and Kim, S H (1985) 'Seoul's super school', *ICDE Bulletin*, May,8.

Hiltz, S R (1995) *The Virtual Classroom*, Norwood, New Jersey: Ablex Publishing Corporation.

Hong, S J et al. (1998) 'KNOU's CATV utilization strategies', KNOU Policy Paper.

Jung, I S, Jun, Y K, Hong, S J, Anh, B K and Hwang, S Y (1995) 'A study on small study group activities at KNOU, KNOU policy paper.

Jung, I S, and Choi, S W (1998) 'Information and communication technology and open and distance education', *Korea Journal of Educational Technology*, 14(2): 163–86.

Jung, I S and Leem, J H (1998) 'Needs assessment of virtual education in Korea', *Journal of Distance Education*, 12(1).

Jung, I S (1999) 'A report on current status of the Virtual University Trial Project', KNOU.

Jung, I S (2000) 'Korea's experiments with virtual education', *World Bank Human Development Network. Technical Notes Series*, 5(2).

Keegan, D (1980) 'On defining distance education', *Distance Education*, 1(1): 13–36.

Keegan, D (1996) *Foundations of Distance Education*, London: Routledge.

KNOU (1994) 'A study on reasons for low registration rate at KNOU', KNOU policy paper.

KNOU (1998a) *KNOU Statistics Overview*.

KNOU (1998b) *KNOU Statistics*.

KNOU (1999) *University Life*.

Korea, Ministry of Education and Korea Multimedia Education Centre (1998) 'Educational informatization white book'.

Korea, Ministry of Education (1998b) 'A report on the Virtual University Trial Project', Bureau of Educational Technology.

Korea, Ministry of Education (1999) 'A plan for introducing ICT in schools', Bureau of Educational Technology.

Korea, Ministry of Information and Communication (1998) 'Informatization white book'.

Korea, Ministry of Education (1998a) 'Educational statistics', Korea Educational Development Institute.

Korea Multimedia Education Centre (1998a) 'Educational informatization evaluation report, in-service teacher training evaluation.'

Korea Multimedia Education Centre (1998b) 'Establishing a cyber teacher training center'.

Kwak, N H (1997) 'The problem and improvement of KNOU evaluation system', *Journal of Student Guidance*, 8, 51–58.

Lee, T L (1997) 'A study on the school year for graduation of KNOU', *Journal of Student Guidance*, 8, 35–50.

Many Voices: Quality in Open and Distance Learning, 1: 101–4, Milton Keynes: International Council for Distance Education and the Open University.

Moore, M (1983) 'On a theory of independent study', in Sewart, D, Keegan, D and Holmbery, B, *Distance Education: International Perspectives*, London and Canberra: Croom Helm.

Open University Network (1999) 'In-depth discussion: universities in Korea', a series of CATV programmes produced by KNOU.

Park, D J (1995) 'The role of the Korea National Open University in the human resource development of Korea', in Sewart, D (ed.) *One World Many Voices: Quality in Open and Distance Learning*, 1: 327–30, Milton Keynes: International Council for Distance Education and the Open University.

Perraton, H (1994) 'Comparative cost of distance teaching in higher education: scale and quality', in Dhanarajan, G, Ip, P K, Yuen, K S and Swales, C (eds) *Economics of Distance Education: Recent Experience*, Hong Kong: Open Learning Institute Press.

Presidential Commission on Education Reform (1997) *Education Reform for the 21st Century*.

Shin, K (1999) 'Use of PC network for distance education at KNOU', *KNOU Weekly*, 15 March.

Wedemeyer, C A (1983) 'Back door learning in the learning society' in Sewart, D, Keegan, D and Holmberg, B, *Distance Education: International Perspectives*, London and Canberra: Croom Helm.

Mongolia

Bernadette Robinson

Introduction

Open and distance education was introduced into Mongolia for the first time in the 1990s as a response to the economic crisis and its social consequences. The 1990s saw sudden and dramatic changes in Mongolian life as the country changed rapidly from a centrally planned command economy to a market economy and from a single-party communist state to a multi-party democracy. The impact on people's lives, whether in cities or in the countryside, was huge. It generated needs for new curricula, new learning opportunities, changes in the formal education system and the provision of non-formal education for adults and young people. However, there were few resources to finance new educational initiatives or even to safeguard existing provision given the severe economic constraints accompanying the transition to a market economy. The means of supporting the changes and introducing new initiatives came largely from external funding (from the Danish International Development Administration of the Danish government (DANIDA), the UK government (ODA), the European Union, UNICEF, the Soros Foundation, the Mongolian Foundation for an Open Society (MFOS), the Asian Development Bank and others).

This chapter describes the circumstances that led to the introduction of open and distance education into Mongolia, outlines its development up to the year 2000 and identifies the factors that have shaped it.

Country profile

Mongolia is a landlocked country in central Asia bordering on Russia and the People's Republic of China. It is a low-income country with an average annual income of US$390 per capita (World Bank 1999). With a population of 2.4 million in a country of 1.6 million square kilometres (half the size of India), Mongolia has a very low average population density of 1.5 people per square kilometre (for comparison, China has an average of 150 people per square kilometre, Australia has 2.3 and the United Kingdom 235). The population is a young one with half under the age of 20 and a growth rate of 1.4% (National Statistical Office 1998). Just over half the population (52.4%) is urban (of these, half live in the capital city of Ulaanbaatar) and 47.5% is rural. About a third of the rural population (371,100) lives in provincial *(aimag)* centres; the remaining two-thirds (764,100) live a nomadic life herding animals. The climate is dry and extreme with long cold winters. The terrain varies between desert (the Gobi), the steppes and mountains. The country has a weak communications infrastructure with limited telecommunications and few surfaced roads. Radio ownership is estimated to be 139 per 1,000 people, television sets 63 per 1,000, one mobile phone per 1,000 and seven to eight computers per 1,000 (World Bank 1999). Mongolian is the first language of most of the population though there is a minority of Khazak speakers in the west.

From being a feudal society under the dominance of Manchurian China, Mongolia became a socialist state from 1921 onwards, assisted by Russia. In 1924, it was the second country in the world to become communist and a centrally planned economy began in the 1930s. Seventy years of communist socialism saw a huge improvement in the country's development, health and education, for the rural as well as the urban population. During this period the country's economy was transformed from a nomadic agricultural economy into one with an industrial sector producing semi-processed raw materials (mainly copper and cashmere). In the 1960s there was a major drive towards industrialization and a large increase in the urbanization of the population (Sanders 1987). Until 1990, Mongolia had a close association with the Union of Soviet Socialist Republics (USSR) though it was never a constituent republic. Russian influence was considerable. Russian was a compulsory second language and the Cyrillic alphabet replaced traditional Mongolian script. The growth of the Mongolian economy was 'robust' until the mid-1980s when it began to fail, hastened by external events (Yusuf and Burki 1992). A peaceful overthrow of the government in 1990 led to elections and a democratic constitution.

Economic and social transition in Mongolia

Though located in Central Asia, Mongolia's economic transition from a centrally planned to a market economy followed the abrupt Eastern European and Russian approach to economic reform rather than the more gradualist one seen in China, Vietnam and Laos (Collins and Nixson 1993). The sudden political changes in Mongolia were driven by severe economic shocks, internal and external. One external shock was the collapse of the former Soviet Union in 1990 and the withdrawal of the 30% subsidy to Mongolia's annual budget by the USSR. Another shock came with the dissolution of the communist bloc's Council for Mutual Economic Assistance (CMEA) which provided three-quarters of Mongolia's trade links and partners.

As a result, Gross Domestic Product (GDP) declined each year between 1990 and 1993 resulting in a cumulative loss of 22% of output. Growth returned from 1994 to 1997 but still left GDP 10.7% below its 1989 level in real terms (NSO 1998). By 1997, annual GDP per capita was US$394 (World Bank 1998), though alongside this existed a large unofficial economy. Inflation rose sharply reaching 325% in 1992 before reducing to 17.5% in 1997. The exchange rate against the US dollar changed from 3 Mongolian tugriks in 1989 to over 1,000 in 1999. In 1996 alone there was a 60% increase in energy prices. Price increases overall were huge and wages failed to keep pace with inflation. Government estimates put prices at 70 times higher in 1996 than in 1990, though an independent analysis claims they were 150 times higher with wages in the state-funded sector increasing by only 22 times (Sodnomdorj 1997). In either case, the real pay cut was extremely large. Income inequality increased greatly in a country where wage differences were previously small because of the compressed wage scales typical of socialist economies. The richest 20% of households in 1999 had 18 times the income of the poorest 20%.

The social costs of transition were high, borne unevenly by different groups within Mongolia's population. Social inequality grew. Unemployment appeared, and social indicators such as school enrolment, maternal and infant mortality declined. Poverty, a new phenomenon in Mongolia after 1990, rose rapidly with an estimated 36% of the population living below the national poverty line (World Bank 1998). Health, social welfare and education services were cut. The position of women in Mongolia deteriorated with higher unemployment rates and greater job insecurity cuts in maternity care, social services and child support; and reduced representation in parliament and other decision-making bodies (Robinson and Solongo 2000). Life expectancy rates reduced, particularly for males, and alcoholism, domestic violence and crime increased. Education in general was greatly affected by all these changes.

Education in socialist Mongolia

In many developing countries open and distance education has been introduced into contexts where the general educational levels were low or where universal primary education was not yet established. This was not the case in Mongolia. During the socialist period (1924 to 1990) large advances were made in education. These included the rural population everywhere despite the country's huge size, harsh climate and small population. By 1990, Mongolia had human development indicators (literacy, education, female participation and health) higher than expected for its per capita GDP and income levels. The government's commitment to education was reflected in its spending levels (Ariunaa 1997). Expenditure on education in the 1980s was more than 10% of GDP, about 17.7% of total government expenditure. This was a relatively high level for a developing country: other Asian countries spent less — Thailand spent 7% of GDP, and South Korea and China each spent 3% of GDP (Yusuf and Burki 1992).

By the end of the 1980s, Mongolia had virtually universal primary education, a high proportion of children completing the secondary phase of education, well-resourced and widespread pre-school provision, high levels of female participation in education (including tertiary education), high literacy rates and a force of fully qualified teachers (Wu 1994; Bray et al. 1994). In 1989, literacy rates were reported as 97% and enrolment rates in education as 98% for primary, 85% for eight-year secondary education and 17% for higher education (NSO 1997; UNDP 1997). All of this was provided by the state. However, the level of resourcing was one that, increasingly, Mongolia could not afford, especially with the change to a market economy and a reduction in government income.

The impact of economic transition on education

The most immediate impact of transition was a fall in government expenditure on education, a decline in real terms of 68% between 1991 and 1997 (Robinson 2000). From this, together with a decline in real wages and an increase in poverty, a number of consequences flowed. Enrolment rates in schools fell, school drop-out and child labour increased, equity of provision decreased, the fabric of schools deteriorated, school textbooks and materials became scarce and expensive, gender differences appeared in participation rates (to the disadvantage of males), pre-school education shrank, vocational education declined rapidly in relevance and quality, adult education almost ceased and illiteracy rose. At the same time, higher education expanded even though student fees were introduced. Higher education institutions were faced with a rapid expansion of students (from 24,100 students in 1990 to over 36,000 full-time students in 1996 to 1997) and a demand for places that was difficult to meet, even with the establishment of private institutions (Weidman et al. 1998). The expansion of student numbers placed extra strain on scarce resources. Library and study facilities were generally inadequate, and up-to-date learning materials scarce, especially in the Mongolian language.

Thus Mongolia in the early 1990s was faced with a disruption to its education system, rapid changes in society, an opening-up of the country to global influences after a long period of isolation (except for contact with other socialist countries), reduced finance for education and a range of new needs for education and training. Adults and children needed to learn new things rapidly. Children needed to learn new subjects, including a new second language, English, to replace Russian. Teachers needed to learn about new curricula, new subjects (social studies, civics and natural science, among others) and new methods of teaching. Adults in general needed to learn about new legislation, income generation and survival skills for a market economy. Nomadic herders needed to learn how to manage mixed herds effectively (instead of the former single species), to become more self-reliant and to have reading materials to maintain literacy levels. Changes were needed in what people learned and where, how and when they learned it. Traditional face-to-face teaching and training could not meet all of these needs or quickly enough, especially given the limited finances available. It was against this background that initiatives to introduce open and distance education were taken. The nature of this background also explains to a large extent the direction that open and distance education has taken in Mongolia.

The development of open and distance education

Before 1992, there were no open and distance education programmes in Mongolia, though there were correspondence courses and adult education evening classes in population centres (in 1980, for example, there were 3,800 adults taking regular evening classes which often included some element of socialist ideology). The form of correspondence courses was usually a block of four to six weeks' face-to-face teaching and tests in the capital city of Ulaanbaatar twice a year, interspersed by periods of relatively unstructured home study. The correspondence courses, mostly small-scale and at university or college level, provided few or no study materials for students and little or no learner support during the periods of self-study. Students sometimes did assignments which they took with them to the residential school for marking. These were not usually part of the final assessment grade, and in any case, in higher education oral examinations played a major role in assessment.

Until the 1990s, Mongolian planners and educators had little knowledge about developments in open and distance education in countries outside the Soviet bloc and little contact with the global community of distance educators. The concepts and practices of distance education were unfamiliar. Education and training were thought of in terms of traditional face-to-face classes to which students travelled. Because of the size of the country and population distribution, travel and accommodation costs often consumed a large part of training budgets. For example, in 1997, 85% of the in-service development budget for teachers was taken up by the travel and accommodation costs required to enable teachers to participate in training seminars.

From 1992 onwards, open and distance education was introduced to Mongolia through several donor-funded initiatives as outlined below. These were seen as ways of extending the reach of educational services, stretching scarce resources, using available finances differently and to better effect and introducing new models and methods of teaching and learning.

Non-formal education

The Gobi Women's Project

The first distance learning project in Mongolia was the Gobi Women's Project (1992 to 1996). This was funded by DANIDA and implemented by UNESCO and the government of Mongolia. It used print, radio, audio cassettes, local learning groups and travelling tutors to provide non-formal education for 16,000 nomadic women in the six Gobi desert provinces. This target group was chosen as one of the most vulnerable groups in the transition process. During the socialist period, animal husbandry had existed in state-owned collectives with state provision of goods and services to support them (Bruun 1996). With the privatization of the herds, nomadic families had to become self-supporting and supply themselves with many of the things previously provided by the state (for example, ready-made clothing, foodstuffs, advice on animal care, and healthcare). They also needed to generate their own incomes for the first time. The Gobi Women's Project aimed to meet some of these needs through providing information, building knowledge, creating opportunities for contact with others and developing skills and crafts.

An administrative framework at the provincial and district level was created in collaboration with local government officials in the six Gobi provinces. Following a needs assessment study, the project developed materials on healthcare, making clothes, processing animal products, family planning, livestock rearing, felt-making for boots and dwellings, the environment, the new laws, making fuel from animal dung, doing business in a market economy and support for literacy. Printed materials (21 booklets) were produced in Ulaanbaatar, delivered by jeep to the provinces and supplemented by locally produced materials. A partnership was established with the state-owned Mongol Radio in Ulaanbaatar where a new project radio studio was installed. Three provincial radio studios (Gobi Altai, Omnogobi and Dornogobi) were re-equipped and training was provided for producers and technicians (these three radio stations reached all six provinces). A mixture of centrally and locally produced programmes was transmitted. Batteries (40,800) and radios (2,040) were supplied to learners who needed them. Though every family had been required by law under the communist regime to possess a working radio, the Russian-manufactured radios were getting old when the project started and replacement parts and batteries were unobtainable or unaffordable. Television was only available in large settlements and very few families had one. International consultants and technical assistants from UNESCO, Australia, Denmark, the UK and the US worked with Mongolian counterparts in Ulaanbaatar to develop the print and radio 'lessons' and to provide training and technical assistance.

Learner support took the form of group meetings at learning centres at the district level, and travelling tutors ('visiting teachers') also met with learners in their homes (*gers*, traditional felt tents), often taking two or three days at a time to complete a circuit of visits (by horse or camel or, occasionally, by motorbike). Tutors worked voluntarily without pay. Because of previous socialist policies, tutors with good levels of education could be found in rural and remote areas and there was a culture of social obligation to help others.

Important outcomes from the project included the development of an administrative framework for non-formal education, a tested model of open and distance learning appropriate for the rural population, the beginnings of policy formulation on non-formal education, capacity-building at central and local levels and the creation of a resource of learning materials. One strength of the project was the high level of activity and resourcefulness at the provincial and district levels often compensating for weaknesses in the central operation (for example, the late production of printed materials and the lack of coordination between radio and print). Despite some shortcomings, the project demonstrated that it was possible to create a form of open and distance education appropriate for Mongolian conditions (Robinson 1999).

'Surch Amidarya' or 'Learning for Life'

A second non-formal education project followed, the 'Surch Amidarya' or 'Learning for Life' Project (1997 to 2001). It was funded by DANIDA together with some other smaller co-funders and was again implemented by UNESCO and the government of Mongolia. The project followed a similar model but with national coverage for 37,000 learners (about 7,000 marginalized or unemployed youth in urban and provincial centres and 30,000 rural women and their families). Its aims were to help young people understand life in a market economy and to prepare them in finding work or generating income and to help rural women and their families improve their quality of life including support for literacy.

The first phase presented a 12-week course on 'Work and business in the market economy' for 3,000 unemployed young people in Ulaanbaatar in 1998, extending after that to the two other cities in Mongolia (Erdenet and Darkhan) and all provincial centres across the country. The course provided a series of radio programmes on the market economy (presented in magazine formats that reflected the emerging 'pop culture' of the age group, 16 to 25), a self-study book on work and business in a market economy, weekly meetings at local learning centres, talks and demonstrations by local business people and people skilled in trades and crafts, social activities and tutor support. Classes for skills training were also provided in shoe-making, hairdressing, metalwork, basic accountancy, dress-making, baking and woodwork. 'Finding work' was a new concept in a society where formerly jobs were provided for all by the state. The programme was run in partnership with city officials who were active and supportive out of concern about the large rise in youth unemployment. A small tracer study of Ulaanbaatar learners completing the programme shows positive results (Nymann-Berryman and Robinson 1999).

The model of open and distance learning used was similar to the Gobi Women's Project except that the first phase was city-based and for young people. The second phase of the project, to reach the rural population, faced more challenges of distance, communication, logistics and coordination in an environment where provinces varied widely in their levels of income and resources. A characteristic of the project has been its collaboration with a range of organizations including non-governmental ones. For example, some materials on child development for young parents have been prepared jointly with Save the Children UK, Mongolia. At the time of writing this chapter, the project is ongoing and the second phase is in preparation.

Teacher education

The use of open and distance learning for teacher education, both initial teacher training and further professional development, has been successful in a number of countries (Perraton 1993; Robinson 1997). Sometimes it has been the first step in establishing distance education in a new context. Mongolia offered considerable potential for this to happen because throughout the 1990s all teachers in the country were faced with wide-ranging changes, and some donor funding was available to meet teachers' needs. Teachers needed rapid updating and orientation to the new education curricula, teaching approaches and textbooks being introduced to Mongolian schools. The means of providing in-service education and training also needed re-thinking since traditional practices could not be sustained to the same extent nor were they all efficient. For example, existing in-service teacher development budgets needed to be used differently (as mentioned earlier, about 85% of the national in-service teacher education budget was being spent on the travel and accommodation costs at one point and only 15% on the actual training itself, an approach that also limited the number of teachers who could participate). However, the use of distance education for teacher education in Mongolia has met with mixed success so far.

Two projects using open and distance learning have taken place for teachers, one funded by UNICEF, the other by DANIDA as part of a wider project for school curriculum reform and school development. Both projects began in 1994, with introductory and planning workshops in Ulaanbaatar provided with technical assistance from the United Kingdom. The UNICEF project was for primary teachers led by the primary curriculum 'methodologist' at the National Institute of Educational Studies (later to become the School of Educational Development and part of the National Pedagogical University). It used print, radio, audio cassettes and video materials together with meetings for local and regional teachers' groups. Its purpose was to support changes in the curriculum and to encourage new teaching approaches in child-centred education, multi-grade teaching and subject integration in the curriculum. The project began with pilot activities in a few provinces and by 1998 had reached over half of Mongolia's primary teachers (it continues to 2001). A feature of the project was the high level of activity and ownership by regional and local groups of teachers who, mobilized by the central coordinator, generated new materials for their own use as well as sharing them through radio programmes and print materials. The UNICEF project, which is ongoing at the time of writing this chapter, has proved fairly vigorous and, in some aspects, sustainable. This can be attributed to energetic leadership by its Mongolian coordinator, a high level of commitment to the project by UNICEF in Mongolia, the use of a systematic strategy for generating regional groups in a gradually expanding number of provinces and the involvement of grassroots teachers in materials creation and trialing. The project was closer in some ways to open learning than to distance education, consisting of a cumulative and ongoing collection of materials initiated at central and local levels and used by local groups of teachers in different ways rather than a planned and structured course.

Distance education for in-service teacher development was also one part of a DANIDA project for primary and secondary education (one component of 9 or 10). This project (1994 to 1999) aimed at a reform of the school curriculum, changes in teaching approaches (including child-centred education), school development, management training and the preparation of new textbooks. The project was based in the School of Educational Development (the national centre for in-service teacher development in Ulaanbaatar) in an institutional linkage arrangement with the Royal Danish School of Educational Studies, Copenhagen. Outcomes from the distance education component included improvements in the design of textbooks developed in other parts of the project and institution, some guides for teachers, limited experimentation with audio and video cassettes, the establishment of a small distance education centre, and capacity-building in materials design, print production and understanding of open and distance learning. In addition, each provincial education centre (part of the country's administrative system) was provided with a computer, printer and copier, and centre staff ('methodologists') from each province participated in basic training in the design and production of learning materials. The subsequent level of provincial activity and output in generating materials for teachers varied widely in quantity and quality, in some cases limited by lack of basic resources and consumables (such as ink cartridges for the copier), in others showing considerable local initiative and creativity. The decision to decentralize materials production to provincial centres (about 20 in total) opened up opportunities for locally relevant materials but reduced the possibility of achieving economies of scale. This was because provinces sometimes duplicated effort in producing similar materials on the same topics for very small numbers of teachers and few mechanisms operated for collaborative planning. At the distance education centre in Ulaanbaatar, a short, small-scale distance education pilot course was planned around a proposed package of learning materials (on child-centred approaches to teaching and learning) but it was not implemented so no model or system of distance education was tried and tested. Though adequate financial resources were available for the distance education component, distance education activities had more or less ceased before the project finished.

Much scope remains for the use of open and distance education in both initial training and continuing professional development for teachers and teacher educators. Given Mongolia's economic situation at the end of the 1990s and the cost structure of distance education, this would need support from a donor. At the time of writing this chapter, another (small-scale) teacher education project has begun, sponsored by MFOS and making some use of electronic communication.

Higher education

At the university level some small initiatives have been taken to introduce open and distance learning. One was the development of a course in accountancy as part of a degree programme at the School of Economic Studies, National University of Mongolia (NUM). This was a small-scale, low-cost print-based pilot course for 50 students in 1998 to 1999 with a further 50 students taking the same course through the College of Economics in Zavkhan (western Mongolia). The expectation is that the programme will be able to expand and make use of more media, including videotapes produced by the Video-Lab Unit at the university (set up in the late 1990s with Japanese funding), if funds can be found. One reason for developing the pilot course was to improve the quality of its predecessor, an 'old style' correspondence course.

A second initiative was the establishment of an Independent Learning Centre, also at the School of Economic Studies. This provided learning materials and resources to support on-campus teaching and learning and to assist staff experimenting with more learner-centred approaches to teaching. Both of these initiatives were part of a TACIS project (1996 to 1999) funded by the European Commission and implemented by the University of Manchester in the UK together with the NUM School of Economic Studies. The project aimed at institutional strengthening and the development of a new economics curriculum for a market economy.

Other initiatives have included the establishment of a computer network (intranet) for several universities (the first attempt was not sustainable because the online costs were unaffordable after the project funding finished). A contribution to capacity-building in open and distance education has been made by a UNESCO-UNITWIN partnership agreement. The partners to NUM were three other distance education institutions in the Asian region (the Open University of Shanghai, the Korean National Open University, and the Open University of Hong Kong). Although only a few small initiatives began in the 1990s, there was considerable interest in developing open and distance learning by several higher education institutions such as the National University of Technology and the Medical University. This was clearly expressed at the first National Round Table on Distance Education in Mongolia held in Ulaanbaatar in 1998 and sponsored by MFOS and the UNESCO 'Learning for Life' project. However, the growing wish by some to set up an autonomous open university in Mongolia seems unrealistic in the current economic situation (in 2000).

Opportunities, constraints and challenges

The situation of Mongolia offers scope for the use of open and distance learning of different kinds (Robinson 1995; Aabenhus and Kenworthy 1996). However it presents a challenging operational environment, though not an impossible one. There are three main obstacles to be overcome in realizing the potential of open and distance learning: the country's weak infrastructure, the limited communications technology and high cost of using it, and the shortage of funding for investment in open and distance education.

Infrastructure

Some kinds of development are dependent on a basic level of infrastructure (public utilities such as postal services, power, telecommunications and public works such as roads and public transport). This is illustrated by the example of China's investment in infrastructure for rural development, leading to the improvement of transport, telecommunications and power supply at the village level and opening up new conduits for the delivery of educational services. Some operations in open and distance learning are dependent on a minimum level of infrastructure: for example, the delivery of learning materials, contact with others (learners, tutors and course providers), the sending and return of assignment work, supply of timely advice and information, and gathering evaluation data about the programme for remedial action by the provider. Where distances are large, the infrastructure limited and the population small and dispersed, as in Mongolia, then some of these things are difficult to do, and the solutions are not within the control of the providers of distance learning courses. For example, the delivery time for printed learning materials in the Gobi Women's Project was six to seven weeks to reach all learners; speedier electronic alternatives did not exist, even if affordable. In Mongolia the postal service is slow and uncertain. Electricity supplies are unreliable and not available to the nomadic population (though a few have solar-powered generators). Telephone lines are few and depend on old landlines and analog signals outside of Ulaanbaatar (the sound quality is poor and connections unreliable). There are few surfaced roads and limited railway lines or public transport. Low levels of disposable income for individuals and acute shortage of funding for the education sector further limit the options available in designing and delivering open and distance education. All of this makes the operational logistics of open and distance education problematic and requires careful project planning and design to fit the circumstances.

Media and technology

Interactivity of different kinds is emphasized as a desirable feature of open and distance education programmes for supporting isolated learners, for promoting dialogue in open and distance learning and for giving feedback on progress and assignments. Interactivity over distance is difficult to achieve in the Mongolian context. So far, it has been built into projects at the local level, and this has worked well up to a point. In the case of both non-formal education projects, the level of local group and tutor activity has generally been high, often as a result of strong community support. For programmes of this kind, open and distance education in Mongolia can take advantage of the good levels of education to be found throughout the country. Local tutors with appropriate levels of education can usually be found in rural areas. However, there can be problems in finding tutors with specialist and up-to-date knowledge at the local level, especially for formal courses that require assignment submission and feedback (as was the case with the accountancy course mentioned earlier).

One-way media, especially radio, have wide reach in Mongolia through Mongol Radio and half a dozen local radio stations, though local radio stations are limited to broadcasting for only a few hours a week as permitted by the legal framework and Mongol Radio. In the mid-1990s, several independent, privately-owned commercial stations were set up in Ulaanbaatar for coverage within the capital city. Cable television is available in the capital city of Ulaanbaatar, and national television from the former state television service reaches most of the country. Television (including Russian television) reaches most provincial (*aimag*) centres though television ownership is low. However, radio and television, especially at the local level, faced major difficulties as Mongolia attempted to deregulate the media and privatize broadcasting stations. This created a climate of acute uncertainty in the late 1990s; in some cases, stations closed down for periods or broadcast limited schedules for lack of funds and staff lost their jobs or sought other employment or second jobs. Electricity supply and costs have also affected the transmission quality of broadcasts. As radio stations (including Mongol Radio) have increasingly needed to generate their own income, costs to distance education providers have increased.

Electronic communication in Mongolia is slowly being established. Access to computer communications by 2000 was very limited, being expensive in terms of both equipment and connectivity. The cost of computers was high (more than in neighbouring China) — a computer costs more than the average annual per capita income). Ownership of computers was very low, existing mainly in the capital city. The Internet became available in Mongolia in 1996 and, until 1999, the country had only one Internet service provider (ISP), in practice holding a monopoly and charging high fees for services. By March 1999, there were 2,100 registered Internet account users in total and two ISPs. The cost of an Internet account per month was higher than the average monthly salary of US$25 to US$40. Access to computers and Internet connections was mostly achieved through institutional facilities (though not all institutions had these in 1999). Some businesses in Ulaanbaatar began using the Internet from 1998 onwards, and several Internet cafés appeared in the capital city of Ulaanbaatar in 1999.

Despite these difficulties, several initiatives in the use of information and communications technologies (ICT) were started in the late 1990s with the help of the UNDP (United Nations Development Programme) and MFOS. Government task groups were established to develop policy and provide training. Local computer networks linking libraries and government offices in Ulaanbaatar were established, and ICT use began to increase in some schools and universities in the capital city. Local government offices in provincial centres were linked to Ulaanbaatar. Six Citizen's Information Service Centres across the country were established in 2000 to provide email access and training in ICT for public users. An 'Internet for Schools' project in 1999, sponsored by MFOS, provided access to the Internet for 35 secondary schools in Ulaanbaatar and later on to some rural schools. A consortium of higher education institutions within Mongolia formed to try to develop an electronic network, and some projects to assist this began with donor support. Because of the availability of radio and scarcity of computers, ICT was introduced to large numbers of the population through radio and telephone. In 2000, Mongol Radio broadcast a weekly one-hour programme which answered 'on-air' questions from the public about ICT. The radio station presenters surfed websites in real time in response to live phone calls from listeners, helping the public to understand the use of ICT and the Internet as well as providing the particular information requested. This initiative was made possible through support from the UNDP (who donated hardware) and DataCom, the first ISP in Mongolia (who provided the Internet links and who have been active in supporting ICT initiatives in education).

Funding constraints

Open and distance education requires high initial investment to reap cost savings over time and economies of scale. High initial investment for education is the opposite of what Mongolia could afford in the 1990s because of its economic situation. Even relatively small sums to support open and distance learning ventures were not available. During the 1990s, Mongolia made no capital investment in education in general but instead struggled to maintain existing provision with decreasing resources. In these circumstances, the diversion of funds to distance education was seen as impossible. Any investment in open and distance education has needed to come from donor-funded projects, though the government of Mongolia has also contributed resources to projects (personnel, office accommodation and other forms of support).

The challenges of a transitional society

In addition to the constraints characteristic of some developing countries, the features of a transitional society experiencing rapid economic and social transition presented some extra challenges (Robinson 1999). In these circumstances educational planning and implementation take place in a rapidly moving economic and legislative environment, often with high inflation rates which affect costs and in a context where the lifestyles and income levels of learners and tutors alter greatly within a short time. Transition also generates a flow of policies, directives, regulatory frameworks and organizational restructuring not just in the domain of education. This can destabilize the national administrative system and organizational infrastructure for educational services and create a climate of uncertainty. Rapidly changing circumstances also require flexible and speedy responses to situations, with high levels of contingency management skills from planners and implementers. These are generally unfamiliar skills and practices to managers trained for a planned economy and authoritarian structures with centralized decision-making. New ways of doing things take time to establish.

The context of a transitional society had several consequences for implementing the distance learning projects in Mongolia. The rapidly changing economic and legislative environment was difficult to keep pace with, and change sometimes ran faster than the materials development process affecting content, plans and costs. It also threatened to destabilize some of the operational structures and administration on which project planning and implementation relied (for example, the availability of local education officers, the continued existence of provincial education centres and their staffing levels, and the functioning of radio stations). This affected programme delivery and learner support. The changing circumstances and lifestyles of learners required that the relevance of plans, materials and support services needed frequent monitoring and realignment to the changing realities, especially in non-formal education for rural learners. International projects are often constrained by initial agreements, contracts and reporting requirements with donors or partners — donors, too, are bound by their own procedures and accountability mechanisms that arise from a different set of assumptions about the project environment. The media most able to respond quickly to changing circumstances were particularly valuable. Radio proved very effective in providing topical programmes and in reaching large numbers of learners rapidly despite the high levels of uncertainty created by deregulation of the media and privatization.

Changes of government were frequent. For example, by December 1998 three sets of cabinet ministers had been in post during the year. Changes at national level were followed by changes of personnel in local government and some of the staff replaced were key partners at the local level. Changes in personnel meant new relationships had to be formed, new agreements or contracts made, and repeated briefing and training provided for local officers and agents. Changes of policy also affected open and distance learning plans.

Education, too, experienced some transitions during the 1990s (summarized in Table 1) and it can be argued that at least a few of these were influenced by the open and distance learning projects.

Table 1   Educational transitions in Mongolia 1992–1999 (Robinson 1999, p. 201).

From	*To*
• Ministry (MOSTEC) responsibility for formal education for young people.	• Broadening of Ministry (MOSTEC) responsibility to include non-formal and continuing education for adults.
• Centrally planned and administered provision. MOSTEC as policy maker, decision-maker and implementer.	• Decentralized planning and local administration of services. MOSTEC as policy maker and monitor.
• Compulsory participation, directive (and some choices, e.g. in vocational education, made for students).	• Voluntary participation, freedom to choose.
• Education as the province of 'experts' or specialist curriculum developers at government research institutes.	• Education as meeting locally-expressed needs and legitimating local expertise and skills.
• Heavy emphasis on and high status of theoretical knowledge and low status of 'practical knowledge'.	• Broader interpretation of what constitutes valid knowledge from a widening range of sources. Increase in the status of 'practical knowledge'.

Table 1 cont.

• Single form (institution-based and classroom-based teaching, provided by professional teachers).	• Multiple forms (including use of the media such as radio, self-study and local learning groups, led by members of the local community).
• Exclusion and discouragement of traditional Mongolian culture, folk-knowledge and skills.	• Revival and renewal of traditional Mongolian culture, folk-knowledge and skills.
• Teacher-centred and teacher-dependent education.	• Learner-centred and learner-initiated education.
• Densely written, theoretical textbooks with few illustrations, written for teachers as the primary audience. Heavy ideological bias.	• More user-friendly accessible texts, with illustrations, written for learners as the primary audience. A variety of information sources used.
• State provision and state funding.	• Growth of self-help, cost-sharing with families and users, project funding by donors or NGOs (Non-Governmental Organizations).
• Heavy influence of Russia and USSR.	• A range of influences, from the West and Asian countries such as Japan and Korea.
• A highly literate population.	• An increasing range of literacy levels, including illiteracy.
• Based on a single Russian-influenced model of education and narrow knowledge base (previously based around a single ideology).	• International influences, multiple knowledge sources and models, diversity.

(Note: MOSTEC, Ministry of Science, Technology, Education and Culture, is later known as the Ministry of Enlightenment.)

Establishing distance education through the project approach

As has been the case in other countries, the means of initiating open and distance education in Mongolia was the donor-funded project. This approach has both advantages and disadvantages. On the one hand, it can introduce new ideas and practices within a relatively short timescale and bypass the inertia of existing institutions. It can focus on specific goals, build new capacity, demonstrate new approaches and share international experience. It is sometimes the only way of achieving particular educational goals. On the other hand, projects may come and go without much impact. Distance education projects, especially in new contexts, run the risk of being marginalized from the mainstream of policy and resource allocation and, as a consequence, find it difficult to achieve sustainability once external funding has ceased. The timespan of projects may also be too short to establish new structures, systems, practices and attitudes, especially if projects only run for one cycle as some projects in Mongolia have. A one-cycle project gives implementers no time to consolidate learning from the experience or to do better next time round, and project personnel are often dispersed at the project's close. Donor timelines for projects tend to be too short to match the slow process of educational change, and projects may be unsustainable in the longer term with activities coming to a halt with the expiry date of the project.

Conclusions

The initiatives so far in open and distance education were made possible through donor-funded projects, and this makes their sustainability a key issue. So far, none is self-sustaining or institutionalized. One teacher education project has achieved sustainability in some aspects (for example, it has generated regional and local professional development groups which have taken on a life of their own) but needs some continuing external support for other aspects such as further materials development and revision. A second distance education project for teachers was not fully implemented, though some of the ideas and skills developed (for example, in materials design) continue to be reflected in other work. The few higher education applications have, up to this point, been small-scale and tentative and, in at least one case, very under-resourced (putting its quality at risk). The Gobi Women's Project, though large-scale and successful in many ways, was not sustainable after the project finished though it had a positive impact which continued in several ways. In particular, this project and its successor ('Learning for Life') have influenced policy development for both non-formal education and distance education and have introduced new approaches to adult education. However, in parallel to these two projects a non-formal education centre (with minimal funding) was established in 1997 under the Ministry of Enlightenment, and it is not yet clear how some project activities might be institutionalized within this in the longer term, if at all.

Some indication of political will to support open and distance learning is given in the Education Law of 1991 and of 1994, which make the commitment 'to provide the people the right to learn' (section 1) while recognizing that new kinds of provision are necessary to achieve this: 'Citizens can have an education through formal or non-formal channels' (section 6.1), and 'The government will provide alternative and open education' (section 3.2.5). Reference to open and distance learning has been included in more recent legislation and policy documents as a result of the efforts of those involved in the distance education projects. However, political approval is one thing; funds for implementation are another. Policy statements at the highest level also need to be translated into practical strategies and plans, and this remains to be done. Following the first National Round Table on Distance Education (held in Ulaanbaatar 1998) and chaired by a senior member of the Ministry of Enlightenment, a draft national policy for open and distance education in Mongolia was prepared at the beginning of 1999. However, frequent changes of government and personnel have slowed its progress since then, and other priorities have taken precedence. An enabling policy framework for open and distance learning in Mongolia is needed.

Distance education was in its infancy in Mongolia in the 1990s, and only time and more experience will tell if its full potential can be realized. There is much scope and need for it if appropriate working models, systems and funding can be found. However, the country's weak infrastructure, size and current economic situation present major challenges to planners and practitioners. Mongolia also faces the dilemma of some other developing countries in that the remote and rural populations who could benefit most from open and distance education are the ones with least access to the communications infrastructure needed for it. Nonetheless, a start has been made, and more initiatives are likely to develop over the next decade. A key factor in the future development of education in general in Mongolia will be its level of economic growth. A major risk to the development of distance education will be inadequate funding leading into the negative chain of consequences found elsewhere, of low quality leading to low status leading to marginalization.

References

Aabenhus, O and Kenworthy, B (1996) 'Distance education in Mongolia's political and economic transition', in T Evans and D Nation (eds), *Opening Education: Policies and Practices from Open and Distance Education*, London: Routledge, pp. 33–47.

Ariunaa, D (1997) 'Government budget expenditure on education', *Mongolian Journal of Demography*, 2(1): 119–120.

Bray, M, Davaa, S, Spaulding, S and Weidman, J C (1994) 'Transition from socialism and the financing of higher education: the case of Mongolia', *Higher Education Policy*, 7(4): 36–42.

Bruun, O (1996) 'The herding household: economy and organisation', in O Bruun and O Odgaard (eds), *Mongolia in Transition: Old Patterns, New Challenges*, UK, Richmond: Curzon Press.

Collins, P and Nixson, F (1993) 'Managing the implementation of "shock therapy" in a land-locked state: Mongolia's transition from the centrally planned economy', *Public Administration and Development*, 13, 398–407.

National Statistical Office (1997) *Literacy and Education of Mongolia's Population*, Ulaanbaatar: Government of Mongolia.

National Statistical Office (1998) *Mongolian Statistical Yearbook*, Ulaanbaatar: Government of Mongolia.

Nymann-Berryman, L and Robinson, B (1999) Preparing Unemployed Youth for Work in a Market Economy: The Case of Mongolia, Proceedings of the19th World Conference of the International Council for Open and Distance Education, Vienna, June 20–24.

Rana, Pradumna B (1995) 'Reform strategies in transitional economies: lessons from Asia', *World Development*, 23(7): 1, 157–69.

Robinson, B (1995) 'Mongolia in transition: a role for distance education?', *Open Learning*, 10(3): 3–15.

Robinson, B (1999) 'Open and distance learning in the Gobi Desert: Non-formal education for nomadic women', *Distance Education*, 20(2): 181–204.

Robinson, B and Solongo, A (2000) 'The gender dimension of economic transition in Mongolia', in F Nixson, B Suvd, P Luvsandorj and B Walters (eds), *The Mongolian Economy: A Manual of Applied Economics for an Economy in Transition*, UK, Cheltenham: Edward Elgar.

Sanders, A J K (1987) *Mongolia: Politics, Economics and Society*, London: F Pinter.

Sodnomdorj, D (1997) *The Legal Framework Regulating Child Labour in Mongolia*, Ulaanbaatar: Mongolian Labour Institute.

United Nations Development Programme (1997) *Human Development Report: Mongolia*, Ulaanbaatar.

Weidman, J C et al. (1998) 'Reform of higher education in a national undergoing transition to a market economy: the case of Mongolia', *Tertium Comparationis*, Germany: Waxmann Verlag.

World Bank (1998) *World Development Report 1998*, Washington, D.C.: World Bank.

World Bank (1999) *World Development Report 1999*, Washington D.C.: World Bank.

Wu, K B (1994) *Mongolia: Financing education during economic transition*, Discussion Paper 226, Washington, D.C.: World Bank.

Yusuf, S and Burki, S J (1992) *Developing Mongolia*, Washington D.C.: World Bank.

Taiwan

Caroline Sherritt and Wang Cheng-yen

Introduction

The Asian open university movement

As emergent economies in the last two decades, many Asian nations have adopted what Wallis calls 'human capital orthodoxy' (Wallis 1996) with its corollary need for adult education and training. One by one, Asian nations are adopting lifelong learning principles. Asian open universities proliferate. Korea, Indonesia, Thailand, Turkey and India, for example, have between 200,000 and 500,000 students in their open institutions; China has nearly one million (OUHK 1999, 4). There are open universities in Malaysia, Bangladesh, Sri Lanka, Singapore and Viet Nam. Tam noted that open and distance learning are becoming 'the main vehicles for addressing the education, training and human resource development needs of Asian nations' (OUHK 1999, 2). The National Open University of Taiwan (NOUT) is one such vehicle.

The NOUT began in a promising climate. With a highly literate population, cultural respect for learning, relative stability, and prosperity, Taiwan is an ideal place to study incipient open and distance learning in Asia. Based in a suburb of Taipei with 13 regional centres throughout the island, the NOUT serves thousands of Taiwan citizens until now denied access to the limited spaces in higher education.

The value of education in Taiwan

Traditional Chinese education

Chinese culture is characterized by a hierarchy of social classes, a meritocracy at least as old as the Tang dynasty, subordination of human rights to a sense of social obligation, and respect for scholarship (Fei 1991, 55). For over 2,000 years, Chinese education evolved in a traditional

Confucian way where examinations were used to select young men for entry into public service. The values inherent in this system prevail in Taiwan today: rigorous examinations, elite education institutions, education as a means for upward mobility, rote learning, and teacher-centred formats. Fei noted that Chinese education serves to preserve rather than challenge traditional values (Fei 1991, 9). Huang described Taiwan traditional higher education as better suited for young students than for adults or people with disabilities. She wrote, 'Older learners are not attracted to and do not learn effectively in this type of (traditional) environment' (Huang 1997, 246; EDRS 411 890). Interestingly, Huang equates adult learners with special needs students. Her statement illuminates a value judgement pervasive in Taiwan: 'real education' is that which serves traditional learners who have proven themselves through years of rigorous testing.

The ancient education legacy is both strength and weakness in modern Chinese education. At the NOUT, the Confucian heritage ensures motivated students. On the other hand, historic education values militate against the types of change essential to successful adult education. For example, according to Huang, more than 70% of Taiwan adult students are 'teacher-dependent' (Huang 1997, 11). They function best in a teacher directed, face-to-face venue. Open and distance learning require learner autonomy, which, in turn, develops skills for modern life. Huang noted that independent inquiry and critical thinking skills are increasingly important in the workplace (Huang 1997, 11). So, while respect for scholarship produces eager adult students, it does not equip them with the types of skills and attitudes that are ultimately useful in open and distance learning.

Taiwan education

Taiwan education has generated international interest for its apparent success. Laudatory articles on education in Taiwan have appeared in the *London Times* and *Newsweek* (Budge 1996). Taiwan is a highly literate society; its people enthusiastically support education; and children in Taiwan regularly perform well in global maths and science comparisons. Virtually all children in Taiwan go to school, but few are privileged to attend one of the prestigious Taiwan universities. The ancient Chinese system of rigorous examinations weeds out thousands of potential students, many of whom go abroad to study. There is no loop back into the traditional Taiwanese higher education track for those who fail to gain entrance. Before the establishment of the NOUT, thousands of Taiwan citizens had few options for formal learning. The concept of formal learning for non-traditional students is relatively new in Taiwan, and there is potential for growth in this area (Wang 1997a, 55).

The NOUT in Taiwan's education infrastructure

Establishment of the NOUT

Taiwan experienced extraordinary economic growth and political stability in the post-war era (Clark 1991, 15). In addition, Taiwan is a young democracy, the measure of which lies with educated, satisfied and informed citizens. This climate precipitated the establishment of the NOUT in 1986.

The NOUT is the purview of the Department of Supplementary Education under the aegis of the Taiwan Ministry of Education. In a 1997 booklet describing education in Taiwan, published by the Bureau of Statistics, the National Open University is mentioned briefly only twice (NOUT 1994; MOE 1997). The NOUT falls into the 'Supplemental' category of schools. This implies a somewhat marginal position in the whole system; it is not included with other universities, nor is it affiliated with any other appropriate government ministry. Instead, it is one of a category of schools including supplementary elementary, junior and senior high schools, a venue that offers education to 'out-of-school citizens as well as employed youths' (Bureau of Statistics 1997, 41). The category of schools into which the NOUT falls suggests some confusion in distinguishing between adult basic education (literacy and basic numeracy) and alternative university systems. A 1997 Ministry of Education document described in some detail supplementary primary and secondary institutions. Of the NOUT, it merely stated: 'In addition, an open university was set up in 1986' (Bureau of Statistics 1997, 15). It seems that the NOUT holds a rather nebulous place in the structure of Taiwan education.

The NOUT has an open entry policy; hence, students may attend particular classes without pursuing a degree. To obtain a degree, they must meet standards that include accumulation of credits and an entrance examination. In 1991, the first class of 58 students graduated; however, the Legislative Yuan did not formally recognize NOUT Bachelor's degrees until 1994. After the merger of the NOUT and the Supplementary Junior College in 1992, the graduating class expanded. By 1994, 551 students obtained baccalaureate degrees from the NOUT, and 1,639 obtained diplomas from the affiliated Supplementary Junior College (NOUT 1997). The NOUT is currently seeking accreditation for postgraduate study.

In most ways, the NOUT illustrates the exigencies of open and distance learning in other parts of the world; for example, the NOUT:

- Opened in the 1980s when Taiwan was moving rapidly from manufacturing to technology-based industries;

- Uses distance technology as the primary mode of course delivery;

- Offers open admission;

- Confers baccalaureate degrees;

- Has a high graduation rate and appears to enjoy wide public support;

- Has more or less standard academic departments: social science, business, public administration, life science, and general studies;

- Has an infrastructure that would be recognized by academics anywhere, including a Department of Academic Affairs, Department of Student Affairs, Department of Research and Development, a Department of Programming and Production, and audio-visual and library facilities;

- Maintains 13 regional learning centres (in Keelung, Taipei, Luchou, Hsin-chu, Taichung, Chiayi, Tainan, Kaohsiung, Ilan, Hualian, Taitung, Penghu and Kinmen (NOUT 1997, 7).

Despite similarities between the NOUT and open universities the world over, it is quintessentially Chinese in mission, purpose and priorities. This orientation is best understood within the context of traditional Confucian-based education ideals.

The mission of the NOUT

Caffarella wrote that programme planners must have a clear understanding of why they are doing what they are doing (Caffarella 1994, 23). To be successful, programmes must have policy and mission statements that 'clearly and precisely outline the "why, what, who, where, and how" of the unit' (Caffarella 1994, 60). Policy and mission statements related to the

NOUT's conception and operation tend to be abstruse and reflect cultural notions of lifelong learning, to: 'uphold character', 'pursue academic studies diligently', 'everyone can study and classrooms everywhere (sic)', 'uplift cultural standards of the populace', and so on (Bureau of Statistics 1997, 4, 27). While these are guiding principles for an open university and provide a basis for a code of ethics, they do not translate into operational guidelines, nor are operational guidelines for the NOUT easily located. Above all, the belief statements quoted above are Chinese.

Common in Confucian-based cultures is the belief that a paternalistic government will take care of deserving, virtuous citizens but that the citizens have no right to make demands on the political father (Fei 1991, 55). This perspective is illustrated in the NOUT's motto:

> It is hoped that students will join in honouring long upheld virtues and values in traditional Chinese cultures. It is important to teach them the concepts of teamwork and showing respect toward their work. This in turn will contribute to Taiwan's stability and prosperity (NOUT 1994, 4).

The paternalistic message in this statement of purpose is clear: the benevolent government is caring for its citizens by providing education to enhance their quality of life (Fei 1991, 55). The Confucian ideal of filial piety (contributions to the whole of society; respect for leaders and elders) and regard for education drives the mechanisms of the NOUT. This appears to be true in mainland China as well where, according to Guo, 'It is clear that the purposes of adult education in China are different from those advocated by Western educators. ...Individual needs are not regarded as a high priority' (Guo 1996). Thus, both Taiwan and the People's Republic of China entertain similar assumptions about the purposes of education. The difference between the two is that the PRC is attempting to reconcile cultural values with lifelong learning as a means to economic development. Wallis wrote:

> ...the Chinese government has expanded factory-based schools and has increased the number of higher education institutes linked to technical and scientific practice. On top of these efforts to upgrade workers' skills, there has been a concerted effort to retrain...workers shaken out of inefficient industries. ...This constitutes a major training revolution (Wallis 1996, 32).

The role of the NOUT

As clearly shown in its educational ideals, the NOUT is intended to 'be an institution of advanced learning for adults utilizing distance instruction and aims at promoting social education as well as lifetime learning throughout the nation' (NOUT 1999a). Within the whole educational infrastructure, although the NOUT is classified as a social education, in terms of its practical educational functions, we can conclude that the NOUT plays two major roles, i.e., as 1) an institution of higher education and 2) an institution of adult education.

The NOUT as an institution of higher education

The NOUT is a university in terms of its legislative status and its practical operation. For instance, the employment of staff and the distribution of the budget occur in accordance with the legal procedures of higher education institutions. Although entrance policy and the learning and teaching process differ slightly from those of traditional universities, the NOUT is set up as a higher education institution that has a special structure and operation that fulfil the functions of a university.

The NOUT as an institution of adult education

The differences between the NOUT and traditional universities result from its status as a professional adult education institution. Its target students are aged over 18, and it forms particular policies in entrance, learning and teaching specifically to suit the traits of adult learners. This characteristic gives the NOUT a unique role that combines the functions of both adult education and higher education institutions.

As an institution of both higher and adult education, the NOUT faced a series of challenges in the 1990s when there were many shifts in Taiwan society. At such a turning point of a new age for Taiwan, it is time for the NOUT to redefine its roles and enrich its functions.

The NOUT currently

A bird's-eye view

The NOUT had seven departments in 1999 (NOUT 1999a, 2). It admits three categories of student: regular students, non-diploma students and auditing students. In 1997, there were 29,310 regular students, and 1,815 graduates obtained a Bachelor of Arts degree (MOE 1998a). The NOUT has in total over one hundred thousand students. It can thus be considered the largest university in Taiwan compared with the other 139 higher education institutions which include 38 universities, 40 colleges and 61 junior colleges (MOE 1998a, 5).

Based on the major teaching methods via television, radio, classroom lecture and correspondence, the NOUT is continuously improving its teaching. In addition to printed teaching materials, the NOUT also applies computer-assisted instruction in languages and computer instruction via regional learning centres. The NOUT also recently published a manual on classroom teaching for lecturers with the aim of promoting their tutorial skills (NOUT 1998). As the Internet has taken on importance in distance learning, so the NOUT has designed learning tracks through intranet teaching, Gopher, FTP and BBS, based on its website.

The NOUT also places an emphasis on academic exchange. In July 1991, it signed an agreement with Macao's East Asia Open Institute. In June 1992, the NOUT joined forces with mainland China's Beijing TV & Radio University and Shanghai TV University to host a seminar on distance education. NOUT staff have been dispatched to Japan, Korea, South Africa, Thailand and Macao to study the operations of its counterparts (NOUT 1998, 44). Academic exchanges through different approaches and channels will undoubtedly help the NOUT learn from other open teaching institutions to improve the quality of its educational services.

The NOUT and national economic development

Forty years of research in the West on adult student motivation reveal a strong correlation between formal learning and individual vocational interests. Adult students tend most often to go back to school in order to either get a job, keep a job, get a better job, or change jobs altogether. This illustrates the Western cultural bias towards the development of individuals to meet human capital needs. Rubensen ascribed the growth of adult students in the last twenty years to 'the increased demand for adult education by people wanting to be more competitive in the labour market' (Rubensen 1991).

Interestingly, vocational goals are not what is of primary importance to students at the NOUT, or at least to those who graduated in or before 1997. A 1997 study by the Director of the Department of Research and

Development, Li I C, the results of which remain unpublished, found that NOUT graduates did not change careers after graduation. They reported the greatest satisfaction from an enhanced self-respect and respect from others, as well as the personally edifying opportunity to acquire something (an education) that they did not acquire in their youth.

It appears, especially for non-diploma and auditing students, that Taiwanese adults value learning for the benefits it confers to their society and families and as an end in itself rather than as a means to a better job. This may be more a self-fulfilling prophecy than cultural bias. NOUT students may not perceive the NOUT as a means for upward job mobility because the NOUT does not advance this as a part of its identity. It is in the realm of policy that this lack of vision occurs. The role of the NOUT in workforce development appears to elude NOUT policy-makers.

The weak link between human capital development and adult education and training in Taiwan is also illustrated in the student body profile at the NOUT. Women outnumber men, and humanities and social sciences are the preferred majors. One reason may be that the total number of non-diploma and auditing students is larger than the number of regular students who may, by comparison, focus their learning on a need for employment. The Open University of Hong Kong (OUHK), however, has more male than female students, and these students seem to show a preference for courses in business and computer science (OUHK 1998). This implies that vocational interests can be accommodated in a culturally Chinese institution if that institution articulates a role in workforce development.

Insufficiency of technology resources

Distance education came into being to provide learning opportunities for place-bound, working adults. The NOUT serves adult learners by delivering classes at a distance, supplemented with on-site tutorials; however, the instructional technology available to the NOUT is obsolete even though, as mentioned above, the NOUT has utilized intranet, Gopher, FTP and BBS facilities via its website.

Moore posits four generations of distance education technology:

- Correspondence;
- Broadcast media, such as video cassettes, television and radio;

- Two-way video and audio hook-ups;

- Computer-based technologies (Moore and Kearsley 1996).

Using broadcast media to deliver instruction to adults prevails in less well-developed countries where the infrastructure does not support more advanced instructional media. Taiwan, however, can support advanced multimedia; it has a national education infrastructure and its technology industry is globally competitive.

However, in Taiwan state-of-the-art learning technologies are reserved for traditional universities currently experimenting in distance learning. As Sherritt found when gathering information on distance education between traditional universities during visits to Taiwan institutions, interviews with faculty and administrators, and observations of two distance learning projects, a university in one city, for example, may deliver courses via computer or interactive video to a university in another city (Sherritt 1997). The NOUT, on the other hand, uses second-generation broadcast media almost exclusively for adult learners. This consists of videotaped lectures, television and radio supplemented with print materials.

The problems with this approach are three-fold. First, broadcast media are non-interactive and reinforce passive learning. Second, NOUT students are denied technology experiences; hence, they remain on the outside of a digital world unless, of course, they obtain experience elsewhere. Third, the use of obsolete technology in the education of citizens of a technologically sophisticated, globally competitive nation is wholly unacceptable. In contrast, the OUHK, a Chinese institution of approximately the same age and size as the NOUT, uses multimedia tools, compressing its own CD-ROMS in Chinese and has nearly half a million volumes in its online library (Sherritt 1999, 1997a; 1997b).

The NOUT and the vision for a learning society

To achieve a learning society has been an international trend of education innovation in many advanced countries (Van der Zee 1991; Williamson 1995). Taiwan, too, has been involved in this current and announced 1998 as its National Lifelong Learning Year, referring to the European Lifelong Learning Year of 1996. To launch and carry along this Lifelong Learning Year, the Ministry of Education published a White Paper entitled 'Towards a learning society', as the blueprint of its educational policy agenda (MOE 1998b). Accordingly, one concrete approach is the development of multiple models of higher education institutions. Distance teaching is one of these.

The NOUT as a lifelong learning institution

A learning society is composed of many institutions and organizations that can offer lifelong learning resources to the public. The NOUT can and should be one such institution in Taiwanese society. It can achieve this by expanding its educational contributions based on its achievements and its technological capability.

Although the NOUT's target group is people over the age of 18, it can extend its educational services to under-18s as well. Among the NOUT's educational objectives is the obligation to promote lifelong learning. As setting up a learning society has been a national target of the goal of innovation in education, the NOUT has to expand its educational functions and transform itself so that it can move on from its current status as an institution of higher and adult education to become an institution of lifelong learning.

Lifelong learning is necessary for the individual as well as the national growth in a global, information age. Open universities are a preferred venue for its provision. In design, most open universities are the same; however, cultural and national differences affect their identities, as evidenced at the NOUT.

A vibrant economy and political stability characterize post-war Taiwan, which has developed an effective education system that is recognized around the world. Inevitably, when the time was right, Taiwan joined other rapidly developing Asian nations in establishing an open university. Huang cited 'broad workforce development' as the guiding principle behind the NOUT's establishment (Huang 1997, 243). Evidence suggests, however, that this goal is subordinate to a more cherished one: providing traditional academic study for adults to enhance their quality of life and, in turn, benefit society. Indeed, surveys of NOUT graduates indicate that this goal has been met.

Over 100,000 Taiwan citizens have graduated from the NOUT; 30,000 enrol in classes annually. The institution accommodates time and space barriers. The curriculum is guided by theoretically grounded adult education scholars at traditional universities; NOUT instructors are a dedicated group. Graduates report a high degree of satisfaction with their NOUT education and as many as one third return for additional study (Sherritt 1997b). Wang noted: '...the explicit development and incorporation of lifelong learning is encouraging' (Wang 1997a, 61). Indeed, it is. Why, then, argue with success?

The way to go for the NOUT in a learning society

The NOUT cannot be absent from the scene while a learning society is developing in Taiwan. It has to take a more positive and active role in the new age that is now coming.

General improvements

The NOUT is successful but there is room for improvement. Taiwan has a literate population, respect for scholarship, prosperity, technology and a young democratic system behind it. It has the potential to lead the field of Asian open and distance learning. However, in codification, conception, curriculum and resources, the NOUT occupies a marginal place in Taiwan society. It receives neither the resources nor the respect granted to the traditional universities, a common enough situation with open universities. However, since the NOUT is not directly linked to national goals, it loses parity with other schools and resources from business and industry. In other words, it is not able to do what it does best. As a result, NOUT students and Taiwan citizens view it mostly as the means to a personally edifying learning experience.

The position of the NOUT illustrates national preferences for academic over vocational and traditional over non-traditional learning venues. However, open universities are essentially vocation-oriented, non-traditional venues. Herein lies the ambiguity of the NOUT. It is not respected, nor should it be, as an academically excellent university on a par with research institutions. However, it can gain status and find its place by:

• Continuing to be a vehicle for the learning and personal needs of its students using best practices supported by research in adult education;

• Becoming a nexus for national development goals in the areas of business, health, welfare, transportation, the environment, trade and technology;

• Finding a home (governance) that reflects its potential as a diverse institution serving cultural, economic, political and social segments of society;

• Articulating with public and private sectors to broaden its representation, services, and resources.

Without clear policy and informed guidance, the NOUT is neither an outstanding academic institution nor a centre for training. As long as the NOUT is neither this nor that, Taiwan looks almost exclusively to traditional universities to provide human capital, ignoring the enormous potential of non-traditional learners.

Specific strategies

Besides the above improvements, the NOUT needs strategies to fulfil its greater functions in a learning society. The following can be used as strategies in specific areas:

* Enriching independent and updated teaching media. With the continuing development of communication and information technologies, the NOUT has to keep applying new teaching media. This is one area where it can realize its potential and which the Department of Research and Development plans to push ahead with (NOUT 1999a; 1999b). But progress has to be faster. Above all, the NOUT is still dependent on one of the four wireless TV stations, Chinese TV, to produce and broadcast its programmes via UHF. The lack of an independent station has brought many drawbacks for the NOUT such as high cost and low efficiency. It is difficult for it to have its own TV broadcasting station, although more recently it has been able to cooperate closely with the non-profit TV station, Public TV with which it has more in common in terms of educational services. In addition, the NOUT has to increase the use of the Internet as its fifth teaching method and follow in the footsteps of the Kaohsiung City Open University.

* Enhancing learning support via regional learning centres. The functions of learning centres have to be fostered. Currently, these are mainly responsible for classroom lectures, examinations, student services and administrative affairs. Current learning support provision is inadequate. The major difficulty that the 13 regional learning centres have is a lack of manpower to serve as learning support. The NOUT needs to reorganize its learning centres and staff them with the necessary numbers of full-time and professional people with a background in adult or distance education through pre-service and in-service education and training. It being difficult to increase full-time staff, the NOUT could employ part-time professionals from neighbouring higher education institutions. Besides this, the learning support itself needs to be expanded from general student affairs to

tutorials and guidance for self-study students and towards the formation of learning groups.

- Establishing a collaborative distance-learning network. In addition to international academic exchanges, the NOUT also needs to promote domestic collaboration. Due to the growing popularity of cable television in Taiwan and the lack of its own TV broadcasting station, the NOUT has been looking to collaborate with satellite channels and local cable television system owners. The mechanism is still under development. More importantly, a collaborative distance-learning network is required to advance the NOUT's delivery of its programmes — for instance, taking advantage of the capabilities that cable television and satellite can offer, i.e., cable television's accessibility that can link the NOUT with the community (Wang 1997b), and the suitability of satellite broadcasting for national and regional reach. Besides the mass media, other institutions such as schools at different levels, public and private social educational institutions such as libraries and museums, professional associations and enterprise are all potential partners in such a network. The NOUT needs to analyse the relevant conditions for collaboration in order to formulate a distance-learning network that will be effective and advantageous to all parties (Wang 1996). Indeed, in a learning society, the NOUT cannot stand alone; it requires a closely linked partnership to be as effective in the delivery of its programmes and the achievement of its objectives in its aim to establish and maintain its role as a lifelong education provider.

- Extending education provision to other target groups. To be a lifelong learning institution, the NOUT has to extend its educational services from adults to other younger groups. By establishing lifelong learning among adults, the lifelong learning culture can be established at the family level, thus rooting an acceptance for lifelong learning in the family and adapting slightly that familiar adage to 'lifelong learning begins at home', rather than leaning on traditional learning mechanisms which can lead to an overdependence on schooling. The NOUT can in this way increase the diversity of its provision and its methods of delivery by offering its open learning resources to other, younger groups and by using different media to do so. For example, it can produce learning programmes that have been designed specifically with the non-adult learner in mind via TV, radio or the Internet. The services of regional learning centres can be expanded to encompass provision suiting younger groups through the hosting of a variety of learning activities, either independently or as a collaborative project.

Conclusion

The NOUT was set up at a time when open education was needed. It is now a new time and the NOUT needs to move with it. Like other open universities around the world, the NOUT has obligations and responsibilities in the areas of higher and adult education, especially for the educationally disadvantaged. Founded to embrace and fulfil traditional Chinese values of education, the NOUT has provided adult learners with opportunities to pursue ongoing learning in Taiwan and has made valuable contributions to continuing adult learning. To make even greater contributions in education and aware of its need to consider the appropriate course for its future development, the NOUT is expected to gradually reform itself as an institution of lifelong learning. At a time when the vision of developing a learning society has been high on the educational policy agenda, the NOUT has had to consider how to overcome current shortcomings and enrich its potential to be an established and effective provider of a much-needed service within society by expanding upon the framework and the foundations it has already successfully put in place. Moving into the 21st century, the NOUT should be ready now to face the new challenges ahead that we have outlined above in cooperation with and alongside its counterparts throughout the world.

References

Budge, D (1996) 'Nothing succeeds like a siesta' *London Times Higher Education Supplement*, 3 May, in C Murphy 'How Good is Taiwanese Education?' <www.geocities.com/Tokyo/Towers/5657/TaiwanEd.htm>

Bureau of Statistics (1997) *Education in the Republic of China*, Taiwan Ministry of Education, 41.

Caffarella, R (1994) *Planning Programs for Adult Learners*, San Francisco: Jossey-Bass, 23.

Clark, C (1991) 'Economic and political development in Taiwan: a reciprocal relationship' in W Chai and C Clark (eds) *Political Stability and Economic Growth: Case Studies of Taiwan, South Korea, Hong Kong, and Singapore*, Chicago: Third World Institution for Policy Research, 15.

Eric Document Reproduction Service, document no. ED 411 890.

Fei, J C (1991) 'Prosperity and stability in Hong Kong: a cultural approach,' in W Chai and C Clark (eds) *Political Stability and Economic Growth: Case Studies of Taiwan, South Korea, Hong Kong, and Singapore*, Chicago: Third World Institute for Policy Research, 55

Guo, S (1996) 'Adult teaching and learning in China', *Convergence*, XXIX(1): 21–32.

Huang, J (1997) 'Distance education: a key strategy for lifelong learning in Chinese Taipei', *Lifelong Learning: Policies, Practices, and Programs*, 246.

Ministry of Education (1997) *Education in the Republic of China*, June, Taipei.

Ministry of Education (1998a) *Education Statistics of the Republic of China*, Taipei.

Ministry of Education (1998b) *Towards A Learning Society*, Taipei.

Moore, M and Kearsley, G (1996) *Distance Education: A Systems View*, California, Belmont.

NOUT (1994) *Introduction to the National Open University*, Taipei.

NOUT (1997) *Introduction to the National Open University: The Republic of China*, Taipei.

NOUT (1998) *The Teaching Manual for Tutorials*, Taipei: NOUT, Department of Research and Development.

NOUT (1999a) *Introduction* <http://www.nou.edu.tw>

NOUT (1999b) *Prospects*, NOUT: Department of Research <http://www.nou.edu.tw/~research/a3.htm>

Open University of Hong Kong (1998) *Openlink*, 2(1), April.

Open University of Hong Kong (1999) *Openlink*, 8(1): 4.

Rubensen, K (1991) 'The sociology of adult education' in Sharan Meriam and Phyllis Cunningham (eds) *The Handbook of Adult and Continuing Education*, San Francisco: Jossey-Bass.

Sherritt, C (1997a) Discussions with President Professor Tam Sheung-wei in Hong Kong during November 1997.

Sherritt, C (1997b) Interviews with NOUT staff.

Sherritt, C (1999) 'Hong Kong and Taiwan: two case studies in open and distance learning', *Asian Affairs Journal,* 1(Spring): 37–42.

Van der Zee, H (1991) 'The learning society', *International Journal of Lifelong Learning,* 10(3), 213–230

Wallis J (1996) 'China and the tensions of modernization: implications for adult education', *Convergence,* XXXIV(4): 30–36.

Wang, C-Y (1996) Collaboration between education institutions on distance learning, *Kaohsiung Normal University Journal,* 7, 23–49.

Wang, C-Y (1997a) 'Advancing lifelong learning through adult education policy in Chinese Taipei', *Lifelong Learning: Policies, Practices, and Programs,* 55.

Wang, C-Y (1997b) 'The role of cable television in community distance learning networks for adults', paper presented at the 3rd Symposium Distance Education and Open Learning: Future Visions, 17–20 November, Bali, Indonesia.

Williamson, A (1995) 'Australia as a learning society: Issues, trends and prospects', *Australian Journal of Adult and Community Education,* 35(1): 3–12.

Thailand
Vietnam   Philippines

Malaysia

Indonesia

Southeast
Asia

Indonesia

Tian Belawati

Introduction

Distance education was introduced in Indonesia in 1955 with the establishment of a correspondence diploma programme aimed at upgrading teaching qualifications. However, it was not until 1981 when two distance education projects to provide in-service training to secondary- and tertiary-level teachers were started that distance education became widespread. These programmes were established as crash courses in teacher training to meet the demand for more teachers. Subsequently, only distance education has been able to effectively upgrade teaching skills, as regular training is too expensive and replacing teachers while they go for further training is difficult. These programmes later went to make up part of the Indonesian Open Learning University or Universitas Terbuka.

Universitas Terbuka (UT) is a state university and the only one in Indonesia that is a wholly distance education institution. It was established in 1984 with three main missions: 1) to increase access to higher education, especially for senior high school graduates, 2) to train increasing numbers of students in areas demanded by the economic and cultural development of the country, and 3) to upgrade the qualifications of primary and secondary school teachers who had graduated from the short-term programmes to enable them to obtain a full teacher training degree. UT was intended to be a flexible and inexpensive university catering to people unable to attend campus-based face-to-face higher education institutions.

The acceptance of distance education as an educational system has been proved by the fact that UT's student body increases from year to year and because more and more institutions are offering distance education programmes. The acknowledgement of distance education as a way to develop human resources was marked by the establishment of the Indonesian Distance Learning Network (IDLN) in 1993. IDLN is an organization consisting of 13 institutions, which share training, research and information as a cooperative venture to improve open learning and distance education practices across sectors in Indonesia. IDLN members have grown to include agriculture (Ministry of Agriculture), education and culture (Ministry of National Education), finance (Ministry of Finance), banking and management (Indonesian Banking Institute and Institute of Management), health (Ministry of Public Health), manpower (Ministry of Manpower), industry and trade (Ministry of Industry and Trade), religious affairs (Ministry of Religious Affairs), home affairs (Ministry of Home Affairs), and telecommunications (the National Telecommunications Corporation), which now use distance education programmes for human resources development. IDLN's objectives are to assist its members with institutional development, to plan the effective use of resources, to share materials and production facilities where appropriate, to coordinate training, and to provide information on development in the field of distance learning in various sectors.

The development of distance learning in Indonesia has also been accelerated by the establishment in 1997 of the South East Asian Ministry of Education Organization Regional Open Learning Centre (SEAMOLEC), which is based in Jakarta. Together, IDLN and SEAMOLEC have organized training seminars on distance learning programme development and management for both IDLN members and other institutions. SEAMOLEC shares the same objectives as IDLN but operates for the benefit of all countries in the region, i.e. Thailand, Malaysia, the Philippines, Myanmar, Indonesia, Singapore, Brunei Darussalam, Laos, Viet Nam and Cambodia. As a result of their joint efforts, almost all IDLN members have used distance training for staff development.

Universities such as Gajah Mada University, Surabaya Institute of Technology, and Bandung Institute of Technology are still developing appropriate distance education systems, i.e. trying out and/or studying the feasibility of offering several courses at a distance. Therefore, when we talk about Indonesian formal post-secondary distance education, we are basically referring to UT. This chapter therefore focuses on the system and development of UT since its establishment in 1984.

Universitas Terbuka

Organization and networking

UT is one of the biggest universities in the world with over 350,000 students, and thus needs a strong management system that will ensure the smooth operation of its daily activities. With the Head Office located in Jakarta, UT has 31 regional offices throughout the country. The university is headed by a Rector with four Vice Rectors for academic affairs, general administration and finance, student affairs, and operational affairs and collaboration.

UT has both a centralized and decentralized style of management. Institutional policies such as those for quality assurance (namely development and production of course materials, development of test and examination items, and examination data processing) are centrally managed from the Head Office. The regional offices are responsible, among other things, for carrying out daily operational activities. Those activities include student registration, tutorials, some administrative counselling, and examinations. Furthermore, since the heads of the regional offices come from and are nominated by the Rector of the local state university (but are appointed by UT's Rector), regional offices are also expected to maintain UT's partnership with the local public (conventional) universities in their region. Thus, regional offices are an important part of UT's organization and management system.

Collaboration with external institutions is also an important part of UT's organization. UT has established long-term collaboration with several institutions such as with the National Postal Service (PT Pos Indonesia) for distributing registration forms and delivering course materials, Bank Rakyat Indonesia (BRI) for accepting student tuition fees, and provincial governments for making school buildings available for examinations. With such a large area to cover, it is impossible for UT to carry out its mission without such collaborative efforts, which provide the necessary supporting infrastructure. It is this network that has enabled UT to reach and provide educational services to almost all Indonesia's inhabited islands.

While the other three faculties are open for high school graduates as well as working adults, the Faculty of Teacher Training and Educational Sciences offers only in-service training programmes for practising primary and secondary school teachers. Starting in 1990 when UT was appointed by the Indonesian government to upgrade primary teacher qualifications to Diploma II level, the DII-Primary School Teacher Training programme (for classroom teachers) has been the largest with an average of 50,000 students per intake, making UT a mega-university (Universitas Terbuka 2000).

Study programmes

UT offers more than 700 courses within 32 study programmes under four faculties. The study programmes within each faculty are shown in Table 1.

Table 1   Study programmes offered by Universitas Terbuk

Faculty	Level of education	Study programme
Faculty of Teacher Training and Educational Sciences	Degree programme	Bahasa Indonesia
		English
		Mathematics Education
		Physics Education
		Biology Education
		Chemistry Education
	Diploma III	Secondary School Teaching
		Bahasa Indonesia
		English
		Mathematics Education
		Natural Sciences Education
		Social Sciences Education
	Diploma II	Primary School Teacher Training (for classroom teachers)*
		Primary School Teacher Training (for Physical Education teachers)*
		Social Sciences Education
		Civic Education
	Certificate	Teacher Training
	Degree programme	Economics and Development Studies
		Management
	Diploma II	Manufacture and Industrial Services Supervision

* Qualification upgrading programme for primary school teachers and known as DII-PGSD

Table 1 cont.

Faculty of Social and Political Sciences	Degree programme	Business Administration
		Public Administration
		Government Science
		Communication Science
		Sociology
	Diploma III	Fiscal
		Extension Communication
	Diploma II	Library Studies
Faculty of Mathematics and Natural Sciences	Degree programme	Mathematics
		Statistics
	Diploma III	Agricultural Extension
	Diploma I	Environmental Management Studies

Course materials

Print materials are the main medium of instruction. The courses are developed by teams made up at the minimum of a subject matter specialist and an instructional designer. Each course, depending on its credit units, is presented in several modules. The modules are designed to be self-instructional so that students can use them with minimum assistance from instructors.

The subject matter specialists are usually invited and hired from nationally recognized conventional universities. The standard method of writing follows the writer-editor pattern of course development, in which the subject matter specialist writes the manuscript and UT's instructional designers format the content to UT standard. The designers are also responsible for ensuring that each course is broken down into several modules (each module representing three credit units), and each module containing general and specific instructional objectives, introductory parts, study materials, exercises, summary, and formative tests. Moreover, since printed materials are the most accessible medium to most UT students, it is mandatory that these modules contain 100% of the course's content stated in the course's syllabus.

Besides printed materials, UT also develops non-print materials as a supplement. In its initial stage, UT mostly developed audio and television programmes, which were broadcast via national public television (TVRI) and radio (RRI) stations. However, with increased use of computers, in 1998 UT began to develop computer-based materials such as Computer Assisted Instruction (CAI) and Web-based materials (Internet-based supplement) and distribute them via the Internet. These materials are still limited.

Learner support services

Universitas Terbuka, which started with 65,000 students registered in six study programmes, was able to provide two free tutorial services for each course offered within a semester. However, evaluation studies (Belawati 1996) showed these tutorials to be poorly attended. One reason among the most frequently mentioned by students was that the locations of tutorials, which were usually held in the capital city of the province, were considered too far from where the students lived. Some students claimed they had to travel for at least a day to attend. This made tutorial provision inefficient, and UT decided to halt them. After that, tutorials were only provided when requested by at least 20 students. Evaluation studies again showed that only small numbers of students ever requested tutorials.

At the same time, however, students living in relatively urban areas with access to good tutors, tended to set up study groups and invited tutors themselves. They usually hired their own tutors and set regular study times. This seemed to work so well that UT encouraged all students to set up study groups for their own benefit. UT's regional offices also now organize initial gatherings for new students so that they can meet their fellow students and set up study groups. UT also helps these groups find tutors when necessary. Data show that up to present, over 1,000 study groups have been established and are working well.

Besides growth in the student body, UT's study programmes have also increased to more than 700 courses per semester. With such a large number of courses, UT needs to find alternative ways to provide tutorials in addition to face-to-face sessions. Based on the availability and accessibility of technologies as suitable for UT's students, UT has been employing a supermarket model of learning support services. As indicated by the term, learning support services (i.e. tutorial services) are designed to employ various technologies from print (or even hand-written materials and correspondence) to computers. Models include correspondent tutorials, face-to-face tutorials, tutorials by radio, written tutorials via the Internet; and written tutorials by fax and the Internet.

Correspondence tutorials

Correspondence is the most accessible medium. It basically means written tutorials by post. They are intended to reach students in isolated areas that have postal services. Even if turn-around times are long, there are students who still prefer this mode. Telephone tutorials are not popular. Even though UT provides special telephone lines for this, students seldom use the telephone for 'real' tutorials as telephone calls are expensive, especially if they are long distance.

There are three types of correspondence: 1) question-based, 2) assignment-based, and 3) supplementary material-based (Universitas Terbuka 1999a). In the question-based correspondence, tutors give tutorials based on questions raised by students. Tutors are not to initiate contact but rather respond to student initiatives. In the assignment-based correspondence, tutors are required to prepare certain materials based on the main learning materials (i.e. modules) and some assignments, and to comment on the students' responses. Students are expected to do the assignments and submit them according to a certain schedule. In supplementary materials-based correspondence, tutors are supposed to write an article highlighting the central issues of the module being studied, and publish it in a pre-arranged local newspaper. Based on the published article, students are expected to ask questions or make comments on which the tutors then give feedback.

Face-to-face tutorials

The target students for these tutorials are students living in relatively urban areas and those who have access to the nearest face-to-face tutorial locations, which usually are in districts. These tutorials, however, are fees-based and are provided according to demand. In other words, regional offices will only organize tutorials when requested by at least twenty students.

Tutorials by radio

Radio has the unique characteristic of being able to reach remote and difficult-to-reach areas. Radio is therefore an effective medium for reaching students who live in such areas. It is also relatively affordable and easy to use. In fact, almost every household in Indonesia can be assumed to have at least one radio. Besides the ordinary one-way radio broadcasts, radio tutorials are also designed to have follow-up two-way interaction between tutors and students by telephone. Materials are supposed to be developed and recorded, then the pre-recorded audio programmes are sent to regional offices to be broadcast locally. Students are then given the opportunity to phone in (when it is feasible) to ask questions and or give comments, to which a tutor responds from the radio stations (Universitas Terbuka 1999b).

Tutorials by the Internet

An experimental study conducted to test the feasibility of using the Internet for counselling at a distance showed the Internet to be an effective medium for communicating with students (Belawati 1998). Despite concerns of high costs and low computer literacy among students, students who participated in the experiment expressed their satisfaction at having been able to directly communicate in a fast way with counsellors at UT.

This model is therefore intended for students who live in relatively urban areas and can afford the costs, but who are too busy to attend face-to-face tutorials. It is considered to be a feasible alternative since Internet facilities are now available to the public in many Telecommunications Kiosks (known as Wartel), as well as in post offices in big cities. The rental cost for using public Internet facilities is also relatively affordable, especially if it is shared among students within a study group. Data show that the cost can be as low as Rp. 3,500 (US$0.50) per hour. The cost for a subscription to an Internet Service Provider (ISP) is around Rp. 35,000 to Rp. 45,000 (US$6.50 to US$7.00) per month for 20 hours of access.

Tutorials via the Internet are similar to face-to-face tutorials as they allow students to interact with both tutors and fellow students, the main difference being that such tutorials are not real time and therefore feedback is also delayed (Toha et al. 1999). The major advantage of tutorials via the Internet is in overcoming scheduling problems often encountered in face-to-face tutorials as students can post questions, raise issues and read tutors' or other students' responses to questions at any time and at their convenience. Similarly, tutors also have the flexibility of scheduling tutoring times and to prepare materials and look for answers to questions. It is intended that these tutorials will use the mailing list application offered by the Internet; every course having its own mailing list.

Tutorials by fax-Internet

Even though there is public access to the Internet, UT students are mostly low-income working people, and still find the cost high. To overcome this, UT is now developing an alternative model that combines use of the Internet with use of facsimile, which expands the provision of tutorials via the Internet. The only difference between the two lies in access points.

Using tutorials via the Internet, students are required to have access to the Internet and some computer skills, at least opening and sending emails. In tutorials combining use of fax and the Internet, students are only required to have access to a fax machine, which are now widely available to the public in Wartels throughout Indonesia to district level. And since students would communicate by fax, they do not have to be able to use a computer (Hardhono and Belawati 1998). The cost for sending and receiving faxes in Wartels ranges from Rp. 1,000 to Rp. 5,000 (US$0.14 to US$0.70) depending on the destination (local or long distance). With the integration of fax messages into the Internet system, students would send their faxes to the closest fax gateway, which would be installed in UT regional offices. Therefore, fax charges to be paid by students will be either local rates or long distance to the closest regional office, but not to UT's office in Jakarta where the tutors are working. On the tutors' side, student faxes would be received as emails. Tutors will therefore send their replies as an email. This way, messages from tutors would be sent to students through the Internet and therefore would also save communications costs to be covered by UT.

The belief that different technologies are appropriate for different students is the basis for the provision of the above tutorial models. They are developed with one intention: to give students the choice of medium that is most accessible, affordable and convenient to them.

Registration and evaluation system

UT's registration is open all year long so that students can sign up at any time. However, UT only conducts sit-in examinations twice a year, in February and August for DII Primary School Teacher Training Programmes, and in June and December for other programmes. Therefore, students who register too close to the examination time may have to wait and take the examination in the next/closest semester. UT has approximately 360 examination sites, which are generally located in local schools. Table 2 shows UT's academic calendar for registration and examination.

Besides the sit-in examination that must be taken at the end of the semester, each course requires students to submit a self-test (home test), which will contribute to their final grade. Furthermore, some courses also require students to do a practicum or micro-teaching (for teachers) and write reports to be submitted for grading. For such courses, UT has established long-term collaboration agreements with relevant institutions nation-wide, such as with local universities, local schools and other training centres. For example, in conducting and assessing the practica of students of the Agricultural Extension Study Programmes, UT collaborates with the Agricultural Extension Academy (in six locations) and the Husbandry Academy (in two locations) owned by the Ministry of Agriculture, which have the necessary facilities and supervisors.

Table 2   UT's academic calendar

Programme	Registration period for respective examination times	Examination time
Diploma II – Primary School Teacher Training Programmes (for classroom and physical education teachers)	1 March to 10 June	August, weeks 2 and 3
	1 September to 10 December	February, weeks 2 and 3
Other programmes	1 January to 10 April	June, weeks 2 and 3
	1 June to 10 October	2 and 3 December

Facts and figures

UT's 65,000 students in September 1984 had grown to number 372,233 by 1999 (Universitas Terbuka 2000). Table 3 shows UT's active student numbers and data in the first semester of 1999.

Table 3   The number of UT active students* in first semester 1999

Faculty	Number of students		
	Male	Female	Total
Economics and Development Studies	29,339	13,129	42,468
Social and Political Sciences	28,467	14,212	42,679
Mathematics and Natural Sciences	4,123	1,226	5,349
Teacher Training and Educational Sciences	125,827	155,910	281,737
Total	187,756	184,477	372,233

* Active students are those who are registering for at least one course

These students come from every corner of the country, especially those following the diploma programmes of the Faculty of Teacher Training and Educational Studies. Table 4, which illustrates the spread of students by their residential islands, shows that the majority of students live on the island of Java.

With regard to student profile, Table 4 also shows that UT's students are mostly (95.41%) working adults, with an almost equal ratio of male and female as indicated by Table 3 and Table 4. Table 5 further shows the student profile with regard to age and that over 80% of UT's students are aged 30 and above.

Table 4   The spread of students by island

Island	Number of students*			
	Working		Not working	
	Female	Total	Female	Total
Sumatra	48,685	83,830	928	1,661
Java	87,320	177,372	6,094	13,605
Kalimantan (Borneo)	10,249	25,135	399	806
Sulawesi (Celebes)	16,570	32,508	193	374
Irian (Papua)	2,101	6,207	66	120
Bali and Nusatenggara	7,059	19,435	147	299
Maluku (Moluccas)	3,203	6,064	66	140
Others (outside Indonesia)	1,354	4,603	43	74
Total	176,541	355,154	7,936	17,079
	(47.43%)	(95.41%)	(2.13%)	(4.59%)

* Based on data of active students of first semester 1999

Table 5   Student profile by age

Age	Number of students	Percentage
Up to 24	20,736	5.57%
25–29	36,277	9.75%
30–34	80,244	21.56%
35–39	118,438	31.82%
40–44	61,545	16.53%
45 and over	54,993	14.77%
Total	372,233	100.00%

As in any other distance education institution, UT also faces the problem of low persistence rates. As an illustration, Table 6 shows the completion and persistence rates of UT's regular students (that is students in the non-Primary School Teacher Training Programme) who first registered between 1991 and 1994. As the table shows, the average rate of degree completion (persistence measurement) of UT students whose first registrations were in the first semesters from 1991 to 1994 was below 15%. Table 6 also shows that among those who have not graduated, only 14% of students or less were still actively taking courses by February 1997. This means that over 71% of students of these cohorts (groups of students who register in the same academic semester) either withdrew or did not continuously maintain their studies before graduation. This completion rate is lower than the average completion rate of 48.8% in the UK Open University's degree programmes, of 22% in the Indira Gandhi National Open University's diploma programmes, and 17% in Thailand's Sukhothai Thammathirat Open University's degree programmes (Belawati 1998). As the table shows, the average rate of degree completion (persistence measurement) of UT students who first registered between 1991 and 1994 was less than 15%.

Table 6   Completion and persistence rates of students from 1991 to 1994 cohort*

Cohort	Enrolment	Graduated by semester Feb 1997	%	Still registered in semester	%	Total	%
91.1	3980	733	18.00	329	8.00	1062	26.00
92.1	5308	946	18.00	624	12.00	1570	30.00
93.1	5679	706	12.00	891	16.00	1597	28.00
94.1	8817	943	11.00	1632	19.00	2575	30.00
Average			14.75		13.75		28.50

* Excluding Primary Teacher Training Programmes

With regard to re-registration rates, Table 7 shows that the average rate of students re-registering in a second semester of study without interruption was only 61%. Data presented in Table 7 indicates that 39% of these new enrolees did not pursue their studies continuously, either taking time off, withdrawing from, or even dropping out of their studies altogether. Data shown in Table 6 indicates that on average only 13.75% eventually came back and continued their studies in later semesters.

Table 7   Re-registration rates immediately following second semester

Cohort	Enrolment	Re-registration	%
91.1	3,980	2,241	56
92.1	5,308	3,262	61
93.1	5,679	3,300	58
94.1	8,817	6,068	69
Average			61

Despite the relatively low persistence rates, UT has produced over 300,000 graduates during its 15 years of operation. This high number of graduates shows that quantitatively speaking UT's contribution to the development of Indonesia's human resource pool has been significant.

Table 8   Total number of graduates by faculty and level of study

Faculty	Level of study	Number of graduates*
Economics and Development Studies	Diploma II	45
	Degree	4,931
Social and Political Sciences	Diploma II	366
	Diploma III	1,698
	Degree	10,799
Mathematics and Natural Sciences	Diploma I	79
	Diploma III	181
	Degree	658
Teacher Training and Educational Sciences	Certificate	5,523
	Diploma II	270,751
	Diploma III	27,151
	Degree	10,736
Total		332,918

* On 9 August 2000

UT's other significant product besides graduates is learning materials; printed and non-printed. Table 9 shows the number of printed course materials, audio programmes, video programmes and computer-based learning materials developed by UT over its 15 years of education provision.

Table 9   The production of non-print materials/programmes by December 2000

Materials	Number of titles produced
Printed materials/modules	982
Audio cassettes	3,000
Video cassettes	500
CAI	49
Web-based supplements	100

Difficulties and challenges

Entering the new millennium is an exciting time but is also intimidating for institutions that operate in countries such as Indonesia. The general consensus that we have entered the information age and that we have to keep pace with technological developments and effects of globalization (Taylor 1998), have been acknowledged and realized, yet not without raising concerns. Along with the effects of the economic crisis of 1997, the most important of these concerns for UT has been maintaining and increasing the quality of its materials and learning support for students.

This concern for quality relates to questions such as: can UT deliver the same quality of education as 'good teachers' in the classrooms? Can interaction between teachers and students be accommodated with such low access to education-related technologies? Can UT provide feedback to its students? UT has been struggling to answer these questions and convince people that distance education can offer as good an education as conventional methods.

The quality of learning materials has to do with the up-to-date nature of the content: how fast can UT revise its course materials? With the rapid changes in the national social, economic and political systems within the last three years, updating materials has become an essential task. For example, the materials for 'Banking' within the Study Programme of Economics and Developmental Studies was revised in 1997. By the time the materials were re-written, in 1999, some banks were already in liquidation, thus rendering a proportion of the new content obsolete.

Enhancing the quality of learning support has also been difficult for UT. Almost all the surveys conducted to determine what kinds of support students need reveal face-to-face tutorials to be the top requirement. However, data also show that face-to-face tutorials are usually poorly attended, except for courses that students consider to be difficult. On the other hand, distance tutorials (correspondence and electronic tutorials), also provided, are only used by a small number of students. While these facts show a dilemma that is yet to be solved, in the meantime UT continues to provide the support it believes to be an integral part of distance learning.

Conclusion

That increasing numbers of institutions in Indonesia are adopting distance education as a means by which to train and educate their staff, clearly shows that learning at a distance will become a genuine alternative for people wishing to continue their education but without the ability to pursue such study by conventional means. This trend will be enhanced by the fact that the skills needed in today's professional as well as daily lives are constantly changing, as noted by Bardman and Franzpotter:

> ...today, production methods, communication technologies, perceptions on problems and problem-solving strategies can be overdue and obsolete tomorrow (Peters 1999, 5).

Furthermore, as Indonesia's IT infrastructure improves, so access to high technology will increase. This will, in turn, increase the use of computers and connections to the Internet as a major part of the distance learning process. However, even though communications technology such as the Internet will without any doubt enhance the quality of the learning process, the role of printed materials will remain central over the next ten years.

Also, improvements in the quality of distance education programmes will only encourage potential students to enrol in distance courses. This will ultimately change Indonesians' perception about distance education and raise it from being a form of 'second class' education (as it is now widely perceived) to being an alternative equal in quality to face-to-face education. Once this new perception becomes widely accepted, distance education will become a mainstream educational model that is likely to best suit the geographic distribution of the Indonesian archipelago.

References

Belawati, T (1998) 'Increasing student persistence in Indonesian post-secondary distance education', *Distance Education*, 19(1), 81–106.

Hardhono, A P and Belawati, T (1998) 'Base-line surveys for the utilization of fax-internet technology for distance learning supports', Proceedings of the 19th World Conference on Open Learning and Distance Education, Vienna, 20–24 June.

Peters, O (1999) 'The university of the future — pedagogical perspectives', Proceedings of the 19th World Conference on Open Learning and Distance Education, Vienna, 20–24 June.

Taylor, J C (1998) 'The death of distance: the birth of the global higher education economy', plenary address presented at the ICDE Standing Conference of Presidents, Hyatt Coolum, Queensland, Australia, 13-16 September <http://www.usq.edu.au/DEC/STAFF/TAYLORJ/confer.htm>

Toha, A, Belawati, T, Hardhono, A P, and Sigit, A (1999) 'Written tutorials through the Internet and Fax-Internet: pilot project proposal', unpublished manuscript, Universitas Terbuka, Jakarta, Indonesia.

Toha, A, Belawati, T, Hardhono, A P, and Sigit, A (1999) 'Written tutorials through the Internet and Fax-Internet: operational guidelines for regional offices', unpublished manuscript, Universitas Terbuka, Jakarta, Indonesia.

Universitas Terbuka (1999a) 'Panduan penyelenggaraan tutorial tertulis [Guidelines for administering written tutorials through correspondence]', unpublished manuscript.

Universitas Terbuka (1999a/b) 'Panduan penyelenggaraan tutorial radio [Guidelines for administering radio tutorials in regional offices]', unpublished manuscript.

Universitas Terbuka (2000) 'Statistik Universitas Terbuka [Students and alumni statistics]', Jakarta: Universitas Terbuka.

Malaysia

Gan Siowck-lee

Introduction

In many parts of the world today, especially in rapidly developing countries such as Malaysia, the higher education sector is facing the dilemma of how to cope with change and how to meet the challenges arising from change. The changes themselves are a result of rapid development, industrialization and more recently of the onset of the information age and the emergence of a knowledge-based society, all of which are placing new demands not only on the role that institutions have to play in this new society, and their performance, but on individuals as well. The challenges are how to meet these escalating demands, such as a retooling of the workforce, professional updating, and continuous lifelong learning.

In response to such change and challenges, higher education in Malaysia in recent years has undergone fundamental reforms in terms of both its policy and orientation to groom a human resource base for long-term and sustainable economic growth and global competition. Higher education is perceived as one of the strategies of nation-building in Malaysia, and as a key to progress that plays a role in the national agenda, it has been given high priority and much attention. For example, under the Seventh Malaysia Plan (1995 to 2000), a massive allocation of RM10.1 billion or 15.4% of the total public development fund under the plan has been set aside for education and training, compared with 13% under the Sixth Malaysia Plan. This high allocation for education is an indication of the government's commitment to increase access to education and improve its quality for the benefit of all Malaysians.

At the beginning of the 21st century, there is a pressing need in Malaysia to further reform higher education in tandem with market mechanisms. Education legislation, including the New Education Act 1996, the National Council on Higher Education Act 1996, the Private Higher Education Institution Act 1996, the Universities and University Colleges (Amendment) Act 1996, the National Accreditation Board Act 1996 and the

National Higher Education Fund Board Act 1997, has been promulgated for such purposes (Gan and Azahari 1998). These reforms have far-reaching implications for higher education in the coming years and have already resulted in a dramatic increase in access to higher education for Malaysians. (For example, the number of undergraduates enrolled in eight local public universities has increased from 15,964 in 1995 to 29,968 in 1997; and the number of students registered in distance learning programmes has increased about four-fold from 3,472 in 1995 to 12,597 in 1997 (Malaysia 1998)). Also, the establishment of private universities by the private sector — made possible by new legislation — is intended to propel Malaysia towards becoming a regional centre of excellence in education.

Another aim of the new legislation is to expand access to quality higher education locally to reduce the huge amounts of foreign currency that students studying abroad are having to pay out. The number of Malaysian students studying abroad has steadily increased since the 1960s as many qualified candidates were unable to gain admission to the limited number of local public universities. At the same time, the Malaysian government has been sponsoring tens of thousands of scholarship holders in universities and colleges abroad, in particular in the UK, the US, Canada, Australia and New Zealand. According to an estimate, over 50,600 Malaysian students were studying abroad in 1995 (Malaysia 1996). About 40% of them were sponsored by the government (Malaysia 1996). These figures are certainly much higher now. All this means that there has been a substantial outflow of foreign exchange which translates into a significant deficit in the nation's balance of payments.

Expanding access to higher education locally is timely and welcome in view of the current economic downturn and the currency problems of countries in Asia, including Malaysia. As the Malaysian public is increasingly distressed at foreign academic degrees becoming priced beyond their means, the provision of cheaper higher education locally will ease the burden on parents who would have to make heavy sacrifices to have their children educated abroad. It will also help save enormous amounts in taxpayers' money currently spent on government-sponsored scholarships overseas.

Another growing trend, due in some part to the economic slowdown, is the increased popularity of distance and online learning. Most public universities now offer distance learning programmes that cater to the needs of tens of thousands of working adults who wish to further their education while remaining employed. Among those joining such programmes are people who have been retrenched from their jobs.

While expanding access to higher education within Malaysia is hoped to reduce the dependence on foreign institutions for tertiary education, the Malaysian government also intends it to promote the development of a vibrant local education industry at the international level (Gan and Azahari 1998). The Malaysian government is advocating making the nation a regional centre of education excellence by extending higher education opportunities and facilities to students from other countries, particularly those from ASEAN and the Asia Pacific. This approach is anticipated to generate a new source of national income. More importantly, with the establishment of branch campuses by foreign universities and locally conducted foreign degree programmes, the higher education sector can become an 'education superstore' of sorts, capable of offering a wide range of courses and programmes to students in the region at lower prices. In 1996, there were only 5,635 foreign students in Malaysia, mostly from Indonesia and Thailand (Malaysia 1997). In 1998, this figure increased sharply to 11,733 to include students from Singapore, China and Korea (Lee 1999). According to an estimate of the Ministry of Education, this figure was expected to multiply ten-fold in the year 2000.

The last few years have also seen a push by the government for the introduction of more corporate-style management practices, in tandem with a rapid expansion of public universities. This reform is supported by amendments in the Universities and University Colleges (Amendment) Act 1996, which enable public universities to be 'corporatized'. Corporatization is intended to empower public universities by offering them greater autonomy to operate in a more dynamic and proactive manner in a market context specifically as they need to be able to respond quickly to changing times and needs. It is also meant to increase the competitiveness of public universities in local and regional education markets by enabling them to operate on an expanded revenue base generated from their own business ventures. With corporatization, the challenge faced by public universities now is to ensure that they can not only maintain their supplementary income from operating in the market sector but that they can use it to further improve existing standards of teaching and research.

The aim of corporatization, as officially stated by the government, is therefore to streamline the universities to enable them to play a more dynamic role in developing Malaysia into an industrialized nation by the year 2020. It is also hoped that the changes in the management of public universities will allow them greater financial and administrative autonomy. In the long run, if implemented well, corporatization is expected to free the universities from the perceived cumbersome processes of the civil service, thereby improving the efficiency of university management and making them more competitive in the global economy.

The following is based on data and information gathered from a questionnaire survey of all 11 public universities. Some institutions did not respond, some returned incomplete responses, only four (UPM, UiTM, UM and IIU) returned fully completed questionnaires.

Brief background and the institutional framework of ODE in Malaysia

How does ODE fit into the scenario described thus far? ODE has a definite place in the government's efforts to democratize higher education and make it accessible to the masses, rather than only to the elite as in the past. Distance learning has become increasingly popular over the past few years as it allows working people to study without having to sacrifice financial security. Rapid developments are also creating a need as well as a demand for 'just-in-time learning', a concept currently under the purview of all universities and colleges offering distance learning programmes.

All of Malaysia's 11 public universities, with two exceptions (USM and UiTM), first began offering ODE programmes in or after 1995 in response to a directive from the Minister of Education to increase access to higher education through distance learning. Universiti Sains Malaysia (USM) pioneered ODE programmes as far back as 1971, offering a wide range of degree programmes including Bachelor of Arts degrees in geography, history and literature; Bachelor of Social Science degrees in anthropology, sociology, economics and political science; and Bachelor of Science degrees in maths, biology, chemistry and physics. Institut Teknologi MARA (ITM) — upgraded to a university (UiTM) in late 1999 — first started offering ODE programmes in 1990. These included Diploma programmes in Business Administration, and Public Administration. Other dual-mode universities are Universiti Putra Malaysia (UPM), which started distance-learning programmes in November 1995, offering Bachelor of Education and Bachelor of Computer Science degrees and a Master's in Human Resource Development; Universiti Malaya (UM), which started ODE programmes in May 1996 offering Bachelor of Engineering and Bachelor of Computer Science degrees as well as short courses for professionals, and

Universiti Kebangsaan Malaysia (UKM) which has also started offering ODE programmes, albeit on a modest scale.

The main mode of delivery for most of these ODE programmes has been printed lecture notes and audio and video cassettes supported by face-to-face meetings or tutorials. UPM's Bachelor of Computer Science was the first to use Web-based instruction while UM delivers lectures at its centres in and around Kuala Lumpur by videoconferencing.

So far, ITM has already graduated 1,757 students while USM has as many as 6,500 graduates from its ODE programmes to date. UM also graduated a first cohort of 50 students in late 1998.

The drop-out rate has been surprisingly low across ODE programmes. According to their own estimates, ITM had about a 30% drop-out rate during the first semester, but this tapered off to 15% in the second semester and less than 5% in subsequent semesters. USM has an average 5% drop-out rate, UM recorded a rate of 10% to 15%, and UPM about 10%.

USM has, over the last twenty years, conducted many research and development projects on ODE. According to UM, graduate students, mostly from its education faculty, have used ODE programmes as the subject of case studies, but results have not yet been published. A few isolated individual studies in ODE have also been conducted at UPM.

Student profile/enrolment patterns/geographic spread of ODE

USM, ITM, UPM's ODE students are mostly working adults studying part-time. In UM, about 75% of students are part-time. UPM has the highest enrolment for the 1999/2000 academic year with about 7,000 students. UTM has 6,568 registered students, and USM has 6,500. As of December 1998, UM had 644 students enrolled in its ODE programmes.

In terms of geographic spread, all institutions have students from all the 14 states in Malaysia, including Sabah and Sarawak in East Malaysia. In general, in most of the ODE programmes almost a quarter to half of the students are from Kuala Lumpur and the state of Selangor. This is not surprising as UPM, UM and ITM are located in these areas; USM is situated in the northern part of peninsular Malaysia. It is noteworthy that UPM has a total of 1,096 students from Sabah and Sarawak while ITM and UM have 1,460 and 207 students from these two states respectively.

Manpower requirements, demand for learning and credential needs

Education and human resource development have constituted a major challenge for the government in the past few decades. This challenge seems all the more daunting as the nation needs to increase its competitiveness and be able to manage new technologies. There is an urgent need to groom a productive and highly skilled labour force with a strong work ethic and commitment to excellence. The rapid move towards industrialization in the last ten years has highlighted the need for tertiary education and professional and technical training. Talent in science and technology is essential to overcome the acute shortage of technology-based human capital. Currently only about 10% of the workforce in Malaysia has had any form of college or university education. The government hopes to raise this figure to 25% by the year 2020 by increased access to higher education. A strategy to achieve this is the development of ODE to upgrade, update and retool the workforce. Within this context, the Minister of Education issued a directive in late 1995 urging all public universities in the country to embark on ODE projects. In fact, the government has set an ambitious target for 50% of graduates to be produced via ODE in the long term (The Star 1998a).

A quick historical survey shows that higher education in Malaysia, up to 1990, has been preoccupied with two main concerns: expanding progressively to meet the educational needs and demands of a growing population and distributing tertiary education opportunities to redress ethnic imbalances. Traditionally, Malaysian society puts a high premium on education and looks upon education as an important means of social mobility and economic advancement across lines of class and race. To the government, higher education is vital in that it determines the quality and efficiency of a workforce required to realize Vision 2020. Considered by many as the most significant document to appear in Malaysia in recent years that propels IT to the forefront is the Malaysian Prime Minister's speech to the inaugural meeting of the Malaysian Business Council in 1991 entitled 'Malaysia — The Way Forward'. Exhorting a concept now widely known to Malaysians as Vision 2020, this document declares for the first time that Malaysia's objective is to be a fully developed nation by the year 2020. The main concern in recent years, therefore, has been how to reform higher education to effectively accomplish the government's goal and the citizenry's aspirations.

In the move towards democratization of higher education, expansion in terms of access has been dramatic. Before 1969, Malaysia had only one university, the University of Malaya. Today, there are 11 public universities, six private universities — including a virtual university, Universiti Tun Abdul Razak (UNITAR) recently set up to offer distance learning programmes using Internet technologies and an open university — and about 500 private colleges that run twinning programmes with foreign universities. These twinning programmes were initiated by the private education sector in response to higher education needs during Malaysia's recession in the late 1980s. Students in these programmes obtain degrees from foreign universities and pursue their final one or two years of study at the partner universities abroad. The Private Higher Educational Institutions Act 1996 officially recognized the role of private higher educational institutions in providing an educational infrastructure to meet the demand for higher education.

A key goal for ODE is to eliminate differences in the quality of outcomes between on- and off-campus programmes. However, with public universities facing staff shortages and a growing intake of both on-campus and ODE students, serious doubts have arisen as to quality. Doubts have also been expressed among academics and professionals about whether rigorous mathematical and laboratory-based courses like engineering are suitable for ODE — a case in point, the Board of Engineers of Malaysia (BEM) has differentiated between degrees earned on campus and through ODE (The Sunday Star 1998b). In a ruling effective in early 1998, students who earn degrees through ODE are considered graduate engineers with restrictions. In order to sit the professional assessment examination, they must have a minimum of six years work experience. Their counterparts who graduate through on-campus programmes need only four to sit the same examination. Similarly, the Legal Profession Qualifying Board of Malaysia accords graduates of ODE programmes either partial recognition or imposes additional requirements for recognition.

The government is aware that there have to be stringent measures to ensure that the quality of higher education is not compromised by its rapid expansion in a number of forms, one of them being ODE. Through legislation, the LAN (Lembaga Akreditasi Negara) or National Accreditation Board was established in 1996 to formulate policies on the standard and quality control of courses of study. The Board is also empowered to monitor, review and oversee the standard and quality of courses of study in all institutions of higher learning for accreditation of certificates, diplomas, and degrees.

Programme management and quality assurance

The four institutions surveyed each has a separate unit dedicated to the management of ODE programmes. In UPM, this unit is called the Institute for Distance Education and Learning (IDEAL).

With regard to the management of ODE, most institutions do not perceive the lack of expertise in ODE as a problem. However, a lack of necessary human resources is seen as a major challenge. This problem is compounded by perceived faculty indifference or the lack of interest towards efforts in staff training and development for the updating and upgrading of skills for the teaching and management of ODE programmes. Generally speaking, neither technical nor student support services give rise to major problems in the management of ODE.

In all but UM, where materials development is the confine of academic faculties, ODE learning materials are developed by the academic staff from relevant faculties/departments as well as staff members of the ODE units. For example, at UPM the learning modules are largely developed by academic staff who teach similar courses on campus, but because some staff members at IDEAL were originally from these academic units and also taught these courses on campus, they too are involved in materials development. IDEAL also has a curriculum specialist who provides instructional design/support services to faculty and staff.

Support services are provided for academic staff involved in ODE. UPM, UM and UiTM provide media production support in graphics, desktop publishing, audio/video recording, computer courseware and Web-based materials. They also provide formal training in how to teach at a distance. However, only two institutions (UPM and UiTM) provide formal training in how to prepare learning materials.

Most responses to the questionnaire survey already referred to indicate that the above-mentioned institutions have mechanisms for quality assurance. These include a preplanned academic calendar to monitor teaching-learning activities, a well-defined schedule for course and materials development, a procedure for quality control of materials before dissemination, procedures for monitoring and supervising instruction and tutors, ongoing research and development projects on ODE, ongoing systematic assessment of learner needs, and ongoing systematic feedback and evaluation from learners and instructors. Elements that seem to be missing in most of the institutions surveyed are the ongoing systematic feedback and evaluation from learners and instructors.

Financing ODE

Funding for ODE is not perceived to be a problem. In general, the four institutions were financially supported by the universities when they first started operation. All institutions, however, are moving towards becoming self-financing as the increasing ODE student population is beginning to generate a substantial income. In some universities, the income generated from distance learning programmes is so sizeable that their ODE units have come to be looked upon as cash cows for the larger institutions! The fees paid by students in these ODE programmes tend to be higher than their on-campus counterparts, often three times or more. For example, the cost of an ODE degree programme at UPM is about RM24,000 (about US$6,000) spread over a period of three to four years. However, this higher price for ODE is still considered very reasonable by those working adults who earn an average monthly income of about RM2,000 (about US$500). Government policy has kept tuition costs low in public universities.

National and international collaboration in ODE

All universities in Malaysia are moving quickly into the distance education market, each following a different path in planning and implementing distance education programmes. While some are adopting a carefully charted decision-making and planning process, most seem to follow a rather ad hoc process of implementation. There is a need now for each institution of higher learning to assess the situation and recognize that some innovations and changes have to be made at institutional, and even the national level, to avoid unnecessary competition and lend more credibility to the distance learning courses they offer both on and off campus.

By its very nature, distance education has the potential to transcend all campus and even national boundaries. As such, it is important that national strategies for distance education be adopted to coordinate efforts in this area. This would maximize the use of local resources and collectively explore the possibilities of international collaboration with institutions and organizations abroad.

Collaboration among both public and private institutions of higher learning could be further explored and developed through the formation of a distance education consortium (Gan 1997b). Gan (1997a) made the following recommendations that may be helpful in delineating its roles and functions.

Through such a consortium, institutions delivering similar courses could pool their resources to produce a set of courses rather than each institution struggling to produce its own, sometimes sub-standard version. Such collaboration would be advantageous to the production of quality distance education materials, especially those requiring technology, expertise and high capital costs. Institutions would save on development costs, and the quality of the final products would likely be even and generally better. More importantly, parallel or duplicative work in the development of learning materials would be avoided. Institutions would eventually be able to share a pool of quality course materials developed and contributed by individual institutions together.

Collaboration in a consortium should, of course, draw on the profiles, specialities and professional expertise of the different institutions. This strategy would increase both the breadth and depth of learning for students. The consortium would be able to provide a greater variety of courses and programmes to learners than any one of the institutions could manage on its own. This would go a long way to addressing related concerns about flexibility mentioned earlier.

This kind of collaboration would also be an impetus for individual institutions to put more effort into the development of and the delivery of knowledge through such one-of-a-kind programmes. By emphasizing such specialized programmes, they would be able to attract and serve the needs of students from not just Malaysia but throughout Southeast Asia or even beyond. Needless to say, setting up a consortium and initiating collaboration would require extensive study and planning by curriculum experts. But if low-cost and quality distance education is the final goal, such a national collaboration model would be well worth the cost and effort.

Collaboration with foreign universities, other enterprises or consortia (Gan 1997b) should also be explored. UNITAR is collaborating with computer corporate giant, Oracle, to offer programmes. Local partners such as publishers and IT industries within the Multimedia Super Corridor (MSC)[1] — an area 15 km by 40 km, in and around Kuala Lumpur, to be developed

---

1 The MSC encompasses the Kuala Lumpur City Centre, Putrajaya, and the new Kuala Lumpur International Airport (KLIA). World-class multimedia corporations are invited to locate their business units and research and development facilities in this area, which is to be used as a high-tech testing area and springboard to serve the local, regional and world market for multimedia products and services.

as a multimedia catalyst centre — must necessarily play a part in such cross-organization endeavours. However, the availability of foreign resources, especially instructional materials, must not lull Malaysians into thinking that all is well for such international distance learning programmes. Foreign materials may lack local content and context — important elements in some courses and programmes. Also, not all students have the necessary English language proficiency to benefit from imported materials. Learning support in the form of regular interaction with instructors is a must in any education process, on campus or off. Can international distance education programmes cater to this need? Perhaps then, one of the most vital roles of the national distance education consortium would be to consider and evaluate all these issues before embarking on or advising any local institution about international collaboration.

In late 1998, the Ministry of Education announced the setting up of a consortium called Multimedia Technology Enhancement and Operation Sdn. Bhd. (METEOR), which is supposed to involve all the local public universities. METEOR Distance Learning Sdn. Bhd. (MDLSB), one of METEOR's three subsidiaries, was set up to provide quality and affordable distance learning programmes for the 'average Malaysian'. METEOR's other two subsidiaries are METEOR Technology Sdn. Bhd., which deals with information technology, and METEOR Research and Services Sdn. Bhd., which handles research and consultancy services.

Initially, MDLSB's role seemed to be limited to the management of electrical engineering distance learning programmes offered by UTM with programmes in information technology, accounting, economics and business administration from UM and Universiti Utara Malaysia (UUM) in the pipeline. For its debut intake in August 1999, it shortlisted 250 out of 500 applicants in UTM's electrical engineering distance learning programme. It claims to offer this programme at a lower cost than other local public universities. At first, the medium of instruction was Bahasa Malaysia, but from the year 2000 onwards, this programme will also be conducted in English to attract students from the region and other parts of the world. As publicly announced, MDLSB's task is to spearhead the open university concept by maximizing resources from local universities and tapping facilities from the MSC (The Star 1999a).

At the moment, only 21% of those aged between 17 and 23 have had a university education. It is hoped that the open access policy on education will help to increase this to 40%. A new private university, the Open

University of Malaysia or Universiti Terbuka Malaysia (Unitem), the country's sixth, was set up in late 1999 to provide distance learning programmes more efficiently and at a lower cost (The Star 1999b). MDLSB was invited to set up Unitem, which will be jointly owned by the 11 local public universities. In other words, Unitem is entrusted with the task of coordinating the distance learning programmes of the local public universities, eventually taking over the distance learning operations from all universities. This move is supposed to be in line with the government's open access policy on education. Unitem would be working with the UK Open University. Unitem began operations with its intake of 238 undergraduates in the Bachelor of Electrical Engineering at the UTM campus on 7 August 1999.

Unitem will adopt a multimode approach to learning using a combination of printed self-study modules, videoconferencing, face-to-face tutorials at designated learning centres and support through the Internet (The Star 1999c). With the collaboration of Telekom Malaysia Berhad, the first batch of students would be able to 'attend classes' at six Telekom studios in Penang, Perak, Sarawak, Sabah, Johor and Kuala Lumpur. In addition, the students will have access not only to UTM facilities but also facilities at all the other public universities in the country.

Priorities for the policy on the national ODE consortium

To ensure success in ODE, priorities for the policy on the national ODE consortium must be set. Based on the survey mentioned above and an analysis of the current situation, the author believes that the following priorities need to be considered:

National needs assessment

An in-depth needs assessment analysis should be conducted to determine demand for courses and programmes offered at the national level. This is because the initial outlay of quality distance education programmes is often very high, particularly those requiring new and expensive technologies (Birk and Coscarelli 1997). Such a needs assessment will provide a platform for the planning and initiation of a working distance education consortium, not to mention the avoidance of costly miscalculations.

Broad-based planning

Careful planning is imperative with regard to time and people costs, especially when a consortium involves several institutions (Sedlack and Cartwright 1997). Such planning not only requires leadership with the right expertise, it also necessitates broad-based faculty, administrative, student and technical input. In addition, attention to and careful consideration of the success and failure of other cross-institutional efforts in distance education is a must. Distance education projects have been known to fail, usually due to a lack of planning rather than to anything inherent in the delivery methodology.

Institutional commitment

One crucial element in the success of a distance education consortium is commitment on the part of each participating institution to provide support as well as human and material resources (Haugen and Ask 1997). Commitment would also be shown by a policy of mutual recognition of credits, courses and modules among the different institutions and, more importantly, a policy of not discriminating between an on-campus course or programme and one that is taken off campus via distance learning.

Students, both on-campus and those registered for distance learning, should be allowed to choose modules and courses from the consortium's larger menu. To address concerns related to the issue of flexibility, students should be permitted and encouraged to combine the offerings into more varied and specially tailored lines of study. It is, however, still up to the institution that issues the certification — if not the consortium itself — to recognize and endorse the final course combinations. To these ends, each participating institution should also develop an efficient organizational structure to support and monitor the implementation of these policies.

Technology applications

Information technology is definitely a boon to distance education. But, technical expertise alone will not make a distance education consortium a success. In the selection, production and evaluation of distance learning materials for one particular subject or course, curriculum and instruction experts within the consortium should choose from a range of technologies that can best handle the subject matter in question and address the most common and obvious learning problems associated with it. Very often a combination of media may be the best way to address different learning needs and problems. A team is often required for the production of distance leaning materials — no-one can be an expert in all the skills needed to produce effective course materials, especially those which are computer-based or multimedia. In Malaysia, higher education is an area ripe for the new information technologies, some of which already exist on campuses such as UPM and many of which are forthcoming with the establishment of the MSC. The initial cost of developing multimedia interactive software is high, but if local and regional universities can coordinate and collaborate on programme and courses offered, this will increase market size and lead to reasonable cost.

Quality assurance

To attain the goal of educational excellence, whether at institutional or national level, decision-makers in the consortium must pay enough attention to the assurance of instructional quality. This will help avoid quality being compromised and such scathing remarks that the diploma is not worth the paper it is printed on! To assure quality, the selection of appropriate instructional design, materials, delivery and support systems, feedback strategies, and secure and equitable evaluation methods are of the utmost importance.

Learner performance evaluation should explore alternatives other than the usual tests to take into consideration the relevant work experience of working adult learners. These may take the form of offering experiential learning courses where evaluation is based on a portfolio developed by a learner. These portfolios provide evidence that he/she has learned by experience what in-class students have learned from books. While it is not strictly an evaluation strategy, offering distance learners the option of getting credits by examination is another way of taking into consideration adult learners' work experience or on-the-job training.

Finally, to assure academic quality, strong communication links between instructor and learner and among learners are crucial. Not only must the necessary technology infrastructure be in place to facilitate such communication, but human resources must be available to provide meaningful and effective instructor-learner communication and interaction.

Conclusions

To propel Malaysia into the 21st century and to equip the nation for the attainment of the various aspirations, inter alia, Vision 2020 and the MSC project, increasing access to higher education through ODE is a requirement. This chapter has attempted to examine some of the trends and strategies in this endeavour as well as suggest some priorities for national policy in ODE. In some respects, what is happening in Malaysia in ODE is merely a variation of international trends. These include the dramatic expansion of student numbers in a climate of changing needs and demands, the alignment of institutional goals with national priorities, and the more direct contribution from higher education to national economic well-being. However, in many other respects, the Malaysian experience in ODE is somewhat divergent as exemplified by the liberalization of its education policy not only to encourage the participation of the private sector but also to forge alliances with foreign universities from all over the world.

References

Birk, T A and Coscarelli, W C (1997) 'Benchmarking decision-making for distance education at US colleges and universities', Proceedings of ED-MEDIA/ED-TELECOM 97, Calgary, [CD-ROM].

Gan, S L (1997a) 'Towards educational excellence: national and institutional strategies for higher education and distance learning', paper presented at Academia '98 Conference, Kuala Lumpur, <http://edtech.kdu.edu.my/webpage/staff/gansl/acad98.html>

Gan, S L (1997b November) 'Some models of technology innovations', *The Star*, In-Tech, 41–42, <http://thestar.com.my/intech/112597/drgan.html>

Gan, S L (1998 January) 'Digital diploma mills?', *The Star*, In-Tech, 10, <http://thestar.com.my/intech/012798/slgan.html>

Gan, S L and Azahari (1998 July) *Education Reform Towards the 21st Century: New Trends and Market Mechanisms in Higher Education in Malaysia*, Country Report: The 1998 Association of Southeast Asia Institutions of Higher Learning Seminar, Jakarta, Indonesia.

Haugen, H and Ask, B (1997) 'Telecoms and open Learning — a change to institutional co-operation', Proceedings of ED-MEDIA/ED-TELECOM 97, Calgary [CD-ROM].

Lee, MNN (1999) *Private Higher Education in Malaysia*, Monograph Series, no.2/1999, Universiti Sains Malaysia.

Malaysia (1996) 'Seventh Malaysia Plan, 1996–2000', Kuala Lumpur: National Printing Department.

Malaysia (1997) 'Statistik Enrolmen Pelajar IPTS', Kuala Lumpur: National Printing Department.

Malaysia (1998) <http://www.moe.gov.my/upustat.htm>

Sedlak, R A and Cartwright, P (1997) *Two Approaches to Distance Learning: Lessons Learned*, <http://contract.kent.edu/change/articles/janfeb97.html>

The Star (1998a) 'DL still has some distance to go', *Sunday Star Education*, 26 April, Kuala Lumpur, 3–5.

The Star (1998b) ' The distance learning dilemma', *Sunday Star Education*, 9 August, Kuala Lumpur, 2–3

The Star (1999a) 'One-stop center for DL programs set up', *Sunday Star Education*, 18 July, Kuala Lumpur, 2.

The Star (1999b) 'Easier access to distance learning', *The Star*, 6 August, Kuala Lumpur.

The Star (1999c) 'First open university starts classes', *The Star*, 8 August, Kuala Lumpur.

Philippines

Josefina N Natividad

Background and institutional framework

The Philippines is an ideal site for open and distance learning because of its geographic configuration. An archipelago of 7,100 islands covering 300,000 square kilometres of land area, it is composed of three major island groups, Luzon, Visayas and Mindanao. As a former colony of Spain, the Philippines is the only nation in the Asian region that is predominantly Christian although a sizable Muslim population resides in the southern Mindanao islands. Moreover, being a former colony of the United States as well, English is widely spoken and until 1987 was the official language. English remains a standard feature of the curriculum from the elementary to the tertiary level.

In the 1995 census the Philippines had a population of 68 million, 24% or 16 million of whom are in the 6 to 16 age group, the age for basic compulsory education, and about 7 million or 10% in the 17 to 21 age group, the majority age for college students. The Philippines has one of the highest literacy rates in Southeast Asia, registered at 93.9% in 1994 with no significant gender differential; males have a literacy rate of 93.7% as against 94% for females.

The educational system of the Philippines is patterned after the American system except that pre-collegiate education is shorter at ten years. Government supervision and regulation of formal and non-formal education is shared by three departments: the Department of Education, Culture and Sports (DECS) for basic education, the Commission on Higher Education (CHED) for tertiary education and the Technical Education and Skills and Development Authority (TESDA) for technical-vocational training. This three-part system was instituted in 1994, before which time all formal and non-formal education was under one government body, the DECS.

Since the Philippines became an independent republic in 1946, basic elementary education has been compulsory and provided free by the state.

In 1987 the new Philippine Constitution modified the coverage of mandatory free education from the original elementary schooling of six years starting at age seven to include the secondary or high school level for an additional four years. In 1995 further reform in basic education lowered the admission age to six years. Students in the Philippines usually enter college at a much younger age than their counterparts in Asia because of the lower number of years at the basic education level. This new measure will further lower age at entry to college to 15 to 16 years once the cohorts now entering school at age six reach college. Tertiary level programmes, with the exception of Architecture, Engineering, Law, Medicine and a few other subjects, are normally completed in four years.

Data for 1995 show that 16.4 million were enrolled in the elementary and secondary levels while tertiary level enrolment stood at 2 million (Yearbook 1998).

Unlike in other Asian countries, admission to tertiary education in the Philippines is not contingent on performance in a national standardized test. Although a standard test, and while the National Student Achievement Test (NSAT) is administered to all secondary level students in their senior year, results are used by the DECS only as an institutional measurement of the achievement level of high school graduates. There are no national criteria for a desired cut-off grade to qualify a student for college admission. But colleges and universities are allowed to set their own admission criteria for incoming college students, which may include scores in the NSAT as well as in additional qualifying examinations administered by the respective schools. The national university, the University of the Philippines (UP) administers its own admission test — the UP College Admission Test. First-year undergraduate admission to the UP is highly competitive. For example, of the 65,000 or more applicants who take the test each year, only 10,000 qualify for admission.

College education is considered by most Filipinos as an important tool for achieving upward social mobility; hence completion of a college degree is a highly valued achievement. This value is further reflected in the requirement of a college education for many occupations and in the competitive edge in job applications of those with a tertiary education over those without, even for positions where a college degree is not of critical value, for example as a sales clerk or secretary.

To respond to the overwhelming demand for tertiary degrees, there are in all 1,413 institutions officially recognized by the Commission of Higher

Education (CHED) as tertiary-level degree-granting units; of these, 1,147 are private schools while 266 are government owned. These are established in all regions of the country with the highest concentration in urbanized areas, particularly MetroManila. The official figures do not include a number of institutions offering tertiary-level education without formal permits from the CHED and which are thus operating illegally. Since everyone who completes secondary education is eligible for entry into college and can choose from a wide range of schools, actual enrolment is limited mainly by cost considerations and the student's ability to meet additional qualifying criteria set by the respective institutions.

The cost of education varies widely. Private institutions generally charge higher fees; the more prestigious ones charge the most. Private institutions operate on a cost recovery basis and are usually run as business concerns. In contrast, the government heavily subsidizes tertiary education in public institutions. For example, the UP has a socialized tuition fee scheme in place with graduated tuition fees based on family income. Although many UP students pay full tuition as their incomes exceed the ceiling for discounted fees, full tuition students still pay only one-third of the real cost of their education. The rest is borne by government subsidy.

Despite the seeming ease of access to all levels of formal education, a cohort study on new entrants to the formal education system (Grade I pupils in 1982) followed up to graduation from college in 1995 found that of those who entered Grade 1 in 1982, only 65.7% reached Grade 6, 48% reached the last year of high school, 34% enrolled in college and 15.6% of the original cohort eventually completed tertiary education. These attrition figures point to a pool of school leavers who are a potential clientele for open and distance education (ODE) programmes.

Another clientele for formal education are those who seek graduate or post-baccalaureate training leading to a formal degree. This type of training falls under the supervision of the CHED and is customarily provided by institutions of higher learning that also offer baccalaureate degrees. A few institutions offer only graduate programmes. The CHED sets basic criteria as to what types of institutions offering college degrees may also offer graduate-level training. For students, among the major impetus for pursuing graduate education is the need to improve one's qualifications and to gain promotion points in one's current job. For example to qualify for supervisory positions in government (e.g. division chief, school principal, etc.) an employee is required to have a Master's degree. Teaching positions in tertiary-level institutions also require an advanced degree.

In 1997, the CHED instituted a new system that allows the formal accreditation of knowledge and skills gained from actual practice and other experiences towards a college degree in the field closest to these skills. Known as the Expanded Tertiary Education Equivalency and Accreditation Program (ETEEAP), this system has been instituted in recognition of experiences and lifelong learning as legitimate sources of education that can take the place of formal classroom instruction. This represents an initial step towards recognition of the philosophy of open learning.

Seven universities based in MetroManila have been deputized by the CHED to be the first to implement this programme. These institutions have identified specific degree programmes where equivalency and accreditation may be granted to a candidate based on assessment criteria issued by the CHED as well as criteria devised by the institution itself to ascertain adherence to its standards. Equivalency credits may be gained from formal courses, non-formal training such as workshops, short-term training programmes and informal training including self-study. Where a candidate needs further knowledge or skills he or she will be advised to participate in appropriate competency enhancement programmes that include those offered via ODE.

Beyond the need for people to obtain formal degrees there are also institutionalized requirements for further training and upgrading for professionals already in the workplace. In order to renew their professional licences, those in the professions are required to show proof of having updated their knowledge and skills on developments related to their profession through what are known as 'continuing education units'. These are obtained from non-formal courses or training programmes offered by accredited providers. In addition, short-term training programmes for specific skills provide promotion points and improve a person's qualifications for career advancement. A registered professional is a person who has passed an examination given by the Professional Regulatory Board and been issued a Certificate of Registration and Professional Licence (CPE Primer 1997). Among the registered professions are physician, nurse, elementary and secondary school teacher, engineer, chemist, nutritionist, social worker, librarian and others.

Accreditation for this type of training is under the auspices of the Professional Regulatory Commission through its Professional Regulatory Boards for each of the professions. Each Board in turn has a Continuing Professional Education (CPE) Council that accredits CPE providers.

In recent years there has been a sharpening realization by employers, both in government and in the private sector, of the necessity to upgrade the workforce to keep pace and conform with the changing needs of the labour market, particularly one that is increasingly globalized and transcendent of national boundaries. Emerging perspectives on lifelong learning, which are starting to take root in the Philippine setting, have also created a potential market for training programmes that are geared towards the retooling of the workforce, providing new skills to meet new demands without necessarily granting formal degrees. All these provide a receptive clientele for non-traditional forms of education because most of the target groups will be unable to enrol in the usual residential classes.

Another fertile potential market for non-traditional forms of education is middle-level manpower, which requires technical-vocational education and training. Presently the training needs of this sector are addressed by the Technical Education and Skills Development Authority (TESDA) through industry-based programmes that include apprenticeships, dual training systems, etc. This government body also accredits institutions involved in middle-level manpower development.

Innovations in information and communication technology and the entry of new telecommunications providers in the latter half of the 1990s have further enhanced the climate for ODE. The ratio of telephones to households has improved immensely and telephone services are now available in most of the 72 provinces in the country. Moreover, the use of the Internet is increasing, especially in urban centres, although no official estimates of Internet usage are available.

History and current status of ODE in the Philippines

Early attempts

ODE in a variety of forms has been practised unobtrusively in the country for many decades starting in 1940 when the US-based International Correspondence Schools (ICS) set up operations in the Philippines (Librero 1997), but it never gained mainstream attention. Correspondence education did not take off partly for lack of popular acceptance fed by the public impression that it is of inferior quality and open to abuse by those who simply want a degree without having actually learned content. The absence of supervised examinations further strengthened these perceptions. This image of correspondence education in the minds of the majority carried over to distance education when the latter began gaining adherents in the 1990s.

Variant forms of reaching learners outside a face-to-face setting were also in practice prior to the 1990s. The most prevalent format involved the identification of specific target groups and the designing of course content and delivery around their specific needs. The majority were in the nature of non-formal education that did not culminate in the granting of a degree.

The Home Study Programs offered by the University of Life, a now defunct institution created under the Marcos regime, offered non-formal livelihood courses delivered through print modules and supplemented by actual demonstrations and face-to-face interactions between learners and the instructional manager. Target clientele were out-of-school youth and adults who wanted to learn a livelihood skill. The DECS also at various times offered distance education programmes to high school leavers to allow them to complete their high school education through print modules supplemented by face-to-face meetings. One programme was called the *Balik Paaralan* (Back to School) programme; another was the Continuing Learning Delivery System.

Radio was as important as print as a medium for instructional delivery. Given the archipelagic nature of the country and the widespread availability of this medium, radio has been and continues to be the most cost-effective way to reach a mass audience. One of the pioneers in the use of radio was the UP in Los Banos' School on the Air programme. It aimed to equip farm households with applied skills on a wide range of topics from Integrated Pest Management to Cooking Nutritious Dishes. A similar radio-based DECS programme provided enrichment courses to elementary school teachers nation-wide through programmes aired over the government-owned Philippine Broadcasting Services.

Before the 1990s, formal education leading to a degree via distance education had hardly been heard of although it had a handful of practitioners. Four of these were residential universities and colleges and three engaged solely in ODE. The residential institutions were the University of Mindanao (UM), the UP in Los Banos (UPLB), the Polytechnic University of the Philippines (PUP) and the Visayas State College of Agriculture (ViSCA). All four are state colleges and universities, the operations of which are heavily subsidized by the Philippine government.

In 1979 the UM offered a Master's degree programme for elementary and secondary school teachers through a combination of lectures aired on its own radio station and packaged printed learning materials patterned after on-campus materials and supplemented by on-campus weekly tutorial sessions. The programme was discontinued in 1982 following a fire that destroyed all the materials used in the distance education programme. In 1984, UPLB, in collaboration with the Department of Science and Technology (DOST) Science Education Institute, launched a distance learning programme for secondary school teachers, which utilized printed self-study materials supplemented by monthly tutorial sessions. Starting as an enrichment programme the programme was transformed into a post-baccalaureate degree programme (Diploma in Science Teaching) in 1987. In 1985, ViSCA, in collaboration with Massey University of New Zealand, transformed its extramural programme for agriculture teachers and rural extension workers into a graduate-level distance learning programme. The PUP likewise transformed some of its extramural programmes into distance education format.

In 1972 the Southeast Asia Interdisciplinary Discipline Institute (SAIDI) began offering the first and so far only academic programme that operated under the principles of contract learning, a variant of open learning. The degree programme was entitled Organizational Development and was offered at Master's and doctoral levels. The Asian Institute for Distance Education (AIDE) and CAP (Collegiate Advancement and Proficiency) College offered undergraduate programmes. CAP College began operation in 1989 as a correspondence school. All three institutions have no residential programmes, are privately owned, do not receive government subsidy and are reliant on student tuition fees and non-government sources to cover their costs.

In general, all ODE institutions before the 1990s had small-scale operations; none had a nation-wide reach and enrolment figures were low, never reaching beyond a few hundred. SAIDI deliberately kept its enrolment to less than a hundred. There is a noticeable divergence between public and private institutions in the types of programmes offered and the target clientele with public institutions targeting teacher training.

Given the high number of residential institutions offering tertiary-level education in all parts of the country and the prevalent conception about the dubious quality of distance education courses, there was little impetus for learners to turn to the distance mode. Those who had no time to spare for regular class hours enrolled in extension classes. These were residential courses held in off-campus locations during weekends under compressed time schedules with lecturers from the main campuses flown in to conduct classes face-to-face. For some institutions extension classes were considered distance education classes because the teacher travelled some distance outside of the campus to meet a class. This notion persists to this day and some schools who claim to be engaged in distance education are actually running extension programmes.

ODE in the 1990s

The 1990s saw the gradual recognition of the potential of distance education for degree-granting programmes even in a setting saturated with tertiary-level residential institutions. There is no single set of factors that can be pinpointed to account for this development, but the growing ODE movement outside the country certainly contributed to it. The 1990s also saw the emerging role of television as a tool of delivery of educational materials for both degree and non-degree courses.

In 1995 the Continuing Science Education for Teachers via Television (CONSTEL), a consortium project of the DECS, DOST, the UP Institute of Science and Mathematics Education and PTV 4, the government-owned television channel began broadcasting the country's first educational television programme. CONSTEL broadcasts were well-researched and professionally produced telelessons for science teachers. The coverage later expanded to include telelessons for English teachers. Currently aired every Saturday for an hour and a half the programme is viewed nationally via satellite transmission to 16 provincial stations. The lessons are to provide enrichment for teachers but not credit units.

In 1994, a new player in ODE, the Philippine Women's University (PWU), a private university in Manila, launched PWU EdTV, the first cable television channel exclusively dedicated to educational programmes. Its broadcasts lasted for only two years, however, and its reach was limited to those who subscribed to cable TV. PWU then entered into partnership with PTV 4 for the broadcast of telelessons for its degree offering by distance education mode of a Master of Arts in Education.

CAP College, which began with home study or correspondence-type courses, transformed itself into a distance learning institution with the use of what it calls 'learning support collaterals' comprised of print modules, and audio and video materials including computer-assisted learning modules. It has a half-hour daily radio programme to broadcast audiotaped lessons. Moreover, it has a network of Distance Learning Centres equipped with communication equipment and where Distance Learning

Coordinators may be reached for information. Table 1 shows the programme offerings of CAP College.

Table 1   Programme offerings of CAP College

Level	Degree programme
Graduate	Master in Business Administration
Undergraduate	Business Administration Criminology Economics English Entrepreneurship History Journalism Mathematics Political Science Psychology Sociology

The PUP and ViSCA transformed from distance learning organizations into 'open universities' in 1990 and 1997 respectively. Thus, the PUP Open University and the ViSCA Open University were born. The PUP currently offers four Master's and two undergraduate programmes in distance mode (see Table 2), while ViSCA has not added any new programmes to its original extramural programme.

Table 2   Programme offerings of the PUP Open University

Level	Degree programme
Graduate	Master in Public Administration Master in Educational Management Master in Mass Communication Master in Construction Management
Undergraduate	Bachelor of Broadcast Communication Bachelor of Entrepreneurial Management

In the latter half of the 1990s, a number of state colleges and universities also began claiming to be 'open universities' in addition to being residential universities, a sign that distance education was starting to attract the attention of the mainstream universities. A major impetus behind these moves was the promise of funding from the government for this new idea boosted by the belief that this would open up access to many people who until now are unable to avail themselves of higher education. But with very little funding and no clear idea of how to operate an 'open university' all remained so in name only. Moreover, these developments brought with them only a muddled sense of what ODE was and what open universities were all about. Some courses run via distance mode were actually extension classes under a new name. At worst these efforts only served to give ODE a bad image as there were no clear quality controls in place.

In 1995, the Board of Regents of the UP system created the UP Open University (UPOU) as the fifth constituent university within the UP system with the mandate to offer distance education degrees and non-degree programmes. The other autonomous universities within the system (UP Diliman, UP Los Banos, UP Manila, UP Visayas and UP Mindanao) offer only traditional residential programmes. The goal of the new university was to improve access to a UP education, deemed more prestigious than most in a country of numerous tertiary-level institutions. The Diploma in Science Teaching, which originated in the Los Banos campus, was its first programme offering. Initially all programmes were at the post-baccalaureate level and with the exception of the Diploma in Science Teaching, consisted of the transformation to distance mode of existing residential degree programmes. An undergraduate programme was launched in 1997.

The UPOU is currently the most comprehensive distance education provider in the country covering all levels of tertiary education. It consists of four faculties: Education, Management Sciences, Health Sciences, and the combined Faculty of Social Sciences and Humanities/Science and Technology. In all it offers 15 post-baccalaureate programmes: 14 diploma/Master's programmes, one doctoral and one undergraduate programme, the Associate in Arts (Table 3).

Because admission to the undergraduate programme in the UP system is highly competitive and contingent on performance in an admissions exam, undergraduate admission to the UPOU has to conform to the same yardstick. Thus, unlike in most open universities entry to the Associate in Arts is also dependent on each applicant's performance in an assessment test which is designed specially for UPOU applicants. Moreover, to be admitted to the undergraduate level a student must be at least 20 years old and a high school graduate, or have passed the high school equivalency examination.

Enrolment in the UPOU per semester runs to a total of about two thousand students. The undergraduate programme has an enrolment of 157 students. The programmes with the most enrolees are the diploma/Master's teacher training programmes of the Faculty of Education. Another popular course is the Master of Public Management, a programme that attracts mostly government employees. Since 1995, the UPOU has graduated more than one thousand students, the majority of them from the teacher training programmes.

Table 3   Current programme offerings of the UPOU

Faculty	Programme offerings
Faculty of Education	Diploma in Science Teaching Diploma in Mathematics Teaching Diploma/Master in Language Studies Education Diploma/Master in Social Studies Education PhD Science Teaching
Faculty of Health Sciences	Master of Hospital Administration Master of Public Health
Faculty of Management Sciences	Master of Public Management Master of Environment and Natural Resource Management Diploma in Research and Development (R&D) Management
Faculty of Social Sciences and Humanities/Science and Technology	Associate in Arts Diploma in Agriculture Diploma in Computer Science Diploma/Master in Social Work Master of Professional Studies in Development Communication

The UPOU also offers non-formal courses that do not lead to a degree. Two such courses are in entrepreneurship.

Course materials used by the UPOU are mostly print-based, supplemented by audiotape, videotape or CD-ROM-based materials where applicable. The UPOU relies on the human resource potential of the entire UP system as faculty members from all the constituent universities are tapped to write the course materials and to act as faculty-in-charge. By sharing the services of faculty members in the residential units the UPOU is able to keep down the cost of running a fully fledged university. Courses that require laboratory work are conducted in residence. All courses follow a semestral schedule.

Student support consists of monthly tutorial sessions, which can be face-to-face, via telephone (teletutorials) or electronic mail (email). Face-to-face tutorials and teletutorials are held in 26 learning centres located all over the country, from Luzon to Mindanao. A learning centre is also located in Hong Kong. Learning centres are equipped with library materials for the courses as well as communication facilities where there is the available infrastructure (e.g. telephone lines, an Internet connection, etc.). The tutor-student ratio is kept to a maximum of 1:30 and is actually lower in many courses.

Grades in the UPOU are derived from tutor-marked assignments and final examinations graded by the faculty-in-charge. Students sit their final examination in the learning centres. Overall course development and course delivery is patterned after the UK Open University system, an institution with which the UPOU maintains a linkage. An active partnership with the Simon Fraser University in Canada also allows the UPOU to learn from the Canadian experience in ODE. Other institutions with which the UPOU maintains linkages are the Open University of Israel and the Open University of Hong Kong.

In the past year a new unit in the university was created to take charge of development and delivery of courses via the Internet. This initiative puts the UPOU squarely at the forefront of new technologies that further recreate the environment for open and distance learning. Using a platform for course delivery on the Web developed by the National University of Singapore, the UPOU is now moving towards offering more courses online. Among the first to utilize this technology are two courses, Health Informatics and Philippine Art and Popular Culture.

The decision to deliver courses via the Internet is based on the same vision of making a UP education available to students who have access to this technology but who are not able to enrol in residential programmes. This clientele would include Filipinos based abroad. However, it is not envisaged that online course delivery will take the place of print and multimedia materials in the foreseeable future, lest the greater number of students whom the UPOU wants to reach be unduly disadvantaged by the inaccessibility of Internet technology in their places of residence or work.

Prospects for ODE

Of the eight institutions identified and acknowledged by the CHED as having offered ODE programmes before the 1990s, seven remain in operation. Only one other institution has been added to the pre-1990 official list. This list has not expanded so far because the CHED only recently (in December 2000) issued an updated set of policies and guidelines for open learning and distance education country-wide that contain the rules that will guide the operation of institutions offering ODE programmes including the obtaining of the initial permit needed to commence operations. The new guidelines provide for the formation of a Technical Committee that will evaluate the worthiness of any proposed ODE programme at the tertiary level. As the newly formed committee has yet to meet there has been no opportunity so far to ascertain how many applications for permission to operate ODE programmes will be forthcoming.

The issuance of the guidelines is motivated by CHED's concern that ODE will erode even further the quality of tertiary education in the country if allowed to operate unchecked. The perception of CHED is that this delivery system is susceptible to abuse both by clients who want a degree without much effort and by providers who need a market. As the CHED Chair observed in one forum, quality education is difficult enough to ensure in the residential institutions, and ODE can further open the floodgates to spurious degrees obtained via this mode. Unfortunately such a perception is not totally unwarranted.

This kind of situation may be peculiar to the Philippines where almost everyone wants a college degree and practically everyone has a chance to go to college though not necessarily to the institution of their choice. The proliferation of public and private universities offering residential programmes attests to a huge demand for tertiary education. Ultimately, in this buyer's market, institutions that offer ODE programmes will have to convince would-be enrolees that their brand of education will give the same value for money as a residential degree.

Recent developments in information and communication technology in the 1990s have changed the climate for tertiary education in the Asia Pacific region in general giving ODE a boost. Local tertiary-level institutions, whether residential or distance, now face competition from foreign universities that offer courses online thus allowing access to a foreign university minus the costs incurred from actual stay abroad. In the Philippines such developments will probably have less impact than anticipated. While it is true that a degree from a foreign university, especially from an industrialized country will always be regarded more favourably than most locally obtained degrees, a major consideration in opting for online courses from foreign universities will be their relative affordability. Although they are an attractive alternative to studying abroad, not many will be able to afford the fees. In any case, studying abroad has never been a popular alternative for local students because the costs have always been prohibitive and affordable only to a small affluent minority.

Online courses developed and offered locally, however, will become more prevalent as more students become connected to the Internet. The trend will probably go the way of online delivery in American and Canadian universities with residential students given the option to be educated in a mixed mode of residential and ODE courses. The major obstacle in the short term for the widespread adoption of this delivery system is the unequal access to the technology among students and among the various regions and provinces in the country. While some places have full access, others do not even have electricity.

The learning needs in the non-formal, non-degree, continuing education sector is another potential area for growth in ODE. Continuing education in the professions lends itself well to the ODE format, especially those that use online delivery, because the target clientele are more likely to be able to afford the technology requirements of this mode. Moreover, ODE can respond quickly to new learning needs of people already in the workforce and can provide quick updates on cutting-edge developments in the professional fields without the clients being required to leave the workplace to obtain them. The Health Informatics course being developed by the UPOU is a test of health professionals as a clientele for online delivery of continuing education. It is envisioned that the UPOU will develop more courses to cater to the learning needs of this sector.

In charting its future direction a state institution like the UPOU will be guided by its original mission to widen access to its programme offerings and to reach those sectors that would otherwise be unable to obtain a UP education. With this mandate the considerations of market forces will not always be a prime factor in deciding programme offerings. It is assumed that government will subsidize the cost of providing training to such groups as teachers, rural extension workers, government employees, social workers and the like because their skills need to be upgraded in the interests of the nation in general.

Private institutions respond to market forces and will likely offer programmes that are popular and marketable. With the growing desire to venture into ODE among residential colleges and universities and non-traditional education providers, the CHED will have to play a more pro-active role to ensure that the quality of ODE programmes is observed and guaranteed.

References

Felix Librero (1997) *Distance Education in the Philippines: Status and Trends*, country paper presented in the Regional Seminar on Satellite Applications for Distance Education, Manila, Philippines, 9–12 September.

1998 Philippine Statistical Yearbook (1998) Republic of the Philippines: National Statistical Coordination Board.

Continuing Professional Education Primer (1997) Manila, Philippines.

Thailand

Chaiyong Brahmawong

Introduction

The major changes in Thailand's distance education system over the past decade have mainly been related to the use of new telecommunications networks, with greater use of satellite communications and the Internet, and the establishment of new distance education providers using interactive Web-based instructional systems. Most important is the Education Law enacted in 1999 pursuant to Article 40 of Thailand's 1997 Constitution, which now requires the sharing and distribution of telecommunications, radio and television frequencies for education and human development.

In addition to the three distance education providers covered in the 1991 NIME Report, namely Ramkamhang University (RU), Sukhothai Thammathirat Open University (STOU) and the Department of Non-Formal Education (DNFE), two other distance education projects are running: 1) the Klai Kangwon Royal Satellite Project, an educational project offering secondary education via satellite under the initiative of the King of Thailand and operated jointly by the Department of General Education, the Ministry of Education (MOE) and the Education via Satellite Foundation established 5 December 1995; and 2) the Borderless Education Project (BEP), Suranaree University of Technology (SUT) utilizing integrated on-screen interactive (OSI) and Web-based interactive media in the SUT delivery system for students in various educational centres.

Background

Thailand is located in central mainland Southeast Asia. With an area of 514,000 square kilometres, it is bordered by Laos and Myanmar in the north, Laos and Kampuchea in the east, Myanmar and the Andaman Sea in the west, and Malaysia in the south. It has been a constitutional monarchy since 1932.

Thailand has a market economy. In 1999 it had an estimated GDP growth rate of 4.2%. Exports of agro-industrial products and the tourist industry are the major sources of national income. Thailand has a population of 62 million, 43% of which are under 15 years of age, and with an overall growth rate of 1.6%. About 8.5 million people live in the capital, Bangkok, while 90% of Thai people live in rural areas.

The medium of instruction is Thai, which has its own writing system and which, according to ancient inscriptions, was developed 6,665 years ago. Thus it was not derived from Pali and Sanskrit as earlier believed, in fact quite the reverse. Foreign languages are not allowed to be used as a medium of instruction except in international schools and in teaching and learning languages. There are three major dialects: southern, northern and north-eastern. Speakers of one dialect understand the other dialects without much difficulty.

Education

Up to the year 2002, education in Thailand will be handled by three government agencies, with the National Education Commission (NEC) in charge of the national educational plan and educational policies, the MOE in charge of formal, non-formal and vocational education, teacher training, religious affairs and fine arts, and the Ministry of University Affairs in charge of higher education. After 2002, in accordance with the Education Law, all three educational agencies will be incorporated into one organization, the Ministry of Education, Religions and Culture.

Thailand's general educational system follows the 6:3:3 format, i.e. compulsory elementary education (7 to 12): lower secondary education: upper secondary education. Pre-school education is also available for children aged two to five.

Higher education (Bachelor's, Master's and doctorate degrees) is provided by 24 national universities and institutes. There are more than 20 private universities and a number of private colleges. It usually takes four to eight years to complete a Bachelor's degree, two to five years to complete a Master's degree, and two to five years to compete a doctorate. Students with higher vocational certificates or associated degrees may take only two to four years to obtain a Bachelor's degree. Distance education institutions in Thailand allow students to spend from four to 12 years to complete a Bachelor's degree programme.

Teacher training is provided by the faculties of education in national and private universities under the Ministry of University Affairs, and by 36 Rajabhat Institutes in the MOE offering a variety of certificates and first degrees in Education, Management Science, Sciences, Humanities and Communication Arts.

Technical and vocational education are provided by 120 technical colleges and schools in the Department of Vocational Education, and the Rajamangala Institute of Technology (with 30 technical colleges and eight faculties) under the MOE.

Non-formal education is provided by the DNFE under the MOE, which offers functional literacy programmes as well as normal elementary and secondary education programmes via distance learning, and face-to-face schooling.

Communications infrastructure

Thailand has a comprehensive communications infrastructure of domestic satellite services (ThaiCom), radio, television, telephone, postal services, printing and transportation. In 1998 there were more than 523 AM/FM radio stations and more than 30 million radio sets. There are six television networks (Channels 3, 5, 7, 9, 11 and ITV) reaching 15 million television sets covering 90% of populated areas. Pay TV via cable and Ku-band direct broadcasts are available in Bangkok and big cities.

About four million people use domestic and international telephone services, through mobile phones (470, 800, 900MHz and digital GSM, 1800 and 1900MHz) and personal cordless telephones (PCT).

Internet services are provided by 15 Internet service providers (ISPs) nation-wide. There were at least 600,000 users, mostly in Bangkok and big cities, as of mid-2000.

Postal services are very reliable. There are post offices in every district reaching all villages. Postal services are operated by both public and private ventures.

Printing services are available in all parts of the country including high quality gravure and non-impact printing technology.

Institutional framework for distance education

Up to the year 2000, distance education in Thailand has been legally institutionalized in five institutions: RU, STOU, the DNFE, the Klai Kangwon Royal Satellite Project, and the BEP.

The purposes of distance education in Thailand are threefold:

- To provide multiple opportunities for secondary school graduates and working adults to pursue higher education certificates and degrees;

- To meet the increasing demand for continuing, lifelong education for those in the workforce to upgrade the qualify of their life and their professional ability and to keep pace with advances in science and technology;

- To provide non-formal education to those who have not earned elementary and secondary education certificates.

Distance education in Thailand was first developed in 1933 with the establishment of the University of Moral and Political Sciences and further developed by RU in 1971. Distance education was developed and has been implemented at STOU since 1978. The borderless education concept was initiated by SUT in 1996. At the elementary and secondary levels, distance education programmes were started by the DNFE in the early 1950s and the Klai Kangwon Royal Satellite Project in December 1996.

Institutional concepts and formats

The University of Moral and Political Sciences operated with an open admission policy offering a general degree, Bachelor of Thammasart (B.Th) via the so-called 'academic market approach' (*Talard Wicha*) for government employees and the general public to work towards degrees in law and business administration. Students bought texts and handouts for self study or attended classes on campus. There were no special distance education courses for home-based students. The university became a conventional university and was renamed Thammasart University in 1957, at which time entrance examinations were required for admission.

RU, with an academic market policy originally modelled after the University of Moral and Political Sciences, was established as a public university by Royal Charter on 26 February 1971 to serve the needs of secondary schools leavers. Its distance learning approach included producing better texts and using radio/television programmes for direct teaching. RU is an open-admission institution providing a triple-mode instructional system to three groups of students: class-attending students; home-based distance learning students; and mixed type students both attending classes and studying by themselves.

Since 1996, RU has expanded its services to provincial students by establishing Regional Academic Resources Centres (RARC) in different parts of the country. Teaching and learning activities in each RARC are supported by videoteleconferencing systems with two-way communications links to the main campus in Bangkok.

The DNFE began its distance education programmes via radio correspondence programmes for home-based students who had not completed elementary or secondary school. Presently, the DNFE's distance education activities have expanded to cover the needs of all groups of students. This is aimed at providing opportunities for people to study for elementary and secondary education certificates.

In 1996 the DNFE established the Education via ThaiCom Satellite Foundation, with an initial investment donated by the Shinnawatra Corporation, the then concession operator of Thailand's domestic satellite. The Foundation provided a Ku-band channel for an Educational Television Station (ETV) operated by the Centre for Educational Technology. It also donated a number of Ku-band receiving disks for the DNFE's Provincial Non-Formal Education Centres. The ETV broadcasts educational programmes nation-wide for various non-formal education groups.

In addition to the ETV station, the DNFE broadcasts radio programmes via Radio Thailand Education Network and broadcasts its TV programmes via the Department of Public Relations' Channel 11.

SUT, the first autonomous university in Thailand, was established on 27 July 1990 as a state-owned but non-governmental university of science and technology in Nakorn Rachasima Province (Korat) located 254 kilometres north-east of Bangkok. SUT began its distance education project in 1996 aiming at providing education to remote students in its Education Centres initially commencing in Udorn Thani and Buriram provinces using OSI and Web-based instruction as the core media, supplemented by print, audio-visual media and telecommunications.

The BEP has begun to produce the first sets of 46 courses. In the year 2002, the first batch of 300 BEP students will begin their studies in Udorn Thani

Education Centre, about 300 kilometres north-east of Korat, and 300 BEP students in Buriram Education Centre will begin in the following year. A total 313 courses will be offered via the BEP by 2010.

The Klai Kangwon Royal Satellite Project was a royal initiative marking His Majesty the King's 68th anniversary. The Project is located at Klai Kangwon School, a royal patronage school established within the compound of Klai Kangwon Summer Palace in Hua Hin District, Prajuab Kirikhan Province. The Project is operated jointly by the Distance Education via Satellite Foundation and the Department of General Education. The Project received technical support for installation of direct-to-home (DTH) TV stations mainly from Shinnawatra Satellite Corporation (operator of ThaiCom satellite) and the Telephone Organization of Thailand (TOT). Shinnawatra Satellite Corporation provided six Ku-band channels, transmitters, control rooms and equipment for classroom studios capable of live broadcasting six instructional programmes for Matayom Suksa 1 to 6 (Grades 7 to 12) simultaneously to 1,400 participating secondary schools. The TOT provides signal linkage via optical fibre from Hua Hin to Nontaburi where TV signals are linked to ThaiCom for direct broadcasting to homes and schools. The Klai Kangwon's six Ku-band programmes are also broadcast via Thailand's only cable TV provider (UBC) reaching more than 200,000 homes in Bangkok and regional major cities.

Student profile

Distance education students' profiles vary according to the level of educational institution. For elementary and secondary education under the DNFE, students are mostly young professionals, aged 18 and over, pursuing certificates at three levels of secondary education: Sixth Grade Certificate (Elementary), 10th Grade Certificate (Secondary) and 12th Grade Certificate (Secondary). The DNFE has established study centres within existing secondary schools and factories. Face-to-face tutorials are held regularly at the designated centres. Students also view TV programmes via ETV Channel broadcasts on a Ku-band satellite station operated by the DNFE's Centre for Educational Technology.

Students in the Klai Kangwon Royal Satellite Project are regular students in more than four thousand secondary schools mostly in the provincial areas. Lessons are broadcast via six Ku-band satellite channels from Klai Kangwon School.

There are two groups of RU students: 1) secondary school graduates who failed the entrance examinations to campus-based universities of their choice; and 2) working adults young and old. Students may also be categorized into three groups: campus-based, home-based and mixed.

- Campus-based students are those who attend classes at one of the two campuses in Bangkok. Some wear student uniforms and form informal discussion or tutoring groups within the campus. In the provincial areas these mostly graduate students attend videoteleconferencing sessions at RARCs.

- RU's home-based students rarely attend classes on campus. They are the real distance education students who study mainly from texts purchased on campus and TV programmes broadcast via Channel 11.

- The mixed group of RU students are those who occasionally attend classes on campus but mostly study at home or at their workplace.

STOU students are mostly working adults categorized into three groups: degree, non-degree or certificate students. Degree students work towards a Bachelor's degree or a Master's degree in one of 12 schools (Liberal Arts, Education, Management Sciences, Law, Economics, Home Economics, Health Science, Nursing, Political Science, Agricultural Extension and Cooperatives, Communication Arts, and Science and Technology. As of 2000, Master's degrees are being offered in the School of Education and include Economics, Management Sciences, Home Economics, and Agricultural Extension and Cooperatives.

Bachelor's degree programmes are four-year programmes offered to students with secondary education certificates and two-year degree programmes offered to students with Higher Vocational Certificates (five years vocational education after secondary schools) or associated degrees. Non-degree students work for a one-year certificate and a semester-based single certificate of achievement. A one-year certificate programme requires each student to study for two semesters to complete 36 to 40 credits, while a single-certificate of achievement (SCA) is granted to anyone registered on a five-credit or six-credit course who passes the final examination. Applications may be made to convert accumulated SCA courses to a regular degree programme.

SUT, the first autonomous university in Thailand, plans to admit its first batch of undergraduate students in the Institutes of Engineering, Social Technology, Agricultural Technology, Sciences, and Natural Resources under the BEP in 2002. Students will study via OSI using video-teleconferencing and computer-assisted instruction (CAI) and / or Web-based instruction at education centres in Udorn Thani and Burirum Province. OSI and CAI are augmented by print media (in the form of study guides, comprehensive texts and course bulletins), audio-visual media and telecommunications.

Enrolment patterns

Enrolment patterns are different among students of various distance education/open learning institutions.

DNFE students apply for admission once a year in May at designated provincial secondary schools, factories, workplace-based study centres or Provincial Non-Formal Education Centres. Once admitted, they register and take courses according to the programme of study designed by the DNFE.

For the Klai Kangwon Royal Satellite Project, regular students enrol in secondary education courses offered via satellite by Klai Kangwon School. The programmes are not available to the general public, although broadcast programmes via satellite are re-run or simultaneously broadcast via cable TV.

Students are enrolled at RU once a year and begin their first semester in the first week of June. About 100,000 students are admitted each year, mostly secondary school graduates, without taking entrance examinations.

Students at STOU apply for admission during January and May. After being admitted, they begin their first semester on 1 July and the second semester on 16 December. Orientation sessions are conducted for new students in the last week of June. Although undergraduate and certificate students are not required to take an entrance examination, the selection of graduate students is based on the qualifications, proposed work plans and research projects indicated in their application forms.

SUT will admit 600 secondary school graduates enrolled in undergraduate courses in the Institutes of their choice, 300 each for the Udorn Thani Education Centre and the Buriram Education Centre.

Geographic spread

Distance education in Thailand is offered to students nation-wide.

The DNFE offers distance education courses to young adults at its Provincial and District Non-Formal Education Centres and study centres located in selected factories and workplaces.

The Klai Kangwon Royal Satellite Project offers access to secondary schools in remote areas as well as participating private schools located in Bangkok and other parts of the country.

RU provides access to half a million students in the north, north-east, central and southern areas of Thailand.

90% of STOU's students live in rural areas. STOU has established nine Regional Distance Education Centres (located nation-wide in Nakorn Nayok, Nakorn Sawan, Ubol Rachathani, Udorn Thani, Lampang, Sukhothai, Petchaburi, Nakorn Srithammarat, and Yala) to act as coordinating centres for library, information services, counselling and guidance, OSI and Web-based instruction, Internet, seminars and workshops for undergraduate and graduate students.

SUT also has plans to establish Border Education Centres (BEC) nation-wide. Although initial projects have been set up at Udorn Thani and Buriram, more BECs are planned for the north, the central region and the south. Existing regional universities such Walailak University in Nakorn Srithammarat Province and the Princess Mother University (Mae Faluang University) also have plans to join SUT's BEP via UniNet, a telecommunications network launched by the Ministry of University Affairs.

Manpower requirements

Thailand's 8th Economic and Social Development Plan stated manpower development to be a top priority. Distance education is considered the most economical and effective way to provide education and training to a large number of learners in a short period of time.

The most urgent requirements for manpower development are in the area of educational reform in compliance with Thailand's Education Law.

The Office of Educational Reform, an ad hoc organization to last only three years (from 2000 to 2002) established under a special provision of the Education Law, plans to provide short-course training for more than 600,000 administrators and teachers to prepare them for the educational reforms. Delivery of training will be by distance.

According to the Law, all teachers and administrators at elementary and secondary educational level are required to be qualified for their positions. Distance education is the only way to provide timely training to provide half a million teachers and administrators with these qualifications.

With the advancement of distance education technologies, especially information technology and the Internet, and the need for personnel in the public and private sectors to upgrade their knowledge and skills without having to leave their work, distance education is considered the most effective alternative for personnel in the public and private sectors to attain knowledge and experience that will enable them to keep pace with the changing world.

Aside from the use of traditional, face-to-face techniques, many colleges and universities are seriously planning to make use of distance learning approaches such as Web-based or online computer-based instruction for home-based students. Thus it appears that the number of dual-mode distance learning providers in Thailand is set to grow.

Curriculum content

Although distance education has proven effective in many countries as an alternative to providing science and technology-based courses, curriculum content provided via distance learning in Thailand is mostly in the area of the social sciences. The exceptions are the science and technology programmes offered at STOU and technology-based programmes to be offered by the BEP in 2002.

STOU's School of Science and Technology offers two two-year degree programmes: Printing Technology and Business Information Technology. There are three course levels: basic (theory), practical, and professional experience. Students at the basic level study at home via print-based distance learning packages and partly by CAI via the Internet. Students at the practical level are required to do certain practical work exercises at home via computer following guidelines in a tutorial manual. They are then required to join a four-day intensive workshop at STOU's main campus in Park Kred, Nontaburi or at an affiliated computer centre in other colleges or universities. Students at the professional level are required to attend a six-day professional experience enrichment workshop to do practical work in simulated labs or real labs set up for each type of skill required of them before their graduation. SUT's BEP plans to offer courses in engineering, science and technology at its education centres.

Courses of study

Courses of study include certificates and undergraduate and postgraduate degrees.

Certificate programmes cover one-year programmes and a single-course certificate of achievement. All distance learning institutions offer certificate programmes.

Undergraduate degree programmes include four-year Bachelor's degree programmes for secondary school graduates and two-year Bachelor's degree programmes for students with higher certificates (two-year vocational programmes after secondary education), associated degrees and Bachelor's degrees.

Postgraduate degrees offered via distance education include doctorate and Master's degrees. STOU offers some doctorate programmes through cooperation with Charles Sturt University in Australia and plans to offer a joint doctorate degree with the University of Minnesota in the US.

Master's degree programmes via distance learning are available only at STOU. RU and SUT offer Master's degree programmes via face-to-face instruction. At STOU, nine Master's degree programmes are offered: six in the School of Education; one in Economics; one in Management Sciences; one in Home Economics; and one in Agricultural Extension and Cooperatives.

Teaching staff

Academic staff in colleges and universities generally have to fulfil four basic roles: teaching, research, providing professional services to the community, and upholding the national cultural heritage, culture and tradition.

In the areas of distance education, the roles of teaching staff vary according to the type of distance learning institution. For an open admission university such as RU, teaching staff spend most of their time teaching class-based students. Although class attendance is not compulsory, nearly 60,000 students come to the campus and attend face-to-face lectures.

For an open education university such as STOU, as no regular classrooms are permitted, the academic staff conduct their teaching by writing self-learning units and modules, joining radio and TV programmes as either moderators or resource persons, conducting tutorial sessions, writing the final examinations for each of their designated self-learning units or modules, and coordinating final examinations at local study centres nation-wide.

Learning support services and study centres

Presently, only RU and STOU maintain their own main campuses and study centres. The learning support services needed at the main campus will vary according to the type of distance learning institution. STOU and RU provide regional and provincial study centres. The DNFE, on the other hand, has its own community learning centres in all provinces.

Ramkamhang University

At RU, large classrooms or lecture halls are needed for face-to-face instruction. CCTV systems are installed in big lecture halls. In addition, sound and TV production studios, videoteleconferencing studios and Internet servers are installed to provide online and offline services to homes and RU's RARCs.

RU's second campus is at Tung Sethi in Samut Prakarn province and has RARCs nation-wide. The RARCs offer classrooms, two-way full duplex videoteleconferencing systems linking the RARC to RU's main campus at Hua Mark and Tung Sethi campus, Internet access, and library services. The RARCs provide administrative and counselling services to students who are not able to come to the main campus in Bangkok. RU does not operate provincial study centres, although some informal student clubs are established in some provinces.

Sukhothai Thammathirat Open University

At STOU, learning support services comprise seminar centres and accommodation for students at STOU's headquarters so as to enable them to attend practical workshops and professional experience intensive workshops. Three seminar centres can accommodate up to 500 students at one time. Halls and rooms are available for small-group discussion. In addition, the Office of Educational Technology provides six radio studios and four TV production studios for producing radio and TV programmes as supplemental media for STOU's distance learning packages. The microwave link is available to transmit radio and TV signals from STOU to Channel 11 and Radio Thailand Education Network, and to Ku-band satellite stations of the Klai Kangwon Royal Satellite Project.

STOU's Regional Distance Education Centre (RDEC) or RARC learning support services include a library, Internet access, tutorial and seminar rooms, satellite downlink, and counselling services.

STOU's local study centres are provincial study centres located at a provincial secondary school in each province. Learning support services provided by the host school include a classroom for tutorials and seminars, a rest area for instructors/tutors from STOU, and book corners where texts from STOU can be deposited.

Department of Non-Formal Education

The DNFE does not have its own campus. Thus, teaching and learning take place at regional and local study centres. The operating units are established at various secondary schools and selected factories where learners from all walks of life can enrol as DNFE students.

The DNFE's regional study centres are in the form of Regional Community Learning Centres (RCLC). Each RCLC acts as the central administrative and service provider. Each educational region coordinates its activities though the DNFE's study centres.

Local study centres are lower operational levels of CLC divided into three levels: provincial, district and village.

Suranaree University of Technology

Most face-to-face and master classrooms are located on SUT's main campus in Korat. Instruction is via OSI videoteleconferencing and Web-based instruction at SUT's education centres.

SUT's local study centres are education centres (a type of IT campus under the IT networking policy) established in Udorn Thani and Buriram provinces for the BEP. At both centres, students are linked to SUT's main campus by OSI videoconferencing and Web-based instruction.

Student assessment

Student assessment in Thailand's distance education institutions, with the exception of a few practical work-oriented programmes, are mainly paper-based examinations. RU, STOU, DNFE and SUT students in most courses must sit a final examination at a designated study centre. However, in certain courses, practical work accounts for 30% to 40% of assessment and students are required to submit project reports and written assignments as part of assessment requirements within these programmes.

Under the new Education Law, actual professional experience may be considered eligible for transfer as credits in all colleges and universities.

Programme management and quality assurance

The management of all study programmes is carried out by individual distance learning institutions under the policy and guidelines set forth by the MOE (for the DNFE) and the Ministry of University Affairs (for RU, STOU and SUT), which will become the remit of the Ministry of Education, Religions and Culture formed from these three organizations after 2002.

Quality assurance is the top priority issue in Thailand's higher education system. All colleges and universities are encouraged to develop their own quality assurance systems and are supported in this endeavour by guidelines and provisions laid down by the Ministry of University Affairs.

Financing distance education

All of Thailand's distance education institutions, with the exception of SUT, are self-funded. The government budget is mainly allocated for salary and construction costs and basic infrastructure. Funds are mostly collected from student tuition fees, endowments and income from selling books, radio and television programmes, and other instructional materials.

STOU receives only 20% to 25% of its annual budget from the government. RU receives about 60% of its annual budget from public funds.

SUT, as an autonomous university, receives nearly 90% of its annual budget from the government in the form of a block-grant and manages its own finance under the supervision of its Financial Committee. Student fees account for less than 10% of SUT's annual budget amount.

The DNFE is principally funded by tuition fees from, according to the DNFE's claim, nearly 30 million learners. The MOE's contribution mainly goes towards the salaries and wages of instructors and service personnel.

The Klai Kangwon Royal Satellite Project receives around THB125 million to THB200 million annually (US$2.8 million to US$4.6 million) from the Department of Secondary Education in operational funds and donations from the private sector.

Technologies for distance education

The technology used in distance education falls into three categories: print-based, broadcast-based and computer-based.

Since 1980, STOU has been employing the print-based approach in which print materials and audio cassettes are used as core media supplemented by radio programmes, TV programmes, limited CAI, and face-to-face tutorials. The new STOU Plan 2000 was designed to offer the dual-track print-based and Web-based instruction so that it can reach a wider range of students.

RU operates all three for its three groups of students: class-based, home-based and mixed structure. Class-based students attend large lecture halls equipped with CCTV and audio-visual aids to enable the instructor to reach thousands of students at the same time. Home-based students use self-study texts supplemented by directed teaching television and radio programmes.

As mentioned, SUT plans to use a computer-based approach making use of OSI and CAI and Web-based instruction supplemented by print materials (study guides, comprehensive course synopsis and course bulletins), audio-visual media and telecommunications media (fax, telephone, mobile phones, etc.). Videoteleconferencing systems and Web servers will also be established. SUT has already signed with Philips (Thailand) for the turn-key establishment of a Digital Multimedia Production Centre to be used by the BEP.

The DNFE teaching and learning system makes use of both broadcast programmes and interest groups. Radio programmes are broadcast via Radio Thailand Education Network and television programmes are broadcast via the ETV Channel on UBC's Ku-band satellite network.

The Klai Kangwon Royal Satellite Project operates under the broadcast-based approach. TV lessons are broadcast via six Ku-band channels from Klai Kangwon Secondary School and reach more than 3,000 schools, mostly in the remote areas.

International collaboration

All distance education institutions in Thailand work in collaboration with international agencies, in particular UNESCO and RIHED.

The UNESCO Principal Regional Office for Asia and the Pacific, located in Bangkok, plays a major role in promoting distance education in the region.

RIHED (SEAMEO), UNESCO and certain distance education institutions such as STOU are planning to set up the Mekong Delta Virtual University Project to provide access to education to people of Mekong Delta member countries.

Priorities for policy and national direction

Thailand's priority now is developing programmes and curricula, setting up an infrastructure and central organization for technologies for education, innovating more effective distance education approaches, and providing appropriate educational environments and contexts for use by distance education institutions and their students.

Developing programmes and curricula appropriate for delivery via distance education is the most urgent priority, especially in the areas of science and technology. Since Thailand is in urgent need of more scientists and technologists, distance education, with the support of IT and computer technology, can be an effective tool to produce a large number of educated and qualifed personnel in science and technology within a short period of time.

Such a system needs to run within a well-designed and adequate infrastructure. To make this a reality an autonomous organization to support technologies for distance education, such as the National Institute of Technologies for Education (NITE), needs to be established that will incorporate the use of educational technologies, mass communications, IT, telecommunications, and learning resources for education, religions and cultures.

Educational technology must not be viewed as mere media in education. It should consider and embrace the full range of current and future approaches and system design, the performance of instructors and learners, methods and techniques for delivery and teaching, communications processes and necessary media, educational environments management of the system, and methods for effective evaluation and improvement.

Distance education is not just a way of education in which learners and teachers are physically distant. More effective distance education approaches suitable to Thailand's diversified needs and cultures must be developed to better serve the needs of learners nation-wide.

Most important of all is the provision of an appropriate educational environment for use by distance education institutions and their students. Distance education policy-makers need to ensure that a viable infrastructure becomes an integral part of Thailand's distance education system.

Viet Nam

Bernadette Robinson, Le Van Than and Tran Duc Vuong

Introduction

Education in Viet Nam engaged in a process of change and reform at all levels throughout the 1990s, a trend which is set to continue in the 21st century.

The 1990s saw new policy development and legislation for education, a re-statement of the Education Law, an expansion of access and participation, improvement in quality and a new inflow of international funds and assistance in support. The changes were driven by three main forces:

1 Recognition of the limitations of the existing education curriculum and system for a market-oriented economy and for competition in a global economy.

2 A concern to improve the quality as well as quantity of provision.

3 The achievements of other Asian countries in both education and economic development.

While aiming to modernize its educational system in line with international standards, the government of Viet Nam is still concerned with marrying new influences and developments with cultural and socialist values. The Education Law defines Vietnamese education as 'a socialist education with popular, national, scientific and modern characteristics, based on Marxism-Leninism and Ho Chi Minh thought' (The Education Law of the Socialist Republic of Viet Nam 1999, Article 3.1).

Open and distance education (ODE) has played a role in these changes, though it is difficult to quantify it for two reasons: problems in defining 'open and distance learners' in the Vietnamese context, and limitations in available data. In Viet Nam, the term 'open learning' has a very particular meaning that is different to its meaning in international literature and practice, where it generally refers to a set of values relating to the removal of barriers to learning and access, flexibility of provision, choice on the part of the learner and provision of resources to support learning. In Vietnamese, 'open learning' translates as *dao tao mo rong, dao tao* meaning 'training', and *mo rong* meaning 'expansion' or 'extension'. Between 1989 and 1994, institutions were permitted to admit, on a cost-recovery basis, more students than officially approved. These students did not qualify for 'regular' admission, paid higher fees and were described as 'extra plan' or 'open study mode' students. Though the system has changed somewhat the meaning has carried over. The term 'distance education', *dao tao tu xa*, is used loosely in Viet Nam to refer to several arrangements of teaching and learning. These include courses where teachers are sent to distant locations to provide face-to-face teaching sessions, courses where a student registers with an institution then studies through 'self learning' (*tu hoc*) either with or without learning materials being provided, the provision of educational radio or television programmes, or part-time courses providing summer schools of face-to-face teaching in between periods of 'self learning'. 'ODE' in Viet Nam places a heavy reliance on face-to-face teaching and the teaching approaches, curriculum and methodology are close to those found in traditional institutions.

With these definitions in mind, this chapter addresses three main questions:

1   What role does ODE play in education and training in Viet Nam at present?

2   What developments have there been during the 1990s?

3   What direction is ODE likely to take in Viet Nam in the future?

We begin by locating ODE in the context of Viet Nam and outlining its development.

Viet Nam in transition

The Socialist Republic of Viet Nam is in Southeast Asia and borders on China, Laos and Cambodia. It covers 330,363 square kilometres and has a varied terrain (mountains, plains, river deltas and islands). In 1999, the population was 77 million with an average growth rate of 1.6% in the 1990s. About 45% of the population is under the age of 15 years. Viet Nam is largely an agricultural economy, with 77% of the population living in rural areas. It is the third most densely populated country in Southeast Asia, after Singapore and the Philippines, with an average density of 231 people per square kilometre. This distribution is very uneven, with 75% of people concentrated in the Mekong Delta in the south and the Red River Delta in the north.

The average annual income was about US$330 per capita in 1999, yet Viet Nam's human development indicators are higher than might be expected from its income levels. Literacy rates were 94% (91% female) in 1999. Primary school enrolment rates (net) in 1998 were 90.7% for males and 92.1% for females. Lower secondary school enrolment was 62.1% for females and 61.3% for males, and upper secondary level was 27.4% for females and 30.0% for males. Government expenditure on education is about 9% of its total annual expenditure though the intention is to increase this as the economy progresses. Poverty levels have declined, though there is a widening rural-urban gap and most of the poor are rural. There are 53 ethnic minorities (about 13% of the population), living mainly in mountainous and rural areas. The main minority groups are Chinese, Muong, Khmer, Tai, Miao and Cham. Vietnamese is the official language though generally used by minority groups as a second language. English was introduced into secondary schools after 1990 to replace Russian as the major foreign language and during the 1990s the government ran a programme to retrain 2,000 teachers of Russian to teach English.

The transport and communications infrastructure is limited but being improved. Transport is a key ingredient of rural economic development and is a conduit for services such as health and education (including distance education where communications technology is limited). At present it does not reach all rural areas (World Bank 1999a). Vehicle operating costs are nearly twice those in countries with well-developed roads, largely because of high levels of wear-and-tear caused by poor quality surfaces. Three-quarters of the rural population does not have year-round access to all-weather roads and more than half have no access to electricity (World Bank 2000). Viet Nam's telecommunications sector lags behind that of many other countries in Southeast Asia even though during the 1990s all provincial switchboards were digitized and fibre-optic and microwave transmission systems extended to all provinces from Hanoi, Danang and Ho Chi Minh City (HCM City).

Viet Nam has spent the last two decades recovering from thirty years of war. The struggle for north-south re-unification was driven by a socialist ideology, which led to the establishment of a centralized command economy. The period since 1976 has been characterized by efforts to rebuild the country and its economy, and to provide education as a route to development. This has not been easy, especially with a lengthy US-led oil and trade embargo in 1975 and, until the end of the 1980s, separate education systems for the north and south.

The 1990s have seen Viet Nam move towards a 'socialist market-oriented economy'. The process began in 1986 with the *doi moi* ('renovation' and 'open door') macroeconomic reforms followed by a period of rapid economic growth (World Bank 1997a; World Bank 1998). GDP grew at an annual average rate of around 8% between 1990 and 1997, inflation was reduced to single figures, per capita income increased by over 5% each year and agricultural production doubled (Viet Nam moved from being an importer of rice to becoming the world's second-largest exporter). This was accompanied by increases in development indicators (life expectancy, literacy, real incomes, health and nutrition, gender equity, participation in education, material well-being and poverty reduction). Ownership of consumer durables has increased, so that in 1999, 47% of households owned a radio, 58% a television, and 76% a bicycle (Viet Nam Development Report 2000, 7). The country has gradually opened up and is now linked to the global economy though it still faces formidable challenges in maintaining the pace of economic progress.

Doi moi also resulted in some education policy changes. These permitted the establishment of private institutions, promoted 'people-founded' and community education centres, encouraged non-formal education and self-instructional activities and established greater cost sharing (Sinh and Sloper 1995). Three kinds of financing of educational institutions resulted from these policy changes: public, private (*tu lap*) and 'semi-public' or people-founded (*ban cong*). The public institutions are fully funded and operated by the state, though in practice can and do charge fees from learners or parents. The private institutions receive no funding from the state and are run by private groups. In 'semi-public' institutions, the facilities, equipment and curriculum are provided by the state while operating costs, teachers' salaries and maintenance are financed by student fees. The use of family or personal finance for education has become common in Viet Nam, even when students attend public institutions. Viet Nam's two open universities are funded differently, one as a public institution (Hanoi Open University) and one as a semi-public institution (Ho Chi Minh City Open University). Though it still reflects characteristics of a command economy (strong centralization, control of the curriculum and strict compliance with policy) the system of education (*giao duc*) and training (*dao tao*) is changing in line with reforms initiated during the early 1990s.

The development of open and distance education in Viet Nam

ODE was introduced to Viet Nam in 1960. In the first phase of its development between 1960 and 1988, ODE mainly took the form of correspondence courses, evening classes and part-time courses provided by state institutions. Its purpose was to meet the country's needs for economists, technicians, skilled workers and teachers generated by the government's first Five-Year Plan (1960). In-service courses, part-time courses and evening classes for workers were provided at factories, offices and workplaces by different ministries. Courses were provided in Hanoi by the Polytechnic Institute, the Teacher Training College and the Economics and Finance College. During the war period (1965 to 1975), despite the disruption caused, local centres for part-time education were established in most of the provinces in northern Viet Nam. After 1975 and re-unification, several provinces in the south (HCM City, Minh Hai, Ben Tre, Nghia Binh and Binh Tri Thein) also set up part-time courses based on local centres. The curricula and teaching methods were the same as for the formal education system though the courses offered some flexibility. Learners needed nomination and approval by the authorities and were supported financially by the government; often their work organizations or agricultural cooperatives paid the costs involved. Learners had no fees to pay and their incentives for taking the course were usually a pay increase or advancement at work or a requirement that they took the course.

The creation of Viet Nam's second Five-Year Plan (its implementation delayed by the war) aimed at reconstructing the country. Education tried to cater to a wide range of needs, including around half a million demobilized soldiers. However, the efforts were directed towards too many targets, and were too heavily subsidized and centralized to be effective. To remedy this, major education reforms were initiated in 1979, including new methods of teaching (the idea of student-centred education was introduced at this time). In 1986, influenced by the radical changes to communism taking place in other countries, Viet Nam introduced new policies and reforms, centring on the notion of *doi moi* (renovation) and an 'open door' policy. This led to the expansion of educational opportunity and greater diversification of forms of education, including ODE.

In Viet Nam ODE is classified as 'non-formal education', and from 1986, as the private economic sector and foreign investment grew, people of any age were allowed by the Ministry of Education and Training to take 'non-formal' courses. At the same time, traditional institutions were allowed to admit students in addition to the official government quotas for higher fee payment as 'extra plan' or 'open mode' students. This led to a rapid rise in numbers. Entry to ODE courses was generally by competitive entry, with about 50% of applicants admitted and completion rates of 45% to 50% (Tran Dinh Tan 1991). The total number of students completing ODE courses between 1960 and 1990 was 662,833 at post-secondary level and 275,475 at secondary level (a detailed breakdown of numbers by year is not available on record). From 1989 to 1990, 38,842 students were enrolled in diploma-level open learning courses and 6,000 more took correspondence plus videotape courses. In addition, an estimated 700,000 more were described as taking part in distance education as audiences of radio and television programmes (Tran Dinh Tan 1991).

By 1990, 26 provincial distance education centres existed, set up by provincial People's Committees and recognized by the Ministry of Higher Education. Finance was provided mainly by the provincial People's Committees and the cooperatives and organizations that sent its workers to the centres for courses. Each centre had a director, teaching staff and assistants who monitored activities or helped to made contracts with universities for teaching services. They supported the visiting lecturers and made arrangements for the examinations held by the contracted universities. Foreign language teaching was a major focus as a means of gaining access to technological information. Distance education centres were also set up in industrial areas, such as the Da River power plant, Hongai coal mine, Thay Nguyen steel factory and Lao Chai Apatit mine.

Distance education provision in universities and provincial centres was supervised by the Department of Distance Education in the Ministry of Education and Training, and played a significant role in expanding access to education and training. 'Distance education' courses were offered by 53 universities and 73 secondary vocational colleges (Arger and Tran Dinh Tan 1990). The curricula and teaching methods were similar to those of formal courses. Typically, lecturers travelled to regional distance education centres for concentrated periods of time to give face-to-face classes. Some printed materials and assignments were left for students to complete between visits by lecturers. Not much was provided in the way of specially prepared learning materials or local support.

Open and distance education in the 1990s

ODE provided valuable additional access to learning throughout the 1980s, but the system had weaknesses. It was fragmented and varied in quality. No one centre had responsibility for the development of ODE or for acting as a centre of expertise or materials development. The limitations were described by contemporary observers as follows:

'The enrolment ceiling is low, the range of courses is limited, and the dropout rate is 50%. Rectors of participating colleges are often too busy managing on-campus courses to pay much attention to correspondence courses, and they are not inclined to upgrade the content and method of teaching in correspondence courses because of the time and labor needed … Students learning at a distance have to go a long way to reach the colleges where face-to-face teaching is provided. Many cannot afford the time and costs involved and eventually drop out' (Arger and Tran Dinh Tan 1990).

To remedy this situation, the Viet Nam People's Open University was set up by the Ministry of Higher Education and approved by the Central People's Committee. In 1988, this became the only institution in Viet Nam offering distance education and was renamed the Viet Nam National Institute of Open Learning (VNIOL). By the early 1990s, it was operating two divisions, one in Hanoi, the other in HCM City, and with 22 study centres in the provinces. Radio and television programmes were introduced in collaboration with the State Radio and Television Centre. These two divisions eventually became the Open Universities of Hanoi and HCM City in 1993. By 1995, they had 52,582 students, 14.8% of the total higher education enrolment or about one in seven of all higher education students. Fewer than half of these were studying through distance education.

Since 1993, ODE has been used to meet changing labour market needs and unmet demand for higher education, though ODE providers are not allowed to duplicate the course offerings provided by traditional universities. The market economy has generated new motivations to learn, either for advancement in the workplace or for change of occupation. ODE has also been used as a resource by some students at traditional universities, who simultaneously enrol in open university courses in order to add computing and English language skills to their degree subjects, in preparation for a competitive job market on graduation.

Higher education

Higher education in general in Viet Nam expanded enormously in the 1990s, rising from 124,484 students in 1991 to over 750,000 (full-time equivalents, 850,000 individual students) in 1999, at over a hundred universities and colleges. Entrance is by examination and capacity is still insufficient to meet demand. One consequence is that the pressure on institutions created by the expansion is causing concerns about quality. There are five categories of higher education students in Viet Nam (World Bank 1997b, 23): regular full-time (*sinh vien chinh quy dai han*); 'short-term training' (*ngan han chuyen tu*) taking upgrading courses, usually full-time, to degree level following a diploma qualification; graduates taking specialized or retraining courses (*boi duong va dao tao lai*); in-service training (*tai chuc*), usually civil servants on part-time courses; and a group referred to as 'other' (*khac*), which includes open universities and those taking ODE courses. ODE for higher education has not expanded at the same rate as traditional forms, though provision has grown since 1991.

In 1999, apart from the two open universities, ten institutions provided distance education: Hué University, Hanoi National University, Hanoi Pedagogical University, Hanoi Foreign Languages College, Hanoi Foreign Language Teachers College, the College of Culture, the National Economics University, Danang University and the College of Foreign Trade. Some courses are small-scale, in limited subject areas or pilot courses, while others are substantial. Hué University established a Distance Education Centre in 1995, providing courses in law, business studies and education, which had around 11,000 students by 1999 (2,500 of these were part of a Belgian-funded teacher education project). Hanoi Pedagogical University provides part-time courses for around 7,000 teachers (1,500 of them part of a Belgian-funded project). The National Economics University offers a Diploma and Master's level course in economics in collaboration with the School of African and Oriental Studies (SOAS), London University, UK. This programme was created in the UK and first presented in English in Viet Nam, though gradually adapted to local conditions, and provided in the Vietnamese language. After initial experience as students of it, staff at the National Economics University took over its local support, management and administration, establishing a network of experienced Vietnamese staff who could act as tutors and explain the meaning in Vietnamese of technical English terms in economics. As a result, a Distance Learning Centre was established at the National Economics University, with core staff trained in the UK.

Overall, an increasing number of international linkages are being built in the field of ODE, with UK and Australian universities, the University of Quebec, Canada, the Sukothai Thammathirat Open University, Thailand, and with Asian open universities, among others.

The open universities

The two open universities, one servicing the north and one the south, were established in 1993 out of existing institutions and structures. Hanoi Open University (HOU) is a public institution in the north:

'a university which is concerned with training and researching all modes of education including distance education, face-to-face education etc. in order to meet variable learning needs of the people contributing to increasing the scientific and technical potentiality of the country' (The Prime Minister on establishing the Hanoi Open University, Decision code 535/Ttg).

The university has eight faculties, offering courses in business management, accounting, information technology, bio-technology, industrial design, English language, telecommunications, law, fashion design, accounting and architecture. More courses are planned. In 1996/97, of HOU's 26,074 students, 13,248 were taking distance education courses in business management, English, accountancy and information technology (Ministry of Education and Training). There are three categories of students: full time, part-time (both taught in face-to-face classes) and distance. The degree-level courses are strictly controlled and supervised by the Ministry of Education and Training (MoET). Before providing a course, the curriculum content has to be formally approved by MoET; usually the distance education courses follow the content and standards of conventional courses. HOU comes under the control of both the Higher Education Department within MoET and the Department of Continuing Education (unlike the traditional universities) because it is seen to provide non-formal education. In July 1998, HOU was allocated 2,000 places in the national university entrance examinations for the first time, taking students qualified to enter traditional universities but unable to get a place.

Ho Chi Minh City Open University (HCMCOU) is a semi-public institution in the south. It has eight faculties teaching foreign languages, business management, bio-technology, Southeast Asia studies, rural industry, women's studies, journalism and law. In 1999, 17,000 students were enrolled, including 5,000 students taking distance courses.

Both open universities receive less government funding than traditional universities. HOU receives around 10% of its budget, HCMCOU around 5%; traditional universities receive about 50%.

Teacher education

Many teachers have upgraded their qualification levels through ODE in Viet Nam. The teaching force, especially at primary school level, has a wide range of educational qualifications, from those with seven years of basic education (or less) and two years of teacher training to a minority with 12 years of basic education and four years of teacher training to degree level. Government policy to upgrade all teachers to a national standard of 12 + 2 is currently being implemented, and ODE plays a role in this. The form it takes is typically blocks of face-to-face teaching by university and college staff in vacations (mostly the summer), with 'self-learning' periods in between. Few materials other than textbooks and lecture notes are generally provided and little tutor support has been available. Courses are generally organized by provincial education authorities in partnership with universities and teachers' colleges. Student numbers are generally controlled by MoET and the provincial authorities. The curriculum mirrors that of the conventional system and the courses tend to focus on academic content and theory rather than practice. In upgrading courses for teachers through ODE, Hanoi Pedagogical University and Hué University have taken a leading role in this. In 1999 HOU provided degree-level courses for over eight hundred lower secondary teachers of English.

Some teacher education programmes are being provided through donor-funded projects and are introducing some new approaches to ODE. One new initiative is a Belgian-funded project for primary and lower secondary teachers in six provinces (1997 to 2000). This aims to upgrade 1,500 primary and 2,500 lower secondary teachers to Bachelor of Education level. Degrees are awarded by Hanoi Pedagogical University (for primary teachers) and Hué University (for lower secondary teachers). Over 200 items of printed self-study materials have been prepared, including translations of articles from other countries (Viet Nam does not yet have copyright laws). This has provided a valuable learning resource not previously available for teachers, and is much sought after by conventional colleges and students. There is a little use of video, and the project team has prepared some materials which focus on the practicalities of teaching, while the universities have concentrated on theoretical and academic subject content. Again, the model relies on university staff travelling to teach at provincial or district centres, though less than for some other programmes.

Another initiative is the English Language Teacher Training Project (ELTTP), 1998 to 2001, funded by the Department for International

Development, UK Government. This is designed to strengthen the English teaching of lower secondary school teachers and teacher trainers, including provincial educational training personnel. One component of the project is a distance learning course. Between March 2000 and October 2001 nearly one thousand junior secondary teachers of English in ten provinces will take the course. The teachers use textbooks, study guides, audio and videotapes, and local learning groups with tutor support. Assignment work is set during periods of self-study and new methodologies of teaching and learning are introduced both in the approaches to teaching English and in the teacher-training course itself. The Hué University, Can Tho University and Viet Nam National University organize delivery of the course and provide learner support, as well as examining students.

Policy framework for ODE

The legal status of distance education was first established by Prime Ministerial Decision, signed by Le Thanh Nghi, the Deputy Prime Minister, on 11 October 1992. This aimed to consolidate and further develop 'Open Learning Institutions and courses aiming at training cadres at higher and secondary levels'. This legislation defined the purposes of ODE, its forms of instruction, types of learners to be trained, curriculum and teaching methods, and the duties of teaching staff and learners. Achieving good quality in the basic essentials of a courses curriculum was emphasized. Priority groups were identified as 'cadres holding a leading position, dominant scientists and researchers, cadres or workers with good professional experience, with a good reputation to the revolution, labour heroes, outstanding farmers, soldiers and workers', women, members of ethnic minority groups and 'regrouped southern people'. It was also stated that 'The Ministry of Education will give detailed instruction in the designing' (Le Than Nghi 1992).

In response to changing times, in January 1993 the government reemphasized the priority of *doi moi* in education through the resolution 'Continued Renovation of the Stages of Education and Training' (MoET 1993). Key priorities were identified as increasing quality and improving the curriculum, training and teaching methodologies to enhance learning. The Education Law of 1999 includes a reference to 'in-service learning, distance learning and guided autodidact learning' under the heading of Non-Formal Education (Article 40, 1d). The Government's Strategy of Education and Training for 2010 to 2020 identifies the goals (among others) of quality improvement, increased levels of education and training, the creation of a skilled and flexible workforce, recognition of the importance of life-long learning and more dynamic approaches to teaching and learning with the goal of achieving 'a Vietnamese modern education with national colour'. It includes ODE as one means of achieving these goals, proposing the establishment of more distance education centres. While ODE has been referred to in recent policy documents, references to it are brief and the policy framework for it needs further development. The prospects for this were strengthened in July 2000, when a proposed Resolution was issued in preparation for the 9th Congress of the Viet Nam Communist Party (to be held in 2001). This places new emphasis on distance education: 'Distance education will be widely developed and improved (*Phat trien manh dao tao tu xa*)' and the national system of distance education will be restructured,the two open universities (HOU and HCMCOU) playing a key role.

While there is support at a policy level for ODE, there may also be a continuing shortage of funds to develop it, especially given the cost structure and high initial costs of ODE. In relation to policy for information and communication technologies (ICT) and their use in education, there is little so far but work is being done to develop a national strategy for the use of ICT in general and a new Information Technology Management Agency has been set up in the Ministry of Science, Technology and the Environment.

The use of technologies in ODE

The main technologies used for distance education in Viet Nam are print, radio, television, and audio and video cassettes. Print is the dominant medium. Many of the printed materials are similar to traditional textbooks, though projects and the open universities have begun to introduce self-instructional design features found elsewhere. Instructional design is a relatively new field in Viet Nam. The use of visual and audio media tends to run in parallel with printed materials, or stand alone, rather than be closely integrated with the print.

In 1997, the national television and radio station, the Voice of Viet Nam, signed an agreement to devote 25% of air time to educational broadcasting. Radio and television signals can reach most regions of Viet Nam though not all may have access. It is estimated that there are 106 radios and 180 television sets per 1,000 people (World Bank 1999b). HOU has produced radio and television programmes (Viet Nam Television Channel 2) on agriculture, rural development, computing and business management. The number developed is limited by the small amount of funds available for programme development; transmission is provided at no cost to the university. Foreign language courses have been provided by the College for Foreign Languages and the Foreign Language Teacher Training College, in cooperation with Hanoi Television and Viet Nam Television. HCMCOU, in collaboration with HCM City Television and other provincial television stations, provides courses on rural development and business management, among other things. Hanoi Television has begun to provide courses on general education to widen the knowledge of school students and teachers. There is still further scope for the use of radio and television in education and in distance education.

The telecommunications infrastructure

Viet Nam illustrates some of the problems of introducing the use of information and communication technologies in low-income countries. The telecommunications infrastructure in Viet Nam is weak, limiting the opportunities for its use in distance education. Up to 1991, tele-communications was 'an extremely under-developed, not comprehensive system, with very limited capacity and low efficiency' (Viet Nam Development Report 2000). Investments and improvements were made during the 1990s, changing from analogue to digital technology. By 1996, there were about 21 telephone mainlines (that is, a unique dialling number to which calls are billed) per 1,000 people (compared to an average of 50 per 1,000 for East Asia and the Pacific, and 506 for high income countries). Rural access to telephones is much less than urban, and not available in all villages so far. It is estimated that there are five personal computers per 1,000 people (World Bank 1999b) though this may be an underestimate. The use of mobile phones is growing fast, especially in urban areas.

Internet development in Viet Nam

According to the General Department of Post and Telecommunications (GDPT) there were about 60,000 subscribers to Internet accounts in May 2000. There were four officially approved Internet Service Providers (ISP): VNN, run by GDPT, FPT (Financing and Promoting Technology Company), Saigon Net and NetNam. VNN has about 65% of the subscribers. HCM City has 40,000 subscribers: 5.7 in 1,000 people there use the Internet. Many Internet shops have opened in urban centres since 1999 and have proved popular. Prices are falling though costs are still high. One obstacle to wider use is the limited amount of Vietnamese language information on the Internet though many people are learning English.

One ISP has a particular interest in education and training. In 1997, the Institute of Information Technology obtained access to the Internet, developing a link with a West German institution and with the Australian National University in Canberra. It also formed alliances with some universities in Viet Nam. Following this, the Institute set up as an ISP, as a state-owned company in June 1999. Any enterprise wishing to establish itself in telecom-related activity in Viet Nam must first register as a state-owned company, although after a year, it can decide whether to continue as a state-owned or private company. NetNam is one of a few new-style companies created by a decision of the 8th Congress of the Communist Party. This allowed a research institute or university to create a company and reclaim tax paid during the year provided it is re-invested in the company. Internet services provided are defined by the Ministry of Planning and Investment, and include Internet facilities, advisory services and training in information technology. NetNam also collaborates with universities in less-developed provinces in Viet Nam, providing intranet and information services.

At present, forms of ODE involving new technology (such as computer communications) are not an option for most learners in Viet Nam. It is estimated that only one Vietnamese in every 2,000 has Internet access compared to a world average of 17 per 1,000, and subscribers are charged relatively high fees in relation to income. Up until January 2000, 30 hours of Internet services cost about US$47. Line costs were later reduced by 25%.

Despite the constraints some initiatives have begun. A few limited networks (intranets) have been established between universities for research purposes; a Viet Nam-Canada ICT (VCIT) Project has been funded by Canada to develop IT policy, to support improvements in the government's IT strategy and management, and promote female participation in ICT (in 1999, about 17% of Vietnamese university students following IT courses were female). The VCIT project is supporting the development of a new national five-year strategic plan for the use of IT (2001 to 2005) and an IT Management Agency has been set up in the Ministry of Science, Technology and the Environment.

So far, the use of ICT for teaching and learning in ODE is largely limited to the participation of Vietnamese students in international postgraduate courses. Though the use of ICT in Viet Nam has been slow to develop, rapid acceleration may occur when the decreasing costs of access and bandwidth availability and increasing numbers of users coincide. However, continued economic growth will be a factor.

Conclusions

ODE in Viet Nam has continued to make an important contribution to education and training provision in the country throughout the 1990s though it is difficult to quantify the extent for lack of official detailed data and records and clear categorization of what counts as open and distance learning. Nonetheless, many who have obtained qualifications would not have been able to do so without the access to opportunities that ODE courses provided. The establishment of the open universities has been significant in progressing the use and status of ODE and in parallel, traditional universities are increasingly adopting more flexible and varied modes of course delivery. The range of learning needs generated by transition to a market economy is wide and it is likely that, in the future, ODE will need to play an increasing role in meeting these. So far, ODE has been used mostly for target groups in the higher and post-secondary sectors of education, and relatively little for others, such as school-level or basic education, non-formal education for rural communities, minority groups or those rural and mountainous areas most in need of educational services. The challenges over the next decade will be to realize the full potential of ODE for a wider range of target groups, and to improve the quality of existing provision.

Though much has been achieved in ODE in Viet Nam during the 1990s, in some ways ODE has been slow to develop beyond its earlier conceptions. The predominant models in 2000 are similar to those existing at the start of the 1990s, relying heavily on face-to-face teaching, short of specially designed learning materials, using media to a limited extent and giving minimal learner support. However, some reconceptualization of open and distance learning has begun, assisted by increasing interaction with other countries and influenced by new ideas and examples of different models. One challenge facing ODE in Viet Nam, as in many other countries, is the achievement of parity of esteem and a quality equivalent to, or better than, that of traditional providers and modes. Another is capacity building in ODE: in instructional design, systems design, use of media, evaluation and training staff for learner support. A third challenge relates to funding. While there is debate in Viet Nam about the most efficient and effective ways to provide ODE and the organizational issues involved, those working within ODE point to a lack of adequate funding as a major handicap in putting new thinking into practice and in achieving desired standards. A new challenge will come with the use of ICT. So far, the use of ICT for open and distance learning in Viet Nam has had little impact, because of the lack of infrastructure and affordable facilities. However, this is likely to change over the next decade. New options as well as new challenges are sure to present themselves.

References

Arger, G and Tran Dinh Tan (1990) 'VIPOU, Vietnamese People's Open University: the evolution of an ideal', Proceedings of the XVth International Conference of the International Council for Distance Education, Caracas, Venezuela.

Government of Viet Nam-Donor-NGO Poverty Working Group (2000) 'Viet Nam Development Report: Viet Nam attacking poverty', Hanoi: The World Bank.

Government of Viet Nam (1999) 'The Education Law of the Socialist Republic of Viet Nam', Hanoi.

Robinson, B (March 2000) 'A review of learning and training materials for primary Teacher training and development in Viet Nam', internal report to the World Bank/DfID Primary Teacher Development Project, Hanoi.

Sinh, Hoang Xuan and Sloper, D (1995) 'An entrepreneurial development: Than Long University', in D Sloper and L T Can (eds) *Higher Education in Viet Nam: Change and Response*, Singapore: Institute of South-East Asian Studies.

The Government of the Socialist Republic of Viet Nam (1996) 'Public Investment Program 1996–2000', Hanoi.

Tran Dinh Tan (1991) 'Viet Nam', *Distance Education in Asia and the Pacific*, vol. 1, UNESCO and NIME.

World Bank (1997a) 'Viet Nam: deepening reform for growth', Economic Report No. 170 31-VN, East Asia and Pacific Region.

World Bank (1997b) 'Viet Nam: education financing', Washington: The World Bank.

World Bank (1998) 'Viet Nam: rising to the challenge', an Economic Report, Report No. 18632-VN, Washington: The World Bank.

World Bank (1999a) 'Moving forward: achievements and challenges in the transport sector', Report No. 18748, East Asia and Pacific Regional Office.

World Bank (1999b) 'World development indicators', Washington: The World Bank.

Pakistan
Bangladesh

India

Sri Lanka

South
Asia

Bangladesh

M Aminul Islam and Hasibul Haque

Introduction

Bangladesh is a green flat land covering 147,570 square kilometres and has a population of 130.5 million. It is characterized by a low per capita income (about US$386), a low literacy rate (about 64%), a high drop-out rate at the primary (about 65%) and secondary (about 56%) education levels, and very limited and inadequate educational resources and facilities. Although the Constitution of Bangladesh upholds the right to education for all, and universal primary education to a certain level is compulsory by law, the government has been struggling to educate its people since the country's independence in 1971.

Bangladesh's economic infrastructure, which is mostly agriculture-based, is poor, and the country badly needs trained professionals. Education is seen as a primary solution to developing this manpower, as the Fifth Five-Year Plan states:

'Education is the basic need for socio-economic transformation and advancement of a country. It is the prime ingredient of human resource development... . Education plays the most important role for creating trained workforce for a nation.' (p.427)

Bangladesh's traditional educational system has, however, very limited intellectual resources and is without the institutional capacity to meet this demand.

Distance education can thus play a major role at the very least in providing training programmes for professionals. Bangladesh Open University (BOU), the only national institution providing ODE in Bangladesh, has undertaken to conceive and design programmes to meet this need.

ODE in Bangladesh

Although BOU was established in 1992, the history of distance education in Bangladesh goes back about forty-five years. In 1956, the then Director of Public Instructions of East Pakistan had already understood the significance of distance education and, in 1957, the Education Reform Commission recommended that a correspondence school be established on a trial basis. In 1956, the Government of East Pakistan allotted 200 radio receivers and 400 car batteries to the Education Directorate to be distributed among the educational institutions of the province via a small 'Audiovisual Cell' created under the Education Directorate. Subsequently, in 1962, production of an 8mm film and silk screen printed educational charts led to the establishment of East Pakistan Audiovisual Education Centre (AVEC) with the broader objectives of printing and distributing educational charts, developing a 16mm educational film and 35mm filmstrip library, and offering a loan service and regular training to school teachers for the preparation and use of low-cost audio-visual educational materials. Accordingly, arrangements were made with Radio Pakistan, Dhaka, to air an educational programme.

In 1980, the School Broadcasting Programme (SBP) was approved by the National Evaluation Committee as a project under the Education Directorate, but independent of AVEC. The elaborate programme of regular school broadcasting was inaugurated on 1 January 1981.

A British team from the UK Open University and the British Council was invited to visit Bangladesh in November 1980 to study the feasibility of introducing distance education programmes in Bangladesh. Following discussions with that team, a high-level Bangladeshi team visited the UK Open University, the British Broadcasting Company, the University of London and UNESCO, Paris. The delegation agreed that a formal distance education system would be introduced in Bangladesh and, accordingly, funds were earmarked for this purpose in the Second Five-Year Plan (1981–1985). This was followed by another visit by a four-member British team which prepared a draft scheme for primary teacher training and the training of mass education squads by distance.

In 1983, the SBP and AVEC merged to form the National Institute of Educational Media and Technology (NIEMT). Meanwhile, the local committee appointed by the Ministry of Education to conduct a feasibility study on the establishment of an open university submitted its report indicating that there was potential for a Bachelor of Education (BEd) course through distance education as the first phase of an open university. Following the recommendations made in 1985, NIEMT was renamed as the Bangladesh Institute of Distance Education (BIDE) and undertook the trial distance education BEd programme (Islam 1986).

Encouraged by the tremendous response to the BEd programme, the Ministry of Education, with financial support from the British Overseas Development Administration (ODA), undertook a project in 1987 to assess the feasibility of setting up the BOU. In October 1988, again with ODA support, a high-powered team was formed with representation from the Ministry of Education, the Government Planning Commission and the University Grants Commission. The team toured India, Pakistan, Thailand and the UK and, in 1989, with the help of British experts, drew up a plan for the BOU. At the same time an information-gathering mission from the Asian Development Bank (ADB) came to Bangladesh at the invitation of the Bangladesh government. Supported by the ADB, the Technical Assistance Project was launched to conduct another BOU feasibility study.

With a view to setting up the BOU, a contract was signed between the ADB and the government agreeing that the ADB would grant the government a loan of US$34.33 million to cover 80% of the costs involved in the establishment project, with the government bearing the remaining 20%.

In October 1992, the BOU was formally recognized by an Act passed in the National Parliament. Following this the BIDE was merged into the BOU.

Bangladesh Open University

BOU is the only distance education institution in Bangladesh. The Prime Minister is Chancellor of the BOU, while the Vice-Chancellor, appointed by the Chancellor, is chief executive.

The Vice-Chancellor is supported by more than one Pro-Vice-Chancellor and a Treasurer appointed by the Chancellor. There are a number of statutory bodies such as the Board of Governors and the Academic Council formed by a representation of professionals and chaired by the Vice-Chancellor. These formal bodies make policy decisions on administrative and academic matters of the University.

The University has six academic schools (Faculties) and ten support divisions, as shown in the organizational chart in Figure 1, to organize and launch the academic programmes. The University has a wide physical infrastructure-based network of 12 regional resource centres, 80 local centres and more than 650 tutorial centres.

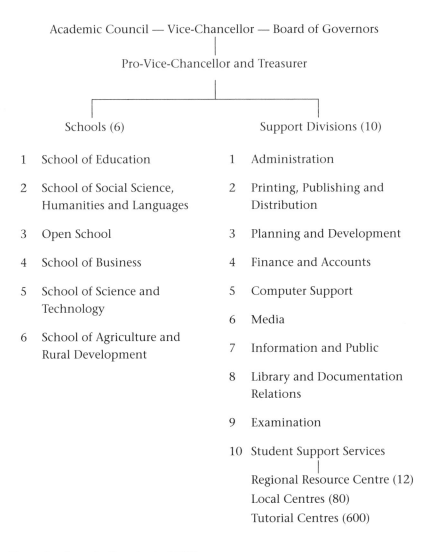

Figure 1   Organization chart of BOU

Student profile and geographic spread

Since its establishment, BOU has developed and launched 19 formal education programmes that offer courses from certificate level to diploma and degree level. BOU also offers a number of non-formal and informal education programmes.

Currently more than 200,000 students attend BOU, and this figure is projected to exceed 300,000 in a couple of years.

The majority of students are enrolled in the Secondary School Certificate (SSC) programme, followed by the Higher Secondary Certificate (HSC), the BEd and the Graduate Diploma in Management (GDM).

Student enrolment is country-wide. However the majority of students are from the Dhaka region, followed by the Jessore region. Of all the students 60% are from urban areas and the remaining 40% from rural areas. The enrolment of male students in both urban and rural areas (57%) is a little higher than for female students (43%). Interestingly, the students are from a wide range of occupational sectors, and include professionals, unemployed youth, job-seekers, school drop-outs, regular students, housewives and seniors.

Manpower requirements and the demand for learning

Bangladesh is fighting to eliminate illiteracy, alleviate poverty and develop its human resources into a self-sufficient productive force, but the resources available to achieve this goal are very meagre against the increasing demand for education and training.

In the formal and traditional education sector, the country has 12 public universities, 989 public colleges including 10 teacher training colleges (TTC), 20 polytechnic institutes, 35 vocational training institutes, 13,526 secondary schools, 95,886 primary schools, 6,172 madrashas (religious institutions) and 54 primary teacher training institutes. Besides these public institutions, there are some private universities, colleges and schools, but these offer not only expensive but also limited facilities for education and training.

In the teacher education sector, the 10 public TTCs offer a BEd degree to secondary school teachers with a total capacity of 5,000 students per year. There are also five non-government TTCs offering the same programme that have a total capacity of 1,000 students per year. The 54 primary teacher training institutes offer a CEd to trainee primary school teachers, with a total yearly capacity of 8,100 students. In addition to these teacher training institutions the country has five Higher Secondary Teacher

Training Institutes offering short courses (56 days) to higher secondary (Grade 12) teachers. These have a total yearly capacity of 1,750 students.

Bangladesh's health education sector has 13 government medical colleges, two dental colleges, one college of nursing, and a number of nursing training institutes affiliated with the government hospitals. However, total capacity is highly inadequate in the context of demand although there are some private medical education institutions offering medical education programmes.

The management education sector has an Institute of Business Administration (IBA) under the University of Dhaka offering BBA and MBA programmes to around 300 students per year. The University of Chittagong also offers a BBA programme. Although some private university enterprises are emerging, access is very limited due to high cost and limited capacity.

Meanwhile, the rural development and agricultural education sector has two agricultural universities and three agricultural colleges offering courses to a limited number of students.

In addition to these formal education and professional programmes, various organizations occasionally arrange short training courses and non-formal education programmes for professionals. But demand always exceeds provision.

Curriculum content and courses of study available by ODE

BOU develops the curricula of its educational programmes itself. Each programme usually has its own Curriculum Committee formed by the experts and practitioners related to that programme or course. The Curriculum Committee develops the curriculum, which is then reviewed by the members of the Schools and finally approved by the Academic Council after further review.

The following table shows the formal programmes on offer at BOU, their respective Faculties (Schools), levels and the years they were launched:

Table 1   Formal programmes at BOU

School	Formal Programmes	Level	Year of Launch
Open School	Secondary School Certificate (SSC)	Certificate	1995 July
	Higher Secondary Certificate (HSC)	Certificate	1998 July
School of Agriculture and Rural Development	Certificate in Agro-processing	Certificate	1998 July
	Poultry and Livestock	Certificate	1998 July
	Pisciculture and Fish Processing	Certificate	1998 July
	Bachelor in Agricultural Education (BAgEd)	Bachelor	1997 Jan
	Diploma in Youth in Development (DYD)	Diploma	1999 Jan
School of Education	Bachelor of Education (BEd)	Bachelor	1992 July
	Certificate of Education (CEd)	Certificate	1998 Jan
	Master of Education (MEd)	Master	1999 April
School of Social Science, Humanities and Language	Bachelor of Arts (BA)	Bachelor	1999 July
	Certificate in English Language Proficiency (CELP)	Certificate	1994 Jan
	Certificate in Arabic Language Proficiency (CALP)	Certificate	1996 Jan
	Bachelor in English Language Teaching (BELT)	Bachelor	1997 July
School of Business	Graduate Diploma in Management (GDM)	Diploma	1995 Jan
	Certificate in Management (CIM)	Certificate	1995 Jan
	Master of Business Administration (MBA)	Master	1998 July
School of Science and Technology	Diploma in Computer Applications (DCA)	Diploma	1998 Jan
	BSc in Nursing	Bachelor	1999 July

The Open School provides secondary (Grade 10) and higher secondary (Grade 12) education to adults, early school leavers and working people. It follows the curriculum suggested by the National Curriculum and Textbook Board with some modification to distance format. Both the SSC and the HSC are two-year flexible courses that can be completed in five years.

The School of Agriculture and Rural Development provides needs-based education to rural youth, extension workers and agriculture teachers. The duration of the certificate programmes is six to twelve months. The duration of the Diploma in Youth in Development is two years. The Bachelor of Agricultural Education (BAgEd) is a three-year course for practising teachers of agriculture.

The BEd and CEd of the School of Education are mainly teacher training programmes for secondary and primary teachers. The BEd takes two years to complete, and the minimum duration of the CEd is one year. The MEd is a higher degree programme for teachers and education professionals. It has four branches of specialization: Science Education, Language Education, Educational Administration, and Development Economics Education.

The School of Social Science, Humanities and Language has two language proficiency courses in English and Arabic: CELP and CALP. Their duration is six to twelve months. The Bachelor in English Language Teaching (BELT) is a two-year professional development programme for practising English language teachers. The Bachelor of Arts (BA) is a first degree programme with options for majors. This programme takes three to four years to complete depending on the majors.

The School of Business provides management and business education through certificate, diploma and MBA programmes. The Certificate in Management takes six to twelve months to complete, the Graduate Diploma in Management two years, and the MBA lasts two years and is designed for practising and prospective business executives.

The School of Science and Technology offers a two-year Diploma in Computer Applications for information technology and communication technology professionals. The BSc in Nursing is a three-year Bachelor degree programme for practising nurses.

Besides these formal education programmes, the University also has a number of non-formal and informal programmes for training and building awareness of different development issues.

Table 2   Non-formal programmes at BOU

School	Programme
Open School	• Basic Science • Mathematics
School of Agriculture and Rural Development	• Agriculture • Pisciculture • Fish Processing • Afforestation • Horticulture • Poultry • Livestock
School of Business	• Bank Loans • Marketing Management
School of Business/ School of Agriculture and Rural Development	• Preparation and Preservation of Food
School of Science and Technology/ School of Business	• Health, Nutrition Population Studies
School of Science and Technology/ School of Education	• Maternity and Child Care Environment
School of Social Science, Humanities and Language/ School of Agriculture and Rural Development	• Irrigation Management • Women in the Workforce
School of Social Science, Humanities and Language/ Open School	• Religion and Ethics

Teaching staff roles and characteristics

BOU follows a centralized system of course development and delivery. The courses are developed by the Schools. There are a total of 82 teachers (Faculty members) attached to the six Schools.

The Schools are mainly responsible for the development and delivery of the academic programmes. The Schools take the initiative to start courses, form the Curriculum Committee, hold workshops for curriculum developers and members of the course development teams and organize the development of the curriculum and courses.

As members of the Schools, the teaching staff have to perform a wide range of activities, and require skills in multiple areas. The teaching staff provide the necessary leadership in initiating, organizing, developing and delivering the academic courses, and have a central role in curriculum and programme development. They have to frame rules and regulations for each academic programme, organize and guide the members of the Curriculum Committee, train and guide the course-writers, coordinate and take part in the course development process, write part of the courses in teams, edit and review courses written by external resource persons, do the necessary instructional design for the courses, give necessary direction to the graphic designers and supply the camera-ready manuscripts to the Printing, Publishing and Distribution Division of the University for printing of study materials and production of audio and video materials.

The University also often draws upon expertise from the traditional universities and other research and educational institutions, and these external experts often join the curriculum and course development teams.

BOU uses self-instructional print materials, radio and TV broadcasting and limited face-to-face tutorial sessions for delivery of and back-up for programmes. During the delivery phase, the teaching staff must select the tutorial centres, tutors and coordinators of the programme and design the academic calendar for that programme.

Tutors at BOU are usually teachers from conventional educational institutions who work with BOU on a part-time basis. These tutors provide face-to-face tutorials to students twice a month during holidays. As BOU's tutors are from the conventional educational system, and are not course developers, the central teaching staff of the University train them to ensure successful implementation of the curriculum and courses and tutoring for distance education purposes.

During delivery the central teaching staff are also required to monitor the quality of the programmes in different regions of the country by visiting some tutorial centres. The members of the teaching staff usually provide feedback and any necessary back-up to students through radio and TV broadcasting, in which they act as principal presenters.

The members of the teaching staff of the University are also responsible for student assessment and evaluation of the courses. They set the student assignments, write the question papers for the end-of-course examinations, mark the answer scripts, act as head examiners and give necessary instructions to the Examination Division of the University with regard to the conducting of the final examinations and publication of the grades.

The teaching staff are also expected to do their own academic research and follow study programmes. This can be in the area of distance education in general, evaluation/revision of a particular course, or research in their specialist field of study.

In addition, as members of various statutory bodies and committees, teaching staff at BOU are also required to participate in policy-making, planning and programming at management level. They are in fact the nucleus of the University and provide the academic leadership in the distance education field.

Learning support services

Student learning support is provided both by the Schools and through the network of the Student Support Service Division of the University. The Schools incorporate this support mechanism into the course materials when developing the courses. This mechanism includes instructions to the learners, self-assessment questions and answers, and feedback provided in the study materials.

For reinforcement and back-up, the Schools use radio and TV broadcasting, which is made possible by the BOU's Media Division. However, such broadcasting is mainly one-way communication and students can use telephone or postal correspondence to communicate with members of the central teaching staff for feedback and advice on coursework.

However, most of the two-way learning support occurs during the face-to-face tutorial sessions held at selected tutorial centres close to where students live or work. The tutorial centres are in fact the meeting point between the students and the University. Students come to the tutorial centres to enrol, to obtain course materials and information, and for counselling and guidance. They can consult their tutors on appointed days for any academic problems that they may encounter during the course.

Some of the BOU's programmes (such as the BEd programme and the BELT programme) arrange 'Summer School' and 'Winter School' programmes for teaching practice and practicals. The students are also encouraged to form self-directed study groups to discuss their problems and to have the opportunity to meet other students, i.e. for learner-learner interaction.

The tutorial centres are selected by the Schools and follow the instructions given by the Schools and the Student Support Service Division. The Student Support Service Division administers the 12 regional resource centres. Under each regional resource centre there are local centres and under each local centre are a number of tutorial centres. The distribution of the tutorial centres depends on the programmes. While the regional and local centres are run by University staff, the tutorial centres are usually conventional educational institutions run by the staff of those institutions who work part-time for BOU.

The regional and local centres of the University deal with the local management and administration of the academic programmes. They deal with the dissemination of programme information, enrolment of students, distribution of course materials, monitoring of the tutorial sessions, conducting the course examinations, and providing counselling and guidance to students.

The regional and local centres also act as the clearinghouse of the University by taking charge of local promotional activities for University programmes, and supplying the necessary input for managing student information, and by collecting student queries, tutor-marked assignments (TMAs) and answer scripts and forwarding them to the central campus.

Assessment of student achievement

BOU uses both formative and summative evaluation systems to assess student achievement. Formative evaluation is continuous and takes place through self-assessment questions that are incorporated into the course materials. There are also TMAs, which the students have to submit to their tutor as required throughout their course.

The self-assessment questions are designed to allow students to monitor their progress as they proceed through a course and do not count towards their final grade. The TMAs, however, are worth a certain percentage of the final grade and students should receive feedback from the tutor on these, and, hence, on their progress.

The final stage of student assessment comes at the end of the course in the form of an examination conducted by the University at selected examination centres. These are usually the tutorial centres. Students come to the examination centre to take the end-of-course examination, which is overseen by tutorial centre officials and monitored by University staff.

The Examination Division of the University conducts the examinations and student answer scripts are collected centrally and marked by a pre-approved panel of examiners. The setting of examination papers, moderation, marking, scruting and publication of the examinations are done under the supervision of an Examination Committee formed from members of the Schools and the Academic Council.

Except for the SSC and HSC programmes, BOU follows a grade point system for all other programmes. Grade points are counted according to a maximum four-point scale as shown in Table 3.

To progress through a programme, students have to carry at least a cumulative grade point average (CGPA) of 2.5 with not lower than a C (2) grade in a single course. Students must resit the end-of-course examination if they receive a D+ (1.5) or lower grade in that course.

For the SSC and HSC programmes, BOU follows the traditional norm-referenced division system of 1st division (60% or above), 2nd division (45% or above) and 3rd division (33% or above).

Table 3   The BOU grade point system

Grade	Point	Remark
A	4	Outstanding
B+	3.5	Excellent
B	3	Very good
C+	2.5	Good
C	2	Average
D+	1.5	Below average (resit exam)
D	1	Poor (resit exam)
F	0	Fail (resit exam)

Programme management and quality assurance

With six academic schools and ten support divisions, BOU works through a number of statutory bodies, such as a Board of Governors, Academic Council, School Boards, Curriculum Committee, Finance Committee, Academic Planning Committee, Admissions Committee, Works Committee, Disciplinary Committee, and so on.

As chief executive, the Vice-Chancellor chairs the Board of Governors and the Academic Council which take final decisions regarding the administrative and academic affairs of the University. The Schools are headed by a Dean who is usually also a professor. The Dean is appointed by the Vice-Chancellor for three years and chairs the School Boards, Curriculum Committee and any other committee formed within the School.

The divisions are headed by a full-time Director appointed by the University and have no policy decision-making power. The Schools initiate all policy decisions to be approved by the relevant statutory bodies, while the divisions are responsible for their execution.

For academic programmes, the Curriculum Committee, with the initiative of the respective academic school, designs and develops the curriculum which is then approved by the Academic Council. Then a course development team consisting of writers, editor, instructional designer, graphic designer, DTP Operator and referee/validator works on developing self-instructional materials for the course, which is then printed and published by the Printing, Publishing and Distribution Division of the University.

To ensure a standard quality of courses, the University applies a refereeing/validating system. Each course is refereed anonymously by two referees who have the right to accept or reject any part of the course materials and suggest changes.

For quality assurance of programmes, the University has a section called Survey, Research and Evaluation, which monitors and evaluates the quality of courses and student services through individual research and evaluation studies to continuously update courses and to assure their quality.

Financing ODE

BOU is now included in the government's annual revenue budget. However, the government has imposed a condition that BOU should generate and bear at least 30% of the University's total annual costs/annual budget and the government will bear 70%.

In addition to this regular allocation, Bangladesh's universities occasionally receive some irregular allocations from the government's Annual Development Programme (ADP) for development work within them.

Technology and ODE: what's in use and what's in store

BOU uses a range of media, such as print, audio, video and human interaction. However, in terms of using technologies, the University is still in the 'second generation of distance education' employing postal or courier services, radio and TV broadcasting and face-to-face tutorial sessions.

The delivery system of the University is mainly one-way, and back-up largely depends on human interaction at the tutorial centres. The University has yet to set up a national satellite-based communication network system, which may allow audio and video teleconferencing in selected areas. There is a possibility of establishing a satellite-based teleconferencing system by renting satellite facilities from India. However, the University has yet to come to a decision.

The Commonwealth of Learning (COL) has donated a telephone conferencing system to BOU that can connect six sites simultaneously. It can currently connect six regional centres for information dissemination, administration and limited teaching back-up. The University is now thinking of extending the system to 12 sites to interconnect the 12 regional centres.

A widely used computer- and Internet-based electronic communications network is still to be set up. When it is, it will be limited. The University is working on setting up a Local Area Network (LAN) on campus and a Wider Area Network (WAN) to bring its regional resource centres under the computer network. Although there is already limited Internet access and email facilities on the main campus, the University has no reason to plan to launch courses online or to integrate the IT into courseware due to the limited access that students have to technological resources.

However, it is expected that the situation will change soon as IT becomes more affordable and more popular. The University will then at some point be obliged to incorporate these technologies in course development, delivery and back-up services.

International collaboration in ODE

As an institution of open and distance learning, BOU believes in international cooperation and collaboration. BOU is a member of the International Council of Distance Education (ICDE), the Association of Commonwealth Universities (ACU) and the Association of Asian Open Universities (AAOU). BOU is also a member of the South Asian Forum for Distance Education for Development (SAFDED), a forum of open and distance learning institutions in South Asia.

BOU staff members regularly take part in international seminars, symposia and conferences and contribute to international fora. The University also moderates a listserv called SAFDED-L, which connects more than 175 distance educationalists around the world.

Through initiatives of the COL and the Commonwealth Secretariat, the University has taken part and continues to take part in a number of international projects, such as the Commonwealth Youth Programme (CYP) initiated by the Commonwealth Secretariat for the youth of Commonwealth countries and in the Commonwealth Executive MBA programme jointly developed by BOU, Indira Gandhi National Open University of India, Allama Iqbal Open University of Pakistan, and the Open University of Sri Lanka.

In collaboration with the COL, BOU has also developed a non-formal education programme for women rural business owners called Management of Small Enterprises Skill Training for Rural Women Using Open and Distance Learning Materials. Funded by the UK's Department for International Development (DfID) and initiated by the COL, BOU is also collaborating in a basic education and literacy project with India and Zambia.

The University recently hosted an international meeting of policy-makers from the CYP. It is also taking part in a number of collaborative projects with COL and other international agencies. These projects include designing training materials for the garments manufacturers and conducting training needs and feasibility study for the rural farming women.

The University hopes that its international collaborative activities will increase with globalization and the growing use of technologies.

Priorities for policy and national direction

The government is making it a priority to be being prepared for the challenge of the 21st century. Bangladesh has to be able to face the challenges of increasing globalization, compete in an increasingly competitive marketplace, provide high quality products and services, and effect a smooth and successful transition from the current labour-intensive economy through a market-oriented economy to become a knowledge-based economy.

Education, in this changing environment, is crucial in enabling people to meet these challenges. The workforce will not only need formal education and training, they will also need continuing education, retraining and life-long learning. ODE has to lead the way in fulfilling this country's huge demand for trained professionals.

In its struggle to enable provision of basic and higher education to all its citizens, Bangladesh's priorities in terms of policy and national direction are both horizontal and vertical. They are horizontal in that it has to accelerate the reach of its education and training programmes from literacy to tertiary education. Equally important is the priority to grow vertically. Bangladesh has to develop quality educational programmes to catch up with and stay alongside global trends and achieve excellence in education and training.

Only ODE has the potential to grow horizontally and vertically at the same time, to reach a large target group and provide an excellent quality of education.

It has been said that the priority of the universities in the 1960s was academic freedom and self-governance. In the 1970s it was greater access and distance education. In the 1980s this became quality assurance of educational programmes. And in the 1990s the demand was for greater accountability of universities and a meeting of national needs and priorities.

Bangladesh has to achieve excellence in ODE to ensure all of these.

Conclusion

Although BOU is the only and a comparatively new ODE institution in Bangladesh, ODE is not a new concept in the subcontinent. Within a short period of time, the total number of students enrolled at BOU has exceeded the total intake of all other universities in Bangladesh. The extent of the demand and need for ODE in Bangladesh could not be clearer. To meet this demand in the 21st century, it is not only BOU that must provide ODE. The traditional universities also have to offer ODE options and thus operate as dual-mode or multi-mode institutions.

References

Islam, K M Sirajul (1986) 'Distance Education in Bangladesh', country paper in Proceedings of the Regional Seminar on Distance Education, Manila: Asian Development Bank.

Planning Commission (March 1998) *The Fifth Five-Year Plan 1997–2002*, Ministry of Planning, Dhaka: The Government of the People's Republic of Bangladesh.

India

Asha S Kanwar and C R Pillai

Introduction

The search for an alternative response to the growing demand for higher education dates back to the 1960s. Government policies proposed the expansion of places through evening college, correspondence courses and external degree programmes. On the recommendation of a committee appointed by the Ministry of Education in 1961, the University of Delhi established a Directorate of Correspondence Courses in 1962. So began distance education in India.

The response to correspondence courses was not enthusiastic. In the first place, correspondence education was perceived as a poor substitute for full-time formal education. This view was strengthened by policy pronouncements that urged selective admission to full-time institutions to maintain quality and standards. Correspondence education was thus perceived as a device to 'accommodate the spillover' from the formal system. This perception lingered, even though more universities launched correspondence programmes and more students enrolled in them.

The launch of second-generation distance education programmes through open universities in the 1980s was a new beginning. Official policies this time justified the establishment of single-mode distance teaching universities by highlighting the inadequacies of the correspondence programmes, which were seen as neither providing adequate student support services nor utilizing distance teaching methodologies and pedagogical practices. The first open university in India was established in 1982 by the State Government of Andhra Pradesh at Hyderabad. This was followed by the establishment of a national open university, Indira Gandhi National Open University (IGNOU) by the government in 1985. The National Policy on Education announced by the government in 1986 committed itself to the growth and expansion of distance and open education in India in the following terms: 'The open learning system has been initiated in order to augment opportunities for higher education, as an instrument of democratizing education and to make it a lifelong process. The flexibility and innovation of the open learning system are particularly suited to the diverse requirements of the citizens of our country, including those who had joined the vocational stream' (National Policy on Education 1986, para 5-35). The policy also committed support to the establishment of open universities in the states.

Three more open universities were established in Bihar, Rajasthan and Maharashtra in the 1980s.

Institutional framework of ODE in India

The institutional framework for ODE in India is complex. There is a multiplicity of authorities and regulatory bodies on the one hand, and a very large number of institutions offering ODE programmes on the other. The institutions include dual-mode universities, single-mode universities and private institutions which may, or may not, be affiliated to a university.

Dual-mode universities

Before the advent of the single-mode open university in 1982, there were 34 universities offering correspondence education programmes. Though the first of these launched its programmes in 1962, it was not until 1967 that another four universities ventured into this area. In 1970, there were only nine dual-mode universities. The 1970s saw a major expansion of correspondence programmes. This was primarily due to the government policy that unplanned proliferation of universities should be contained.

Most of these institutions did not create a separate infrastructure for the correspondence programmes. They were assigned to a department, redesignated in recent times as Directorate/Institute. The functional responsibility was mostly administrative: enrolment, distribution of materials and examinations. Instructional materials were written by teachers in the regular departments. The curriculum, syllabi and examinations were the same as for courses taught in the classroom. Most of these institutions also organized personal contact programmes for students.

As the apex body for higher education in the country, the University Grants Commission (UGC) is responsible for determining and maintaining the standard of education in universities. In pursuance of this responsibility, the UGC framed guidelines for correspondence programmes specifying minimum requirements in terms of personnel, services and contact hours. However, there has been no meaningful attempt to monitor observance.

The emergence of single-mode open universities did not discourage the expansion of correspondence programmes in the dual-mode universities. In fact, the initial success of these new universities prompted more universities to launch such programmes.

Table 1   Growth of distance education in the dual-mode universities

Period	New universities offering correspondence education	Total no. of universities offering distance/ correspondence education
1962	1	1
1967–1970	8	9
1971–1975	13	22
1976–1980	10	32
1981–1985	6	38
1986–1990	8	46
1991–1995	16	62
1995–1999	8	70

Source: Adapted from M S Yadav and S K Panda (1999)

Total enrolment in the correspondence education programmes of conventional universities in 1995 was 669,000, which was a little over 10% of the total enrolment in higher education in India.

Single-mode universities

The first open university was established in 1982 in Andhra Pradesh, followed by the IGNOU in 1985, and eight more state open universities subsequently.

Enrolment in the open universities in 1995 was about 200,000, accounting for about 3% of the total enrolment in higher education.

Table 2   Establishment of single-mode open universities

University	State	Year of establishment
Dr B R Ambedkar Open University, Hyderabad	Andhra Pradesh	1982
Indira Gandhi National Open University, New Delhi	National	1985
Kota Open University, Kota	Rajasthan	1987
Nalanda Open University, Nalanda	Bihar	1987
Yashwantrao Chavan Maharashtra Open University, Nashik	Maharashtra	1989
Madhya Pradesh Bhoj University, Bhopal	Madhya Pradesh	1992
Dr Baba Saheb Ambedkar Open University, Ahmedabad	Gujarat	1994
Karnataka State Open University, Mysore	Karnataka	1996
Netaji Subhas Chander Open University, Calcutta	West Bengal	1997
UP Rajarshi Tandon Open University, Allahabad	Uttar Pradesh	1998

When IGNOU was established in 1985, it was envisaged that the fledging open university system should be developed independently of the constraints of the organization, management and funding that governed the conventional universities. A Distance Education Council (DEC) was thus set up in 1992 with the express mandate to promote and coordinate the open university and distance education system and to maintain quality and standards in the system. A unique power vested in the DEC is the establishment and development of an open university network comprising the IGNOU and state open universities and other distance education institutions in the country.

The establishment of DEC was significant in many ways. Its notable success has been in establishing a system of sharing programmes, courses and facilities among open universities. In a multilingual country like India, this networking arrangement has not just extended the outreach of higher education programmes, but has, more importantly, widened the access to such programmes through the medium of several languages. This arrangement encourages universities to acquire programmes offered by others and use them by means of adoption, adaptation and/or translation. It has also significantly reduced the cost of developing programmes for the new universities.

Emerging as a national apex body for distance education in India, the DEC has assumed the role that the UGC has been performing. With this, a major reform process in correspondence programmes has also been initiated. The reform measures include transformation of the correspondence education packages into self-instructional format, diversification of the media mix of the instructional packages, induction of distance education technologies in the teaching-learning processes, organization and delivery of more effective student support services, training of personnel and critical institutional reforms essential for distance education management.

Private sector in distance education

The 1990s were a watershed in India's development. The economy opened up and policies of liberalization, privatization and globalization were introduced along with new technologies; information and communication technologies the most significant among them. The induction of these technologies required personnel trained in their application, and the more enterprising institutions foresaw the opportunities for training personnel for the global workplace rather than meeting just local needs. The significant outcomes of these developments relevant to ODE were:

- The major players in the training industry are seeking collaboration/ affiliation with established universities.

- Those involved in business education and information technology in particular are moving over to distance education methods and practices offering their programmes and courses through virtual class-rooms and websites.

- A large number of foreign education providers, especially from the UK, Canada, Australia and the USA, are also offering distance education in India and are reportedly attracting significant enrolment.

The new developments have had an unsettling effect on India's education system. The emergence of private enterprise in Indian education has introduced an element of competition, which will mostly be in the area of distance education.

Enrolment patterns and programme profiles

The available database for any comprehensive and critical analysis of the enrolment patterns and student profiles in distance education institutions in India is inadequate, but to give an idea of certain broad trends and to identify the broad category of student groups in ODE, we will look at the enrolment patterns in three representative institutions, namely, IGNOU, BRAOU, a state open university, and the School of Correspondence and Continuing Education of the University of Delhi.

Indira Gandhi National Open University, New Delhi

IGNOU offers certificate, diploma, postgraduate diploma, and Bachelor's and Master's degree programmes. A vast majority of its programmes are non-traditional, and are structured on a modular pattern. Programmes in the professional/technical fields attract very large enrolments.

Table 3   Enrolment in IGNOU by level of programme during 1995 to 1999

Levels	1995	1996	1997	1998	1999
Non-credit	263	160	26	-	-
Preparatory programmes for Bachelor's degree	8,881	7,461	12,657	10,392	10,793
Certificate	5,833	11,274	23,587	26,255	30,029
Diploma	5,709	7,196	12,614	12,423	8,409
Postgraduate diploma	18,894	35,072	3,216	2,299	5,921
Advanced diploma	-	1,375	2,220	1,274	568
Bachelor's degree	28,081	34,821	48,435	56,223	69,035
Master's degree	23,737	32,869	59,890	50,817	47,793
Total	91,398	130,228	162,645	159,683	172,548

Source: Annual Reports, IGNOU

Table 4   Enrolment of students during the same period by programme area

Programme area	1995	1996	1997	1998	1999
Management	42,301	62,571	58,388	44,852	35,351
Arts and Commerce	322,212	32,092	39,401	39,643	31,530
Science	3,504	4,140	3,924	5,005	4,753
Computer Science	1,535	14,614	44,162	57,697	71,187
Education	1,783	1,685	1,527	1,119	2,184
Health, Nutrition, Nursing, etc.	4,315	4,747	3,930	4,011	4,523
Tourism Studies	2,186	4,082	3,749	1,233	3,335
Library and Information Science	1,246	2,025	1,915	1682	2,031
Journalism, Mass Communication, Creative Writing	791	1,732	1,993	1,876	2,888
Rural Development	1,525	1,777	1,436	1,427	2,343
Engineering and Technology	-	763	2,220	3,586	559
Total	91,398	130,228	162,645	163,131	172,548

Source: Annual Reports, IGNOU

Table 5 IGNOU student profile

Year	Male	Female	Socially	Rural	Urban weak	Employed
1995	77.75	22.25	6.28	18.81	81.19	61.52
1996	77.98	22.02	5.45	8.77	91.23	57.00
1997	77.18	22.82	6.01	16.48	83.52	67.54
1998	71.52	28.48	NA	17.89	82.11	NA
1999	73.53	26.47	4.60	22.40	77.60	NA

Note: Figures are in percentages. NA = not available

A vast majority of IGNOU students are working (60% or more), and IGNOU insists on work experience for most of its professional programmes; thus the proportion of mature students (aged 25 and over) in its programmes is very high. This requirement also partly explains the relatively low enrolment of women (on average under 25%) in IGNOU programmes. Although 75% of India's population is in rural areas, there is no definitive rural-urban divide of the student population.

B R Ambedkar Open University, Hyderabad

The major programmes offered are traditional Bachelor's and Master's degree programmes in arts, commerce and science and, more recently, professional programmes in business studies at Master's level.

Table 6   Distribution of enrolment across programmes

Year	Certificates	Diplomas	Bachelor's degree	Master's degree	Research	Total enrol.
1990–1991	949	1,145	42,051	-	17	43,707
1991–1992	452	730	55,958	-	27	57,171
1992–1993	350	462	57,554	-	22	58,388
1993–1994	210	312	54,264	4,990	-	59,796
1994–1995	1,166	311	46,428	7,113	-	55,018
1995–1996	1,156	312	71,000	7,357	-	79,825
1996–1997	416	228	64,922	6,976	709	72,514

Source: Pushpa Ramakrishnan in Panda (1999)

What is striking in the above data is the majority of enrolments in BRAOU in its first degree programme leading to the Bachelor's degree in arts, science and commerce. This accounts for almost 90% of the total enrolment. This is because BRAOU admits students with no formal qualifications into its Bachelor's degree programme, and because these programmes are offered by the university in the regional language Telugu as opposed to English.

Table 7   BRAOU student profile in the 1990s

Year	Students without qualifications*	Students with qualifications*	Male*	Female*	Socially weaker groups*
1990–1991	71	29	73	27	48
1991–1992	76	24	73	27	50
1992–1993	70	30	74	26	52
1993–1994	64	36	72	28	54
1994–1995	71	29	72	28	55

* Figures are in percentages
Source: Ibid

Also worthy of note are that 80% of the students are aged 25 or under; nearly 85% of the women enrolled are housewives; and about two-thirds of those joining the university are unemployed youth.

School of Correspondence and Continuing Education, University of Delhi

Typically, the major features of dual-mode institutions are that the correspondence programmes that they offer are mainly offered to full-time regular students; are mainly traditional first degree and postgraduate programmes; and students enrolled are mainly school leavers unable to gain entry into full-time formal institutions.

The number of students from Delhi's schools wanting to go into higher education far exceeds available places by about 45,000. A large number of these students register with the School of Correspondence and Continuing Education.

The programme menu of the school consists of BA and BCom as well as MA and MCom degree programmes. All these programmes are in the fields of the humanities and social sciences; there are no programmes in science or technical/vocational fields. The students have to fulfil the minimum eligibility requirement of successful completion of senior secondary education. Master's degree programmes are open only to those who are graduates.

The university conducts Personal Contact Programmes at selected colleges outside hours or on holidays. Unlike open universities, the school does not have any multimedia facilities or academic counsellors (1998).

Table 8   Enrolment by programme and gender, 1997 to 1998

Programmes	Total enrolment	Female enrolment	% of women enrolled
BA degree	52,690	28,869	54.80
BCom degree	44,038	13,595	30.87
Master's degree	3,889	2,867	73.72
Total	100,617	45,331	45.05

Source: DEC database

It should not be assumed that these three institutions represent three distinct and exclusive models of distance education institutions in India. At best, these are three typologies and, in practice, institutions share many features. For example, the Institute of Correspondence Education of the University of Madras offers a Bachelor's degree programme under what it calls the 'open university system', which does not insist on the usual entry level qualification, and professional education programmes: Library and Information Science, Teacher Education, Computer Applications, and Labour and Taxation Laws.

Table 9   Enrolment at the University of Madras by programme and gender, 1997 to 1998

Programmes	Total enrolment	Female enrolment	% of women enrolled
Bachelor's degree for school leavers	59,038	29,522	50.00
Bachelor's degree under open university system	31,858	8,769	27.52
Master's degree	17,185	9,805	57.05
Professional education programmes	7,797	2,987	38.31
Total	115,878	51,083	44.08

Source: DEC database

Learner groups and learning needs

Although the Indian higher education system is huge, participation is only about 6% of the relevant age group, so learner demand and expectations are also huge. The government's 1986 Programme of Action to implement the newly formulated National Policy in Education lamented: 'Higher education programmes have to be redesigned to meet the growing demands of specialization, to provide flexibility in the combination of courses, to facilitate mobility among courses, programmes and institutions, to update and modernize curricula, to integrate work/practical experience and participation in creative activities with the learning processes, and to facilitate reforms in the evaluation procedure. The present rigid structures do not permit these reforms' (p. 42).

The ODE system at the national level was expected to address these critical issues. In fact, the agenda for the 1990s, articulated in the revised Programme of Action of 1992, proposed that ODE focus on education and training in areas related to employment and self-employment, involving existing institutions and organizations. It also emphasized the need for modularity in programme structures, flexibility in course combinations, transfer of credits and development of programmes jointly with employing sectors.

IGNOU's response to the above through bold initiatives and a willingness to innovate has made it one of the 11 mega universities in the world. Despite this, however, its share in overall ODE enrolment in India is no more than 12% to 15%.

Today every third university in India offers distance education programmes. Unfortunately, however, this is often because distance education is a seller's market. A number of private institutions, and industry, have entered education and training because they find it convenient to seek the collaboration of a university for the purpose of certification so that the question of validity does not affect marketing and sales. In the process, the classical functions of the university, namely, prescribing curricula, developing courses and setting standards have been appropriated by market-savvy private enterprises. Universities also find this arrangement convenient. It is easier to give away certificates and degrees without taking on the responsibility of framing curricula.

Roles and responsibilities of teachers

That brings us to the crucial question of the roles and responsibilities of teachers in distance education. One of the inevitable consequences of the 'massification' of higher education across the world has been a progressive 'devaluation' of the university, and the degrees awarded by it. Today, in the multimedia age of the Internet and other communication networks, and virtual universities, the university teacher finds his/her traditional role seriously eroded. This decline in the academic authority of the university has led to a significant 'de-institutionalization' of higher education in India.

It is against this background that the teacher's role in distance education has to be examined. The distance education teacher is quintessentially a team member rather than an icon of authority. The transition from the pre-eminent position of teacher to that of a facilitator of learning is not easy to accomplish. To be successful and effective in a distance education environment, academics have to assume multiple roles involving:

- Course team coordination;
- Discipline coordination;
- Programme/Course coordination;
- Curriculum development and instructional design;
- Competence in preparing self-instructional materials;
- Organizing and controlling delivery of programmes and services;
- Proficiency in the application of multimedia technologies;
- Telecounselling.

Learning support services

Open universities in India have generally followed the UK Open University in designing their instructional system. The IGNOU has developed multimedia learning packages for most of its programmes and uses print and electronic media delivery. The state open universities rely largely on print media, supported marginally by audio or video cassettes. A student pursuing a programme with the open university receives self-instructional learning packages, may attend counselling sessions at a local study centre, completes assignments at regular intervals as part of a continuous process of evaluation and finally sits end-of-term examinations. Depending upon programme requirements, there are also experiments, practical work, projects and fieldwork.

A network of regional and local study centres provides support services. The local study centre is the student's contact point with the university. A typical IGNOU study centre, for instance, is a facility provided by a local educational institution that provides certain services, including access to supplementary reading materials, audio and video cassettes along with playback facilities, tutorial support and practical lessons or experimental work. Students submit their assignments at these study centres and the local tutors evaluate them, give feedback and send in their assessment for the students' grade records.

The management of these study centres, mainly coordination and monitoring of their functions, is the responsibility of the regional centres. They identify the study centres, recruit the part-time staff and academic tutors to run them and supervise their expenditure and accounting. A core group of academics is appointed at each regional centre to provide academic guidance and professional support to the study centres. The following table illustrates the vastness of IGNOU's learner support service network.

Table 10   IGNOU's student support network

Regional centres	21
Academic staff at regional centres	85
Study centres	382
Study centre coordinators	600
Academic tours	18,991

Source: IGNOU Report, 1998

A similar, much smaller network provides student support services for each state open university.

The Indian national television network Doordarshan transmits programmes throughout the week, and selected stations of All India Radio in the metros as well as in the less densely populated hilly regions broadcast audio cassettes. The state open universities do not yet apply electronic media in any substantial measure, although some do broadcast radio lessons, and the older among them are now in the process of setting up media production centres.

In 1995, the IGNOU launched a satellite-based telecounselling experiment using facilities provided by the India Space Research Organization. Academic counselling held at the Central Studios in Delhi was beamed to all the regional centres, which were equipped to receive both voice and image signals. The video transmission was one way only, but students assembled at the reception centres could interact with the academic counsellors by two-way audio transmission. Despite students having to get to the regional centres to participate in these telecounselling sessions, there was sufficient enthusiasm and positive feedback to embark on an expansion and strengthening of this technology. Reception facilities are now set up at over 125 centres country-wide, which deliver about 480 hours of telecounselling.

The state open universities are also now linked to this network. The initiative is costly if all the expenses involved are considered, but since satellite time is available on the Indian national satellite systems and promotion of any new technology in the initial stages involves substantial cost, and given that these technologies will soon play a key role in education, the cost can be justified.

The dual-mode universities have still to embark upon the application of distance education technologies. Their courseware is predominantly print materials, and extended personal contact programmes support the students enrolled in them. There is a growing sense of urgency now for the transformation of their programmes into mainstream distance education format and the induction of newer technologies for this purpose is high on their agenda.

Financing ODE

India spent 3.85% of GDP on education in 1995, but the national goal of 6% is still a distant dream. About 23% of total state expenditure goes on education. Of this, 11.31% is higher education. Of that, no more than 5% is for non-governmental resources, including fee income (National Accounts Statistics 1996).

Recently, there has been a serious attempt to raise funds for higher education from private sources. The argument that higher education should pay for itself is gaining some force and feeble support. Prestigious professional education institutions like the Institutes of Technology and Management have raised their fees substantially, but the general universities are still reluctant to do so and expect the government to help.

Privatization of education is being talked about, but there are still no major initiatives. Universities in India can be established only through legislation. Degree-granting power belongs exclusively to universities. Private institutions in India function within the regulatory discipline of the universities to which they must seek affiliation if they wish to offer degree-level programmes. Their expenditure is met by the sponsoring management. The role of the private sector is thus confined to providing more of the same; there is no incentive for them to initiate any meaningful reform.

There is no doubt, however, that distance education is cost-effective. Even though IGNOU's per student costs are about one-third of the cost of conventional universities, the state open universities offer programmes at a still lower cost (Kulandai Swamy 1995). This cost differential between the IGNOU and the state open universities could be attributed to the levels of operations, the nature and extent of technology applications, and the cost involved in mobilizing the physical and intellectual resources nation-wide as against making do with what is locally available.

Distance education cannot be left entirely to be governed by market forces. It has to conform to the principles and guidelines of national policies and has to be integral to the overall educational process within the nation. In a country like India where millions of people still remain outside the reach of the established education system, the objective of distance education is to reach out to the people who cannot afford the costs involved.

International collaboration

Today, there are more than 1 billion young people in school, as against a mere 300 million in 1953 (UNESCO Report 1996). The pressure put on the education system by this unprecedented growth can only be dimly visualized.

With the onset of globalization, nations across the world and institutions within those nations must cooperate to empower the vast masses of people and raise general standards of living by providing access to information and knowledge. Distance education is surely the most appropriate medium by which this can be achieved. But while the details of specific programmes must be rooted in the local environment, the larger issues of appropriate methodologies and pedagogical approaches could be evolved through cooperative initiatives.

Conclusion

That education now revolves around computerization and technological application makes their accessibility and use, and the knowledge of how to use them, among students and teachers alike, an essential undertaking in countries where distance education is becoming increasingly a real alternative education option. Such introduction of technologies and their use in the world of education in India, field studies and research on the impact of new technologies on communities at different levels of development could be undertaken with support from international agencies and organizations to evolve new pedagogical frameworks and more people-friendly technologies for exclusive application in education and training.

References

IGNOU Annual Report 1995 to 1999, New Delhi: IGNOU.

Kulandai Swamy, V C (1995) 'How cost-effective are open universities?', *Indian Journal of Open Learning*, New Delhi: IGNOU.

Ministry of Human Resource Development, GOI and Central Statistical Organisation (1996) *National Accounts Statistics*, New Delhi.

National Policy on Education (1986) New Delhi: MHRD.

NPE (1986) Programme of Action, New Delhi: MHRD.

Panda, S (ed.) (1999) *Open and Distance Education: Policies, Practices and Quality Concerns*, New Delhi: Aravalli Books International Pvt. Ltd.

Prime Minister's Committee on Higher Education (1963) 'Robbins Report', HMSO.

Smith, A and Webster, F (1997) *The Postmodern University*, UK: Open University Press.

UGC Annual Report (1995/96), New Delhi: UGC Printers.

UNESCO (1996) 'Report to UNESCO of the International Commission on Education for the Twenty-First Century', Paris: UNESCO.

Yadav, M S and Panda, S K, 'Open and distance higher education: policy and development' in Panda, S K (1999) *Open and Distance Education: Policies, Practices and Quality Concerns*, New Delhi: Aravalli Books International Pvt Ltd., 29–31.

Pakistan

Mussaret Anwar Sheikh

Introduction

Pakistan is facing enormous education problems. Only 47% of the 70% of children under age 12 enrolled in school complete primary school, only 33% of children in the fifth grade can read with comprehension and only 17% can write a short, simple letter.

Education is generally considered to be the concern of the provinces, with policy, planning and coordination as the major responsibilities of the federal government. There is formal and distance education at pre-primary, primary (Grades I to V), middle (Grades VI to VIII) and high (Grades XI to X) school, post-secondary and higher education levels. The distance education system, such as that in the Allama Iqbal Open University (AIOU), also operates at the federal and provincial levels.

The national language, Urdu, is compulsory and is used at most levels. English is introduced much later and is used at Master's level, and regional languages such as Sindhi, Pushto and Punjabi are used at basic literacy and pre-literacy levels. Pakistan has a complete communications infrastructure of radio, television, postal and telephone services among which radio and television reach between 50% and 96% of the population.

ODE in Pakistan

The demand for formal education in third world countries has consistently run ahead of available resources and the large part of the population, therefore, remains educationally deprived. At the same time social and economic pressures continue to increase. The illiterate and semi-literate clearly require education, and even among the educated there is a dire need for continuing education.

Awareness of the magnitude and complexity of the problem has led more and more countries to turn to distance education as a solution. Moreover, the continuing economic inability of different countries to fund the formal educational system has compelled their educational planners to explore the possibilities of unconventional methods that can overcome the limitations of the formal system. Over the last three decades, distance education has become increasingly recognized as a real alternative. Both developed and developing countries have seized upon its advantages to meet pressing educational and social needs. Consequently, distance education is maturing rapidly into a discipline in its own right. More importantly, its effects are being felt and seen, often in striking ways throughout the world and it has made its way deep into the educational, social and economic mainstreams of many societies.

The AIOU has successfully used the distance education model in Pakistan. It has established a multimedia, multi-level and multi-mode teaching system. Within a short time, the university has been able to offer courses from literacy to PhD level.

By reaching students in their homes or workplaces in accordance with the principles of openness and lifelong education, the AIOU is filling the gaps left by the conventional system and is providing educational opportunities to people unable to benefit from it.

Establishment of the Allama Iqbal Open University

The AIOU was established in 1974 as the People's Open University. It was renamed the Allama Iqbal Open University in 1977 on the eve of the first centenary of the national poet and philosopher, Allama Muhammad Iqbal. The idea of an 'open university' was presented in the Education Policy of 1972 to 1980 by an enunciation of broad principles upon which this idea was based:

> Open universities are being used in several countries to provide education and training to people who cannot leave their homes and jobs for full-time studies. An open university will, therefore, be established to provide part-time educational facilities through correspondence courses, tutorials, seminars, workshops, laboratories, television and radio broadcasts and other mass communication media....

As the first open university established in Asia, the AIOU started functioning as a recognizable entity in June 1974 pursuant to Act No. XXXIX passed by the Parliament of Pakistan in May 1974.

Objectives

The main objectives of the university are, to the extent that it decides:

- To provide certain educational facilities to people who cannot leave their homes and jobs;

- To provide educational facilities to improve people's education;

- To provide teacher training facilities;

- To provide for instruction in technology or vocational education, and to make provision for research and the advancement and dissemination of knowledge;

- To hold examinations and award and confer degrees, diplomas, certificates and other academic distinctions.

During its 26 years of existence, the University has made every effort to realize the above objectives, and to offer a second chance — often indeed a first chance — of access to education to people who would otherwise have been unable to advance their careers, satisfy their inner need for knowledge or equip themselves as better citizens. Above all, the University has tried to reach out to the disadvantaged and those in greatest need of education, across Pakistan. Many are in the remotest parts of the country. Most of those in rural areas have inherited skills and practices built up over the generations, but times change, knowledge expands and materials, tools and techniques become obsolete and new ones are introduced. To meet these challenges and to benefit from new technology, people everywhere need education. Moreover, just as knowledge is expanding, so too is our population. Indeed, both are expanding at such a rate that our present educational system simply cannot cope, either at school or higher levels. It was in response to this situation that the AIOU was established.

The programmes of the University are offered at a distance throughout Pakistan and even in some Middle Eastern countries. Its programmes offer a wide choice of courses at a variety of levels for the general public as well as for professionals.

With its main campus in Islamabad, the AIOU extends its educational facilities to the remotest parts of the country. It does this principally through the mailing of learning packages, its radio and TV broadcasts and, secondly, by tutorial services through its country-wide network of regional centres, via campuses and study centres established in almost all the country's major cities. The University arranges tutorial support to students at the local level, through the study centres established in various formal educational institutions. This collaboration at the local level is an example of the partnership nature of the University's cooperation practices. It works hand in hand with government departments and agencies at all levels, as well as with a range of national and international non-governmental agencies to advance education and development throughout the country.

The institutional framework of ODE in Pakistan

The University Act has laid down the powers and functions of the AIOU's authorities and officers. The President of the Islamic Republic of Pakistan is the Chancellor of the AIOU. The Federal Minister for Education is the Pro-Chancellor, and the Vice-Chancellor of the University is its principal executive and academic officer.

Being an academic institution, the AIOU has an academic structure at its core, which consists of faculties, teaching departments and institutes as shown in Figure 1. Administrative, servicing departments support these.

Staffing

Through distance education, the AIOU has become the largest institution of learning in Pakistan with a course enrolment of almost one million people. Distance education has thus emerged as the most effective method of imparting education in this country of limited resources. The University supplements the efforts of the federal and provincial governments without placing any burden on their resources.

In its first 25 years the University did not focus on the postgraduate programmes as it did not wish to compete with formal universities in this area. In view of the increasing demand for admission in such programmes, from working people and women, the AIOU has started more than fifteen postgraduate degree programmes in the last few years including MPhil and PhD programmes.

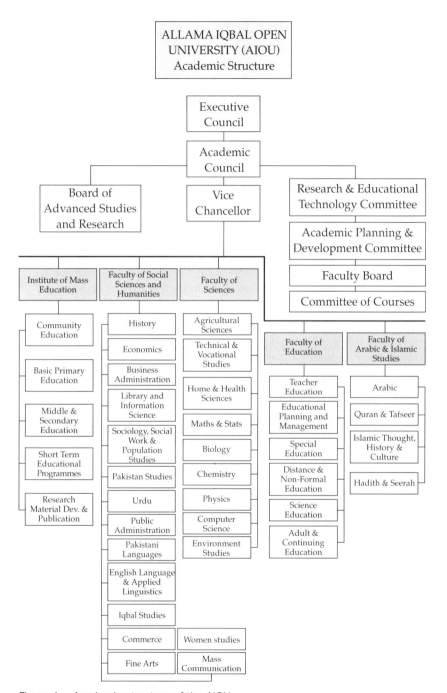

Figure 1   Academic structure of the AIOU

Source: Research and Evaluation Centre, AIOU (1999)

In order to manage and meet the country's vast educational needs, the University is carrying the job through its four faculties and Institute of Mass Education. The collective academic strength at the main campus in Islamabad is 97, with 627 supporting staff and 206 staff in the regions. Compared to the other formal universities, academic staffing positions for the 631 courses on offer in the 1999 semesters are very meagre. The basic pay scale (BPS) for academic staff starts at Lecturer (BPS-17) and rises through Assistant Professor (BPS-18), Associate Professor (BPS-19) and Professor (BPS-20). The entry point requires the applicant for a position to hold a 1st division degree in his or her subject of specialization. Each tier also has requirements of experience, research and publications. A continuing ban on the creation of posts has been in place since 1989. Course enrolment in 1988 was around 80,000 only. Since then, course enrolment in the University has increased almost 12-fold and has reached almost one million. The University's academic and administrative staff, numbering around 1,250, were stretched to their limit. The regional campuses were under particular stress to coordinate and organize educational activities in the regions with skeleton staff. The average number of staff per Regional Office was only one officer of BPS-17, yet the University was offering more than 700 courses and more than 50 degree programmes. It became extremely difficult for Regional Offices to administer such a large number of programmes and courses.

After a great struggle, the government allowed the University to open 149 posts, created with the approval of the Chancellor, mostly for academic departments and regional centres. This has provided some relief. However, at least 800 additional posts are required to strengthen the academic departments and our regional campus in the coming years.

All 149 posts have been created with the undertaking by the University that their financial impact will be entirely borne by the University from its own resources, which the University has accomplished through the continuously increasing income from the new degree programmes.

Staff development

The induction of academic staff in the AIOU system is based on selection by merit with a 1st division Master's degree in the specialized subject. Experience in distance education is not a pre-condition for employment. Until the late 1980s, staff development in distance education involved sending staff from the different faculties on a three-month course in distance education at the University of London in the UK through the Overseas Development Authority (ODA) sponsorship scheme. Locally this was done through externally sponsored workshops. Thereafter until the mid-1990s this was done through a series of short one-week training sessions organized by the Department of Distance and Non-formal Education. This local in-service training by faculty members who have had exposure to distance education through ODA sponsorship has proved a useful practice in acquainting staff with current practice. Unfortunately it only became a regular feature in 2000, until which time the need had perhaps not been felt because of the ban on appointments. Its recommencement is positive for staff development. The professional growth of staff in higher studies until the mid-1990s was done through the government Central Overseas Training (COT) Scholarship scheme. Some staff benefited from Commonwealth of Learning (COL) and British Council scholarships. But in some cases the University did not gain from their professionalism on their return and lost out as staff left to join other institutions either in the private sector in Pakistan or abroad, for more lucrative jobs and better benefits. These factors have offered a few individuals greater opportunities (Mustafa 1999).

In order to move ahead with staff development, in 1999 the AIOU started its own system, by establishing an Endowment Fund. With a sizeable allocation of income from the Endowment Fund, the University has launched a staff development programme that includes scholarships for at least two teachers every year for a PhD programme in recognized universities abroad. Under this programme, two faculty members were sent on PhD programmes in the UK and Australia in Business Administration and Women's Studies respectively. In addition, two more faculty members joined overseas PhD programmes on other sponsorships. The doctoral studies of four other faculty members are also being supported in Pakistani universities.

Meeting educational demand through the formal system

Demand for distance education in Pakistan is increasing by the day. Despite the AIOU's manpower and financial constraints, it is fulfilling demand for education through its collaboration with academics in colleges, universities and schools of the formal system. These academics participate in course development as members of course teams, course committees, unit and script writers. For the implementation of courses, the AIOU relies very heavily on part-time tutors from the formal system. The tutors in the

1998 to 1999 academic year numbered 18,780. These part-time tutors are again academics from the educational institutions of the formal system. A very crude formula of three tutors for 100 students is used. In exceptional circumstances and hard-to-reach areas, a tutor is provided for ten students. Where student numbers are too low, only a correspondence tutor is provided.

Qualifications

The acceptance of AIOU diplomas and degrees did not proceed as easily. The first major step forward in the fight for credibility of its qualifications occurred in 1980, when the University Grants Committee (UGC) issued a notice stating that AIOU qualifications were equivalent to those of other universities and requiring all universities in Pakistan to acknowledge this. The UGC said, 'It is a strange thing that the university whose Chancellor is the President of Pakistan, its degrees are not acceptable to a federal (authority) whereas the Universities for which a governor is the Chancellor, its degrees are accepted' (Mustafa 1999).

Accreditation has opened new channels. A Memo of Understanding has since been signed between the AIOU and the Pakistan Atomic Energy Commission (PCSIR) to offer an MSc in Physics. The PCSIR is offering the services of its experts in the writing of textbooks and to provide instructional support to AIOU students, in addition to allowing students to use their laboratories for practical training.

Curriculum content and courses of study

The AIOU is a unique educational institution, which offers degrees, diplomas and certificates from basic to doctorate and research level. All these programmes have a wide variety of clusters and courses, which are developed and launched by the four faculties — the Faculty of Education, the Faculty of Social Sciences and Humanities, the Faculty of Arabic and Islamic Studies and the Faculty of Sciences — and the Institute of Mass Education.

The main components of its multimedia package are as follows:

- Correspondence materials including self-learning study packages and supplementary study materials (readers, textbooks and study guides);

- Radio and television broadcasts generally related to the study materials;

- Satellite transmission — the AIOU is airing its educational media material on PTV-2, which beams transmission via satellite to more than 45 countries;

- Non-broadcast media including slides, audio cassettes, flip charts, and leaflets (generally for basic functional and literacy level courses), and audio and video cassettes as an integral part of learning materials;

- Tutorial instruction through contact sessions and academic guidance facilities at study centres (mostly in the afternoons);

- Face-to-face teaching, which has recently been started for courses that require intensive practical and lab work or skills development;

- Group training workshops for postgraduate programmes, generally at MA, MSc, MPhil and diploma levels;

- Short- and long-term internships in industrial or business concerns for BBA and MBA programmes;

- Written assignments as an instrument of instruction, continuous assessment and general academic guidance. Tutors evaluate the assignments;

- A final examination for each course at the end of the semester.

The teaching system described above shows the components that make up the AIOU teaching methodology, which is where the difference between the AIOU and the traditional formal system of instruction. The curriculum does not differ so greatly as the University is part of the UGC system and abides by mutually agreed curricula. The different teaching methodology and the way the curriculum is presented in the form of course materials means the roles of distance educators also differ. Distance education teachers undertake a range of roles simultaneously, such as planning, curriculum development, writing, evaluation, monitoring, coordination, pre-testing, tutoring, training, demonstrating, resource linking, managing, researching, reviewing, giving feedback, supervising, leading, field coordination and revision.

In view of the requirements of the distance education teaching methodology, the Registrar of the AIOU requires educators to:

- Conduct feasibility studies;
- Initiate course of programme proposals;

- Develop course outlines (curricula) for courses and programmes;
- Write course units (chapters);
- Coordinate the development of courses and study guides;
- Revise and update course materials;
- Compile related reading materials in the form of readers;
- Teach in course-related workshops and course revision sessions at the head office and in the regions;
- Supervise and coordinate orientation or end-of-course workshops;
- Participate in tutor training and briefings;
- Supervise postgraduate level research;
- Write scripts for media, radio and TV and non-broadcast programmes;
- Participate in the production of media programmes;
- Prepare assignments for each semester and monitor assignment evaluations;
- Visit tutorials to obtain feedback;
- Review the three drafts of each unit of every course at the development stage;
- Proofread units, assignments, student and tutor guides and publicity materials;
- Maintain links with other agencies for needs assessment and course production and course offerings;
- Prepare working papers for statutory bodies;
- Maintain courses.

With the latest developments in communication and information technology, particularly by satellite and the Internet, the role of teachers will change further. The correspondence method and tutorial system are likely to be replaced by distance teaching via satellite and the Internet. The University has already taken steps in this direction. More on these developmental activities can be found under the section entitled 'Technologies for ODE' and 'Future technologies'.

The development of course materials in distance education and unit writing is more challenging. A written unit must go through three drafts before it can be finalized. Thus, in comparison to teaching under the traditional formal system, it is a more demanding and time-consuming process. As a result, distance education teaching staff do not have much time for individual research, which becomes a hurdle to promotion. Since unit writing and distance education course materials are published work, they should be given some weight for their scholarly nature, and considered in addition to research articles in staff promotion. The AIOU needs to make a policy decision with regard to its teaching faculty promotion criteria and implement a set of promotion criteria that reflect the differences in the distance system and that will differentiate it from the formal system that it currently imitates. It should, of course, not in any way be considered an inferior system.

Research-based activities should be encouraged as the second generation of distance education has gained momentum and the third generation already has a whole new set of research directions in terms of new technology in view and, no doubt, that will soon come into use around the world and will need to be matched.

Until the mid-1990s, as part of teaching staff assessment, self-assessment forms were given to teaching staff at the end of an academic year. The benefits of this activity were two-fold. In the first instance the teaching staff had an opportunity to review their own performance and their place in the University, and it provided feedback for the preparation of the Annual Confidential Reports (ACR). It was a good practice and it would never be too early to revive it.

Learning support services

Directorate of Regional Services and the Student Advisory and Counselling Cell are the major providers of student learning support services.

Directorate of Regional Services

The Directorate of Regional Services is a distinctive aspect of the AIOU that differentiates it from the formal universities. Through this service the University extends its educational facilities to people's homes. It comprises the following broad spheres of activity.

Tutor support and study centres

This is arranged through part-time tutors (teachers of formal institutions) who evaluate students' home assignments and hold tutorial meetings at the local study centres in the evenings and at weekends.

Tutors are specially appointed to provide academic guidance for all courses offered during a semester. There are currently between 8,000 and 9,000 tutors. They belong to local educational institutions and work with the AIOU on a part-time basis.

The University has established over 500 study centres (in the premises of other institutions) where tutorials are held according to a study schedule. Of these study centres 70 are equipped with audio-visual aids. A number of centres are exclusively for female students.

Face-to-face workshops for students joining professional courses provide opportunities for interaction. Extended practical sessions for technical and vocational courses are arranged usually at weekends.

Enrolment in AIOU courses is increasing by semester, and the number of tutors and study centres is also increased accordingly. This increase in regional services outreach is shown in Figure 2.

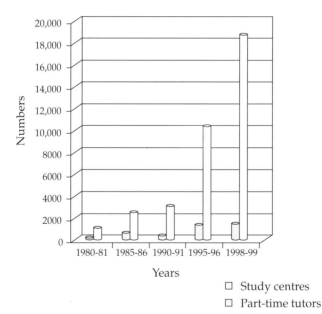

Figure 2   Study centres and part-time tutors

Source: The AIOU from 1974 to 1999 (1999)

The AIOU evaluates each student's progress through continuous assessment and a final examination. Regional Services undertakes all continuous assessment through its part-time tutors and also identifies examination centres and supervisory staff, and facilitates inspection of university examinations conducted in most districts twice a year.

Regional Services constitutes the field operation side of the University and its campus; centres are the focal point of all student support services. It is through activities in the regions that the University is recognized in the large cities as well as remote areas.

Today Regional Services caters to the needs of around one million students enrolled in courses from all over Pakistan. The beneficiaries of the AIOU spread from the coast around Karachi to the heights of the Himalayas, such as Siachin and the far-flung areas of Chitral, i.e. Wah Khan near the border with Tajikistan (Central Asian State). Every year more than 1,200 tutors are appointed and over 1,000 study centres provide face-to-face guidance to students on over 600 courses from basic to PhD level.

Regional Services is today equipped with PCs (both in the offices and the library) and photocopiers, and the use of modems and the Internet to enable the transmission and retrieval of data to and from the main campus, and vice versa, is in progress so that students' complaints, etc., can be addressed locally.

In addition to the activities mentioned above, the Directorate also takes care of the arrangements for promotional activities, student support services and co-curricular activities for students in all regions.

Student Advisory and Counselling Cell

The Student Advisory and Counselling Cell was established in 1984 with the main objectives of providing academic assistance to students to enable them to continue and complete their studies. The major activities undertaken by the cell for the students are as follows:

- The cell provides guidance and counselling services to distance learners through the media, by telephone and by post;

- Individual and group (face-to-face) counselling sessions are also conducted for students on campus as well as in the regions;

- The cell acts as a link between the students and the campus, and aims at promoting interaction among students through curricular and co-curricular activators so as to motivate them to become active learners throughout their course of study;

- The cell attracts new learners and can facilitate their choice of courses and programmes, and introduces them to the distinct features of distance education;

- A weekly radio programme 'JAMIA NAMA' written and conducted by the Director of Student Affairs provides current information regarding University programmes for students and the general public. It also highlights pressing issues experienced by students and offers advice as to how to remedy such problems;

- The cell responds to general queries, and draws up standard letters regarding University programmes and procedures;

- Staff of the cell help to resolve problems that students may have by liaising on their behalf with the relevant academic and serving departments.

In addition to providing these services to students based locally, the advisory cell also has the assigned task of coordinating overseas students. The overseas cell has also been made a part of the advisory cell. Coordination includes:

- Admission of Overseas Pakistanis residing in the Middle East and Gulf states and Saudi Arabia;

- Providing information on guidance and academic counselling to overseas students;

- Liaising with Pakistani institutions abroad for student enrolment and provision of tutorial support where possible;

- Coordinating with the Foreign Office and Embassies abroad for the conducting of examinations and imparting admissions information to Pakistanis living within their area of jurisdiction;

- Replying to queries of students and the general public abroad;

- Study packs are also delivered via the supervision of the overseas cell;

- The assignment schedules, supplementary materials and student guides are also prepared and provided to overseas students by the overseas director;

- The assignments of the overseas students are received in the cell and evaluation is arranged by the Director of Regional Services;

- The final examinations are arranged and conducted by the Examination Department, however the overseas cell is responsible for conveying any information regarding examinations and results;

- Complaints regarding examinations are handled and conferred by the overseas cell.

The advisory role of the cell responds to student queries and requests for help, etc., by the use of:

- Standard answer sheets;

- Personal and specific letters;

- Telephone counselling;

- Face-to-face guidance;

- Regular communication through the media.

Student assistance and the funding of activities

To provide assistance to needy students, especially those on costly courses such as Computer Sciences, Physics, Business Administration, etc., a fee of Rs10 per course is levied from each student with the approval of the AIOU Executive Council. Similarly, a fee of Rs5 per course per student is levied for the organization of student activities. The income from these two sources is approximately Rs15 million per annum.

In order to distribute the Student Assistance Fund equitably, an elaborate system for the evaluation of applications has been put in place in the regions as well as in the AIOU headquarters.

Assessment of student achievement

Each student can usually take a maximum of two full credits or four half-credit courses in a semester. A full-credit course has a study period of 18 weeks. A full-credit course has 18 units, which require students to complete four tutor-marked assignments. A half-credit course has nine units with two assignments. Correspondence units are designed to require one week of study comprising 10 to 12 hours of study. A student may not take more than two credits in one semester. A special concession is granted to those approved to take three credits in courses where 80% attendance is compulsory for practical and lab work. Most courses include nine or more radio programmes during the semester and several courses also include television programmes. Some courses also have a workshop component.

Each student is required to complete his or her assignments and send them to the assigned tutor for assessment. The evaluated assignments are returned to students with instructional notes. The marks obtained in these assignments are sent to the Controller of Examinations for the record and for preparation of the final grade.

The Examinations Department conducts the final examinations for each course (as the other Boards and universities in the country) at the end of each semester. The main examinations are conducted twice a year, i.e. in March/April and August/September each year. A student may resit the final examination three times.

The overall result is based on a combination of the grades obtained in continuous assessment (30%) and the final examination (70%). The minimum pass mark for each course is 33% but the aggregate mark for the award of a complete certificate (e.g. for a BA) is 40%.

Programme management and quality assurance

Programmes are managed through close collaboration between the Bureau of Course Production and Academic Planning (BCPAP) and the faculties and academic departments. The BCPAP is central to the course development process as it functions in close collaboration with the Course Committees, Faculty Boards, Group for Academic Policy and Planning (GAPP), Research and Technology Committee, Academic Planning and Development Committee and the Academic Council. The BCPAP participates in course planning, administers course production and the launching of courses in collaboration with the faculties, academic and servicing departments, as well as with many other bodies that influence the formulation of policy and planning of academic programmes. The overall coordination of course writing and all associated activities are its major responsibilities. In monitoring the progress of course production it endeavours to meet deadlines and arrange meetings with course team and course development coordinators and the personnel in the printing, editing and design sections of the University.

The BCPAP arranges, about a semester ahead of the start of each semester, details of academic courses and programmes, printing and reprinting of course books, assignments and related materials, and the broadcasting schedules of TV and radio programmes of the courses to be launched in the ensuing semester. It also coordinates and consults with the faculties, academic departments, Institute of Educational Technology, Print Production Unit, the Editing and Design Cell, Computer Centre, Admissions and Mailing sections, and the Advertisement Committee, etc., as required. Thus it is in many respects the nerve centre of the University.

The University's academic year is divided into two semesters. Each semester is normally six months, from October to February, and April to August. All admissions are notified well in advance by a notice in the national press. There is always a deadline for admissions for each semester.

Approximately 150,000 forms are received and processed for admission to various programmes each semester. The admission process takes about three months from the receipt of forms to finalization of the admissions. After eligibility for admission to a programme is verified, the forms are coded by the admissions section and sent to the Computer Centre for preparation of enrolment lists and address labels. The Mailing Section then sends instructional materials to students. The admission lists are passed on to the regional offices in all provinces for the appointment of tutors and the establishment of study centres according to the enrolment clusters for each course.

The AIOU's programmes are offered through its faculties and institutions. The departments concerned are responsible for programme initiation and the formation of the course team and the development of course outlines. Project feasibility is done before the formation of the course team. The course team formulates course outlines and proposals, which are discussed by the Course Committee. In some cases the outlines are deferred before recommendation to the Faculty Board or the Board of Study. The outlines and proposals must be approved by various statutory bodies before final approval by the Academic Council. After the final approval the course production stage starts and follows the stages shown in Figure 3. Ideally, before a programme is launched, its courses should be pre-tested. This is not the case with all the AIOU's programmes. Only project courses are pre-tested as there is financial provision for such an exercise. The pre-tested courses, compared to the other courses, are therefore quality assured. However the development process as shown in Figure 3, which the other courses undergo, also ensures quality. At the implementation stage, quality is checked through monitoring. Again, the monitoring of academic programmes is currently possible only for project courses.

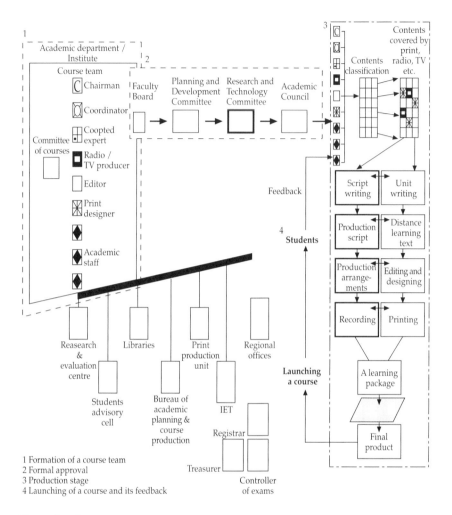

Figure 3   Course development process

Source: AIOU Profile 1999

Course quality is also ensured by the feedback forms, provided with each course, for submission at the end of a course. This feedback helps the University address course administration or academic issues. Based on this feedback, course content is sometimes revised inside the course lifecycle of five years. The Research Centre also undertakes research to monitor the effectiveness and quality of the course.

Monitoring of tutor-marked assignments was a practice in the early years of the AIOU. With the increase in the number of courses it was discontinued.

It was particularly effective as it monitored grading by tutors. The practice needs to be reactivated at the regional office level. It can be addressed by appointing a regional academic coordinator for this purpose. The academic coordinator thus appointed can also help with other activities arranged as part of some courses, i.e. workshops and practicals. In addition, the monitoring of the academic programmes by teaching staff, concerned departments and coordinators needs to be pursued to ensure qualitative input.

If this practice cannot be implemented, then every three semesters a short orientation workshop may be arranged to pinpoint the least effective tutors.

Financing ODE

The University's income and expenses are divided into two broad categories in accordance with government practices — development budget and recurring expenses budget. Development funds cover the cost of construction, equipment and new project development. The recurring budget generally covers fixed expenses like salaries, physical plant maintenance, supplies and other costs.

Over the years the AIOU has generated sufficient funds to ensure its sustainability. With the expansion of activities and diversification of its programmes funds have been able to have been generated from student fees, utilization of Institute of Educational Technology studios and the sale of publications.

In 1999, the total budget of the University stood at approximately Rs503 million, of which Rs423 million was raised by the University from student fees with Rs80 million provided by the government in the form of a grant. In addition, as mentioned earlier, the University earns Rs15 million per annum for Student Assistance and Activities funds directly from the students. The University has also received Rs27 million as grants for donor-sponsored projects such as the new Primary Teachers Orientation Course (PTOC). The government share of the current revenue for the 1999 to 2000 academic year comes to about 14% (Rs85 million) of the University's budget of Rs610 million. The University has thus raised 86% of its budget from its own resources. The AIOU is thus moving well towards self-sufficiency with a well-balanced budget.

Taking the University's total revenue, including the government's development grant, into account, government share for recurring as well as development activities expenses comes to about 12.5% of the total. With the addition of new academic programmes, it is hoped that the income from fee collection will steadily rise in coming years.

Technologies for ODE

The AIOU has realized the need for the introduction of IT in its administrative and academic departments. For this purpose, the AIOU has invested heavily in technology-based infrastructure.

The following are a few notable examples:

- Faculty and staff training — The AIOU has equipped every department with PCs. A total of about 500 have been installed. Staff and faculty members have all attended training courses. Almost all staff members and faculty have signed up for courses in computer applications and course materials development. Internal training is provided by the Computer Science Department.

- Development of databases — Even though initial computerization raised many data-processing problems related to student enrolment, the need was felt to update software and systems. In this connection, applications are being posted to an Oracle database. All administrative systems including admissions, examinations, fees, student services, etc., are posted to an Oracle-based application.

- Internet and Web application — All regional offices are connected to the University mail server and Web server. The University has a sponsored Internet connection to the Internet, which is provided nation-wide to all AIOU regional offices.

- Multimedia courseware — The Computer Science Department is heavily engaged in development of RCD facilities geared towards University computerization. In this connection a multimedia courseware laboratory has been established. This is being used to train faculty and develop the courseware. The laboratory is well equipped with necessary hardware and software.

- Media Laboratory — The Computer Science Department in collaboration with Institute of Educational Technology is developing a media laboratory. This laboratory will be used for the development of video materials for its courses at graduate level and for the general public.

- Development of an Internet-based academic system.

The AIOU is now focused on the development of an Internet-based academic system. The first course on e-commerce is being developed with the help of an expert from New Zealand Open Polytechnic.

Future technologies

The AIOU now has a vision of the technology-supported infrastructure that will be a key component of our distance education system. Serious thought is being given to the development of a virtual University model. The following are the main areas where the AIOU is taking initiatives:

- Online admissions and examinations system;
- Online tutoring and faculty support;
- Development of a Web-based student management system;
- Specialization in multimedia and Web-based courses in all disciplines;
- Rural Internet communication infrastructure development through the Ministry of Science and Technology;
- Development of model study centres in remote areas of Pakistan;
- Digital TV transmission and reception capacity at model study centres to support course study.

We hope that all such endeavours will help to earn the AIOU a respectable place in the world of learning. The University now has a website <www.aiou.edu.pk>.

International collaboration in ODE

The University has enlisted international support from a number of aid-giving agencies under collaborative arrangements. Since its establishment the AIOU has been receiving technical assistance from the UK Open University in the form of staff training, consultancy in distance education and the setting up of the Institute of Educational Technology. The ODA project continued from 1976 to 1994. It not only helped in the University's academic development, it also provided assistance for the setting up of the University Press, the Data Processing Centre, academic programmes at basic level through the Integrated Functional Literacy Project (IFLP), the Functional Education Programme for Rural Areas (FEPRA), and the Basic Functional Education Programme (BFEP). The major hardware necessary for these projects was TVs, video cassette recorders, audio cassette players, 29 Land Rovers, seven motorcycles, and a mobile study centre (AV van) for use in rural areas.

The government of the Netherlands gave the University assistance for the Women's Matriculation Project, which ran to three phases. The project provided educational opportunities to women in rural areas who could not attend the formal institutions for social, financial and cultural reasons. The project has now become a regular programme of the University and is also open to male students.

The government of Norway funded the new PTOC for the training of 50,000 primary teachers over a period of almost ten years.

The following agencies have also helped the University in its formative years:

- The UNDP, which equipped the University's first TV studio;

- UNICEF for Integrated Functional Education Projects in the four regions at Daultala, Sarai Naurang, Samahni and Bhit Shah;

- UNESCO helped in the initial years by helping with staff training and research activities and conducting workshops for the development of distance teaching materials. In the 1990s the AIOU became UNESCO Chair in distance education in the region. In recognition of its pioneering work in the field of non-formal and basic education, the University has received the international UNESCO NOMA Award and the Raja Roy Sing Award;

- The Arab League Educational Cultural and Scientific Organization (ALECSO) has been collaborating with the AIOU in its efforts to upgrade secondary school teachers' qualifications through a crash course for approximately 2,400 in-service Arabic secondary school teachers. Under an agreement with the government of Pakistan and the AIOU, ALECSO provided five trainers and financed education software and audio-visual equipment projects;

- The government of Japan (JICA) helped the University in modernizing and updating its studios and equipment of the Institute of Educational Technology. The AIOU is currently negotiating with JICA to begin the second phase of this project with the provision of the latest digital technology for producing quality educational film. The AIOU was awarded a silver medal by JICA for the documentary film entitled 'Sohni Dharti';

- The COL is assisting the AIOU in offering a diploma in its Youth Development Programme. It is one-and- a-half years (three semesters with five modules per semester), specially prepared by the Commonwealth Youth Programme taken from the Intermediate and F.Sc course of instruction. It is activities-based and concludes with an examination;

- The World Bank is sponsoring matriculation for girls in the northern areas under a project called the Northern Area Education Programme (NAEP) through the British Council as the implementing agency. It is being offered to 150 girls in the two remote districts of Ganchi and Diamer. The programme started in Spring 2000 and will continue until Spring 2003;

- Korea, through technical assistance, sent a list of audio-visual equipment in July 2000, and has asked the AIOU to specify its requirements;

- International linkage of the AIOU through its membership of the International Council for Distance Education (ICDE) and the Asian Association of Open Universities.

The periods for all of these foreign-aided projects have expired. The University is now attempting to secure assistance through the Social Action Programme of the government, which has donor funding.

Priorities for policy and national direction

The advent of modern IT, the use of satellites and most importantly the Internet have opened new vistas in the field of distance education.

As access to the Internet expands, the University will increasingly be in a position to supplement its instructional efforts through the Internet throughout Pakistan. The traditional system of written correspondence and tutorials will be gradually replaced or supplemented by online teaching on the Internet. The University is preparing for this major change in its methodology by training its faculty members in the use and application of the Internet. It is also improving its ability to use this technology for imparting education by creating its own website, and creating a wide area network throughout Pakistan by connecting all of its regional offices to the Data Processing Centre and the academic departments.

The University is also currently applying to obtain a licence to start its own full-time radio and TV stations for use in support of its educational programmes. Presently it has only one hour of air time every day in the afternoon on Pakistan Television network (PTV) PTV-2, which is not only inadequate but also unsuitable in terms of scheduling. As soon as the AIOU is able to start its own radio and TV network and secure the necessary transmission facilities from the Pakistan Telecommunication Corporation (PTC) and PTV, the University's ability to use different media effectively in support of its educational programmes will be augmented considerably (Siddiqui 2000).

The University can also play an effective role in mass literacy through distance education. It has already contributed significantly to this effort by doing basic research, providing quality indigenous literature and by training teachers. If assigned a direct role in the literacy campaign, the University has the expertise and its nation-wide network to make even greater contributions.

The University has already made a significant beginning in the fields of Basic and Applied Sciences. Science and technology will be the focus of academic expansion in the next five years or so. Innovations in IT, and collaboration and cooperation among sister institutions such as the Pakistan Atomic Energy Commission and Pakistan Council of Scientific and Industrial Research (PCSIR) is making the task easier.

The University has begun to make inroads in the field of medicine. It has launched postgraduate diplomas in Eye Care, Nutrition and Dietetics with the expertise of local recognized hospitals. It hopes to start degree programmes in the near future.

ODE use by other educational institutions

The teacher training curriculum in the country has been changed. The change is a positive one and was made possible under the ADB Teacher Training Project Diploma in Education.

Teacher Training Diploma in Education

Under the ADB Teacher Training Project, the Diploma in Education has been created to enhance and substantially improve education for elementary school teachers in Pakistan. The Diploma in Education is seen as part of the 'ladder of opportunity' available for teachers and prospective teachers in Pakistan.

The Diploma in Education will enable graduates to teach from classes 1 to 8. It will be available for both Year 10 and Year 12 high school graduates. Year 10 graduates will take a three-year programme integrating content subjects equivalent to years 11 and 12 higher secondary school subjects, and the final year education subjects. If the course is taken completely through distance education, the Year 11 and Year 12 courses may be undertaken through an approved distance education programme such as that offered by the AIOU.

The Diploma in Education programme will include 12 courses specially geared towards teacher training, i.e. five core courses and seven methodology courses. Teaching practice will be an integral part of the programme. Year 12 graduates will complete one year with teacher training courses and teaching practice.

For Year 12 students these courses would be completed in one-year on-campus study at a Government College of Education (GCE) and in three semesters or 18 months if studying through distance education at a Training Outpost, a unit in the provincial teacher education institute.

The distance education programme

The 12 courses in the distance Diploma of Education are taken in the final 'distance education' year of study if the 10+3 model is used. If the 12+1 model is used, all courses will also be done in one 'distance education' year. i.e., over three semesters or 18 months. The distance education core courses and methodology courses are for students who have completed the equivalent of intermediate study. The Diploma in Education studied at a Training Outpost usually includes the distance education materials, face-to-face tutorials, micro-teaching and blocks of teaching practice.

On-campus or distance education study

The Diploma in Education will be available for study in two modes:

- On campus at Government Elementary Teacher Training Colleges (GCETs) and GCEs;

- Through distance education at Training Outposts.

Normally the Diploma will be completed in one year (two semesters) following Year 12, if studied on campus. Through distance education at Training Outposts, the Diploma will usually take three semesters, although it may be completed over a longer period of time if necessary. Whichever mode of study is chosen, courses studied will be identical, covering the 12 courses, micro-teaching and teaching practice in schools. In addition, regular tutorials will be conducted at the Training Outposts, incorporating micro-teaching practice, materials development and discussion of Study Guide activities and course assignments. The components of the teaching system and approaches to the course of study can be seen in Figure 4.

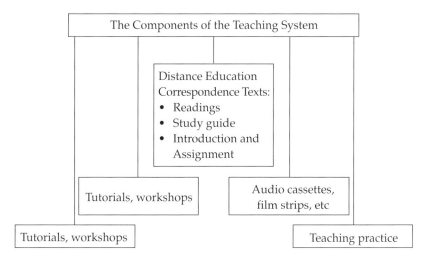

Figure 4   Diploma in Education through distance education

Source: Manual of Operations for Training Outposts (1997).

An important function of the Training Outposts is that they conduct tutorials for the students who are studying the Diploma in Education through distance education.

Six tutorials are held at a Training Outposts each semester. Each tutorial lasts for one day, commencing at 9.00 am. It is highly recommended that student teachers attend these tutorials since sessions cover distance education materials, micro-teaching and teaching materials development. Participation of student teachers in these tutorials is evaluated on an 'Individual semester achievement form'. An attendance register should be kept. Tutors should ensure that all students have access to transport and should deal with attendance problems as soon as these arise.

Army School of Administration

The Army School of Administration uses the AIOU's STEPs management programme as the distance education component in its administration course. A group of 60 officers have gone through the STEPs course in the last two years.

IT Virtual University

The government of Pakistan is giving great priority to the IT sector as it has assumed unprecedented importance in the global economic arena. On 25 July 2000 the Minister of Science and Technology (Prof. Dr Atta-ur-Rehman) and Telecom has announced plans to establish an IT Virtual University. As per this announcement a two-hour slot on PTV will be dedicated to IT education. In this way the AIOU's new IT studio will be utilized to the maximum. In addition, negotiations are underway with a number of reputed foreign universities for affiliation with the IT Virtual University.

The IT policy and action plan has now been formally circulated to all concerned institutions. The policy clauses relating to distance education are reproduced here:

3.4.2   IT Education

3.4.2.9   Establish virtual classroom education programmes, using online, Internet and/or video facilities, to provide distance learning to a large number of individuals (Government of Pakistan 2000, 10).

3.4.2.10   Provide foreign and local universities incentives to set up distance learning or resident programmes in Pakistan (Government of Pakistan 2000, 11).

Under the IT Action Plan and project portfolio, Virtual IT University has been allocated Rs 1,500.00 million (Government of Pakistan 2000, 40).

Conclusion

The distance education system has in the case of Pakistan proved its potential for further expansion and growth. It has greatly supplemented the efforts of both the federal and provincial governments by easing their educational workload. Above all, its contribution in making education accessible to female learners and working people has been invaluable. The 25-year journey has opened more vistas of learning and joint collaborations for making it the largest open and distance learning university.

References

AIOU (1986) *The First Ten Years — 1975–1985*, Islamabad: AIOU.

AIOU (1989) *The Guidelines for Unit Writing*, Islamabad: AIOU.

AIOU (1989) *Vice Chancellor's Report — 1985–1988*, Islamabad: AIOU.

AIOU (1996) *A Brief Introduction of Faculties, Administrative and Servicing Departments*, Islamabad: AIOU.

AIOU (1998) *Chronology of AIOU Courses and Media Support Present and Future Plans*, Islamabad: Bureau of Academic Planning and Course Development, AIOU.

AIOU (1999) *Achievements of IME, 1975–1999*, Islamabad: Institute of Mass Education, AIOU.

AIOU (1999) *Profile Twenty Five Years*, Islamabad: AIOU.

AIOU (1999) *Triennial Report 1997–1999*, Islamabad: AIOU.

AIOU (2000) *Annual Report July 1,1999 to June 30, 2000*, Islamabad: AIOU.

Government of Pakistan (1999) *Economic Survey of Pakistan*, Islamabad.

Government of Pakistan (2000) *IT Policy and Action Plan*, Islamabad: Ministry of Science and Technology, IT & Telecommunications Division.

Kato, H and Wong S-Y (1992) *Asia and the Pacific: A Survey of Distance Education* 1999, Japan: UNESCO and NIME.

Kay, T and Rumble, G (1991) 'Open universities: a comparative approach', *Prospects*, 21(2): 214–26. <http://www1.worldbank.org/disted/management/governance/sys-02.html>

Ministry of Education, Asian Development Bank (1996) 'Pakistan teachers training project, Loan No.1210-Pak (SF)', *First Report of the International PBME, EMIS and Research Specialist*, Islamabad.

Ministry of Education (Curriculum Wing) and Asian Development Bank (1997) *Manual of Operations for Training Outputs*, Islamabad.

Ministry of Education (1998) *National Education Policy (1998–2010)*, Islamabad.

Mustafa, B A (1998) Institution Building and Organizational Development at Allama Iqbal Open University (Pakistan) 'A study of institutional development and technology transfer based on the British Open University model', USA: Indiana, A Bell and Howell Company Michigan, 48106-1346. <http://www.umi.com>

Robinson, B (1996) 'Effective schools/teachers: distance education for primary teacher training in developing countries, in J Lynch, C Modgil and S Modgil (eds) *Innovations in Delivering Primary Education*, London: Cassell Educational.

Siddiqui, A H (2000) *25 Year Success Story: Pioneering Role in Spreading Cost-effective Mass Education*, Islamabad: AIOU.

Taylor, J and Motial S (1990) 'Distance education in South Asia: towards regional cooperation', in M Croft, I Mugridge, J S Danial and A Hershfied (eds) *Distance Education: Development and Access*, Caracas: The International Council for Distance Education, 312–16.

Visser, J (1994) 'Learning without frontiers: distance education for the nine high-population countries', DE9 concept paper, planning meeting on distance education in E-9 countries, Manila, UNESCO, Basic Education Division, Paris.

World Bank Group (1999) *New Approaches to Education: The Northern Areas Community Schools Program in Pakistan, South Asia Brief.* <http://www.worldbank.org/html/extdr/offrep/sas/educbrf/nacsp.htm>

Sri Lanka

N R Arthenayake

Introduction

The Democratic Socialist Republic of Sri Lanka, known as Ceylon until 1972, is an independent state in the Indian Ocean, lying off the south-eastern coast of the Indian peninsula. Sri Lanka covers a total area of 65,610 square kilometres, has a parliamentary form of government and is a member of the Commonwealth of Nations.

Sri Lanka is still basically an agricultural country, but is rapidly becoming industrialized.

An extensive communications infrastructure is already in place, with over a dozen radio stations providing AM and FM broadcasts as well as nine different television channels, with both radio and TV broadcasting in the two national languages, Sinhala and Tamil, and in English. Telephone facilities are extensive and widely available throughout the island, while computer facilities are growing in availability, at present mostly in urban areas. In recent years the number of Internet users has also begun to grow rapidly with several private Internet service providers catering to a large clientele all over the island.

Sri Lanka's population, provisionally estimated at 19.043 million in mid-1999, is composed of several ethnic groups as shown in Table 1.

Table 1   Distribution of population by ethnic group

Ethnic group	Population % distribution
Sinhala	83.86
Sri Lankan Tamils	5.39
Indian Tamils	3.62
Sri Lankan Moors	6.35
Burghers and Eurasians	0.27
Malays	0.31
Other	0.20

The island's indigenous people, the Veddah aborigines, are one of the oldest traditional cultures in the world, though they currently make up only a small fraction of the country's population. In terms of religious belief, Buddhism has been the religion of the majority since its introduction in 250 BC.

Table 2   Distribution by religious affiliation

Religion	Population % distribution
Buddhism	78.24
Hinduism	7.51
Islam	6.71
Christianity	7.51
Others	0.04

The island was colonized in successive waves of migration, the earliest known of which dates back to about 500 BC. Most migrations came from neighbouring India, while the island was briefly occupied by the Portuguese and Dutch in the 16th and 17th centuries. It became a part of the British Empire in 1815, finally gaining independence in 1948. Colonization was to drastically transform the country's face. This gave rise to parliamentary democracy, the rule of law and modern social and cultural structures.

The country enjoys a comparatively high literacy rate (90%).

Education system

Until the arrival of the Portuguese in 1505, the education system largely consisted of *pirivena* education for the Buddhist clergy and the privileged laity, in Buddhist temples. During the years of occupation by the Portuguese, the Dutch and the British, the education system familiar to the West was introduced to Sri Lanka and became the standard, bringing the traditional form of education to an end.

A name that is synonymous with free education in Sri Lanka is Dr C W W Kannangara. He is affectionately remembered as the father of free education for, as Minister of Education, he was instrumental in obtaining the sanction of the State Council of pre-independence Ceylon to introduce free education from kindergarten to university. Introduction of national languages (Sinhala and Tamil) in place of English at primary level and the establishment of Central Schools paved the way to ensuring the provision of equal opportunities in education for Sri Lanka's citizens.

Since 1948, primary, secondary and tertiary education has been free in Sri Lanka. Almost all children between the ages of five and 11 attend school, while a high proportion continue until the age of 16 and the General Certificate of Education (Ordinary Level) examination or the age of 18 and the General Certificate of Education (Advanced Level) examination. The government also provides all children with free textbooks and school uniforms.

The formal education system is as follows:

- General education system: Primary and secondary education;

- Technical/vocational education: Targeted at preparing skilled vocational and technical personnel to meet the needs of a growing economy;

- Higher education: College and university education.

The system of general education comprises pre-school education from the age of three to five and primary education covering Grades I to V. Junior secondary education covers Grades VI to IX, and the senior secondary stage covers Grades X to XIII. Regulations making education compulsory for children in the age five to 14 group were enacted by Parliament and came into effect in January 1998.

The Technical Vocational and Education Training (TVET) sector caters to a large segment of school leavers and others through a number of public and private training institutions. Technical education in Sri Lanka has a history of more than one hundred years. Within the public sector the major provider of TVET is the Department of Technical Education and Training (DTE&T), the largest body, with 26 technical colleges and seven affiliated colleges. The Vocational Training Authority (VTA) and the National Institute of Technical Education of Sri Lanka (NITESL) provide vocational and skills development programmes and training programmes to trainers. The National Apprenticeship and Industrial Training Authority (NAITA) is responsible for the provision of vocational training, specifying training standards and conducting National Trade Tests. All these institutions, namely the DTE&T, VTA, NITESL and NAITA, operate within the Ministry of Vocational Training. The Sri Lanka Advanced Institute of Technical

Education (SLAITE) in the Ministry of Higher Education and Information Technology Development provides courses at a higher level than those offered by the institutions in the Ministry of Vocational Training.

During the period from 1979 to 2000 the university system operating under the University Grants Commission (UGC) recorded an expansion in both student numbers and the number of institutions. However, given the limited number of places available in the universities, admission to conventional universities is extremely competitive. The Open University, where modest fees are charged, offers higher education for a larger clientele through distance education methods. Students of the Open University are provided with self-study course materials and, depending on the need, some face-to-face interaction with the teachers is also offered. Foundation programmes are provided for those students who do not possess university entry requirements.

The government budget still continues to fund about 95% of the total expenditure of the university system. However, it is interesting to note that in relation to the country's Gross Domestic Product (GDP), allocation is rather low (particularly in comparison to other countries in Asia), and stands at a meagre 0.4% of GDP. While university education up to the first degree is totally free, over 90% of Sri Lanka's university students in the country receive financial assistance for their education through scholarships and bursaries.

It is observed that a sizeable number of students (about 107,000 at the end of 1999) had registered for external degrees of five conventional universities. External students who prepare themselves by self-study and private tuition sit the examinations conducted by these universities. This confirms the fact that a large segment of the population is keen to pursue higher education and that they are deprived of the opportunity to join the mainstream conventional universities due to a limited number of available places.

Overview of distance education in Sri Lanka

Methodical attempts to provide education through the distance mode in Sri Lanka are comparatively recent. This is largely due to the fact that Sri Lanka had a fairly wide network of primary and secondary schools, as well as opportunities for tertiary education, even at the time of independence from the British Empire in 1948. This served to create the impression that, in terms of educational facilities, the needs of the population were adequately catered to.

However, the formal education system has been slow in adjusting to the requirements of various age groups in education and training and has been unable to cater to the ever-growing student population. Distance education, as opposed to the formal conventional system relates to the teaching and learning situation in which most of the teaching is conducted by a teacher who is separated temporally and geographically from the student. It has become increasingly apparent that distance education is a necessity. With the establishment of the UK Open University in 1969, and more particularly after the emergence of an Open University in Pakistan in South Asia, several institutions imparting instructions through the distance mode were set up to meet the demand for education in Sri Lanka.

Since 1972, the following five institutions have been involved in distance education:

• The Ministry of Education's Distance Education Branch for Teacher Education (1972);

• The University of Sri Lanka's External Service Agency (ESA 1972);

• The Sri Lanka Institute of Distance Education (SLIDE 1976);

• The Open University of Sri Lanka (OUSL 1980);

• The National Institute of Education (NIE 1985).

At present, only the last two institutions are in operation. The other three have been assimilated by either the OUSL or the NIE, which are government institutions receiving either full or partial grants from the government.

At its inception the NIE, which is a national institution funded entirely by the government, had a Department of Distance Education. The forerunner to this Department was the Distance Education Branch set up in 1981 within the Teacher Education and Curriculum Division of the Ministry of Education. With the establishment of the NIE, the Department of Distance Education developed into a department within the NIE in 1986. This department was responsible for planning and implementing professional teacher education. Since 1984 a number of Distance Teacher Education courses have been conducted at the NIE.

The OUSL is one of the 13 National Universities in Sri Lanka's university system. The UGC, as the apex body in the university system, is expected to function within the Ministry of Higher Education and Information Technology Development as a buffer between the universities and the government. Disbursement of state funds for university education is one of the major functions of the UGC. The Open University receives about two-thirds of its recurrent expenditure from the UGC. The remaining one-third is generated within the OUSL, a major portion of which comes from student fees. The University depends solely on state funds for its capital expenditure.

Other than government grants, sources of financial support include student fees and international assistance. United Nations Educational, Scientific and Cultural Organization (UNESCO)/United Nations Development Program (UNDP), Department for International Development DfID(UK), Swedish International Development Agency (SIDA), Japan International Cooperation Agency (JICA), Korea International Cooperation Agency (KOICA) and the Commonwealth of Learning (COL) have provided significant assistance during the 20 years of the OUSL's existence.

The purpose and objective of establishing these institutions for distance education were to open up education and make it accessible to as wide a range of people as possible by providing opportunities for working people and other people unable to enter a conventional university and follow a full-time course of study.

The Open University of Sri Lanka

The OUSL provides opportunities to adults (preferably employed), to acquire a university-level education through distance education methods that enable support of a large number of students scattered throughout Sri Lanka. It offers education programmes formulated with the aim of developing human resources to aid national development. The only statutory requirement for enrolment in OUSL courses is that a student should be above 18 years of age. No formal qualifications are prescribed except where specified. However, the ideal student enrolling with the University is one who possesses a general education background and, having progressed into some livelihood, aspires to further him or herself academically.

The advantage of this system to the adult learner is that there are no strict timetables or classes that require attendance as in the conventional university system, so an adult learner can easily follow a systematic programme of study at the OUSL while in full-time or part-time employment.

With its three faculties, namely the Faculty of Engineering Technology, Faculty of Humanities and Social Sciences and the Faculty of Natural Sciences, the OUSL at present caters to a Sri Lankan student population of 20,000 with planned expansion in regional services and by launching regular academic programmes. In addition, there are the continuing education programmes, beginners' courses and awareness programmes. The OUSL, from its very inception, also offered programmes in science and technology through the distance mode. These programmes are now well established and have gained the recognition of relevant professional bodies. The two faculties responsible for science and technology are continuing to introduce new programmes. The OUSL is also fully equipped to support postgraduate research.

The programmes of study offered by the Open University at present include:

• Foundation courses;

• Certificate programmes;

• Diploma programmes;

• Bachelor's degree programmes;

• Postgraduate degree programmes;

• Continuing education programmes.

In these programmes, each course is a unit of study normally completed within a period of one year. Several such courses can be offered simultaneously up to a maximum two and a half credits. A programme of study is made up of an approved combination of courses. In addition, the University also offers several beginners programmes, standalone courses and awareness programmes. Exemptions are granted to those who possess approved relevant qualifications.

Control and management

As government institutions, both the OUSL and the NIE are co-authorities empowered as administrative bodies under their respective Ordinances. The authorities of the OUSL are:

- The Council, the executive and governing authority;

- The Senate, the main academic body vested with the authority to control the general direction of instruction, research and examination;

- The Faculty Boards, for initial approval of programmes or courses of study, examinations and other areas of academic interest before submission through the Senate to the Council for final approval.

In addition to these statutory bodies, the OUSL also has two Boards, with the mandate for Regional Educational Services and Educational Technology. The Board of Regional Educational Services is responsible for the planning and development of regional educational services and the provision of resources required for the learning process in the study centres. The Board of Educational Technology is responsible for the planning and use of educational technology for the production of instructional materials for students.

The Open University is headed by a Vice-Chancellor, who is appointed by the President of the Republic of Sri Lanka. He is the principal executive and academic officer of the University.

The authorities of the NIE are:

- The Council, responsible for the administration, management and control of the affairs of the NIE;

- The Academic Affairs Board, responsible for advising the Council on the academic affairs of the NIE concerning courses of study, students, teaching programmes and examinations.

A Director-General heads the NIE. He/she is appointed by the Minister of Education, is the principal executive and academic officer, and is assisted by two Deputy Director-Generals and six Assistant Director-Generals. After a major restructuring process undertaken in 1998, two major divisions were established in the NIE: the Curriculum Development Division and the Systems Development Division (SDD).

The primary function of the SDD is to facilitate the implementation of the curricula developed for the general education system. In the discharge of its duties, the Teacher Education Unit in the SDD, under the guidance of two Project Teams, offer a Trained Teachers Certificate and the Postgraduate Diploma in Education through the distance mode.

Instructional system and media for distance education

Originally, media used in distance education programmes were mainly printed materials written in the traditional lecture-note style. After the establishment of SLIDE, a systematic development of printed materials for distance education students took place.

Like other distance education institutions overseas, the OUSL adopts a multimedia study system in the delivery of its academic programmes, with modifications to suit local conditions. The core element in the study system is a set of printed self-study course materials. Depending on the programme of study, it also provides audio-visual aids to supplement them. These aids are produced in the fully equipped state-of-the-art media house, which was donated to the University by the Japanese government. Where appropriate, discussion classes in the form of face-to-face tutorial sessions, seminars and workshops, etc., are conducted. Laboratory work and demonstrations are built in as an integral part of the science and engineering programmes. The University's main library is located on the Central Campus. It also operates a network of mini-libraries at its Regional Centres and Study Centres. In addition, computing facilities are provided in most of the centres.

Student progress is monitored during the academic year by continuous assessment, which has become an integral part of the evaluation system of the OUSL. Tutor-marked assignments, continuous assessment tests, project work, laboratory work, fieldwork and case studies are some of the components of the University's continuous assessment system. A student's eligibility to sit the final examination, conducted at the end of the academic year, is determined by that student's continuous assessment grade. A student's final grade for each course is determined by combining the grade obtained for continuous assessment and the grade obtained for the final examination.

Announcements of different programmes of study are made through the national press and other news media, while further details on the programmes of study and the method and the time of application can be obtained from the Director of Public Relations of the OUSL.

The major component of NIE study packages are also printed materials. The NIE produces videos as part of its study materials, which are narrowcast as study supplements. Continuous assessment forms an integral part of the evaluation process.

Geographical coverage

Sri Lanka's distance education institutions are located nation-wide. The OUSL has four Regional Centres located in Colombo, the capital city of Sri Lanka; Kandy, the capital of the central province; Jaffna, the main city in the northern province; and Matara, a major city in southern Sri Lanka. It also operates 16 Study Centres, which are located in Ambalangoda, Ampara, Anuradhapura, Badulla, Bandarawela, Batticaloa, Buttala, Galle, Kalutara, Kegalle, Kuliyapitiya, Kurugegala, Polonnaruwa, Ratnapura, Trincomalee and Vavuniya, providing educational facilities to students all over the country. In addition, there are six Teaching Centres, which function without the direct supervision of OUSL staff. Almost all centres provide computing and library reference facilities.

Students are able to attend to most of their learning activities at the centres they are attached to. This includes registration (limited to a few selected centres), the collection of study materials, handing over of home-based assignments, and the use of audio and video cassettes as part of study requirements at the audio-visual Resources Centres. Examinations and limited interaction with tutorial staff are conducted at some selected Study Centres.

At present, the total number of centres operating under the NIE has been reduced to 53 (27 Sinhala-medium and 26 Tamil-medium centres) as the number of teachers enrolling for the programmes has been declining. In due course the NIE envisages transferring the responsibility for teacher training to the Colleges of Education, another state-controlled authority established for the training of teachers.

Research activities at OUSL

Research activities in distance education, conducted as part of Master's and doctoral theses and regular research projects, are in the areas of approaches to distance teacher education, student satisfaction with support services, employer expectations, student performance, student drop-out and the cost effectiveness of distance education. Faculty members themselves have undertaken research after the initial impetus brought in by a DfID-funded project (1996 to 1998) that brought about an attitudinal change by creating a research culture.

The importance of publishing a journal through which findings of distance education research studies can be disseminated has been recognized and the University now publishes the *OUSL Journal* annually.

Enrolment and graduates in distance education programmes

Enrolment at the OUSL in 1998 was 17,040. In addition there are 4,260 associate students. The total number of graduates since 1982 is 12,698.

At the NIE, the total enrolment of students registered for the Trained Teachers Certificate stood at 67,429. Although 66,068 students sat the examinations, 59,070 successfully completed the certificate course. There have been 10,059 graduates since establishment.

International affiliation and cooperation

The OUSL has been actively collaborating with several overseas open as well as conventional universities, and has entered into agreements for academic cooperation with a number of them. The first ever Bachelor's degree in Nursing in Sri Lanka, was made possible through collaboration with the University of Athabasca in Canada.

In addition, the introduction of the Diploma in Youth in Development Work and the launching of an Advanced Certificate in Laboratory Technology, the first of its kind in the country, have been made possible through a working partnership with the Commonwealth Youth Programme and the Commonwealth of Learning respectively.

The University has worked closely with the following international agencies and associations for a considerable period of time:

- The Asian Association of Open Universities (AAOU), of which the OUSL was a founder member;

- The International Council for Distance Education (ICDE);

- The International Association for Continuing Engineering Education (IACE);

- The Association of Commonwealth Universities (ACU).

During its growing years, the NIE has formed strong links with the University of Lund in Sweden through assistance provided by the SIDA. The World Bank is providing assistance for the training of personnel and other related issues in teacher training using distance education.

Priorities for future attention

The following are the priorities that distance education needs to focus on for the future:

- A need to maintain a continuous dialogue with students and to provide them sufficient support and facilities to enable self-learning;

- A need to ensure that there are adequate time and resources to make full use of radio and TV broadcasts and information and communication-based technologies;

- The building of a cultural base for home study, built around the availability of books, papers and media facilities, and a positive attitude towards self-study;

- A need for external support to home-based students to enable them to carry out and continue their learning and to help them move away from the formal style of learning they are accustomed to;

- A need for more systematic interaction to maximize dialogue within groups that are socially and culturally alienated from the mainstream;

- A need for skills practice and learning to learn to supplement theory, especially in the case of students who are entering the education process after a period of time out of education;

- A need to create the necessary infrastructure, such as regional centres, study centres, office buildings, laboratories and workshops as well as media production facilities;

- Create a means of financial support for students, the lack of which results in a high drop-out rate;

- To concentrate on moving the content of distance education programmes available to younger and institutionalized full-time students away from the current mould, which is based more or less on the model of conventional programmes;

- The worrying situation of a diminishing number of students that is leading to institutions having to close courses.

Canada

USA

South Pacific

Australia

New Zealand

Pacific
Rim

Australia

Colin Latchem

Introduction

Australia was one of the earliest pioneers of distance education and is today a world leader in the field. The goal of public education in Australia has always been equality of opportunity for all students, regardless of their geographic, social or economic circumstances and, with a small and widely distributed population occupying the world's largest island continent, it is perhaps hardly surprising that Australia has so readily embraced distance learning and new technology. The so-called 'tyranny of distance' is still a factor in distance education, particularly in regard to the Schools of the Air, but most of today's distance education students live in and around the major conurbations and opt for this mode of delivery for reasons of convenience and flexibility. Australia has always utilized the 'dual-mode' or 'mixed-mode' model in which the courses and awards pursued through distance education are identical to those provided on campus and students can opt for various combinations of off- and on-campus study.

Traditionally, Australian distance education has been primarily concerned with improving access and outcomes for the disadvantaged and the disenfranchised. In today's highly competitive global marketplace, with the drive for a 'user pays' system and work-oriented education and training, Australian colleges and universities also see commercial potential in distance and open learning. They can no longer rely solely upon government funding or traditional markets and, as control passes to the demand side of education and training and student cohorts change and diversify, they find the need to be more open, flexible and entrepreneurial. They are also acutely aware of the threats posed by global and 'virtual' online providers. This 'educational export' contributes significantly to the Australian economy and there is growing interest and involvement in international applications of distance and open learning and technology.

There has been exponential growth in the number of students, institutions and courses using distance and open learning. In 2000, 94,000 students — nearly 14% of all Australian university students — were studying in the distance mode. Many thousands more take some of their courses off campus or study online or use distance education materials in flexibly delivered on-campus programmes. Tens of thousands more study through Technical and Further Education and private colleges, industry organizations and alternative postgraduate providers. Distance learning and technology are also bringing education and opportunity to Australia's indigenous people. Nine thousand students are enrolled in Australian university distance education courses overseas.

The following chapter draws on a wide range of research, literature and comment to provide an up-to-date, comprehensive review from early correspondence education to the latest 'dot.com degrees' and to discuss some of the more contentious and unresolved aspects of open and distance education in Australia.

Country profile

The Commonwealth of Australia is the world's largest island continent with a landmass of almost 8 million square kilometres. Of Australia's 18 million people 86% live in the state capitals or major coastal cities.

Australia's indigenous peoples, the Aborigines and Torres Strait Islanders, have a 50,000 year-old history and culture. Many of these live in rural and outback areas in Queensland, New South Wales, Western Australia and the Northern Territory but there are also substantial communities of Aborigines in the larger cities and towns. Their numbers have declined rapidly over the two centuries since the white man's conquest and today Aboriginals represent less than 1% of the population.

Over 20% of Australia's population was born overseas. The culture is predominately Anglo-Celtic and Mediterranean but in recent decades significant numbers of Asian and other nationalities have emigrated to, or sought refuge in, Australia, enriching the multicultural society.

Australia is a wealthy industrialized nation. Rich in natural resources, it is a major exporter of iron, bauxite, oil, natural gas and other minerals and its wheat, wool and other farm products also contribute to its overseas earnings. With so much wealth generated by mining and agriculture, Australians have tended to regard their land as the 'lucky country'. Today, in the face of fierce global competition and economic setbacks in the Asia-Pacific, Australia is learning the lesson that it must become the 'clever country', value-adding its natural resources and developing new technology-based and service industries. This inevitably places additional demands upon the Australian education system.

The Australian education system

The goal of public education in Australia is equality of opportunity for all students, urban or rural. Each state has a common curriculum for its schools and right across Australia, any difference in the curriculum is more a matter of degree or emphasis than content. Distance education therefore fits into an ethos of equality of educational opportunity and uniformity of practice.

Constitutionally, education is the responsibility of the states. The states' government schools are financed through a redistribution of federal funding, and the 25% of schools that are private, predominately run by religious denominations, also receive some public funding. The language of instruction in schools is English. Traditional languages are taught in some Aboriginal community schools, usually outside school hours, and languages other than English are taught in high schools.

Depending on whether or not they plan to engage in some form of tertiary education (vocational education and training and university) immediately after completing their schooling, pupils leave after completing their compulsory schooling (15 years of age or 16 in Tasmania) or go on to complete years 11 and 12. In 1998, the last year for which such data were available at the time of writing, 51% of 15–19 year olds were still at school and 25% were engaged in tertiary education. In the 20–24 year age group, there is a substantial decline in the proportion participating in education, with 30% in some form of tertiary education (61% studying full-time and 39% studying part-time). Overall, 11% of the 15–64 year age group attend tertiary institutions. Most of those who are 25 and over do so part-time (Australian Bureau of Statistics 2000).

Vocational education and training is provided by Technical and Further Education (TAFE) colleges for which the state governments have prime responsibility. The TAFE sector is currently transforming itself into an industry-led training system operating under the Australian National Training Authority (ANTA) (ANTA 1997) and with a National Training Framework of training packages, skills passports and enterprise-based and competency-based qualifications (Macnamara 1997).

The administration and funding of higher education is the responsibility of the Federal Government and specifically the Department of Education Training and Youth Affairs (DETYA). However, most of the universities were established under Acts of State Parliament and still operate under state government legislation. There are 38 Commonwealth-funded universities and two private universities. The conferring of higher education awards and responsibility for governance lie with the individual institutions. They employ rigorous processes for self-accreditation involving consultations and benchmarking with other universities in Australia and overseas, consultations with relevant professional associations and formal internal processes of review and approval. At the same time, the quality and standards of their performance and outcomes is monitored and made public by DETYA.

University education has become the preferred option for a wide range of school-leavers who would formerly have chosen employment or TAFE study. Since 1983, the number of university places has increased by 80%, and more than fifty Australians per thousand (or 148 per thousand in the case of 17–24 year olds) now attend university. The pattern of enrolment has also changed. Female participation has risen more than the male rate, fewer than 50% of undergraduates now come straight from school, only 59% of students are full-time, and a large and ever-increasing number combine work and study. Distance education is obviously a boon to people in rural and remote areas but 60% of university distance education students live in cities, showing that convenience rather than remoteness is the main determinant. Those who choose to study in this mode are usually mature-aged — 32,146 students out of a total of around 94,000 are in the 30–39 age group, 19,540 are in the 40–49 age group, and only 1,766 20 year-olds study externally. Many have already studied on campus. Women outnumber men, and students tend to come from high to middle socio-economic groups (Richardson 2000).

In the second half of the 1980s and the first half of the 1990s, pursuing deterministic economic and labour market reform, Labour governments forced many radical changes upon higher education (Jakupec 1996; King 1999). These included amalgamation, an increased number and diversity of students, a system of deferred payment for tuition, the encouragement of greater self-reliance in the institutions and the 'export' of higher education. By 1999, the number of overseas fee-paying students, despite Asia's economic woes, had reached 63,683.

Under the current conservative Liberal-National Coalition, there has been an intensification of these ideologies and expectations. The costs of university study have increasingly been transferred from the state to the individual. All Australian students now contribute to a Higher Education Contribution Scheme (HECS) through up-front fees or levies upon their earnings after graduation once these reach a certain level. In 1998, the growth in higher education was almost entirely due to a 14.6% increase in international students, predominantly from Hong Kong, Malaysia, Singapore and Indonesia. South-east Asian students now represent almost 10% of the total student population of 671,853 and there are plans to increase the number of overseas students to 90,000 by 2001.

The colleges and universities have been forced to be ever-more dependent upon alternative sources of funding, in the case of the colleges, by providing fee-for-service programmes for industry and, in the case of the universities, taking in fee-paying domestic and overseas students. The universities can now accept full fee-paying domestic undergraduate students, provided that these do not exceed 25% of the total enrolments in any course. Overall, student numbers increased by 16,000 between 1995 and 1998 but, in the same period, there was a reduction in the number of teachers and support staff and a greater use of part-time and contract staff (<www.detya.gov.au/highered/statpubs.htm>).

The universities are now operating in a highly competitive and accountable environment. They have to compete nationally and internationally for their students and their research income. Their funding is performance-based with penalties for not meeting student enrolment targets. And they are required to be more publicly accountable. As a consequence, they have to ensure that the courses and services they provide for professional, vocational, training and lifelong learning are client-responsive, more cost effective and more entrepreneurial. One consequence of this has been a greater use of technology and distance and open learning.

In 2000, nearly 14% of all Australian university students, or 94,000 compared with 48,000 ten years ago, were studying through distance education (Richardson 2000). What these figures may not reveal is the full extent to which students are taking some of their courses off-campus and using distance education materials in more flexibly delivered on-campus programmes. There are tens of thousands more studying through the TAFE and private colleges, industry organizations such as the Australian Computer Society and alternative postgraduate providers such as the Association of Professional Engineers, Scientists and Managers, Australia and the Securities Institute. Nine thousand students are enrolled in Australian university distance education courses overseas.

The history of distance and open learning in Australia

Australia has one of the longest histories of distance learning in primary, secondary and tertiary education. Distance education dates back to the turn of the century when Australia federated, and it has gone through three distinct phases: correspondence courses and external studies (from 1910 to the early 1970s); distance education (from the early 1970s to the mid-1980s); and open and flexible learning (from the mid-1980s onwards).

Formal correspondence study started because of agitation by people in rural areas — and in particular the politically influential rural graziers — for schooling, technical training and university education without agonizing and expensive family separations. The honours for the first correspondence programmes in Australia appear to go equally to initiatives in 1910 by a Victorian secondary school and Sydney Technical College (Rayner 1949), but the TAFE Colleges only really began to teach regularly at a distance in the late 1920s–1930s and on the School of the Air in the 1950s.

Australian universities were pioneers in distance education and, in the early years, they had to invent ways of developing and delivering programmes. One consequence of this was that the UK Open University, when it was established in 1969, drew heavily upon this Australian experience (Lowe 1997).

King (1999) attributes Australian universities' interest in distance education to two factors: considerations of access and equity and concern for institutional viability. The connection between these is sometimes blurred. The first moves into distance education by metropolitan-based universities were prompted by the need to overcome barriers to access (Guiton and Smith 1984). The 1909 inaugural charter of The University of Queensland (UQ) committed the university to providing external studies programmes. In 1911 it offered the first university distance education programme in the southern hemisphere and one of the first in the world (Cunningham et al. 1997). The University of Western Australia (UWA) followed in 1921, again largely as a consequence of political pressure from non-metropolitan electorates. The Royal Melbourne Institute of Technology (RMIT) was the next higher education institution to offer external courses in 1919.

Immediately after the Second World War, there was an upsurge in distance teaching as universities such as Sydney and Melbourne enabled service or ex-service personnel to continue their studies. In 1955, there was another newcomer to external studies — Australia's first non-metropolitan university, the University of New England (UNE). UNE subsequently received world-wide recognition for its pioneering work in 'dual-mode' provision and influenced many institutions throughout Australia and the world (Northcott 1984).

By 1970, there were six Australian universities offering courses externally. The 1970s saw a review of tertiary distance education and government consideration of a specialist distance education institution on the lines of the UK Open University (Committee on Open University 1974). At that time, there were about 16,000 distance education students in universities and colleges of advanced education (Anwyl et al. 1987) and it was concluded that Australia lacked the population base for such an open university.

By 1985, such was the need to secure off-campus provision and, to a lesser extent, course viability, that 37 higher education institutions were offering some of their programmes in the external mode. The majority of these were the recently established rural Colleges of Advanced Education, which were formerly Teachers Colleges and were now under pressure to rapidly increase their student numbers to ensure their viability (Cunningham et al. 1997). The use of distance education continued to increase in these institutions, which subsequently became universities in their own right (King 1993), but the increased accessibility to local and regional campuses, a declining rural population and huge growth in part-time on-campus studies meant that for a while distance education enrolments failed to keep up with on-campus enrolments (Cunningham et al. 1997).

In 1989, external students comprised 10% of the higher education enrolments (Campion and Renner 1992); in 1995, 12.25% (Atkinson 1996) and today, nearly 14% (Richardson 2000). The four major providers are all regional universities — Charles Sturt University with 16,039 or 17.1% of the 94,000 Australian distance education students, The University of New England with 11,377 students (12.1%), The University of Southern Queensland with 10,806 students (11.5%) and Deakin University with 10,277 students (10.9%) (Richardson 2000).

Distance and open learning are not exclusively at undergraduate level. The rapid growth in enrolments in postgraduate coursework programmes is resulting in an increasingly complex blend of delivery options including distance education and technology-based delivery (James and Beattie 1995, 1996), and students can pursue their studies right up to doctoral level.

The highest numbers of distance education enrolments at undergraduate level are in Business (27,058 or 28.8%), Arts (17,889 or 19.0%), Education (14,654 or 15.6%) and Health (10,727 or 11.4%). Science attracts 7,999 students (8.5%), Law 5,909 (6.3%) and Agriculture 3,526 (3.8%). Architecture and Veterinary Science attract fewer than 1,000 students between them. There are 2,323 students enrolled in non-award courses (Richardson 2000). However, any data on distance education student numbers have to be examined carefully as they tend to refer only to students enrolled as distance education students and not the many others who opt for mixed-mode for some part of their studies.

There is no overall governing body for distance education in Australia. There is a National Council for Open and Distance Education (NCODE), but this is not a governing or policy-making body. NCODE has no official standing with DETYA and is predominately focused on the needs of the tertiary sector. Responsibility for the management, academic standards, resource allocation and infrastructure for distance education is distributed through the state, TAFE and university management structures. This may be seen as one of the great strengths of the Australian system because it means that the standards and services of distance education are those of the existing and mainstream systems rather than separate and marginal institutions.

Distance and open schooling

Families on remote cattle and sheep stations in the Australian outback face major problems in educating their children. The nearest school is usually too far away and there are very limited opportunities for children to mix with other youngsters, so distance schooling, technology and home tutoring are vitally important to the communities of rural Australia (O'Sullivan 1997).

The School of the Air (SOTA) is probably one of Australia's best known distance education systems. It was established in the early 1950s and today serves 4–13 year-old pupils in outback Australia through a combination of correspondence courses, talkback radio via the radio network of the Royal Flying Doctor Service, home tutors (most commonly, the children's mothers) and increasingly, computers, modems and the Internet (made available through special bulk buying and loan schemes). The SOTA pupils spend five to six hours a day, five days a week on their correspondence-based home studies. There is up to half an hour of radio-based teaching a day and every pupil has a 10-minute personal talkback session with his/her teacher once a week.

Australia's largest School of the Air is based in Alice Springs. It serves 1.3 million square kilometres of the Northern Territory, Queensland, South Australia and Western Australia, and its furthest student is 1,000 kilometres from 'the Alice'. This SOTA is resourced by the Northern Territory Department of Education and currently employs 13 teachers and 10 support staff. The cost of educating SOTA pupils is twice that of educating children in conventional schools but the parents are only required to pay a voluntary fee of A$80 per year for the first two children and A$60 per year for any additional children enrolled in the programme.

The Broken Hill School of the Air was established in 1956 to teach students in remote areas in New South Wales, South Australia and Queensland. Today, it comes under the New South Wales State Department of Education and all of its students are within that state.

The South Australian Open Access College comprises three Schools of Distance Education — reception to year 10 (Marden site, metropolitan Adelaide), senior secondary (Marden), and reception to year 12 (Port Augusta site, 300 kilometres by road from the Marden site). SOTA students may be denied educational opportunities commonly available to pupils in regular schools, but they can also enjoy some experiences denied to their town-based counterparts. For example, pupils enrolled in the Port Augusta School of the Air have had the opportunity to speak with astronauts, 747 pilots, captains of ships at sea, members of the Australian Olympics team, members of the British Royal family, and fellow pupils in the US. The Open Access College is also developing Internet options for students with access to the technology, utilizing the medium for the arts, legal studies, social studies, biology, environmental studies, geology, home economics and languages other than English.

The state of Victoria's Distance Education Centre (DEC) offers tuition for a minimum of two school terms to children of five years and over who live far away from the nearest primary school, live with physical or emotional disability, or are recommended for home study as a consequence of school discipline procedures. The DEC also provides tuition for a maximum of two years to children of families on extended holiday or work tours, children temporarily overseas intending to return to Victoria, secondary school students requiring subjects not available in their schools and adults (15 years and over) who do not have access to other education facilities (Lugg 1994).

The various state Departments of Education also provide distance education print materials, audiotapes and videotapes, kits, library loan services and technologies such as telephony, email, interactive multimedia and live television via satellite to broaden and enrich education in remote and rural areas where it is not possible to offer the full spectrum of specialized staff. Where possible, these are supplemented by teachers' visits to students' homes, occasional seminars, annual residential camps for junior secondary students and excursions for senior secondary students.

In Western Australia (WA), the School of Isolated and Distance Education (SIDE) operates under the aegis of the WA Education Department. It is led by an Executive Principal who is responsible for managing the development and delivery of preparatory (primary–age 5), middle (age 6–10) and post-compulsory (age 11–12) school programmes from the SIDE headquarters in the state capital, Perth, and the five Schools of the Air in Kalgoorlie, Port Hedland, Meekatharra, Carnavon and Derby. SIDE also caters for WA students temporarily travelling with their parents in Australia or elsewhere in the world, students whose local high schools do not offer the subjects they wish to study, students suffering from long-term illness and adult students in remote and rural areas who wish to take school, tertiary entrance examination and TAFE courses to improve their education and their employment options.

As part of the Western Australian government's Technology in Schools initiative, the Ministry of Education has installed satellite dishes and decoders in the 350 government country schools throughout the state. This enables students throughout the state to have access to educational programmes transmitted from SIDE's Interactive Television Studio in Perth via the state's Westlink talkback television network. These programmes include Indonesian, Italian and Japanese language teaching, accounting and health sciences and programmes delivered by TAFE. SIDE also broadcasts professional development and information programmes for principals and teachers.

Teachers in small, remote community schools in regions in Australia's far north such as the Kimberley in Western Australia have to contend with limited, expensive and slow Internet connections, high installation and repair costs, Argentine ants that eat through the cables, heat, humidity and lightning strikes, all of which play havoc with the technology. Nevertheless, technology resources are being upgraded, extended and applied to help remote and indigenous pupils, and teachers are supported by an online professional development programme for indigenous students provided by Perth's Edith Cowan University.

There is an Australian Association of Distance Education Schools and the Schools of the Air.

Distance and open learning in technical and further education

Changes in the world of work are having a major impact on the TAFE sector. There is still a need for pre-employment trade, technical and para-professional courses, but there is also growing demand for courses concerned with updating and retraining, preparing for career changes and individual enterprise, and recognition of competencies. Courses are offered at the Certificate, Diploma and Advanced Diploma levels and in accordance with a new Australian Qualifications Framework (AQF), which enables study to be nationally and institutionally consistent and recognized.

The TAFE sector can no longer depend solely upon government funding or traditional markets — in effect, control is passing to the demand side of training. These changes mean that the TAFE institutions have to be more open, flexible and entrepreneurial. They have to establish new markets, products and services, and work to new performance standards and timeframes in course development and assessment. They have to respond to rapidly changing contexts and multiple stakeholders, they have to provide for learners with high levels of dependency, and they have to achieve greater flexibility in staffing patterns and levels.

Under the National Vocational Education and Training System Agreement, the key planning tools are the State and Territory Profiles, which include strategies for on-site multimedia and online delivery, communication networks and open learning centres employed across a range of industry sectors and enterprises to yield measurable training outcomes. TAFE colleges in all states utilize distance education and technology to reach out to remote campuses, the workforce and the wider community.

There has been rapid growth in distance education in the TAFE sector — In 1998 (the last year when such figures were available), 93,299 or 9% of TAFE students were studying through this mode compared with 6% in the preceding year (Richardson 2000). However, the terms 'flexible delivery' and 'flexible learning' are more commonly used than 'distance education' in the TAFE sector, possibly because these are seen as more straightforward and descriptive of a process of customizing courses to learners' needs and preferences. The TAFE colleges tend to concentrate on the practical aspects of flexible delivery rather than engage in debate or research regarding the other aspects of such work (Tinkler et al. 1996; Kay 1997) and to date, it is not easy to identify coherent and illuminating case studies of uses of new technology (Mitchell and Bluer 1997).

One of Australia's largest distance and flexible learning providers is the TAFE New South Wales Open Training and Education Network (OTEN), which delivers more than 250 courses to 31,000 students through strategically placed DECs throughout the state.

Distance and open university education

University distance education is dispersed and delivered through autonomous and competing institutions. Decisions about which courses to teach in this mode rest with individual departments and course teams, sometimes without the capacity or willingness of their institutions to provide appropriate funding or infrastructure. The academics prepare and teach distance education courses concurrently with their on-campus duties, which means that, as a consequence, courses vary in quality, may duplicate offerings by other institutions, may have very small enrolments, and may not be cost effective.

In the early 1990s, the Federal Government attempted to improve quality, control costs, achieve economies of scale and avoid unnecessary duplication by rationalizing university distance education into a system of major DECs. Seven of these DECs were eastern states universities and the eighth was the Western Australian Distance Education Consortium or WADEC, comprising the state's three distance teaching universities (King 1993; Johnson 1996; King 1999). The funding arrangements obliged any other universities wishing to provide courses in the distance mode to contract with these DECs for the development of materials. Such an arrangement was resented by the non-DECs and prevented them from engaging in innovative, technology-based teaching. However, the DEC system was short-lived, failing to survive government dissatisfaction with a creature of its own devising and achieve the somewhat naïve expectations of inter-institutional collaboration and savings in costs (King 1999).

The DEC model evidenced government interest in distance education but was overtaken by a dramatic growth in interest in distance education and open learning by most of the universities. Suddenly, distance education had moved from the margins to the mainstream, being seen as the answer to larger classes and reducing budgets, reaching a wider clientele, exploiting new technology, and generating income (Jakupec 1996).

Such was the level of interest in open and flexible learning that when the Chair of the Australian National Council on Open and Distance Education (NCODE), reconstituted from the government-designated eight-member National Conference of Distance Education Centres, invited all Australian universities to become fee-paying members, 31 of the universities immediately accepted the offer (Le Grew and Calvert 1998). In 1997, NCODE had a membership of 33 (Walker and Walker 1997). Ironically, from that moment of collaboration, the universities also began to compete more aggressively against each other and against international providers which they perceived to be threatening their traditional markets in Australia and overseas.

While some countries have chosen to establish open universities teaching exclusively in the distance mode and granting distinct open learning degrees, Australia has always opted for the dual-mode or mixed-mode model in which the courses and awards pursued through distance education are identical to those provided on campus and students can choose various combinations of off- and on-campus study. Distance education is not necessarily restricted to isolated self-study. Some universities offer summer schools — an idea pioneered by UNE — while others provide academic support through evening classes, local study centres or telecommunications-based 'telecentres' and increasingly, information and communications technology.

The term 'distance education' is increasingly something of a misnomer because more than half of the university distance education students live in and around the state capitals and main coastal cities, often within commuting distance of their local institutions. For most of these students, the barrier to study is not the 'tyranny of distance' but the demands of work and/or family. They are attracted to a mode of study that offers them flexibility in the what, where, when and how of their studies. But there is still a very important minority in the sparsely settled outback and the institutions place great store by serving these students.

The services and standards of the distance education programmes are as close to those that apply on campus as can be guaranteed in the prevailing local conditions. The form(s) of delivery and support depend upon the learners' locations, needs, access to particular technologies and networks, and ability and preparedness to pay for course materials and services. There is a strong and deep-seated commitment to access and equity in Australian tertiary education and so the costs incurred by the students are always given serious consideration.

Attrition and failure rates are typically higher among first-year off-campus students than their on-campus counterparts, but in the subsequent years of study, the retention and success rates are comparable. Psycho-social support and interaction is crucial in learning and the increasing use of online tutoring and peer discussion via the Internet may improve retention and performance rates.

One study suggests that Aboriginal and Torres Strait Islander students are more likely to complete their university studies if they study in the distance mode. While only 59.3% of all Aboriginal and Torres Strait Islander university students succeed in their studies (as compared to 83.3% of all other students), the success rate for those studying externally is 74.2% (Bourke et al. 1996). It would appear that the pressure of assimilation into the dominant culture of the university is a potent negative factor, while study within the community, with the support of family and friends, may be a more culturally appropriate way of learning.

The normal qualifications for admission to university or college may be waived for mature-aged distance and open learning students. Alternative means of entry include special preparatory and bridging programmes, college courses articulating with university courses, advanced standing for prior study, recognition of prior informal learning, credit transfer and study through Open Learning Australia (described in the following section).

Open and flexible learning

In the last decade there have been significant differences in the ways in which distance education has been conceptualized (Walker and Walker 1997). Many institutions now use the term open and flexible learning to capture this combination of educational philosophy, technology and freeing of programmes from geographical and time constraints.

Open learning has been defined as '... an approach rather than a system or technique; it is based on the needs of individual learners, not the interests of the teacher or the institution; it gives students as much control as possible over what and when and where and how they learn; it commonly uses the delivery methods of distance education and the facilities of educational technology; it changes the role of the teacher from a source of knowledge to a manager of learning and a facilitator' (Johnson 1990, 4).

Open and flexible learning can be either on- or off-campus and can take many forms, from autonomous resource-based learning to a mix of off-campus mediated learning and scheduled lectures, tutorials and practical work. It is felt that the pedagogic contract that goes with such arrangements is more likely to encourage active and intellectually independent learners. Instead of being the sole initiator of the learning tasks and outcomes, the teacher combines the roles of 'resource specialist', putting the learners in contact with usable information, ideas and techniques, and a 'response specialist' with whom the learner can discuss and resolve ideas and issues.

An increasing number of universities are introducing open and flexible learning to meet the needs of large numbers of students with differing backgrounds, entrance qualifications, motivations and capacities for learning. One agency that led the breakthrough in increasing the options in access to higher education is Open Learning Australia (OLA). OLA waives matriculation, has no quotas and provides special preparatory and bridging programmes, college-university articulation, recognition of prior informal learning, credit transfer and credit accumulation.

OLA was established as a private educational broker in 1992 (King 1993; Latchem and Pritchard 1994; Atkinson 1996; King 1999). Initially funded and supported by the Federal Government, OLA developed out of the TV Open Learning Project pioneered by Monash University, some partner universities and the Australian Broadcasting Corporation (ABC). In its first four years, OLA attracted well over 30,000 students, people who would not otherwise have had access to traditional campus-based university study. OLA consortium was originally owned by Monash University, but it is now a private company of eight shareholding universities (Monash University, Royal Melbourne Institute of Technology, The University of Queensland, Griffith University, Macquarie University, Curtin University of Technology, Swinburne University of Technology and The University of South Australia) all of which offer units and degree pathways. The OLA contracts with its partners and other universities to provide fee-for-service undergraduate, postgraduate, continuing and professional education programmes in Arts, Social Sciences, Business Studies, Science and Technology, Applied Studies and Australian Indigenous Studies (also known as Warrit Ngulu). It also contracts with TAFE colleges to provide technical and vocational education and training courses and various other agencies to provide bridging units in Academic Literacy Skills, Biology, Chemistry, Computing, Mathematics and Study Skills. In 1999, OLA offered 250 units from 30 universities and TAFE colleges. Some OLA programmes are delivered online, or via ABC television and radio, and some are delivered offshore.

The undergraduate students pay a fee for each 13-week unit of study which is comparable to that payable for conventional university study. OLA does not award its own degrees. The collaborating universities offer degree pathways that can be completed wholly or through OLA or by students gaining sufficient credits to transfer onto on- or off-campus programmes at the university of their choice.

Ironically, OLA subsequently showed signs of becoming the victim of its own early success. Having demonstrated the potential of open learning and technology, it faced increasing competition from the universities and colleges who came to see the commercial possibilities of thus serving the lifelong learning cohort of 25 years and over, and the corporate sector. It also had to head off competition from international, corporate and virtual providers.

Another private company, Professional and Graduate Education (PAGE), was originally established to offer postgraduate and professional development distance education programmes in Business, Marketing, Management, Health Logistics, Procurement, Languages and Multicultural Education, Information Technology and Environmental Management. The members of the PAGE consortium were Central Queensland University, Edith Cowan University, La Trobe University, Macquarie University, Royal Melbourne Institute of Technology, University of Wollongong and University of Auckland, New Zealand. In 1999, there was a merger between OLA and PAGE to capitalize on the former's strengths in vocational and undergraduate education and the latter's expertise in developing and marketing graduate and professional programmes and facilitating new pathways between vocational education and postgraduate programmes for experienced managers lacking formal qualifications.

Yet another corporate distance education provider is Engineering Education Australia (EEA), a subsidiary of the Institution of Engineers Australia. EEA acts as a broker for off-campus university programmes for engineering personnel in Australia and overseas. EEA programmes grant maximum credit for prior learning and include doctoral, masters, bachelors and diploma programmes in Administration, Management, Engineering and Technology.

Australia's universities are now moving quickly to establish online and flexible delivery systems designed with overseas and corporate markets in mind (King 1999).

Technology

Australia is highly dependent upon communications, both externally and internally, as a consequence of its remoteness and the huge distances between centres. There is a comprehensive and rapidly developing infrastructure for broadcasting, information and communications technology and postal services. Satellite services have opened up the outback and the telecommunications industry has been deregulated, leading to greater competition in online costs. Nevertheless, there are still calls to improve access to modern information and communications technology in rural and regional Australia. Australia has a high level of computer ownership and all education institutions have Internet access.

Most Australian tertiary students demand flexibility, so distance education providers tend to make only limited use of the synchronous 'remote classroom' model of teaching using videoconferencing or live interactive television. Such applications are only used where it suits the learners to be at particular places at specific times between campuses (Treagust et al. 1993; Luck 1997), between universities (Knox 1997) or between countries (Burke et al. 1997).

Delivery is essentially based upon the asynchronous 'correspondence' model. The students receive learning packages containing study plans, study guides, readers and reading lists appropriate to their studies. They may also be sent audiotapes, videotapes, slides, computer disks, experimental kits and notes about associated radio or television programmes, which they are encouraged to video-record. (Television has a minor role in distance education, principally because of the costs involved). Tutoring and counselling are provided by means of the telephone, summer/residential schools and/or local study centres or telecommunications-based 'telecentres'. Assignments are delivered, assessed and commented on by post, fax and email. Library services are provided by post or electronically.

The traditional media are found to work well in many contexts; however, the Internet and the Web are increasingly used for the delivery of pre-enrolment information and advice, course materials, assignments, tutorial support, library and information services and support to students with special needs, and for online enrolments, payment of fees and student records.

The ways in which technology can empower marginalized communities is demonstrated in the seven-site videoconferencing network established by four remote Aboriginal communities in the Tanami Desert in the south-western Northern Territory. This network, established in 1992, uses both satellite and ISDN and has been used for mixed-mode secondary education combining videoconferencing with on-site tutoring to provide schooling for remote outback Aboriginal communities, a strategy that opens up the curriculum, reduces recruitment and housing costs, and eliminates the need for boarding schools, which are ill-suited to the needs of the young in these traditional communities. The network has also been used for health education, tele-medicine and government services. Other applications have included a prison links programme, ceremonial links, cultural contacts with the Saami in Finland, First Nations people in Canada and other indigenous groups, presentations to national and international forums and the sale of locally-produced paintings and artefacts in Paris and London. In 1997, the Tanami Network received seed funding through the Regional Telecommunications Infrastructure Fund to help up to 120 remote Aboriginal communities across Australia establish interconnectable but autonomous, indigenous, commercial satellite telecommunications systems. It is planned that 'The Outback Digital Network' will provide room- and PC-based videoconferencing, telephony, electronic banking, radio broadcasting and Internet services and articulate with the various telecentre networks and educational providers (Holt and Japanangka 1998).

Nevertheless, there are concerns about the serious equity problems thrown up by new technology. There are hardware, software and online costs for students to contend with and The National Open and Distance Education Students Network (NODESNet) says that many external students cannot afford to make the transition from print to online. NCODE advocates the wider adoption of such strategies as off-campus outreach and study centres with computer access in regional areas, specially negotiated Internet deals and student loans to purchase computers (Brown 2000).

Support services for students

Evans (1994) argues strongly for recognizing the value and importance of researching student needs and circumstances so that these can be better reflected in the practices of ODE. The size and demographics of Australia and the need to improve rural students' access to and participation in post-compulsory education have led to many innovative projects including the creation of information, technology-based telecentres in remote and rural communities that can be used either for tele-learning or tele-work.

The Queensland Open Learning Network (QOLN) was established in 1990 to provide learning resources and services to the people of Queensland who, because of their geographic or personal circumstances, are unable to attend traditional university, TAFE or other classes. QOLN operates over 40 Open Learning Centres throughout the state. These provide access to computers, video and audioconferencing, meeting and study facilities and course information for registered users (Macpherson and Dekkers 1997). The latest development in the QOLN is its Online Learning Service exploiting all Internet and Web applications (Gooley et al. 1998).

The Western Australian Telecentre Network, established in 1991, performs a similar function serving a relatively small and widely distributed population across the 2.5 million square kilometres of this, Australia's largest state (Oliver and Short 1996). There are currently 76 of these multi-purpose, community-based telecentres across Western Australia and during 2000, with others coming online including eight portable sites, this number should reach 100. Designed originally for tele-education and tele-work, these centres are now also used to provide email, Internet access, electronic banking, tourist information and other regional development services for those travelling through these areas, including tourists, and there are plans to introduce generic e-commerce cards for use in all centres.

Support services for staff

The teachers and lecturers developing and delivering distance education programmes are often conscripted into the work. More accustomed to teaching face-to-face, they are ill-versed in educational theory, student-centred learning practices and technology. There is also the danger of a 'do-it-yourself' approach with teachers producing materials in-house on their own computers, which may result in poor textual design and layout (Andrewartha 1996). It is critically important, therefore, to provide specialist advice and support to help content specialists develop and deliver programmes that provide appropriate and stimulating learning activities, whether in print, audiovisual media or on the Web.

The first institutions to appoint instructional designers to work with subject specialists in the design and development of distance learning packages were Deakin University, Darling Downs Institute of Advanced Education (now University of Southern Queensland) and Royal Melbourne Institute of Technology (Inglis 1991). Now, all universities and some colleges and open schooling providers employ staff developers, instructional designers, instructional editors, media and computing specialists, desktop publishers and graphic designers to assist teaching staff in developing and delivering distance education programmes and services. The reporting lines, structure, status and roles of these specialists vary considerably (Parer 1993; Latchem and Moran 1998), and one of the challenges currently facing the universities is to find an efficient and harmonious organizational framework for academic staff development, instructional design, media and information technology support. There is a potential here for conflicting responsibilities and value systems. The information technology culture, in particular, may be difficult to reconcile with the overall organizational culture of academia.

Cunningham et al. (2000) suggest that the dual legacies of the fast-growing, for-profit higher education sector led by the US will be the professionalization and disaggregation of university teaching, and they predict that such commercialization will have profound implications for academics in conventional Australian universities. They observe that part of these for-profit institutions' intense customer focus is an insistence on training for their teachers, followed by unparalleled and constant monitoring of their teaching. In addition, curriculum development, delivery and assessment can be done by different people — and not necessarily in the organization.

Research in distance and open learning

Australian academics are active in researching and contributing to the in-house, national and international literature of distance and open education. During the 1970s, 1980s and early 1990s, there was a plethora of government-commissioned studies into distance education and associated issues (e.g., Johnson 1983; Ashenden 1987; Johnson et al. 1992; Jevons and Northcott 1994; Tinkler et al. 1994) but under the current government, the flow of such reports has virtually ceased. The former national Committee for University Teaching and Staff Development (CUTSD) funded many university staff to undertake research and development projects on distance education and student-centred learning, about half of which had a computer/multimedia component (Walker and Walker 1997).

The professional organization in this field is the Open and Distance Learning Association of Australia (ODLAA), which, in its former guise as the Australian and South Pacific External Studies Association or ASPESA, developed the world's first distance education journal, *Distance Education*, which is recognized as one of the leading publications in this area. ODLAA also enables leaders, planners, managers, educators, trainers and students (the Association is aligned to NODESNet) to exchange views, research findings and practices through workshops and biennial forums. ODLAA is a regional member of the International Council for Distance Education (ICDE) and has links with the Commonwealth of Learning, Distance Education Association of New Zealand (DEANZ), the Canadian Association of Distance Education (CADE) and the Pacific Islands Regional Association of Distance Education (PIRADE). ODLAA is acutely aware of the need for international cooperation with these professional associations and in 1995, ODLAA and PIRADE joined forces to hold the biennial forum in Vanuatu.

International applications and collaboration

Cunningham et al. (1997) concluded that the concept of the 'virtual university' is currently more rhetorical than real, but as mentioned earlier the Australian universities are acutely aware of the threats posed by global competition and technology. The Cunningham report also showed that institutions are finding the development and support costs of online delivery to be much higher than they originally thought and that most institutions have encountered major failures, technological problems and student resistance in their online trials. Nevertheless, interest in international pariticipation is real. Australia's geographic position, close links with Asian trade and economics, tradition of catering to overseas students, expertise in distance education and technology and sophisticated (although currently expensive) telecommunications provide the country with a considerable strategic advantage in international open and distance education. There is, however, the danger of Australian universities perceiving Asia as a quick market and rapidly developing programmes that lack quality and local cultural relevance. Such a move could be uneconomic and damage Australia's reputation as a distance education provider. Robust consumer protection and copyright regulations, commercial considerations and, in some cases, liaison with other providers, partnerships and consortia will be needed to compete successfully in the lifelong and open learning market. In establishing partnerships with Asian universities, it has been shown that Australian providers may be more welcome as advisers in developing programmes than as marketers of ready-made courses (Cunningham et al. 1997).

Priorities for development

Open and flexible learning are now becoming mainstream activities in Australian education. They and technology are having an ever-growing impact on the organization and operations of educational institutions and are seen as having a global potential to serve people who previously had no or extremely restricted access to education. They are also blurring the distinction between on- and off-campus provision (Jevons and Northcott 1994; James and Beattie 1996).

Distance education and online learning are also being used to help rescue low-enrolment but intellectually and strategically important arts and sciences subjects from closure. For example, with the assistance of DETYA grants, the University of New England is delivering nationally distance courses in Greek, Latin, Archaeology, Linguistics and Education. Six universities in New South Wales and the Australian Capital Territory are using the Internet and multimedia to jointly deliver Arabic, Hindi, Urdu, Thai, Laotian, Vietnamese, Korean and Russian language programmes (Healy 1999).

Traditionally, distance education has been primarily concerned with improving access and outcomes for the disadvantaged and the disenfranchised, and a large proportion of the students have belonged to one or more of the national equity targeted categories (NBEET 1996). However, higher education is now a highly competitive marketplace and a significant number of Australian universities are attracted to the commercial potential of distance and open learning. Moran (1997) observes that the drive for user-pays, profitable, work-oriented distance education programmes is a response to the politics of economic liberalism rather than calls for social justice.

There is a danger that distance and open education and new technology will be seized upon as quick fix solutions for reducing budgets, finding new markets and generating additional income. There is concern over the fact that the tangibility of produced packages can appeal to politicians and senior administrators (Evans and King 1991). Jakupec (1998) observes that Australian universities with a tradition of open and distance education recognize the need for a learner focus and a variety of modes and technologies, and that they have adopted policies and practices that are more 'market' orientated, coherent and strategically focused than those of more recent converts to open and flexible learning. He finds that the newcomers tend to focus more on the 'product' and the digital technology, making the spurious assumption that somehow, the 'product' will take care of the 'market'. His findings suggest a relationship between these orientations and the perceptions and ambitions of the institutional leaders.

New information technology can lead to 'technological determinism' and tempt teaching staff into a 'do-it-yourself' approach. Unfortunately, there appears to be a reluctance on the part of many staff drawn to developing multimedia and Internet applications to utilize the expertise of those staff who are experienced in the more time-honoured practices of course and material development and student support for distance education (Moran 1997; Evans et al. 1997). There is also concern on the part of the National Union of Students that there will be an increasing shift of resources from face-to-face teaching to virtual learning and extra electronic offerings at the expense of access to the more poorly resourced, smaller and regional universities (Healy 1999).

Another misleading and simplistic approach is to assume that open and distance education, and particularly what might be termed 'dot.com degrees', are cheaper than conventional education. Various government-commissioned studies have shown that the costs are differently constituted in different institutions and that it is difficult to establish even indicative costs in open and distance education and technology innovation (Tinkler et al. 1994; Jevons and Northcott 1994).

Australian distance education is moving into a 'post-Fordist' or 'post industrial' phase of high product innovation, high process variability and high labour responsibility (Campion 1995; Campion and Renner 1992). The greater use of computers and the Internet will inevitably mean that course design, materials development and student support are devolved to designated teams and individuals. Internationalization and attempts to achieve economies of scale will need collaboration and strategic alliances between providers of distance education programmes and services. All of these developments have substantial implications for the nature, organization, resourcing, staffing and standing of Australia's educational institutions. They demand envisioning, leadership and management, and careful consideration of the organizational structures, cultural changes, professional development programmes and recognition and reward systems that are needed to encourage and support such practices. As Evans and Nation (1996) point out, the complexity of future endeavours points to a need for dialogue between Australian researchers, policy-makers and practitioners across the various sectors, traditional disciplines and national contexts of education.

References

Andrewartha, G (1996) 'Improving the presentation of printed text for tertiary level distance education: literature review and survey', *Distance Education*, 17(2): 387–411.

Anwyl, J, Powles, M and Patrick, K (1987) *Who Uses External Studies? Who Should?* Centre for Study of Higher Education, University of Melbourne.

Ashenden, D (1987) *Costs and Cost Structures in External Studies: A Discussion of Issues and Possibilities in Australian Higher Education*, Canberra: Commonwealth Tertiary Education Commission.

Atkinson, E (1996) *Evaluation of the Open Learning Initiative: Tertiary Access through a National Brokerage Agency: An Overview of the Final Report*, January 1996, Melbourne: University of Melbourne, Centre for Study of Higher Education.

Australian Bureau of Statistics (2000) *Australia Now – A Statistical Profile: Education and Training*, <http://www.statistics.gov.au/websitedbs/>.

Australian National Training Authority (1997) 'Assuring quality and choice in national training', Brisbane.

Bourke, C J, Burden, J K and Moore, S (1996) *Factors Affecting Performance of Aboriginal and Torres Strait Islander Students at Australian Universities: A Case Study*, Canberra: Australian Government Publishing Service, Department of Employment, Education, Training and Youth Affairs, Higher Education Division, Evaluations and Investigations Program.

Brown, P (2000) 'Students slugged by cost of online future', *The Australian: Higher Education*, Wednesday, 22 March, 46.

Burke, C, Lundin, R and Daunt, C (1997) 'Pushing the boundaries of interaction in videoconferencing: a dialogical approach', *Distance Education*, 18(2): 350–61.

Campion, M (1995) 'The supposed demise of bureaucracy: implications for distance education and open learning — more on the post-Fordism debate', *Distance Education*, 16(2): 192–216.

Campion, M and Renner, W (1992) 'The supposed demise of Fordism: implications for distance education and higher education', *Distance Education*, 13(1): 7–28.

Committee on Open University (1974) 'Open tertiary education in Australia', Final Report of the Committee on Open University to the Universities Commission, Canberra: Australian Government Publishing Service.

Cunningham, S, Ryan, Y, Stedman, L, Tapsall, S, Bagdon, K, Flew, T, and Coaldrake, P (2000) *The Business of Borderless Education*, Canberra: Australian Government Publishing Service, Department of Education, Training and Youth Affairs, Higher Education Division, Evaluations and Investigations Program.

Cunningham, S, Tapsall, S, Ryan, Y, Stedman, L, Bagdon, K and Flew, T (1997) *New Media and Borderless Education: A Review of the Convergence between Global Media Networks and Higher Education Provision*, Canberra: Australian Government Publishing Service, Department of Employment, Education, Training and Youth Affairs, Higher Education Division, Evaluations and Investigations Program.

Evans, T (1994) *Understanding the Learners in Open and Distance Education*, London: Kogan Page.

Evans, T and King, B (eds) (1991) *Beyond the Text: Contemporary Writing on Distance Education*, Geelong: Deakin University Press.

Evans, T and Nation, D (1996) 'Educational futures', in Evans, T and Nation, D (eds) (1996) *Opening Education: Policies and Practices from Open and Distance Education*, London and New York: Routledge, 162–76.

Evans, T, Nation, D, Rennart, W and Tregenza, K (1997) 'The end of the line or a new future for open and distance education?' in Osborne, J, Roberts, D and Walker, J (eds) *Open, Flexible and Distance Learning: Education and Training in the 21st Century*, 13th Biennial Forum of Open and Distance

Learning Association of Australia (in association with the Australian Association of Distance Education Schools), 29 September–3 October, University of Tasmania, 151–55.

Gooley, A, Skippington, P and Towers, S (1998) 'Integrated online services: is this the future?' in Barker, J (ed.) Proceedings of International Conference, Learning Together: Collaboration in Open Learning, John Curtin International Institute, Curtin University of Technology, April, 29–39.

Guiton, P and Smith, M (1984) 'Progress in partnership: external studies in Western Australia', in *Diversity Down Under in Distance Education*, Australian and South Pacific External Studies Association, Toowoomba: Darling Downs Institute Press, 83–7.

Healy, G (1999) 'Rescue bid links universities', *The Australian: Higher Education*, Wednesday, 3 February, 37.

Holt, P and Japanangka R (1998) 'Mixed-mode delivery of health and education services in the Tanami Desert region', in Barker, J (ed.) Proceedings of International Conference, Learning Together: Collaboration in Open Learning, John Curtin International Institute, Curtin University of Technology, April, 53–5.

Inglis, A (1991) 'Eighteen years of instructional design: a personal view', in Parer, M S (ed.) *Development, Design and Distance Education*, 2nd edn, Churchill: Gippsland Institute.

Jakupec, V (1996) 'Reforming distance education through economic rationalism: a critical analysis of reforms to Australian higher education', in Evans, T and Nation, D (eds) *Opening Education: Policies and Practices from Open and Distance Education*, London and New York: Routledge.

Jakupec, V (1998) 'Flexible learning in Australian universities: a comparative study', unpublished report, Faculty of Education, University of Technology, Sydney.

James, R and Beattie, K (1995) *Expanding Options: Delivery Technologies and Postgraduate Coursework*, Canberra: Australian Government Publishing Service, Department of Employment, Education, Training and Youth Affairs, Higher Education Division, Evaluations and Investigations Program.

James, R and Beattie, K (1996) 'Postgraduate coursework beyond the classroom: issues in implementing flexible delivery', *Distance Education*, 17(2): 335–68.

Jevons, F and Northcott, P (1994) 'Costs and quality in resource-based education on- and off-campus, National Board of Employment Education and Training', Commissioned Report no. 33, Canberra: Australian Government Publishing Service.

Johnson, R (1983) *The Provision of External Studies in Australian Higher Education*, Canberra: Australian Government Publishing Service, Commonwealth Tertiary Education Commission.

Johnson, R (1990) 'Open learning — policy and practice, National Board of Employment Education and Training', Commissioned Report no. 4, Canberra: Australian Government Publishing Service.

Johnson, R (1996) 'To wish and to will: reflections on policy formation and implementation in Australian distance education', in Evans, T and Nation, D (eds) *Opening Education: Policies and Practices from Open and Distance Education*, London and New York: Routledge.

Johnson, R, Lundin, R and Chippendale, P (1992) *Changing Patterns of Teaching and Learning: The Use and Potential of Distance Education Materials and Methods in Australian Higher Education*, Canberra: Australian Government Publishing Service.

Kay, D (1997) 'Flexible delivery: the white knight of training', in Osborne, J, Roberts, D and Walker, J (eds) *Open, Flexible and Distance Learning: Education and Training in the 21st Century*, 13th Biennial Forum of Open and Distance Learning Association of Australia (in association with the Australian Association of Distance Education Schools), 29 September– 3 October, University of Tasmania, 226–33.

King, B (1993) 'Open learning in Australia: government intervention and institutional response', *Open Learning*, 8(3): 13–25.

King, B (1999) 'Distance education in Australia' in K Harry (ed.) *Higher Education Through Open and Distance Learning: World Review of Distance Education and Open Learning*, London: Routledge, and Vancouver: The Commonwealth of Learning.

Knox, D M (1997) 'A review of the use of video-conferencing for actuarial education — a three year case study', *Distance Education*, 18(2): 225–35.

Latchem, C and Lockwood, F (eds) (1998) *Staff Development in Open and Flexible Learning*, London and New York: Routledge.

Latchem, C and Moran, L (1998) 'Staff development issues in dual-mode institutions: the Australian experience', in Latchem, C and Lockwood, F (eds) (1998) *Staff Development in Open and Flexible Learning*, London and New York: Routledge.

Latchem, C and Pritchard, T (1994) 'Open Learning: the unique Australian option', in *Open Learning*, 9(3): 18–26.

Le Grew, D and Calvert, J (1998) 'Leadership for open and flexible learning in higher education', in Latchem, C and Lockwood, F (eds) *Staff Development Issues in Open and Flexible Learning*, London and New York: Routledge.

Lowe, I (1997) 'Open and distance learning: education for the future', in Osborne, J, Roberts, D and Walker, J (eds) *Open, Flexible and Distance Learning: Education and Training in the 21st Century*, 13th Biennial Forum of Open and Distance Learning Association of Australia (in association with the Australian Association of Distance Education Schools), 29 September–3 October, University of Tasmania, 256–62.

Luck, J (1997) 'Evaluation of videoconferencing across campuses', in Osborne, J, Roberts, D and Walker, J (eds) *Open, Flexible and Distance Learning: Education and Training in the 21st Century*, 13th Biennial Forum of Open and Distance Learning Association of Australia (in association with the Australian Association of Distance Education Schools), 29 September–3 October, University of Tasmania, 263–68.

Lugg, D (1994) 'Primary and secondary education in Victoria, Australia' in Mukhopadhay, M and Phillips, S (eds) *Open Schooling: Selected Experiences*, Vancouver: The Commonwealth of Learning.

Macnamara, D (1997) 'Igniting innovation: a recipe for the survival of an educational institution', in Osborne, J, Roberts, D and Walker, J (eds) *Open, Flexible and Distance Learning: Education and Training in the 21st Century*, 13th Biennial Forum of Open and Distance Learning Association of Australia (in association with the Australian Association of Distance Education Schools), 29 September–3 October, University of Tasmania, 281–85.

Macpherson, C and Dekkers, J (1997) 'Open learning centres: the perceptions of distance education students', in Osborne, J, Roberts, D and Walker, J (eds) *Open, Flexible and Distance Learning: Education and Training in the 21st Century*, 13th Biennial Forum of Open and Distance Learning Association of Australia (in association with the Australian Association of Distance Education Schools), 29 September–3 October, University of Tasmania, 293–99.

Mitchell, J and Bluer, R (1997) *A Planning Model for Innovation: New Learning Technologies*, Melbourne: Office of Training and Further Education.

Moran, L (1997) 'Flexible learning, technology and change: divining the future from the past', in Osborne, J, Roberts, D and Walker, J (eds) *Open, Flexible and Distance Learning: Education and Training in the 21st Century*, 13th Biennial Forum of Open and Distance Learning Association of Australia (in association with the Australian Association of Distance Education Schools), 29 September–3 October, University of Tasmania, 331–35.

Northcott, P (1984), 'The tyranny of distance and proximity', in *Diversity Down Under in Distance Education*, Australian and South Pacific External Studies Association, Toowoomba: Darling Downs Institute Press, 39–50.

Oliver, R and Short, G (1996) 'The Western Australian telecentres network: enhancing equity and access to education in rural communities', in Carlson, P and Makedon, F (eds) Proceedings of Ed-Telecom, Charlottesville: AACE, 238–43.

O'Sullivan, G (1997) 'Home tutors: the all-important link between the student and the teacher', in Osborne, J, Roberts, D and Walker, J (eds) *Open, Flexible and Distance Learning: Education and Training in the 21st Century*, 13th Biennial Forum of Open and Distance Learning Association of Australia (in association with the Australian Association of Distance Education Schools), 29 September–3 October, University of Tasmania, 347–53.

Parer, M (1993) 'The educational developer's role — present and future', in Nunan, T (ed.) *Distance Education Futures*, 11th Biennial Forum, ASPESA selected papers, University of South Australia, Adelaide.

Rayner, S A (1949) *Correspondence Education in Australia and New Zealand*, Melbourne: University of Melbourne Press.

Richardson, J (2000)'Remote service at your convenience', *The Australian: Higher Education*, Wednesday, 22 March, 46.

Tinkler, D, Lepani, B and Mitchell, J (1996) 'Education and technology convergence, National Board of Employment', Education and Training Commissioned Report no. 43, Canberra: Australian Government Publishing Service.

Tinkler, D, Smith, T, Ellyard, P and Cohen, D (1994) *Effectiveness and Potential of State-of-the-Art Technologies in the Delivery of Higher Education*, Occasional Papers Series, Canberra: Department of Employment, Education and Training, Higher Education Division.

Treagust, D F, Waldrip, B G and Horley, J R (1993) 'Effectiveness of USDN video-conferencing: a case study of two campuses and two different courses', *Distance Education*, 14(2): 315–30.

Walker, J and Walker, M G (1997) 'Review of research in open and distance learning in Australasia and the Pacific', in Osborne, J, Roberts, D and Walker, J (eds) *Open, Flexible and Distance Learning: Education and Training in the 21st Century*, 13th Biennial Forum of Open and Distance Learning Association of Australia (in association with the Australian Association of Distance Education Schools), 29 September–3 October, University of Tasmania, 491–99.

Appendix

Information about open and distance education in Australia

Further information about Australian open and distance organizations and programmes may be gained from:

International Centre for Distance Learning
<http://www-icdl.open.ac.uk/>

Open and Distance Learning Association of Australia
<http://www.usq.edu.au/dec/decjourn/odlaa.htm>

Distance Education, The International Journal of the Open and Distance Learning Association of Australia
<http://www.usq.edu.au/dec/decjourn/deintlj.htm>

Canada

Joan Collinge, Patricia Graca and J Colin Yerbury

Introduction

Distance education has helped to increase access to education in Canada since the late 19th century. The need to serve isolated and chronically ill children provided the impetus for the development of elementary and secondary school correspondence programmes country-wide. Over time, correspondence programmes broadened to include special groups of learners, among them adults seeking basic education and vocational training.

Canada is the world's second largest country, crossing six time zones and covering more than ten million square kilometres, over nine million of which are land and 755,000 fresh water. Canada has ten provinces and three territories, including Nunavut as of April 1999, each with its own capital city. Ottawa, in the province of Ontario, is the capital of Canada (see Appendix I).

The Canadian economy is among the world's soundest. Fully integrated into the global system, Canada is the eighth largest trading nation among the industrialized market economies, and is an active partner in international investment. At the time of the June 1996 census, Canada's population was 29.7 million (1998 — 30.3 million), approximately 0.5% of the global population. According to the 1996 census, 52.8% Canadians aged 15 and over had attended secondary school, and 34% had gone to a trade school or another post-secondary institution. Three million people — 10.1% of the population — had a university degree. Canada's two official languages are English and French. Census data from 1996 indicate that English is the mother tongue of 16.9 million Canadians and French of 6.6 million. However, many Canadians speak other heritage languages. In 1996, First Nations languages were reported as the first language of 185,960 Canadians.

General education system

There is no federal education system in Canada. The British North America Act (1867) assigned the provinces exclusive jurisdiction over education (with the exceptions noted below). The education system varies from province to province and includes six to eight years of elementary school, four or five years of secondary school, and three or four years at university undergraduate level. Other post-secondary options include colleges, university colleges and institutes of technology. These, too, are overseen by the provincial governments.

The exception referenced above pertains to the federal government's role in looking after education in the northern territories and in responding to the educational needs of First Nations people, members of the armed forces, and inmates of federal correctional institutions.

Each Canadian university sets its own admission standards and assesses the qualifications of applicants. There is no national policy regarding equivalencies of qualifications earned abroad or any Canada-wide entrance test.

At the time of Confederation in 1867, there were 17 colleges in Canada, only four of which were independent of denominational control. Public universities are now chartered under the university acts of the various provinces. Provincial governments and ministries use a variety of means to support programme development in distance education and the administrative and communications infrastructures necessary for widespread dissemination. Unlike other jurisdictions, Canada has had few private universities. Those that exist typically have a religious affiliation. The secular private institution, however, is starting to have a presence in Canada.

Canada's universities, both large and small, mirror the unique cultural, social, religious and political mosaic of a vast country, rich in its diversity. They provide a tremendous range of choices with regard to programmes offered, language of instruction, a secular or denominational orientation, and modes of delivery. They are located predominantly in large cities; some, however, are situated in smaller towns; virtually all are on the Internet. While Canadian universities design their own missions and pursue their own futures, they consistently demonstrate a remarkable ability to cooperate with one another and work collectively.

Financial support

While primary and secondary schooling is fully funded by the provincial government, provincial and federal government subsidies to public universities and other post-secondary institutions do not meet all their financial needs. The average student tuition fee at Canadian universities is a minimum of approximately CAD62,500 a year. Provincial governments offer student assistance programmes, and most universities provide scholarships to entering students with exceptional ability. First Nations students are funded through the federal government's Post Secondary Student Assistance Program. In most jurisdictions, international students face surcharges.

Distance education funding

Each province funds distance education initiatives at the post-secondary level. Support for distance education activities varies by institution. Some are funded through the university's budget. Others are solely revenue supported.

Communications infrastructure

The challenges that geography creates have, in part, contributed to Canada developing one of the most advanced telecommunications systems in the world. The Canadian Post Office has also traditionally been at the leading edge of technology as it strives to conquer Canada's vast distances, difficult terrain and often harsh climate. Telephone service is virtually universal. Sixteen million access lines bring service to 99% of Canadian homes. Coincident with the proliferation of technology in the 1970s was the establishment of four provincial education communications agencies: Radio Québec in 1968, TVOntario in 1970, ACCESS Alberta in 1973, and the Knowledge Network of the West in 1980.

Canadians are increasingly hooking up to the Internet. In 1995, close to 30% of households had home computers, and over 40% of those were equipped with modems that allow access to the Internet. Canada now ranks fifth in the world in regard to the size of its Internet population. Furthermore, an Angus Reid survey (September 2000) reveals that 'Canada is near the top of the class globally when it comes to offering Internet access to its students'. These trends are supported at the national level through organizations such as the Canadian Network for the Advancement of Research, Industry, and Education (CANARIE) Inc., a not-for-profit, industry-led consortium the mission of which is to facilitate the development of Canada's communications infrastructure. At the time of writing, CANARIE has proposed a Canada-wide fibre-optic network that would link every home, school, library, hospital and business in Canada and make its residents indisputably the most wired in the world. The CANARIE site <http://www.canarie.ca/frames/startabout_e.html> provides further information regarding the extent of this coverage (see also Appendix 2).

Distance education

Equal access to quality education for all Canadians is a national aim, regardless of geographic and social barriers. Open and distance learning can assist in achieving the education and training requirements of the new knowledge-based economy. With emerging understanding about how people learn and with new technologies for instruction, open and distance learning continues to enrich the Canadian educational system.

Contemporary distance education in Canadian universities grew out of their mandate to provide continuing education services to the wider community. In 1954, the directors of extension and summer schools at several Canadian universities formed CADESS, the Canadian Association of Directors of Extension and Summer Session. And in 1974, following the explosion in the establishment of new institutions for higher education in the 1960s, the Canadian Association for Continuing Education (CAUCE) was created. Its mission is to enhance the stature and expertise of institutions and individuals devoted to providing educational opportunities for adults at university level. To foster excellence in the provision of distance education in Canada, the Canadian Association for Distance Education (CADE) was established in 1983. CADE's *Journal of Distance Education* is a refereed international publication that promotes and encourages scholarly work of an empirical and theoretical nature relating to distance education in Canada and throughout the world. The Journal was founded at the Centre for Distance Education at Simon Fraser University in 1986. In 1998, the editorship was transferred to the Faculty of Education at the University of Alberta in Edmonton. The Journal is one means through which CADE fulfils its aims to advance and promote distance education nationally, to represent Canada internationally, to promote research and access, and to provide a forum for interaction on a national, regional, provincial and local basis <www.cade-aced.ca>.

Establishing distance education programmes

Canada's small and widely dispersed population, separated by imposing geographical barriers, has encouraged the growth of distance education. It was originally undertaken to meet the educational needs of a primary resource-based population of traders, trappers, farmers, loggers, fishers and miners. Distance education also provided learning opportunities for children unable to attend traditional public and private schools because of isolation or illness. The history of distance education in Canada is interwoven with the invention of new communications technologies, the expansion of education, particularly adult education, and the commitment of individual Canadians who had a vision that communications technologies could extend learning opportunities.

In 1889, Queen's University in Ontario began offering university courses by correspondence. In 1919, in response to the request of a lighthouse keeper, British Columbia began to offer correspondence courses (high school completion) and continues to do so today from kindergarten to Grade 12. Between 1921 and 1927, the ministries of education in five provinces established correspondence branches to offer primary and secondary school courses, particularly to students in rural communities. The need to provide current information to Canada's farmers led the Canadian Broadcasting Corporation (CBC), in partnership with the Canadian Association for Adult Education and the Federation of Agriculture, to initiate the pioneering Farm Radio Forum in the mid-1930s. St. Francis Xavier University in Nova Scotia, along with other institutions throughout the country, organized community response groups for this highly influential programme.

In 1938, the International Council for Correspondence Education (ICCE) was formed in Victoria, BC. During the Vancouver Conference of the ICCE in 1982, the Council changed its name and became the International Council for Distance Education (ICDE). In 1989, The Commonwealth of Learning (COL) was created to broaden access to and increase opportunities for learning, by promoting cooperation between universities, colleges and other educational institutions throughout the COL. Its headquarters are in Vancouver, and it is the only Commonwealth intergovernmental organization outside Britain. COL seeks to ensure that distance education programmes and techniques and technologies are developed to suit the particular requirements of the more than fifty current member countries. The 88 institutions of higher learning that make up the Canadian university community offer a wide variety of educational settings. This number contributes to Canada's reputation as a world leader in the provision of distance education.

The 1999–2000 Canadian University Distance Education Directory (CUDED) lists 51 universities in Canada that offer courses through various distance education formats. The number of institutions within Canada precludes a detailed discussion of each. The following section introduces three types of organization (the single-mode university, dual-mode university and consortia) and highlights well-established examples of each. The CUDED lists such institutions at <http://cauce-aepuc.ca/english/directory/institutions/index.html>. Also worth a visit is a world-wide directory compiled by the International Centre for Distance Learning at <http://www.icdl.open.ac.uk/icdl/database/northame/canada/index.html>.

Institutional websites provide more detailed information regarding programming and online teaching and learning initiatives.

Single-mode institutions

A small group of public institutions is dedicated solely to open and distance learning. These universities provide a backbone to the multifaceted Canadian system.

In 1972, Athabasca University <http://www.athabascau.ca> accepted its first students and became Canada's first fully accredited open university specializing in distance education. Between 1972 and 1975, 650 students enrolled in this pilot project, and in 1977 Athabasca University held its first convocation ceremony. It gained permanent status as a university under the Universities Act in 1978. From 1996 to 1999, there was an increase of about 47% in course registrations and head counts. In 1998/99, Athabasca had 30,000 course enrolments in 427 courses and 16,100 students across Canada. Growth in graduate programmes has been higher than in undergraduate ones in this period. Athabasca University offers full Bachelor's degree programmes in Arts, General Studies, Science, Administrative Studies, Commerce and Nursing. Master's programmes are offered in Business Administration and Distance Education. It offers a number of certificate programmes as well. Athabasca University employs its own faculty, mirroring a traditional university in this respect, and has its own design, production and delivery expertise.

Télé-Université <http://www.teluq.uquebec.ca> is one of ten units making up the Université du Québec network, and is the only university in Québec to offer courses exclusively by distance. It began in 1972 and has had 200,000 students since its inception. Students can obtain a Bachelor's degree, a diploma or a certificate recognized by the University of Québec. Télé-Université has a registration of more than 2,400 equivalent full-time students for whom the language of instruction is French.

In 1978, the British Columbia provincial government established the Open Learning Institute, offering college and university courses through distance education. In 1980, the Knowledge Network was created and began to broadcast educational programming. In 1988, the organizations merged to form the Open Learning Agency (OLA) <http://www.ola.bc.ca/ou>. Today the OLA is comprised of four operating components: Open School, Open College, Open University and Knowledge Network. Fully accredited in the public post-secondary system, the BC Open University is a member of the Association of Universities and Colleges of Canada (AUCC). It currently awards 22 degrees in Arts, Business Administration, General Studies, Health Science, Music, Music Therapy, Science, Technology and Tourism. The agency has had more than 70,000 course enrolments since its founding and currently offers more than 270 courses.

Dual-mode institutions

The majority of universities offering distance education programmes and courses across Canada are the traditional institutions, for whom the primary focus remains the campus-based student. These institutions have gradually established distance programmes during the last two decades to serve the needs of part-time, non-traditional learners who are not able or do not want to come to campus for time- and place-bound classes. In addition to providing educational opportunities in urban centres, each provincial institution has adopted a model of delivering a service to rural communities that is designed to meet the unique needs of the learners it serves. Typically, the distance education programme in these dual-mode institutions is administered through the continuing education unit or a separate department established to provide specialized development and delivery services.

The bulk of courseware in the dual-mode, as in the single-mode institutions, continues to be print based. Nevertheless, many dual-mode institutions have a mixed media model of delivery or are moving towards one, sometimes using the services of the provincial telecommunications systems (Knowledge Network, TVOntario, ACCESS Network, etc.) as well as their own video, audio and computer production facilities. Frequently, a common feature of their programmes is the commitment to provide course content and standards parallel to the same on-campus courses. While the telephone continues to be used, student support is increasingly maintained using online technologies.

In the paragraphs that follow we highlight the largest dual-mode distance education providers proceeding from the Atlantic to the Pacific Ocean. We cannot speak for the programmes in all 88 Canadian institutions so we have limited our discussion to the institutions with the highest number of distance education registrations in each of the major regions within Canada.

In Atlantic Canada, the small and scattered population in Newfoundland provided a natural locale for the development of alternatives to traditional educational delivery methods. Memorial University <http://www.mun.ca> was one of the first post-secondary institutions to recognize the benefits of distance learning. With its multimedia infrastructure dispersed throughout the province, Memorial has served as a model for Canadian distance educators to emulate. Typical courses include video, audio and print materials, supported by tutorial services and audioteleconferencing. There are 10,000 single-course registrations in some 250 courses in Memorial's distance education programme.

Other Atlantic universities are active in providing distance learning programming. For instance, Acadia University, Dalhousie University, Mount Saint Vincent and Saint Mary's (all in Nova Scotia) and the University of New Brunswick and Mount Allison University serve their regions in selected programme areas as does the University of Moncton, which provides French-language programming. St. Francis Xavier also offers distance education learning opportunities. Some institutions have only recently begun to offer distance courses, taking advantage of the trend that sees an increasing number of faculty and students alike expecting institutions to provide opportunities to teach and learn online.

In Québec, apart from Télé-Université, which is the main distance education provider, McGill University, the Université de Montréal, the Université du Québec à Rimouski, and the Université Laval in Québec City also provide distance learning opportunities for both English and French speaking students throughout the province.

Ontario's universities and institutes offer many distance learning opportunities, using a variety of delivery modes. In terms of distance˙

learning course enrolments, the largest of these programmes is at the University of Waterloo <http://www.uwaterloo.ca>, which offers 300 courses to an estimated 18,000 registrants provincially and across Canada. The University of Waterloo was created in 1957 and began its correspondence programme in 1968 with audiotaped Physics courses. The programme grew from about 200 student course enrolments in 1968/69 to about 16,000 in 1993/94. They presently offer approximately 250 courses and several degree programmes by distance education.

Other notable providers in Ontario include Laurentian University and Lakehead University (partners in the management of the Contact North/ Contact Nord project). Laurentian has a history of a very strong commitment to the extension of education in both official languages throughout northern Ontario. In addition, Ontario Institute for Studies in Education (offering graduate education courses), the University of Ottawa, Wilfrid Laurier University, the University of Windsor, Guelph University and York University all provide distance learning in a wide variety of subjects. The Open College/Ryerson Polytechnic Institute offers credit courses on CJRT television, which is distributed by cable throughout the province.

Universities on the Prairies have been engaged in extensive distance learning programmes for many years. The University of Manitoba, the University of Saskatchewan, the University of Regina, Lethbridge University, and the Universities of Alberta (Edmonton) and Calgary all have flourishing distance education programmes. The University of Saskatchewan has been very active in satellite delivery of courses. The University of Manitoba is the largest distance education provider with over 4,000 enrolments. The University of Manitoba, in partnership with the Department of National Defence (DND), offers the Canadian Forces University Program. With over 110 education courses available in Arts, Science, Social Work, Nursing, Education and Recreation Studies, the programme is designed to assist Regular and Reserve Force personnel and their families, Retired Members of the Armed Forces, and others in the Department of National Defence to achieve degree completion. Readers with a particular interest in distance education for First Nations people are directed to the websites of the prairie institutions.

Of the six institutions that are part of the British Columbia University Consortium (Royal Roads University, Simon Fraser University (SFU), the Technical University of British Columbia, the University of British Columbia, the University of Northern British Columbia and the University of Victoria), SFU <http://www.sfu.ca> is the largest distance education provider. Since the programme's inception in 1975, enrolment has grown from 55 students in five courses to over 13,000 course enrolments in 275 offerings of 130 different credit courses. The programmes offered include degrees, certificates and post-baccalaureate diplomas in a number of fields.

Consortia

University Consortium (of British Columbia)

In 1984, the provincial government of British Columbia established the University Consortium to increase access to university courses offered at a distance.

Students register through the OLA for distance education courses offered by member institutions SFU, The University of British Columbia (UBC), and the University of Victoria (UVIC), without having to be admitted to these institutions. Currently, 300 courses are offered through this partnership, giving students increased access to a university education through distance education.

New partners Royal Roads University (RRU), the Technical University of British Columbia (TechBC), and the University of Northern British Columbia (UNBC) have joined the University Consortium, which can now offer 17 baccalaureate programmes entirely at a distance. All the partners have recently collaborated to propose the formation of a new British Columbia Virtual University Consortium that will increase inter-institutional programmatic collaboration and coordination.

Contact North/ Contact Nord

Contact North/Contact Nord, with headquarters in Sudbury and Thunder Bay, is described as Canada's largest distance education network. It facilitates the delivery of secondary and post-secondary programmes and courses to over 100 communities in Northern Ontario. It is funded by the government of Ontario to increase and improve access to education and training opportunities. Programmes and courses are offered at local Distance Education and Training Centres, enabling learners to pursue their educational and training goals without leaving their community. The Contact North/Contact Nord website at <http://www.cnorth.edu.on.ca> graphically demonstrates the expanse of its reach. Spanning 880,000

square kilometres in Northern Ontario, its 145 Access Centres meet the
needs of both anglophone and francophone learners.

Campus Manitoba

The Campus Manitoba degree programme which is located at <http://
www.campusmanitoba.com> was established in 1990 and brings together
the three universities in Manitoba — Brandon University, The University of
Manitoba and The University of Winnipeg, all three of which are involved
in the development and delivery of courses for the Campus Manitoba
programme. Students from anywhere in the province may take courses
from any of the three universities. The credits are then transferred to their
home institution. Campus Manitoba allows students to work towards a
university degree without having to move to a larger community with a
university campus. Courses use a variety of technologies, including virtual
classroom software, the Internet and the Web.

Other initiatives and trends

Seven Canadian universities have formed the Canadian Virtual University
(CVU). Members of the pan-provincial consortium are Athabasca
University, Brandon University, The University of Manitoba, Laurentian
University, BC Open University, Royal Roads University, and the University
of Victoria. CVU is a partnership of universities across Canada, committed
to delivering university-level programmes that can be completed from
anywhere in the country or beyond. Its goals include simplifying the
process of identifying accredited online and distance programmes,
facilitating the transfer of credits among the partner institutions and
increasing the opportunities for inter-institutional programme
development and research <http://www.cvu-uvc.ca>.

The Western Deans of Continuing Education propose the establishment of
a Western Canadian Virtual University. While Atlantic institutions have
not yet formed a consortium, there have been attempts to do so, and there
has been some collaboration among partners. For example, the Association
of Atlantic Universities publishes, on a voluntary basis, a directory of credit
and non-credit distance education courses offered by member institutions
<http://www.dal.ca/aau/>.

Media for distance education/instructional systems

In such a large, sparsely populated country, communications have naturally played a significant instructional role. Indeed, it was in Brantford, Ontario, that Alexander Graham Bell invented the telephone in 1874 and two years later made the first long distance call. So it is not surprising that Canadian governments have recognized the potential of communications technologies and have been instrumental in their development and application. Postal systems have helped Canadians communicate for 300 years, shrinking distances by facilitating the exchange of information and the physical distribution of goods. Experiments with satellites in the 1970s demonstrated their viability and led to the establishment and expansion of educational communications agencies and produced other spin-off educational activities.

With this background in innovation, it is not surprising that Canadian institutions are actively exploring the benefits to be derived from more recent technological advancements. Increasingly, online courses are being offered using email and computer conferencing to connect dispersed students for interactive group work. The benefits of print endure, however, and many courses continue to use print-based study guides, textbooks and course readers. Televised programming, face-to-face instruction, teletutorials, audio and videotape continue to be used as well, where content demands and/or student needs deem this appropriate.

Challenges

The responsibility for financing post-secondary education in Canada has long been a shared responsibility between students and the two levels of government. Recently, changing priorities and an overriding focus on the national deficit have brought cuts in government support. In many provinces, tuition fees have been raised, particularly in areas of professional education, but Canadians are reluctant to create financial barriers that limit access.

International affiliation and cooperation

According to a recent statement on Internationalization and Canadian Universities, which was adopted by the membership of the Association of Universities and Colleges of Canada (AUCC) in 1995, internationalization of the university is 'a necessary, vital, and deliberate transformation of how we teach and learn and it is essential to the future quality of higher education in Canada, indeed to the future of Canada...'. Although provincial governments do not fund international projects, many Canadian universities have articulated a commitment to internationalization in their mission statements. The Canadian University Projects in International Development Database (CUPID) contains more than 2,000 records on Canadian university international development projects. The majority of the projects are funded by the Canadian International Development Agency (CIDA), the International Development Research Centre (IDRC), and multilateral development banks. Each record lists, among other things, the universities involved (in Canada and in the developing country), the project's objective, the amount of funding and the duration of the project.

The Mexican, Canadian and United States governments have announced their plan to fund further development of EL NET, the North American Educational Leadership Network, located at <http://www.elnet.org>. The announcement was made on 11 August 2000, when US Secretary of State Madeleine Albright, Mexican Foreign Secretary Rosario Green, and Canadian Foreign Affairs Minister Lloyd Axworthy met in Santa Fe, New Mexico, for a two-day discussion on the progress made on the 'North American Partnership'. Created and administered by the Consortium for North American Higher Education Collaboration (CONAHEC) in 1995 with encouragement and support from the Ford Foundation, EL NET has become a 'one-step shop' Internet site for North American higher education issues.

Canadian institutions are increasingly interested in offering degree programmes at international sites using multi-mode delivery methods. Examples are the delivery of the University of Calgary's online Master of Continuing Education in partnership with the Asian Institute of Technology in Bangkok; the University of British Columbia and the Monterrey Institute of Technology (ITESM) joint development and delivery of postgraduate courses in Technology-Based Distributed Learning; and the new initiative of Shanghai University, L'Université du Québec à Montréal, SFU and Saint Mary's University to establish degree programmes at the Sino-Canadian Institute of Shanghai University.

Research activities

Federal government support for basic and applied research is channelled through three research granting councils — the Medical Research Council (MRC), the Natural Sciences and Engineering Research Council (NSERC) and the Social Sciences and Humanities Research Council (SSHRC). Operating at arm's length from government, the councils are responsible for fostering a strong research base, linking university research activities to Canada's social and economic priorities, and developing highly qualified research personnel. For instance, hundreds of Canadian journals, including the *Journal of Distance Education*, apply to SSHRC for support grants under the Program of Aid to Learned Journals. Eight of the ten provinces have established similar agencies to support provincially funded research programmes.

Canada is a leader in the study and development of effective online education exemplified largely by the TeleLearning Network of Centres of Excellence (TeleLearning NCE). Further information is available at <http://www.telelearn.ca>. Researchers at SFU lead the TeleLearning NCE, which focuses primarily on the design and development of new pedagogies and network technologies to support collaborative learning, knowledge building and lifelong learning. The Network features over 150 researchers from education, cognitive psychology, social science, computer science and engineering science throughout Canada who collaborate online to address some of the major challenges Canada faces in becoming a learning society with a knowledge-based economy. In collaboration with 121 academic and industry partners throughout the world, 80 faculty members from 24 universities across Canada are evaluating the effectiveness of new learning models, analysing the cost benefits and social impact of implementing telelearning, and creating telelearning software prototypes based on innovative learning models.

As of 20 July 2000 an advisory committee for online learning was established jointly by the federal government and the Council of Ministers of Education, Canada (CMEC). This arms-length group will advise the federal and provincial governments and post-secondary institutions on the most successful and cost-effective ways to deliver online learning to all Canadians: <http://www.ic.gc.ca>. With membership including senior representatives from Canada's university, college and business communities, the committee will examine the issues, impediments and incentives involving online learning with the intent of providing educational training opportunities and developing knowledge and skills for all Canadians regardless of their location. The committee will present its report to provincial and federal ministers in November 2000.

References

Association of Universities and Colleges of Canada (1999) 'Higher education in Canada: overview of higher education' <http://www.aucc.ca/english/dcu/highereducation/overview.html>

Bailey, Terrence (ed.) (1997) *Canadian University Distance Education Directory*, Ottawa: Association of Universities and Colleges of Canada.

Bates, T (1999) 'Discussion document on a virtual university of British Columbia', unpublished draft, 14 May 1999.

BCNET: a decade of excellence <http://www.bc.net>

Canadian Association for University Continuing Education (1999–2000) <http://www.cauce-aepuc.ca/english/about>

Canarie Inc. (1998) <http://www.canarie.ca/frames/startabout_e.html>.

Croft, M (1992) 'Single or dual mode: challenges and choices for the future of education' in Mugridge, I (ed.) *Distance Education in Single and Dual Mode Universities*, Vancouver: Commonwealth of Learning.

Daniel, J S (1982) 'Reflections on Rubik's cube', *Distance Education: An International Journal*, 3(1).

Daniel, J S et al. (eds) (1982) *Learning at a Distance: A World Perspective*, Edmonton: Athabasca University/International Council for Correspondence Education.

Department of Justice Canada (1999) <http://www.canada.justice.gc.ca/publications/info%5Feducation/csj/csj%5FEN.html>

E-biz Diary (2000) *Globe & Mail*, 14 September, T2.

Faith, K (ed.) (1988) *Toward New Horizons for Women in Distance Education: International Perspectives*, London: Routledge.

Farrell, G (ed.) (1999) *The Development of Virtual Education: A Global Perspective*, Vancouver: Commonwealth of Learning.

Government of Canada (1999) <http://www.canada.gc.ca/canadiana/faitc/faind_e.html>

Mugridge, I (ed.) (1992) *Perspectives on Distance Education: Distance Education in Single and Dual Mode Universities*, papers presented to a symposium on reforms in higher education in New Delhi, India, Vancouver: The Commonwealth of Learning.

Mugridge, I and Kaufman, D (eds) (1986) *Distance Education in Canada*, London: Croom Helm.

News Watch (2000) *Globe & Mail*, 14 September, p. T2.

Open Learning Agency of British Columbia (1994) *Canadian Studies Resource Guide: Open Learning and Distance Education in Canada*, Ottawa: Minister of Supply and Services Canada.

Rogers, K (ed.) (1993) 'Innovation, risk taking, and collaboration: A celebration and history of CADE/ACED and distance education in Canada', *Journal of Distance Education*, 8(1): 1–7.

University Act (1999) <http://www.qp.gov.bc.ca/bcstats/96468_01.htm>

Verduin, J R and Clark, T A (1991) *Distance Education: The Foundations of Effective Practice*, San Francisco: Jossey-Bass.

Vice Presidents' Academic Committee (2000) 'Proposal for a British Columbia virtual university consortium', prepared by the VPAC Sub-Committee on Distributed Learning and Distance Education.

Appendix I

Map of Canada showing its ten provinces and three territories

Appendix 2

Canada-wide fibre optic network

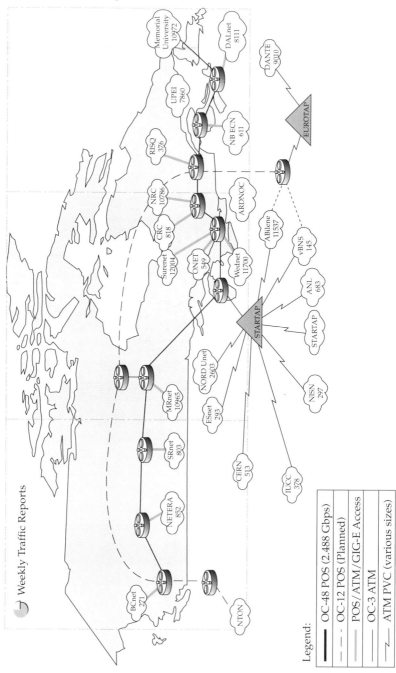

New Zealand

Tom Prebble

Introduction

At the beginning of the 1990s, as part of a similar publication on distance education in Asia and the Pacific, I was commissioned to write a chapter on New Zealand (Prebble 1993). Seven years on, and rereading that paper for the first time, my two strongest impressions are of the ferment in government policy at that time, but also the extraordinary stability and orderliness that could still be observed in the provision of distance education.

At the beginning of the decade the policy and funding environment of public education had been undergoing a revolution. Following on the heels of its deregulation of the economy during the 1980s, the New Zealand Government had begun an equally ambitious programme of deregulating every area of government social spending. The government's aim was to withdraw from the direct provision of education (and most other social services); to make public funding available for locally managed educational institutions on the basis of their performance and their ability to attract students; and to encourage efficiencies in the system by throwing educational institutions into competition with one another. But the impact of these policy and governance changes had yet to be felt in any telling way in the provision of distance education. I was able to describe 'the system' of provision for each sector, the principal institutions and their distinctive features, and the measured march of new technology into distance education. Most of the developments I describe changed only in scale over the previous ten or 15 years.

Confronting the same challenge to survey the state of distance education at the end of the decade, the overwhelming impression I have is one of change and turbulence. In order to make sense of this change it may be helpful to try to identify the important trends and forces that seem to have been at work in distance education over this past decade. Looking back over the 1990s these trends have included:

- An increase in competition among distance education providers coupled with an increase in the number of providers;

- Major restructuring of educational institutions and educational programmes to maintain institutional viability and to maximize market share;

- A system-wide focus on quality assurance driven by consumer expectations and quality validation agencies;

- The application of new technologies to distance education and open learning;

- An increasingly blurred distinction between conventional and distance education as institutions seek to offer students more flexible study options;

- The development of an international market for distance education with all its challenges, opportunities and threats.

Increasing competition

One of the truly distinctive characteristics of distance education in New Zealand right through until the late 1980s was the almost total absence of competition among institutional providers. The market for this form of delivery was dominated by four large, public institutions that between them accounted for well over 90% of all distance education enrolments in any year. These were the New Zealand Correspondence School, The Open Polytechnic of New Zealand, the Advanced Studies for Teachers Unit and the Extramural Studies programme at Massey University. These four institutions provided New Zealand with a comprehensive selection of school-level, polytechnic, teacher education and university programmes respectively. Each institution was created by the national government of the day to satisfy an educational need that was not being met by conventional institutions.

The Correspondence School had its beginnings in the 1920s and, as an arm of the state Department of Education, provided correspondence tuition to the many thousands of New Zealand children that lived beyond the reach of even the most remote rural schools. In more recent years, the Correspondence School has widened its brief to include the provision of specialist subject teaching to smaller rural secondary schools, tuition of the many thousands of students who are unable to study at a conventional school for behavioural, social or medical reasons, and a very large number of adult students taking advantage of a second chance to complete school-level qualifications. The Correspondence School is a specialist distance education institution that operates out of Wellington but provides tuition to students throughout New Zealand and to students scattered throughout the world. With an enrolment of approximately 20,000 in the early 1990s, a staff of several hundred, and a comprehensive portfolio of programmes and services, the Correspondence School was unchallenged in the marketplace.

The Open Polytechnic of New Zealand had its origins during the Second World War when the New Zealand Government set up a unit to provide technical education programmes for servicemen and, later, returned servicemen. From these beginnings, the then 'Technical Correspondence School' mirrored the growth of conventional polytechnic education in New Zealand during the 1960s to the 1980s. By the early 1990s the Open Polytechnic had approved government funding for over 5,000 full-time equivalent students (EFTS), making it one of the largest of the country's couple of dozen polytechnics. Like the Correspondence School, the Open Polytechnic was, and continues to be, a dedicated distance education institution that develops, delivers and services all of its own programmes. It, too, is located in the capital city of Wellington but draws students fairly evenly from throughout the country. One of its traditional strengths has been the variety of its offerings, and until recently it has been obliged to offer specialist qualifications for which there is only a small national market. Up until the 1990s the Open Polytechnic enjoyed a virtual monopoly over distance education provision of polytechnic education, with the exception of a couple of commercial and internationally syndicated correspondence colleges that have maintained a modest presence in the market for several decades.

The Advanced Studies for Teachers Unit was another arm of the former state Department of Education set up in the 1950s to offer continuing education programmes and qualifications to school teachers. As the department began to step back from the provision of tuition to concentrate on funding and policy development, it contracted first with Wellington Teachers College, and later Palmerston North College of Education, to manage the programme. By the early 1990s the Advanced Studies for Teachers Unit, or PACE (Professional and Continuing Education) as it came to be called, was offering a selection of certificates, diplomas and higher diplomas to several thousand students each year, and while other colleges of education were also offering many of these qualifications, they did so largely in a conventional face-to-face mode.

Massey University was the fourth member of the 'club' and enjoyed a monopoly in the provision of university-level distance education for almost thirty years from its inception in 1960. The six universities of the day agreed that the new institution would develop a distance education programme mirroring its campus-based programme and that this programme would serve the distance education needs of the whole country. At the time this decision relieved the other universities of the chore of providing for their more remote students, and they readily conceded the monopoly. Massey's 'extramural' (distance education) programme grew rapidly during the next three decades with its programme and student numbers growing to meet the demand in the workplace for university qualifications.

As mentioned earlier, until the late 1980s these four programmes co-existed with a total absence of competition, either among themselves or from other sources. Unlike the Australian experience, where the government had deliberately encouraged tertiary institutions to embark on distance education programmes during the 1970s and early 1980s, in New Zealand successive governments had seen the advantages to be gained by concentrating resources on single monopoly providers. In practice, the advantages seemed to include economies of scale, a wide array of programmes and the development and concentration of excellence in distance education. If there were disadvantages they probably included a relatively conservative approach to the market and to the adoption of new technology and new systems of delivery.

The educational reforms that began in 1989 and have continued through until the present were intended to open up education to the pressures and the opportunities of the market. Each institution was made more directly accountable to its local community; government funding of state institutions was tied more directly to enrolments; and institutions were challenged to succeed or fail on the basis of their ability to continue to attract and retain students.

At first, the most overt forms of competition occurred between institutions offering face-to-face education. Competition among intermediate (age 11 and 12) and secondary schools has been particularly fierce over the past decade. With the abolition of formal zoning schemes for public schooling, many communities have witnessed alarming surges in the rolls of their schools as their relative popularity has waxed and waned. At the university and polytechnic level, competition has increased, too, as each institution attempts to recruit students from outside its region. This has led to a huge institutional investment in promotion and advertising, with goals of marketing and recruitment replacing the former gentler objective of providing prospective students with sufficient information to enable them to make an informed selection among the various universities and programmes. Competition and deregulation have also encouraged tertiary institutions to try to compete with one another on a programme level. The country's 27 polytechnics, once restricted to delivering certificate and diploma programmes, have been quick to take advantage of the opportunity they now have to offer full degree programmes. There would now be hardly a polytechnic that does not offer a business baccalaureate, and most would boast degrees in Nursing, information systems and social sciences, as well as one or two degrees in their particular speciality areas.

Direct competition by distance education has been slow to develop, though it is now gathering strength. In the vanguard of this competition has been the Open Polytechnic. Like other polytechnics, the Open Polytechnic developed a range of degree programmes during the 1990s, and these have brought it into direct competition with Massey University's extramural programme. Conventional institutions have been slower to develop distance education streams. Most polytechnics and universities have had individual programmes that they offered through some form of distance education during the 1990s. Often these have been speciality subjects where the institution has sought to broaden its market from a regional to a national one. The programme in librarianship offered by Victoria University in Wellington would be one example. Another common approach has been to offer some form of off-campus tuition and support for the region surrounding a university. For a number of years, for example, Waikato University has offered a regional tuition programme in a selection of first year courses, supported by a network of regional centres and polytechnics. Massey University, too, has built up a series of partnerships with regional polytechnics allowing students to undertake their first year of a Massey degree by studying at a local polytechnic. These partnerships have been made possible by the availability of distance education study materials from Massey.

In the past two years competition has begun to intensify in distance education. There seem to be a number of reasons for this recent surge of interest. They include: a recent shift in government funding policy that ties institutional funding more directly to the number of students they recruit; the ability institutions now have to reach a wider catchment by offering their programmes on the Internet; the growing use of international franchising arrangements, where a local tertiary institution can provide tuition arrangements for an off-shore distance education institution; and the growing interest in more flexible modes of teaching and learning. All of these developments will be discussed in later sections.

Institutional restructuring

One of the most visible manifestations of the government's policy of encouraging competition in the education sector is the amount of restructuring that is taking place. Forced to compete for their survival, institutions have been forced to rationalize their operations to live within their means or to better exploit new markets. This trend has been seen among all of the major distance education institutions and many of the conventional institutions that are venturing into distance delivery.

The Open Polytechnic has been affected most sharply by government policies, by changes in vocational training policies, and by a steady shift in market demand away from traditional vocational training programmes. In response, the Open Polytechnic has been forced to shift resources away from these vocational programmes and build up a suite of more generic bachelor's and master's programmes. These shifts of programme emphasis have been matched by a restructuring of the institution's workforce and a reorganization of the whole institution. As the tertiary market has become generally more competitive, the Open Polytechnic has entered into a number of partnership arrangements for the provision of customized training programmes for particular industries. In doing so it has sought to exploit its expertise in instructional design and materials production. Along the way, the Open Polytechnic has also considered strategic partnerships with other conventional tertiary providers, although to date these have not reached the status of full institutional mergers. The most recent announcement along these lines was in April 1999 when the government announced the creation of a taskforce to consider a merger between the Open Polytechnic and the Correspondence School. There are some obvious synergies between these two large, single-mode distance education providers, and they have been cooperating on a project basis for some years, so it will be interesting to follow the outcome of this review.

The second distance education programme to undergo major structural change was that offered by Otago University. In the mid-1980s Otago

University was permitted to break the Massey University monopoly on the provision of distance education with the development of a nation-wide network of audioconferencing suites supporting its 'extension' studies programmes. Some of these programmes were typical of extension studies programmes at other universities around the world — introductory-level courses in general interest subjects drawn from the humanities and social sciences. But others drew on Otago's great strength as a medical university, and for many years the University supported a number of postgraduate, in-service programmes in medicine and pharmacy. The teleconferencing medium was well-suited to the learning needs of both sets of students, and the programmes were both well supported and well received. Unfortunately, the unit costs of this medium were relatively high, the economies of scale from larger enrolments were not attractive, and the teleconferencing network itself could not readily accommodate any major expansion. Another blow was the announcement that the Ministry of Education refused to fund these advanced-level programmes for medical professionals at the normal funding band for medical programmes. Instead, the rate was struck at the much lower 'extramural' rate. At these very modest funding levels, Otago University had difficulty justifying its extension studies programme. This led at least in part to the decision in the mid-1990s to devolve its extension programme and curtail most of its teleconference delivery. Since that time the University has moved some of its expertise in distance education and instructional design into the development of multimedia course materials and Web-based delivery, both for campus-based and off-campus students.

A third distance education provider to undergo restructuring was the Professional and Continuing Education programme offered by Palmerston North College of Education. In 1996, after many years of negotiations and deliberation, the Palmerstion North College of Education merged with Massey University. Since that merger, the programme offerings of the former PACE unit have been integrated within the offerings of what is now Massey University's College of Education. The former advanced and higher certificates of education are giving way to the degrees and diplomas of the University. In terms of servicing, these programmes are becoming increasingly indistinguishable from Massey University's larger portfolio of 'extramural' courses.

Massey University's extramural programme has not been immune from the restructuring wave that continues to sweep the New Zealand education industry. Massey University is just one of seven universities in New Zealand. One of its long-term liabilities was its location in a provincial town of just 70,000 inhabitants with only limited prospects of attracting large numbers of full-time students from the larger cities, all of which had their own universities. The University's strategic response to this situation was to commence on a policy of expansion, first developing its own green-fields campus at Albany in Auckland City, and then committing to mergers with other existing tertiary institutions in Palmerston North, Auckland and Wellington. Within a very few years Massey has become the second largest university in the country and rivals Auckland University as the largest. Alongside this growth of campuses, Massey has also developed a range of alternative teaching modes by which to deliver its programmes. A very recent outcome of this growth in campuses and teaching modes is the recent decision of the University to appoint a principal for each of its physical campuses, but to also appoint a principal for its 'virtual campus' comprising extramural and international students. At the same time, the Centre for University Extramural Studies will give way to a new set of structures that will offer support services more seamlessly across all the different teaching modes of the University.

Finally, in this litany of major distance education providers, there is the Correspondence School. In recent years the School has moved steadily to transform its former organizational structure from that of a typical if very large school, to one that gives due prominence to the critical processes of materials production, programme delivery and student support. The School has also entered into partnership arrangements with literally hundreds of schools around the country that are pleased to take advantage of the School's variety of programme offerings to support their own more limited offerings. Another challenge the School has faced has been to offer worthwhile educational programmes to the many thousands of teenagers who have worn out the patience or the ability of their local schools to contain them. But the greatest change the Correspondence School has faced is the prospect of a merger with the Open Polytechnic that is currently under consideration.

Quality assurance

One of the more laudable thrusts of government policy in New Zealand education in recent years has been to insist on more explicit processes of quality assurance. At the school and non-university tertiary levels, a principal arm of this policy has been the New Zealand Qualifications Authority, the national agency responsible for accrediting all providers, both public and private, seeking state funding. One of the mechanisms for assuring quality has been via the National Framework of Qualifications that provides a set of qualification steps up which all New Zealand students may proceed. The Framework has been an ambitious and a controversial programme, and in this millennium period the government is undertaking a set of adjustments that are intended to ease the worst of this controversy without losing the achievements that have been made. At the university level, the task of institutional and programme accreditation is carried out by a standing committee of the New Zealand Vice-Chancellors' Committee.

At the school level, the ongoing quality of institutions and their offerings is assessed every few years by visitations from the Education Review Office. At the non-university tertiary level, the process is one of institutional and programme review assessments undertaken by teams set up by the New Zealand Qualifications Authority. At the university level this work is undertaken by the Academic Audit Unit, an independent authority that undertakes triennial reviews of each university.

These various quality assurance processes apply equally to distance as well as contact courses. Over the course of the decade, what has been a common claim by distance educators has gradually come to be more widely accepted — that high quality distance education is a match for the very best contact teaching. The processes of distance education lend themselves very handily to processes of quality assurance: it is possible to specify what is required for high quality distance education instruction and then to bring a range of services to bear to make sure that these specifications are met. Once the initial investment has been made into developing a distance education programme, it is generally possible to ensure an acceptable level of course delivery for the life of that course, and the content and the instructional processes of distance education courses lend themselves to easy inspection and comparison. In dual mode institutions, the quality assurance processes of the whole institution have generally profited from the achievements that have been made in their distance education programmes. With only occasional exceptions, New Zealand's distance education programmes have acquitted themselves well in the series of quality audits to which all educational providers have been subjected in recent years.

New technologies

In strictly technological terms there are probably no surprises in the way in which new technologies are being applied to distance education in New

Zealand. While most of the larger distance education institutions can point to examples of all of the major technological options being used around the world, these institutions are seldom right at the cutting edge in this use. Other countries with larger scales of operation, or larger resources to draw on, tend to be taking the big risks or making the most thoroughgoing commitment to new technology.

What is of particular interest about the New Zealand experience in applying new technology over the past decade is the almost total absence of government policy or direct government intervention during that period and the effect of that lack of direction. As a matter of firm principle, the New Zealand Government has left it to the education sector, and specifically to individual institutions, to make their own decisions about the appropriate use of technology to carry out their primary activities. While successive ministers of education over the past decade have urged the sector to make bolder investment decisions in its use of IT, drawing particular attention to the possibilities offered by distance and open education, the overarching free market philosophy of the government has prevented them from intervening more directly. More interventionist governments around the world have moved to shift resources from conventional modes to more flexible distance education and open learning approaches over the past decade. They have set up new purpose-built institutions based on these new technologies or at least have brought industry and institutions together in powerful consortia of shared interest and effort based around these new technologies. The New Zealand Government, on the other hand, has been compelled by the force of its own rhetoric to sit on the sidelines and watch the institutions play the game. That game has not always been as vigorous or as eventful as the government would have liked.

Educational institutions have been forced, through the exigencies of the marketplace, to adopt strongly competitive but essentially conservative delivery strategies. In earlier decades the government had been prepared to fund trial projects in the education system, but in the 1990s an institution's total funding has relied on its ability to attract and retain enrolments. This has encouraged institutions to stick to winning formulas and to avoid capital-expensive and high-risk options. They know that in the event of failure they face the very real possibility of formal bankruptcy and collapse with little prospect that the government will bail them out. Innovations, when they are adopted, are given a limited trial, and if they do not yield early substantial benefits, they tend to be quickly withdrawn. A few examples from the distance education sector will illustrate.

At the beginning of the decade the government was very keen that institutions should take advantage of a relaxation of the broadcasting regulations and make greater use of television, or more recently cable, to deliver educational programmes both to a distance education and a conventional institutional market. The distance education sector was not unresponsive. For some time a consortium of distance education and conventional institutions worked with broadcasting interests to explore ways of cooperating in order to make greater use of these media. Then, when this ambitious project failed to secure the commitment of all parties, several educational institutions formed bilateral partnerships with television companies to produce and screen educational programmes for the distance education market. In all cases these could best be described as qualified successes. Most evaluations of these projects found that the programmes were well received by students and that they complemented the more conventional paper-based study materials being used by distance education institutions. These evaluations also showed that few of these programmes were cost-effective solutions to their particular educational challenges. New Zealand is a small market for any product and a very small market for television. Typically, the use of television might double the potential enrolment for an introductory-level tertiary distance education course, but it also in the process turned a modestly profitable programme into one that barely broke even. This was hardly the sort of encouragement that institutions needed in order to venture further with this technology. As a result, educational television has limped through the decade as a marginal proposition both in educational and commercial broadcasting terms and is unlikely to experience any sort of revival in the foreseeable future.

A second group of technologies that has attracted more interest from educators, and certainly more project funding from government and telecommunications companies alike over this past decade, is that of teleconferencing. Just as the newly deregulated industry broadcasting companies were attempting to woo the education sector in the early 1990s, the newly deregulated 'telcos' adopted the same tactic. These companies invested generously in teleconferencing trials in the first half of the decade. Audioconferencing and audiographics networks were set up between schools in several regions. The hope and the promise of the new technology was that smaller rural schools would be able to link with larger schools to provide wider curriculum options for their students. Funding constraints certainly limited the rate of uptake of this technology. While the telecommunications companies were prepared to seed these projects, their medium-term objective was always to achieve a commercial return on their investment. While the Government was prepared to target some funds to initiate these projects, it too was not willing to subsidize a medium such as this over the longer term. As the start-up money was withdrawn and institutions were forced to bear the full cost of telecommunications, institutions were forced to a realistic assessment of the costs and benefits of teleconferencing. Some of the smaller rural schools have persisted with teleconferencing, but many of the larger schools that were required as 'teacher' schools in any successful network found the costs clearly outweighed the benefits. For such schools, teleconferencing tended to be an additional cost rather than a source of savings elsewhere; they found themselves contributing their teaching expertise with little direct return or recompense from the wider network; and they soon grew impatient with the timetabling demands of a synchronous medium such as teleconferencing.

Teleconferencing is still very much alive in New Zealand education, but it tends to be used most extensively and most successfully in niche areas. Nation-wide commercial and public organizations now use teleconferencing and videoconferencing extensively for their inter-branch training programmes. Educational programmes targeted at medium-sized groups of professionals from a single industry also make successful use of this medium. Two cases in point would be health professionals and school administrators. Both groups have access to institution-based teleconferencing equipment; they are both able to timetable regular synchronous meetings more readily than some others; and they both see a high level of group interaction as an important ingredient of professional development. But these requirements are relatively unusual in distance education in New Zealand. Unlike the North American pattern, where synchronous study in 'linked classrooms' is almost the norm in distance education, in New Zealand most distance education students choose this mode precisely because it is not synchronous. Most distance education students live within an easy drive of their local tertiary institution. They choose to study at a distance because work or family commitments prevent them from conforming to a weekly schedule of classes. These same commitments make it difficult for them to take advantage of synchronous distance education options such as teleconferencing.

The other group of information technologies that warrants mention is the use of the computer-mediated communications. With the very rapid increase in home ownership of computers by New Zealanders in recent years and the blossoming of possibilities created by the World Wide Web and user-friendly authoring software, there would hardly be any sizeable tertiary educational institution that is not using the Internet for the delivery or support of some aspect of its teaching. Just one example of a conventional campus-based institution turning to the Internet to broaden its catchment area would be the Diploma in Education Technology offered by UNITEC, a polytechnic in Auckland, at <http://www.unitec.ac.nz/faculties/arts/education/programmes/edtech/>. But again, what is interesting about this development is not the technology nor even the pedagogy, but the institutional strategies that are being employed and the explanations for these strategies. In other more regulated educational systems, national or state governments have seen the use of the Web for the delivery of educational services as an irresistibly tempting opportunity for intervention. Governments have brought together consortia of educational organizations or created new institutions to take advantage of this new medium. In New Zealand the ethos of deregulation precludes the government's direct intervention in this way, and the climate of extreme competition that prevails among educational institutions, itself the deliberate product of government policy, is also a disincentive to collaborative endeavours of this kind.

There is certainly cooperative endeavour at the margins — the Correspondence School and the Open Polytechnic have a cooperative relationship for the creation and delivery of multimedia and Web-based programmes, for example. But even this example probably supports rather than contradicts the earlier observation about the impact of competition. These two institutions have complementary rather than shared markets, and this always makes collaboration easier. More commonly, each institution has its own individual strategy for developing its own courses and reaching its own market. Most would find the prospect of collaborating with an international partner to achieve a market edge more palatable than seeking such collaboration with an on-shore provider. An earlier section discussed the recent growth of mergers among educational providers. These have tended to replace the collaborative partnerships that were more common at the beginning of the decade.

Another outcome of government policy has been the growth of private commercial ventures to deliver educational services on the Internet. There are currently several such ventures attempting to establish a place for themselves in the education marketplace, either by offering to service the programmes of conventional institutions or by mounting their own programmes. Those attempting the former strategy are finding it difficult to demonstrate to the provider institutions the added value they are able to bring to the enterprise; those attempting the latter are struggling to establish credibility or even visibility in the domestic market.

The emergence of flexible learning

Five years ago the future of distance education seemed to lie in the growing convergence of information technologies. There was a race in progress between the broadcasting, telecommunications and computing industries over which would be the dominant party in the new convergence technology that was being promised to the market. This new technology would provide broadband communications access to every home and workplace through a single integrated user interface. In the educational context it would provide learners with access to an international market of multimedia learning opportunities.

This race is still in progress, of course, and there is now a sense of inevitability about the promised technological developments. But in the meantime, another development is taking place in educational provision and one that owes as much to the demands of the student market as it does to the opportunities offered by technological development. This is the development of increasingly flexible study opportunities for students.

This demand is coming from a variety of sources: from students who can no longer afford to pursue full-time campus-based study and are looking for study options that allow them to earn a living at the same time; from employer groups that are seeking to upskill their workforce but want an educational programme that is relevant and that fits around the time demands of industry; from educational institutions that are trying to maintain a market edge over competing providers; from programme leaders within institutions who are looking for the most cost-effective delivery options in order to live within increasingly tight budgets; and, of course, from teachers and educational leaders trying to make creative use of new communications technologies.

Institutions throughout the country are responding in very different ways to these challenges, and the trend can perhaps best be understood by a couple of examples. The first example is provided by the Universal College of Learning (UCOL), the trading name of the Manawatu Polytechnic. UCOL is a moderate-sized polytechnic in Palmerston North, a city'of just 80,000. Like other polytechnics in New Zealand, it has been forced to compete for students in the newly deregulated educational market, and it has done so by introducing a range of degree programmes and by seeking efficiencies in every aspect of its management and delivery of those programmes. As it was grappling with these challenges in the mid-1990s, it was also forced to undergo a major relocation and re-building programme for the entire institution. This shift provided UCOL with the opportunity to rethink its delivery systems. It became clear that, given existing and projected assets, the institution could not afford to rebuild itself according to the traditional classroom delivery paradigm. Instead it was forced to look to more flexible, self-directed and self-paced study options. Taking advantage of developments in IT, the new campus has provided for student studios and small seminar rooms rather than the conventional large lecture rooms, where students can access and work through some of their study materials on networked workstations. In line with this development, the institution is seeking partnerships with off-shore institutions with a view to supporting the study of local students in these off-shore programmes.

There are significant challenges facing any conventional educational provider committing to such a radical shift in educational delivery. The largest challenge will be to effect a shift in the role and culture of the teaching staff from that of a director of learning to a facilitator of learning. The second challenge will be to ensure that programmes, delivery and support systems are in place and up to standard. The third and probably most difficult challenge will be to meet the expectations of a heterogeneous student market for a rewarding and supportive educational environment. It is too early to judge the success of UCOL in meeting these challenges, but other New Zealand institutions are interested observers of the process.

The second example is drawn from Massey University. Mention has already been made of Massey's large and long-running extramural (distance education) programme. Over 18,000 students enrol in the Massey University extramural programme each year. This puts it among the biggest distance education programmes in Australia or New Zealand. However, the fastest growth in recent years has not been in extramural or even in campus-based study. It has been in 'block mode' delivery, where students have been able to combine some independent distance education study with intensive bursts of campus study; also in 'conjoint' study, where partnering institutions have provided class-based tuition to students in their home regions; and in the use of the Internet to support both campus and distance education study. Massey University has recognized that these developments need to be supported by a new policy of flexible teaching and learning. This policy will replace the traditional bimodal paradigm that has informed its teaching in the past.

In the future it is anticipated that every course will have a standard package of study materials, but that students will access and study these materials in different ways depending on their circumstances and study preferences. A range of 'learning streams' will be provided that will allow students to assemble a programme that suits them best. In the very near future, for example, a full-time student living at the Auckland campus of Massey University might be able to study a couple of science subjects in the conventional lecture-laboratory mode at her local campus, to study a third science subject largely by self-paced Web-mediated study modules, to study a fourth course in policy-making in environmental studies by attending regular videoconference classes linking several of Massey's campuses, and to round out her programme with an advanced level course based at the Palmerston North campus and requiring attendance at a couple of three-day weekend block courses at that campus.

As with the UCOL example, this proposed shift towards flexible learning brings its challenges. The strategy will require strong policies to define each learning stream and the delivery and support services that accompany it. It will also require clear policies and processes for quality assurance. For instance, it will be necessary to ensure the academic equivalence of each offering of a course regardless of mode, location or timing. It will require a sustained commitment to retaining an integrated academic programme for this multi-campus institution, rather than taking the easier option of developing independent programmes for each major campus, or even each major delivery mode.

In these two cases, new technology is just one driver for this shift to new technologies and new educational delivery options, and distance education is not necessarily the outcome of these trends. At Massey University, distance education is just one of a growing number of portfolios of delivery options, though the institution's experience in distance education is assisting in the development and support of these other modes. At UCOL, the development of structured teaching resources is being used to support more independent modes of study by campus-based students rather than by students studying primarily off-campus.

The developing international distance education market

Throughout the last decade, New Zealanders have been able to enrol in a steadily growing selection of distance education programmes offered from off-shore. At first Australia was the only source available, and a small number of postgraduate vocational programmes were available in such subjects as educational administration and nursing. As the selection of programmes widened to include MBAs and other postgraduate business qualifications, the number of source countries expanded to include the United Kingdom, Canada and the United States. In some cases, off-shore institutions have sought to market their programmes directly to New Zealanders and to service these enrolments directly from the off-shore base. More commonly, and probably more successfully, these off-shore institutions have forged on-shore partnerships with New Zealand institutions that have been able to provide marketing, administrative and tutorial services to support these ventures.

The New Zealand Government has been generally supportive of these developments and has tended to view any such developments as providing a measure of competition for New Zealand providers. From time to time the government has expressed itself as not being fully satisfied with the extent of competition among providers on pricing and hopes that genuine competition from off-shore providers may lead to significant economies in the provision of distance and flexible study options. One very recent move in this direction has been the 1999 White Paper on tertiary education, which breaks new ground by indicating that, in principle at least, government funding should be made available to support New Zealanders studying off-shore programmes as well as local ones. There are many technical issues that need to be resolved before this development takes place. For instance, the government will need to assure itself that an off-shore provider meets appropriate quality standards before it releases public funds to support New Zealanders' tuition expenses. It has yet to address the levels of service that would need to be provided by a 'virtual' provider before it qualified for such assistance, but the broad policy commitment has been made, and there is a strong political will to follow through on it.

There will undoubtedly be a significant growth in the numbers of New Zealanders enrolling with off-shore distance education providers over the next few years. A possibly more important development will be the growth of 'franchising' arrangements whereby New Zealand institutions form partnerships with off-shore providers to import the qualifications of these institutions to New Zealand. The Open Polytechnic of New Zealand has formed a partnership with the UK Open University with a view to supporting the introduction of the latter's degrees into New Zealand. At least half a dozen colleges of education and polytechnics are endeavouring to forge similar relationships in order to secure some sort of future for themselves in the face of increasingly aggressive competition within the sector.

New Zealand distance education institutions are engaged in the export of educational services as well as their importation. All the major distance education institutions have several hundred off-shore students. At present these are mostly expatriate New Zealanders whose enrolments generate a government fees subsidy. Increasingly, these institutions are also seeking partnerships with off-shore distance education institutions to cooperate on the development and delivery of selected programmes to the full fee-paying market. Alternatively, they are choosing to market niche programmes to targeted regions in Asia and the Pacific Rim. The principal mode of delivery to date has been intensive blocks of face-to-face study in selected off-shore centres, supported by correspondence education. A very few institutions, and notably Otago University, have used teleconferencing technologies to support off-shore programmes. Increasingly, these institutions are looking to the Internet to provide a more interactive and cost-effective mode of tuition and support for their off-shore students.

The big question for all providers, and for the sector in general, is whether New Zealand will remain a net exporter of education in the coming decade or so, or whether it will be overwhelmed by low-cost Web-supported distance education programmes and become a net importer. Unlike other countries where the national government can be relied on to protect the local educational industry, in New Zealand no such reliance is possible. As in any other free market for services, the battle will be won or lost on cost and quality. In terms of cost, New Zealand students are already heavily indebted by the government's student loan system, and the introduction of markedly cheaper study options is likely to have some appeal. On the other hand, New Zealand students are looking for qualifications of status and quality. It remains to be seen what value the market will give to a qualification that is sourced from a leading off-shore provider but mediated by a regional polytechnic.

The next ten years

The seeds of developments in New Zealand distance education over the next decade have been sown. These are the rapid developments in information technology and their applications to education; the burgeoning international market for virtual education; the development of more flexible modes of delivery by educational institutions at every level of the system; the intense competition among educational providers; and a set of economic and social policies determined to place the essential decisions about educational provision in the hands of the consumer. Any one of these developments would be sufficient to ensure continued change in the provision of distance education; when combined, they virtually guarantee a state of continual ferment in the field. However, one development can be predicted with some confidence: distance education has already thrown off its Cinderella image, and in the coming decade it will be increasingly at the heart of educational policy and institutional endeavour.

References

Ministry of Education (1999) *Tertiary Education in New Zealand: Policy Directions for the 21st Century (White Paper)*, Wellington.

Prebble, T K (1991) 'Quality assurance under conditions of devolved responsibility: a New Zealand case', Proceedings of the Biennial Forum, Australia and South Pacific External Studies Association, July, New South Wales: Bathurst.

Prebble, T K (1993) *New Zealand, Distance Education in Asia and the Pacific: Country Papers*, vol. 1, Japan: National Institute of Multimedia Education, 234–62.

South Pacific

Ruby Va'a, Josephine Osborne and Andrew Nyondo

Introduction

The Pacific region is generally perceived to consist of the island nations to the west of the Hawaii group, east of the Philippines and north of New Zealand. The countries may be grouped as independent or self-governing nations, those affiliated to France (including French Polynesia, New Caledonia, the Wallis and Futuna group) and those associated with the USA (including American Samoa, the Federated States of Micronesia, Guam, Northern Marianas, Palau). The region is also often divided into North, South and Central.

This chapter outlines open and distance learning initiatives in Papua New Guinea (PNG) and in the independent countries of the region served by the University of the South Pacific (USP). This is the region represented by membership of the Pacific Islands Regional Association of Distance Education (PIRADE). The 12 nations of the USP region are: the Cook Islands, Fiji, Kiribati, the Marshall Islands, Nauru, Niue, Samoa, the Solomon Islands, Tokelau, Tonga, Tuvalu and Vanuatu (see Appendix 1).

South Pacific profile

The area covered by the USP is about three times the size of Europe, mostly water, and a total land area of 64,000 square kilometres. The total population of 1.8 million is made up by three main ethnic groups: Micronesian (Kiribati, the Marshall Islands, Nauru), Polynesian (the Cook Islands, Niue, Samoa, Tokelau, Tonga, Tuvalu) and Melanesian (Fiji, the Solomon Islands, Vanuatu). PNG to the west is the largest of these Pacific nations, with a land area of 460,000 square kilometres and a population of around 4.3 million of mainly Melanesian ethnicity. Other ethnic groups are present in the region, e.g. in Fiji, with nearly half of the 800,000 people being Indian, a small proportion of ethnic Chinese and a few Caucasians.

The Pacific islands are still considered part of the developing world. GDP ranges from about US$280 (Tokelau) to US$2,800 (the Cook Islands) per capita (except for Nauru, with an exceptional figure of US$12,000 because of its mineral exploitation). Industrialization has been slow and economies are predominantly at the subsistence level, especially in the rural or outer islands. Other aspects reflect the developing nature of the region: underdeveloped communications infrastructure such as an unreliable or no telephone service, unreliable postal services, poor transportation, no amenities such as electricity and running water, and lack of maintenance through a lack of trained technical personnel.

Education systems and distance education institutions

Education systems at the primary and secondary levels vary but have tended to reflect missionary influence and colonial administrations, the main ones being Britain, France, the USA, New Zealand, and Australia. At the tertiary level, USP as a regional institution is the largest university, with a total enrolment of about 10,000 students in 1999. There are also national universities in the region: the University of Papua New Guinea and the University of Technology in PNG; Atenisi University in Tonga; and the National University of Samoa. Both PNG universities offer distance education programmes. Atenisi University and the National University of Samoa do not. Other tertiary institutions that offer distance education programmes include the Fiji School of Medicine, which has a regional cohort of students; the Fiji School of Nursing; Solomon Islands College of Higher Education; Pacific Adventist College in PNG; Pacific Theological College in Fiji; and teacher training colleges such as Fiji College of Advanced Education and Tonga Teachers College. The Community Training Centre in Tonga also has distance programmes.

Although over 300 different languages are spoken in the region, education systems mainly use English, particularly at the secondary and tertiary levels. In some countries national languages are used at the primary level while English, French and Bislama (Pidgin) have been used in national level school systems in Vanuatu. At the university level throughout the region, the language of instruction is predominantly English.

Pacific society has been able to maintain knowledge, values, skills and attitudes through informal education where the young learn by observing and imitating how knowledgeable and experienced elders perform various tasks. Formal schooling practices or formal education, however, have been brought into the region. In the modern Pacific, both formal and informal education exist alongside each other, providing learning necessary both culturally and in an environment greatly influenced by the Western world. The state has gradually taken part in education provision, its initial focus on improving public services. This gave way to a broader curriculum that included a large array of subject areas with a bias towards the foreign administrations, although curricula have since become more Pacific-oriented.

Communications systems

The geographical barriers of small land masses and great expanses of water have placed huge constraints on communications in and between island nations. Costs are prohibitive both for the individual and governments, so ownership of technologies now considered basic in a Western household, such as the telephone and the computer, are still far beyond the average Pacific island home. Comparative figures from the same study show very low densities for PNG (1.2%), Fiji, Kiribati, Tonga and Samoa, which all had less than 5%. On the other hand, mobile telephony has become quite popular over the last two years, but only in urban areas and only in some countries and mainly in relation to business. The Internet is also new to the region and very welcome. It is expected that improvements in service provision by satellite and the transpacific Southern Cross fibre-optic cable will enhance this form of communication greatly.

Given communication constraints, particularly for rural areas and outlying islands, telecommunications technology is an important factor in the development of the South Pacific. Modern telecommunications and information technology are crucial to the provision of education to people living outside urban areas. The trend towards globalization is placing huge pressure on the small developing island nations to fit the market or face being left behind. Computerization and the Internet have inevitably led to services and goods from outside the region being available. Hence the demand for education initiatives to bring island people up to expected performance levels, and able to access the Internet, has placed a corresponding pressure on the education services available for professional development. Island nations are attempting to catch up and keep pace with this rapid change, and distance education is perceived to be the way to go (Commonwealth of Learning Conference of Education Ministers 2000).

American and French Pacific neighbours appear to be moving at much greater speeds. For instance, Internet connections are widespread in American Samoa, Palau, Tahiti and New Caledonia. However, in the USP region, the satellite-mediated USPNet has helped establish better links (university-related communications only at this point) for the 12 member countries, albeit only between the main urban centres. Use of the Internet has increased efficiency among institutions in PNG, but financial constraints are the main barrier to further development.

Student profile

The range of environments, cultural diversity and association with different developed countries have given rise to a student cohort across the region which is typically homogenous.

Different cultural beliefs give rise to significant differences in gender ratios in student enrolments in tertiary education. The lower status of women in the Melanesian countries is reflected in the much lower proportion of female students, while the Polynesian countries have higher female numbers corresponding to the higher status of women.

For almost all students English is a second, third or even fourth language. The capability of students in the language of instruction therefore varies. In addition the urban-rural (or outer island) divide has resulted in a disparity in knowledge of technology and communications.

Distance education in the region

The University of the South Pacific

USP was established as a regional university in 1968 and developed as a dual-mode teaching institution in 1970. The main campus in Fiji and smaller campuses in Vanuatu and Samoa have face-to-face teaching. Teams at these sites also develop distance education materials for use off campus through university centres, which serve the needs of some 5,000 students studying by distance education throughout the region. With 28% of USP's full-time equivalent students registered in the distance mode (36% if pre-degree programme participants are included), student enrolments in the distance mode are set to increase by 10% per annum to cope with regional demand for university qualifications.

All 12 member countries have a university centre located in their capital, and some have sub-centres on outlying islands. USP is governed by its Council, whose membership includes representatives of all the member country governments, who together contribute 70% of USP's recurrent funding on a pro-rata basis (income from student fees and overseas aid making up the rest).

Courses and programmes offered at a distance are equivalent to those offered on campus and follow the same semester system. Nearly 200 different courses are offered each year. It is possible to complete a certificate or diploma programme at a distance in a wide range of disciplines, which can then be cross-credited towards a degree. At present, however, only a BEd (in-service) can be completed by distance. All first-year degree programmes are expected to be available in the distance mode and many second- and third-year level courses have now been developed. In consultation with regional governments and with a focus on regional development, university programmes in agriculture, environmental management, marine studies, teacher education and tourism have been identified as academic priorities for the current triennium.

Preliminary and foundation programmes at USP are pre-degree programmes available only by distance. They are designed to be equivalent to secondary level forms 6 and 7. Students may enrol in either the Social Science or Science programmes, or in individual courses. Tutors are appointed at university centres and full-time students can attend classes although the study materials are self contained. There is a strong market for these programmes in Kiribati and the Solomon Islands because of the lack of secondary schools there. Tonga, the Cook Islands and Vanuatu are similar, but have opted to follow New Zealand's bursary system for secondary schools; while Samoa has established its own university preparatory programme at the National University.

Continuing education non-credit programmes are offered at a distance to anyone in the region. Certificates are currently available in Pacific Pre-school Teaching, Community Nutrition, and Disability Studies. Around 250 students across the region are enrolled in these programmes at any one time.

Course materials in all programmes are distributed mainly in the print mode, with the additional support of audio or videotapes.

Audio-tutorials may be provided through USP's satellite network, and exciting new developments lie in this direction. Satellite links from USP were first established in the early 1970s when an audioteleconferencing facility was initiated via the ATS-1 satellite, linking centres in six countries of the Pacific region. A major upgrading of the satellite link was completed in 2000 with the express aim of improving the service to distance education in the region. All 12 countries of the USP community are now linked via a dedicated VSAT network for audio-tutorials, voice and data transfer, video broadcast lectures from any of the three campuses and two-way videoconferencing. This USPNet upgrade has been funded as a joint project of Japanese, Australian and New Zealand aid, with additional contributions from USP funds.

A reliable audioteleconferencing link to all 12 university centres in the region has been seen as the single biggest benefit of the system. Making teletutorials available simultaneously in all member countries of the region means students are provided with the opportunity to participate. Some courses have already experimented with online delivery between campuses; degree-level courses from the School of Law, based at the Vanuatu campus, have been extensively developed for Internet delivery over the past two years. Data links to the main university system also offer considerable benefits to the handling of management information. Student records management can now be handled directly from the USP centres; keeping track of study materials despatched and student assignments received is becoming much more efficient.

The developing role of the university centres is seen as central to USP's 21st century vision. They will have to be equipped to provide face-to-face teaching; computer and science laboratories; access through USPNet to teaching and resource materials, including video and live lectures; and improved data and voice communication through USPNet to make them truly an integral part of the university. Students will be taught through blends of traditional and new methods; 'multi-mode' in the current terminology (University of the South Pacific 1999).' While the three campuses are approaching this state, the centres are still evolving and resources are constantly being sought through further aid grants. Much also remains to be done in training and in the development of educational materials suitable for distribution through the network.

Quality assurance awareness has grown apace with the expansion of course offerings at a distance. The academic content of course materials is reviewed by the same external advisors who moderate face-to-face curricula, and student feedback has routinely been surveyed for years. Systems are in place to monitor administrative support systems, turnaround times for student assignments and the quality of markers' comments (both of particular importance across such a large region of isolated communities). A major review of distance education and flexible learning at USP was conducted in 2000 by a international team of experts in the field and their recommendations are currently being discussed.

Other distance learning activities in the USP region

Tonga, Samoa, Fiji and Vanuatu have had primary-level distance education for many years. In each case this comprises radio lessons from a central education broadcasting unit. In Tonga, there is also some use of the radio for special sessions for senior-level (last two years) examination classes and a teachers session every Friday. In addition, another more recent initiative in distance education at the Tonga Teachers College targets in-service teachers. The objective of this training programme is to upgrade teachers to admission level for the Diploma in Teaching programme.

The rest of this section outlines other distance education activities in the countries of the USP region other than those provided by the University. These are mainly at the secondary and tertiary levels. There are both regional and national initiatives.

Fiji

Fiji comprises some 300 islands, and has a population of around 800,000, over 60% of whom are in the rural areas or outer islands. Efforts to provide education face barriers such as the geography, limited communications and postal services, and lack of commodities such as electricity. Compounding the problems, in May 2000 an ongoing political situation disrupted the country and saw schools closed for some seven weeks of the teaching year. Responding to the immediate need, a ten-week programme of televised tutorials was mounted by the Ministry of Education to help senior examination classes. In addition to the main campus of USP and the regional university centre for Fiji, there are four distance education initiatives in Fiji, two of which are also regional programmes:

Pacific Theological College Extension Education (PTCEE)

Based in Suva, Fiji, Pacific Theological College (PTC) is a regional theological college offering non-degree and degree programmes from diploma to Master's level. Students from throughout the Pacific region are resident at the college. The PTCEE operates the distance version of the Diploma in Theology programme (normally a traditional residential course in Fiji) to countries in the region. The programme requires a student to complete 95 credit hours of which 80 are from 16 required courses. The remaining hours are made up from a choice among five elective courses.

The availability of this diploma has met a need expressed across the region and across all denominational lines. As Johnson-Hill (1998, 4) stated, the extension programme is 'a tool for empowerment for several reasons... for women... since theological schools normally provide training for the ordained ministry and most of the Pacific churches do not ordain women...; for lay people in general since the College intake is for those intending to serve in church ministries; and for most Pacific Islanders who find residential theological education financially prohibitive.'

Students can enrol at any time so student numbers fluctuate throughout the year. The programme had 70 students in 1996, 160 in 1998 and 188 in July 2000. Of these 188, 72 are female. The geographical spread of students is Solomon Islands (38%), Fiji (32%) and 30% come from American Samoa, Australia, Kiribati, Nauru, New Caledonia, Niue, PNG, Samoa, Tonga, Tuvalu, the USA and Vanuatu. Study materials are print-based and are sent to students by normal postal service. Student support was minimal until July 1999 when a group of 22 graduates trained as local tutors for the programme during a workshop funded by the New Zealand Official Development Assistance (ODA). This formed the basis for a regional network of tutors for the programme. Fees of US$66 per course are seen as realistic given the financial situation of potential students.

A major new development is the production of courses in French involving translation of existing courses. During 1999, four courses were ready for offer to the francophone population of New Caledonia, French Polynesia and Vanuatu. With the appointment of a full-time coordinator in February 2000, the full programme is expected to be available within 2000. The Solomon Islands has initiated another pilot project in which 50 students have registered and for which a PTCEE course has been adapted for use with study groups throughout the country.

In April 1999, another New Zealand ODA project saw the successful completion of a hands-on course-writing workshop whereby college teaching staff undertook training in preparing and writing materials for distance learning, under the guidance of an expert from an Australian Theological College that also teaches at a distance.

Financial support for the PTCEE is from overseas funding but a more secure endowment fund has been started (with a contribution from a European donor) to ensure long-term sustainability of the programme.

Fiji School of Medicine Postgraduate Programme

The Suva-based Fiji School of Medicine (FSM) is a Fiji institution with a region-wide intake of students. Programmes offered include postgraduate certificates, diplomas and degrees across a range of medical fields including public health, paediatrics, gynaecology, surgery, radiography, pharmacy and dentistry. There is a serious lack of medical specialist practitioners in the region, so returning medical graduates are desperately needed in their home countries, which makes it difficult for them to pursue further study. It is therefore envisaged that the provision of distance programmes will allow them to study from their home countries. In recent years, some have enrolled in postgraduate programmes offered by the Otago University in Dunedin, New Zealand. In the mid-1990s, FSM was given a mandate to provide distance education programmes based on existing face-to-face programmes.

The distance Postgraduate Training Programme began in 1998. It offers postgraduate diploma and master's programmes to doctors in the Pacific region. Five specialities are being offered: Surgery, Obstetrics and Gynaecology, Child Health, Anaesthetics and Medical Sciences. Accreditation of the programmes is being sought from USP, which currently grants FSM's MBBS qualification. The courses are taught at a distance through mainly print-based course materials. The planned provision of interactive support on CD-ROM is yet to be implemented, but there is some tutor/mentor assistance from locally based clinicians. This has limited the programme's reach since there is a dearth of this expertise in the region and the programme requires much face-to-face support.

Given the mandatory requirement for face-to-face support from a clinician and the lack of available expertise, enrolments since commencement have been minimal. In 1998, two students from Tonga and Vanuatu were enrolled in the surgery programme with, in 2000, two more students from the Cook Islands and Vanuatu. Within Fiji, another group of students is studying at a distance from Lautoka.

At the start, funding assistance for the development of distance programmes was mainly from AusAID to get the programme up and running over a five-year period. The development and production of print and audiovisual materials was started with assistance from USP (instructional design/editing/materials production expertise) in return for financial remuneration and the opportunity for staff development in the production of CD-ROMs. It was expected that development of the five programmes would take one year from March 1998, but this was suspended until September 2000. Support using teleconferencing is currently being used within Fiji but the costs involved for this as a regional support network are prohibitive. The Internet is now being explored as a new medium for delivery as is the idea of establishing a Telehealth network via the Internet.

Long-term sustainability was also envisaged and planned by the institution. At the outset, experts from Australia and New Zealand were seconded to work with local counterparts to write the courses and help launch the programmes. At the same time the local counterparts would gradually take over and eventually be the sole lecturers in charge. A new fee structure was put in place to address the increased resource requirements. Despite obvious increases, fees have remained lower than in the developed countries of the Pacific Rim. Another attraction of FSM programmes is that they focus on medical issues pertinent to the region.

Fiji School of Nursing Management Programme

Fiji School of Nursing (FSN), primarily a face-to-face training institution, also offers two distance programmes by radio: Nursing Management (20 students) and General Nursing. Students are in management positions at health stations and hospitals around the country. The WHO and the New Zealand ODA programme provide financial support.

Participation in a satellite network to be established by Japan is being investigated, the intention being to make FSN programmes available to other countries of the region.

Basic Education Management and Teacher Upgrading Programme (BEMTUP)

This is a four-year in-service teacher training Fiji Ministry of Education initiative that by 2001 will have trained some four hundred in-service upper primary teachers. It deals with revised prescriptions in four subject areas: English, Basic Science, Mathematics and Social Science and provides opportunities for professional development in planning, teaching and assessment in these subjects.

This programme combines distance delivery and face-to-face workshops over five school terms. Delivery is though five printed modules prepared by teams of teachers led by subject advisers from Australia and USP. Through its Institute of Education, USP provided staff consultants for the teams in the subject areas and distance education expertise.

'Students'/trainees are practising teachers who are sent the printed study materials throughout the term. During school holidays, trainees travel to one of two 'centres' (Teachers Colleges) to attend face-to-face workshops with their tutors. Support is further provided through audio tapes and radio broadcasts. Tutors are selected from the original 16 teachers in the writing team. It is expected that the programme will continue after the pilot stage using the materials prepared and the tutors selected.

Solomon Islands

The majority of Solomon Islanders (90%) reside outside the capital of Honiara (Paulsen 1998). Distance delivery of education is highly desirable but barriers include limited access to radio, poor mail services and underdeveloped telephone services. Television is only available in Honiara. The USP satellite network (USPNet) from their university centre provides a telecommunications link-up to other USP member countries, but beyond that modern telecommunications remain confined to Honiara and those who can afford it. High frequency radio provides an alternative means of delivery and communication support activities. Transportation is slow. Education opportunities are very limited and there is huge demand for alternatives to formal schooling at secondary level due to the push-out effect at the Form 3 (Year 8) level. Literacy in 1992 stood at 22% overall: 17% for females, 27% for males (Commonwealth Secretariat/USP 1995).

Solomon Islands College of Higher Education: AEPAD and SIDEN

In addition to its USP centre, the country's only other tertiary institution is the state-run Solomon Islands Institute of Higher Education (SICHE), which offers courses at secondary level and higher. Most of the SICHE programmes are for on-campus study, but a highly successful 18-month bridging programme known as the Adult Education Proficiency Award (AEPAD) provides the opportunity to improve literacy and numeracy skills for those who have not progressed beyond Form 3. This is the focus of the Distance Education Centre (DEC) of the college. Initially offered in 1993, AEPAD enrolled 50 students in two courses. In 1998, there were six courses and 1,200 students (Paulsen 1998). An AEPAD qualification requires three courses: Mathematics and English form the core, and the third course is chosen from four electives: Health Studies, Development and Change, Start Your Business and Education Studies. Students use printed materials and attend tutorials at provincial centres. On successful completion of the AEPAD programme, students can enter the college's certificate courses.

Since 1998 more courses have been developed to be included in another programme, the Adult Learners Training Programme (ALTP) two of which are Management of Distance Learning and Instructional Design.

Along with the development of distance education, SICHE has developed the Solomon Islands Distance Education Network (SIDEN), a national partnership comprising study centres and education institutions. By 1998, 18 study support centres had been established countrywide. The network supports learners on both SICHE and USP distance programmes through local tutorials and teleconferencing. The DEC has made a commitment to make more use of radio since access to telephones is restricted to study centres, especially in the provinces. Study centre facilities include space for study, communications technology (radio, two-way audioteleconferencing equipment, telephone, facsimile) and print references on courses, careers and training opportunities. Sixty part-time staff are available to assist students. Ongoing efforts by the DEC have led to regular workshops for both part-time study centre staff and those at the course preparation/production end. For instance, to help staff improve and develop their skills in writing and developing distance learning courses, workshops on course development and instructional design were held in 1997 and 1998. Workshops for part-time staff focus on student support (Paulsen 1998).

A further development saw the establishment of Internet access for the delivery of online courses from the University of Southern Queensland (USQ) to Honiara but high costs led to its being discontinued. However, email is popular for consultation and discussion with other distance educators internationally.

In addition to developing its own courses, SICHE has entered into a partnership with USQ and increased distance education opportunities whereby students have enrolled in USQ programmes including the MBA and the Certificate in Journalism (Paulsen 1998).

Post-basic Distance Nursing Programme

In the late 1990s, this programme was developed with British technical ODA funding. It comprises three courses: Family Planning, Obstetrics and Gynaecology, and Community Health. The programme targets registered or trained nurse aides working at village level in remote communities. In its development phase, under the guidance of the expatriate development officer, the programme was based at the Ministry of Health and Medical Services but the plan was for SICHE to take it over. Curricula were adapted from resources from the African Medical Research and Education Foundation (AMREF). Each course comprises 14 modules, each module requiring 15 hours of study and assessment. Each module comprises a printed Study Guide and reading materials, audio cassettes are used and practical work is a required component. Student support is provided through a mentoring system, a fortnightly newsletter, and radio contact via the available two-way radios (Matthewson 1997).

Commonwealth Youth Programme (CYP)

This regional programme is based in Honiara and provides training for those in social services particularly in the area of work with young people. In 1999, the CYP pan-Commonwealth professional youth workers' training programme Diploma in Youth Development was offered through USP with 90 full scholarships for students in Commonwealth countries in the region. To comply with USP programmes, the diploma was offered as the Certificate in Youth Development. The entire programme is available only by distance using printed materials. A financial subsidy is provided to students and funded local tutors provide student support. The programme is conducted nationally in the Solomon Islands but regionally through the network of USP centres. Successful completion of the certificate allows admission to the USP Diploma in Social Services.

Vanuatu

Vanuatu comprises 83 islands and an anglophone or francophone population of 192,000. Primary-level distance education has been used for over ten years but because of budgetary constraints, especially due to privatization, this effort has been seriously adversely affected. Given the limited access to education by a population living on scattered islands, distance programmes are envisaged to provide better access to education. According to recent figures 'only 74% of eligible school children attend primary school, and of those, only 30% to 40% get through to secondary education' (*SPDEP Newsletter* April 2000).

The remaining 60% to 70% of the Year 6 school leavers are now being targeted in a distance education project aimed to teach them skills to prepare them for continuing life in their villages. The project is entitled Second Chance: Basic Life Skills Trial, and will be delivered through a combined media of print, radio and local tutoring. The project is currently at the writing stage and community involvement is greatly encouraged since local experts are being requested to assist not only in materials preparation but also in the subsequent local tutoring (*SPDEP Newsletter* April 2000).

Papua New Guinea

Distance education formally commenced in PNG in 1952 with the establishment of the Correspondence School, now the College of Distance Education, where annual enrolment stood at 15,600 in 1996 (Kema 1998). Growth in distance education has been rapid. In 1985, 550 students were enrolled with the University of Papua New Guinea (UPNG). This had grown to 10,000 by 1993. Other distance education efforts in PNG include matriculation programmes at the Pacific Adventist College and, from 1993, at the Papua New Guinea University of Technology (Haihuie and Pena 1998). The latter now has an average 2,100 students enrolled each semester.

Distance education has been essential for PNG where the terrain makes getting around difficult and the population is predominantly rurally based, with only about 15% of the estimated population of 4.5 million living in urban centres.

The shift in the National Policy on Education in government provision of primary and secondary education in recent years has resulted in an exponential demand for tertiary education. Unfortunately, the large increase in secondary-level graduates is not matched with a corresponding increase in the number of places available in the tertiary institutions, and National Government Annual Grants to tertiary institutions have been significantly reduced thus leaving thousands of Grade 12 leavers vying for very limited places. Only 5% of students leaving provincial high schools gain places in national high schools and tertiary institutions (Koigiri 1998). The rest drop out of the formal system. The target group for distance education, originally matriculating students, has hence changed dramatically over the years due to the introduction of top-up schools, and demand is now for tertiary education. Appropriate distance education courses thus are not short of takers.

Distance education in PNG is mainly print-based and students come from all over the country, although the majority are based in the cities. For rural students there is a reliance on a slow postal service to deliver learning materials. The alternative is to make an expensive trip to UPNG during registration and collect materials at the same time. Choice of media for the delivery of distance education to more of the population is a major concern of current projects.

College of Distance Education (CODE)

CODE is the national Department of Education's distance education system in PNG. 'The purpose of CODE is to provide a continuing system of education, alternative to that of the formal school system, for those who for one reason or another have been unable to pursue the latter... The college courses follow the national Department of Education's high school curricula, are academic and lead to the college's grade 10 examination' (Kema 1998). More recently, the need to introduce grades 11 and 12 has been recognized. CODE also offers one post-secondary course at a distance: Certificate in Business Studies. 'Unlike provincial high schools and national high schools, the college caters not only to students of school age, but also to mature adult students, often working people' (Kema 1998).

CODE's head office is located in Waigani in the national capital district, and there are 20 provincial centres serving the regions. Provincial centres are responsible for enrolment, counselling, marking of student assignments and the general administration of their studies. Now linked by the computer network CODENET, this has greatly enhanced data collection and processing.

CODE enrolments rose rapidly to a peak of over 40,000 in 1993, when the government removed fees, introduced a Free Education Policy and instituted 'top-up' schools. Governmental financial support has been associated with delays and cutbacks. Enrolments have dropped sharply and the college is perceived as not receiving the priority treatment it deserves (Kema 1998). Additional funding is provided through project grants from the World Bank, UNESC and AusAID.

University of Technology (UniTech)

The Department of Open and Distance Learning at the Papua New Guinea University of Technology in Lae offers two distance programmes through the distance Departments of Applied Sciences, Agriculture and Forestry and is looking at starting a Diploma in Science for Teachers. The national Department of Education is very supportive of this effort.

Conscious of the need to improve access to study opportunities, two specific projects are underway on audioconferencing and multimedia networks in an attempt to reach a wider population through the use of non-print media. Although the majority of the population does not have access to the necessary media, it is felt that those who do should be given a chance to take advantage of the technology whenever possible.

The main objective of the audioconferencing project is to create access at tertiary level for anyone wishing to further their education beyond adult matriculation level. Audioconferencing uses the telephone network to put several learners in remote sites 'on the line' at once (with or without a tutor) so that all can contribute and hear what others are saying; the tutor teaches from an on-campus studio in Lae. The project had teething problems: equipment costs were high and there were unforeseen difficulties in compatibility with the national telephone system. There were also mixed feelings among the potential providers and users of the system. Attitudes changed with experience, however, and tutors involved in the trial runs quickly became enthusiastic contributors.

The multimedia project was an initiative of UniTech's Department of Electrical and Communication Engineering. Using Toolbook II Instructor, courseware authors were able to construct and deliver multimedia-based learning environments that can be delivered on demand to any student with access to the World Wide Web; it can also be deployed on a local area network for easy access. The biggest barrier to setting up a fully operational system is finance. University budget cuts in recent years have left new initiatives without support. Fortunately AusAID has provided some assistance for courseware development.

There has been some criticism that the multimedia network, when fully operational, will serve only the interests of a privileged minority because students will be required to have access to a computer as a prerequisite for enrolment in the courses that will be offered via this mode. However it is believed that the long-term advantages of the new system will have great value, both for the university and students. By exposing the population to technological options, the potential will eventually be realized, thereby hopefully swaying government priorities.

University of Papua New Guinea

UPNG is a state-owned dual-mode institution situated in the capital of PNG, Port Moresby. The distance programme is the responsibility of the Institute of Distance and Continuing Education (IDCE), with its own academics responsible for writing the mainly print-based materials. Some student support is offered through provincial centres throughout the country. As at UniTech, there is a growing recognition at UPNG that technology is moving at a fast rate, and while electronic developments are beyond the reach of much of the population, there is a growing need to provide opportunities for those who are able to make use of them to further their learning (Pena 1999).

Until recently, most courses offered by the IDCE have been at the matriculation level (equivalent to university preparatory or foundation) in sciences and arts. Degree and diploma courses are now available in Education, Arts, Law and Commerce (Kema 1998). This is the result of changes in national policy, which have increased the availability of schooling as well as the demand for tertiary education.

Conclusion

Globalization has effectively put pressure on the South Pacific to fit the market or be left behind. Throughout the region there is a tremendous need for education to address this demand. The diversity among the island states is reflected in their varying needs and priorities for education — the push-out effect at early secondary level in some countries has resulted in the need for bridging programmes such as those available from SICHE, while the demand for higher education has seen an emergence of degree programmes and other tertiary qualifications from universities and colleges in the region. In the last few years, the scope for higher education has increased through the availability of distance education programmes from institutions in the developed world, particularly Australia, and the recent establishment of a physical presence, with regional campuses, has provided competition to local counterparts.

There is a shared view that higher education will lead to better jobs, opportunities for which are more frequently found in the public service rather than the private sector. In the formal education sector, this has led to a higher demand for academic-oriented rather than technical programmes. Nevertheless, there is also a conscious effort to develop programmes to reach those who did not have the opportunity to go in to higher and further education. At the tertiary level there are common areas such as teacher education, agricultural and marine studies, tourism, and the environmental studies. USP has attempted to prioritize these areas in its current triennium. National initiatives, for example in Tonga and Fiji, are dealing specifically with the issue of teacher education.

Faced with prohibitive financial constraints, major geographic barriers and poorly developed communications and transportation infrastructure, the region has turned to distance education to provide much needed education programmes. National and regional initiatives have and continue to be developed although usually relying on outside assistance. Study materials are mainly in print and a strong commitment to student support has led to the provision of tutor-mentor support at local centres to which students have easy access. However, the move into modern telecommunications reflects a vision and commitment to providing education to enable Pacific people to be in line and online with their global cousins.

References

Fiji Ministry of Education Basic Education Management Teachers Upgrading Programme (1997) *Introductory Module*, Suva.

Haihuie, S and Pena, P (1998) 'Bringing universities to the people: an unaccomplished mission', *2nd Huon Seminar '98 Proceedings*, PNG: University of Technology, 174–80.

Hendey, D (1994) *Distance Education: Implications for NZODA. A Discussion Paper*, Wellington: Ministry of Foreign Affairs and Trade.

Johnson-Hill, L (1998) Pacific Theological College Extension Education, *On PIRADE*, 1998(2): 4–5.

Kema, D (1998) *Distance Education Activities in Papua New Guinea*, PNG: College of Distance Education.

Koigiri, A K (1998) 'Proposed administration structure for the Department of Open and Distance Learning at the Papua New Guinea University of Technology', Association of Tertiary Education Managers NSW State Conference, Southern Cross University, 24–26 June.

Matthewson, C (1994) 'Survey in distance education in the South Pacific' in *A Survey of Distance Education in Asia and the Pacific*, UNESCO-National Institute of Multimedia Education, 645–66

Matthewson, C and Va'a, R (1999) 'The South Pacific: kakai mei tahi' in Harry, K (ed.) *Higher Education Through Open and Distance Learning*, London: Routledge, 277–91.

New Zealand Ministry of Foreign Affairs and Trade (1996/7 to 2000/1/2) *NZODA Assistance for Distance Education in the South Pacific: A Development Plan.*

Parsons-Galloway Foundation Pty Ltd (1998) *Pacific Islands Involvement in the Global Information Infrastructure*, South Pacific Forum, Fiji: Suva.

Paulsen, I (1998) 'Solomon Islands College of Higher Education: Distance Education Centre', *On PIRADE*, 1998(1): 4–5.

Pena, P M (1999) 'Partnerships and collaborative efforts are important', *On PIRADE*, 1999(2): 4–5.

South Pacific Distance Education Project Newsletter, 1(1) April 2000.

United Nations Population Fund (1995) *People Count: A Summary of the 1990 Population and Housing Census in Papua New Guinea*, Port Moresby.

University of the South Pacific (1995) *Commonwealth Secretariat Pacific Teacher Education Consultation*, 5–9 June, Fuji: Suva.

University of the South Pacific (1999) *University Grants Committee Report 2000–2002*, Fuji: Suva.

Appendix 1

The Pirade region

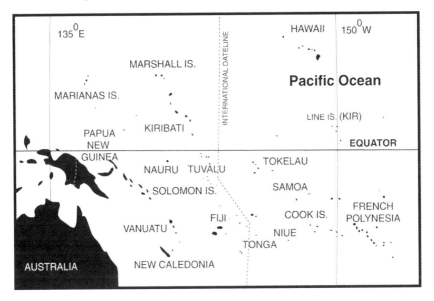

United States of America

Glenn Shive and Peter J Dirr

Introduction

Distance education has been a growing part of the higher education system in the US for a century. Print-based correspondence courses have been offered by many universities, especially the land grant institutions with a mandate to reach out to rural and underserved populations. For the first half of the century, the postal system and print media were the technologies of choice. By the 1950s, the potential of television intrigued educators to enhance the visual and dynamic content of materials.

By the 1980s, the Public Broadcast Service (PBS) and its nationwide affiliates became the leader in the distribution of telecourses to universities. In the 1990s, the Internet diffused rapidly among universities, homes and business organizations. Distance education has been swept up in the dramatic expansion of the Internet and the World Wide Web. This has created new opportunities for some institutions, and has aroused a sense of concern and even threat for many others.

This chapter is organized in three parts. The first, entitled 'Overview of distance learning in the US', creates a statistical snapshot of the state of distance education in the US at century's end by drawing on a major study, *Distance Education and Post Secondary Institutions: 1997-98*, published in December 1999 by the National Center for Education Statistics (NCES) of the US Department of Education.

The second part, 'Developing support services for distance learners in the US', focuses on the state of student support services made available to distance learners in the US. Dr Peter Dirr, co-author of this paper, headed a national study for the Western Cooperative for Educational Telecommunications (WCET).

The third part of this chapter, 'Pedagogical and institutional issues for distance learning in the US', reflects on some of the pedagogical and institutional issues raised in the context of the rapid expansion of distance learning (DL) in the US. These include commercialization, consortium and alliance-building, and the growing tendency to outsource some programme delivery and support functions to specialized service firms outside the university.

Overview of distance learning in US higher education

The NCES study gives a comprehensive survey of the state of distance education programmes and practices in the US and compares them to the benchmark study done in 1995. Here are the highlights of the research.

Institutional involvement and enrolment volume

The percentage of all colleges and universities that offer DL courses grew from 33% in 1995 to 44% in the 1997/98 academic year. The number of course offerings has doubled in three years. Another 20% of institutions that did not offer DL options in that year indicated that they planned to initiate DL programmes in the next three years. So by now, over one half of all post-secondary institutions have programmes using DL in some form.

Total enrolments in DL courses were counted at 1,661,100, of which 1,363,670 were credit courses (mostly at the undergraduate level). Together, the 14.4 million enrolled students in the US probably took 150 million to 250 million courses, of which 1.4 million were DL courses.

The medium and the large-sized institutions tend to be most active in DL, whereas the smaller campuses are less likely to offer DL programmes. This may reflect their lack of resources to invest in new technologies and other programme infrastructure, and/or an orientation that emphasizes the value of face-to-face instruction. About half of the higher education providers in the US report enrolments of 300 or fewer students in DL; the other half have more than 300 enrolments in DL programmes. Half of the providing institutions offered 15 or fewer courses via DL that year, and 23%, probably just beginning to build their programmes, offered from one to five courses.

The total number of courses offered by DL was 54,470. Nearly all, or 49,690 of these courses were for credits towards degrees or certificates at the college level. The major fields represented are English, humanities and the social and behavioural sciences (70%), as well as business management (55%). Most courses were offered at the undergraduate level. Exceptions were in education, engineering and library and information science, in which most courses were offered at the graduate and first professional level.

Public and private initiatives in distance learning

Public institutions are more likely than private to offer DL. 78% of public four-year and 62% of public two-year institutions offer DL, whereas only 19% of private four-year and only 5% of private two-year institutions report that they have DL programmes. Eight in ten DL courses are offered by public institutions; two in ten by private institutions. Public institutions may have access to more state-funded capital to invest in new technology infrastructure. It is somewhat ironic that DL often occurs within a growing culture of educational entrepreneurism, which seems to be as active in the public as well as in the private institutions.

Full degree and certificate programmes via distance learning

Whereas DL courses have proliferated and enrolments have risen, there are still relatively few degree programmes (1,230) and sub-degree certificate programmes (340) offered entirely through DL. Only 8% of total institutions in the US offer such programmes. Only one-quarter of the providers of DL reported they offered a certificate or degree entirely at a distance. Whereas individual courses offered by DL have grown at the undergraduate level, full degrees at a distance tend to be more at the graduate and first professional degree level, especially in the fields of business, health professions, education and engineering.

It appears curious that while more individual course development and deployment tends to be at undergraduate level in the arts and sciences, the full degree packages available by DL tend to occur in graduate and first professional programmes. It takes more time to develop enough courses in distance mode to support whole undergraduate degrees. On the other hand, there may be more philosophical resistance among the faculties at the undergraduate level to move towards full degrees through DL. At the graduate level, which is targeted more at 'non-traditional students', who are working adults, the market forces that emphasize convenience, portability and credential completion make full degrees at a distance more appealing.

Technology change in distance learning

What changes in the technologies of delivery were noted in the three years from 1995 to 1997/98? The Internet. The amount of two-way interactive TV programmes and one-way pre-recorded video programmes (such as telecourses) was about constant. Web-based DL programmes, however, tripled in those three years from 22% to 60%. In general, interactive TV was slightly favoured by four-year publics and one-way pre-recorded video was more popular among two-year community colleges.

The Internet as a new delivery mode, meanwhile, has engaged all categories of two- and four-year public and private institutions. Reported plans for the future indicated strong preferences for the Internet, with smaller increases possible in interactive TV, and probably a plateau for pre-recorded one-way video. In any case, DL has become mixed mode or multimedia, with new permutations likely to emerge as more institutions enter the field and the digital technologies continue to diffuse.

Tuition and fees for distance learning

What about the money? Many advocates of DL expect cost savings over time given that a volume of students are expected to opt for DL for part or even all their degree study. In the short run, however, it is clear that developing and deploying DL courses, especially for whole degree programmes, is expensive. Given these costs, are institutions charging more for DL? Or are they passing on savings to the students in the form of lower costs? What are the expectations of the student market for the cost of DL compared to traditional formats?

The NCES study found that three-quarters of institutions that offer DL charge the same tuition as comparable on-campus courses. Community colleges were especially constrained not to charge more for DL courses.

Two-thirds of all institutions reported they did not add special fees for their DL courses. 'Overall, 57% of institutions are charging both comparable tuition and comparable fees for distance education and on-campus courses.' (NCES 1999, vi)

Given the policy complexity of raising tuition or fees in public institutions, and the overall public sensitivity to increases in costs of higher education generally, it appears difficult for campus-based providers of DL to charge students more for technology-based delivery. The newer, fully virtual providers do not have the same comparative bases for setting their prices.

Given strong public sector involvement in DL and general supply-demand factors that shape consumer expectations, it may be difficult for most campus-based providers to secure an early return on their investments in DL. Even so, expectations of eventual revenue from DL courses based on market position have propelled many institutions to invest considerably in this new mode of delivering education programmes and services.

The NCES report concludes that, 'distance education appears to have become a common feature of many post-secondary education institutions and that, by their own accounts, it will become only more common in the future' (NCES 1999, vi). While more common, DL will also provoke more questions for the stakeholders and constituencies involved. The questions cited by the study include issues of:

- Equity of access to post-secondary education;
- Cost of developing and implementing DL programmes;
- Accreditation and quality assurance;
- Copyright and intellectual property rights;
- Changes and challenges to the faculty;
- Pressures on existing organizational structures and arrangements.

The overall picture of the NCES study is confirmed by two recent studies for the IT industry, which has a large stake in the growth of DL applications. The IDC, a Massachusetts-based market research firm for the IT industry world-wide <http://www.idc.com> conducted market projection research in which they estimate 'the number of college students enrolled in DL courses will reach 2.23 million in 2002, up from 710,000 in 1998'. That is more than a tripling of enrolments in the space of four years, moving from 5% to 15% of all higher education students.

The IDC research points to the Internet as the major catalyst attracting both colleges and students to this new mode of learning. They estimate that 85% of the two-year colleges will offer DL courses in 2002, up from 58% in 1998; and 84% of four-year colleges will do so, up from 62% last year.

The general trends described in the NCES study are reflected in the *Survey of Distance Learning Programs in Higher Education 1999* conducted for the New York-based Primary Research Group <http://www.primaryresearch.com>. They estimate that 57% of all DL programmes in the northern US use the Web in combination with email for course delivery.

Their random sample of 61 college and university DL programmes shows an average of 1,719 enrolled students, with a maximum of 50,000. The sample programmes offer an average of 66 online courses per semester, ranging from two to 550 courses. In 1999, instructor salaries accounted for 32% of programme costs (down from 37% in 1998), with 37% serving as adjunct faculties (up from 27% in 1998). 87% indicate their programmes earn a profit. 13% of programmes claim that they operate at a profit of over 50%.

This growth vector for distance education in the US is anybody's guess. Some analysts predict that new demands for learning, especially from a growing knowledge-intensive workforce that must continually retrain itself, will far exceed the capacity of traditional academic delivery systems. Michael Dolence and Donald Norris (1995) estimate that 'just to keep even, each individual in the workforce will need to accumulate learning equivalent to that currently associated with 30 credit hours of instruction every seven years. This can translate into the full-time equivalent (FTE) enrolment of one seventh of the workforce at any point in time'.

This new demand would add, they estimate, 'over 20 million FTE learners from the workforce' to universities and other providers of advanced learning. If all this learning were to be accommodated by a campus and classroom mode of delivery, the US would have to open a new university every eight days over the next decade (Dolence and Norris 1995).

What would such a growth rate in learning demand mean for any country trying to expand capacity to keep up with demand? Given the globalization of the economy, especially in the service sector, and the significance of human resources in the next stage of that economic growth, a small elite-oriented education system is not feasible.

If new technology is a major force creating new social demand for learning and re-learning, then the same technology will be used to satisfy that demand.

In the industrial revolution in the US, the new universities were created from the land grant system. New land was the resource used to establish universities in the early industrial era. With the information revolution well underway, the new resource for creating new teaching and learning services is not land, but bandwidth. Our new academic programmes will be built in virtual space.

Developing support services for distance learners in the US

Until recently, the major focus for new DL initiatives in the US has been on the delivery of instruction. The major challenge seemed to be how to provide geographically dispersed students access to effective teaching and learning activities. To move beyond the classroom, recasting the delivery of instruction has been the *sine qua non* for DL programmes. However, it is also becoming clear to many institutions of higher education (IHE) providers that a successful DL programme does not depend only on accessible and effective delivery of academic content. Academic success for students at a remove from campuses also depends to a great extent on the quality of the support services available to them.

For colleges and universities initiating and expanding DL courses, and especially whole degree programmes, it has become necessary to rethink and redesign the whole range of non-academic interactions they have with their students. This has led innovative institutions to create new technology-based applications for building these relationships from initial recruitment to lifelong alumni relations.

Many of these innovations, especially in online support services, began initially as attempts to find solutions for relating more effectively to distance learners. As the IT revolution expanded, many of these applications specific to DL had broader implications for improving the quality and user-friendliness of customer-oriented services for all students, whether they be residential, commuter or distance learners. The major challenge for support services has become not just overcoming distance for a few remote students, but saving time for all students.

WCET's overview of distance learning programmes

In the spring of 1997, the WCET surveyed over 1,000 institutions of higher education (IHEs), mainly in the 14 western states in the US. 'The 417 responses (40.5%), along with the follow-up telephone interviews with a small sample of non-respondents, provide a strong basis for believing that the responses represent a true picture of the state of student support services (in IHEs) all across the country.' (Dirr 1999, 16)

The survey found that the primary institutional motivation for offering DL courses and programmes was 'to respond to student demand for distance education (74%)' (Dirr 1999, 3). Significant secondary imperatives were stated as: to compete with other IHEs that provide DL (31%), to enable marketing to business and industry (28%), and to reduce the costs of increasing student access (27%). These reported policy motivations suggest the extent to which the DL movement in US higher education is a market-driven and competitive process.

In line with the NCES survey, the WCET study found that more institutions offer DL courses at the undergraduate level (92%) than at the graduate level (42%). Over one-third of IHEs (37%), more than the NCES study, reported offering non-credit courses via DL. Interestingly, WCET found more four-year IHEs such as state universities offering non-credit courses (55%) and certificate programmes (41%) by DL than community colleges (26% and 12% respectively). This seems at variance with the perception nationally that community colleges have been more pro-active than four-year institutions to use DL to deliver non-credit and certificate programmes.

Technologies in use for distance learning

As for types of technology used, WCET found a variety of delivery strategies. These are listed in order of popularity of use:

Live interactive video to two or more sites	64%
Videotapes (materials recorded by video cassette tapes)	63%
Internet-based training	59%
Broadcast or cable TV (video course materials televised by broadcast or cable)	54%
Two-way video (satellite, videoconferencing)	47%
Correspondence study (primarily print-based courses)	30%
One-way video with audio talkback (ITFS, cable satellite, desktop video)	27%
Stand-alone computer-based training (via CD-ROM, or linked to a LAN or WAN)	26%
Instructional TV fixed service (ITFS) from a central tower	21%

WCET found that four-year IHEs generally make more use of Internet-based and traditional correspondence study than two-year institutions. In particular, four-year publics make more use of interactive video, pre-recorded videotapes, and ITFS. This may relate to the history of vocational and technical colleges included in this category offering professional education to engineers and other technical professionals in the workplace.

Locations of distance learning programmes and their students

The WCET study reports that two-thirds of students are within the state of the provider and one-third are based outside the institution's home state. Naturally, community colleges are less inclined to reach out for out-of-state students (20%) than four-year publics or privates. The DL programmes of private four-year universities have more out-of-state than in-state students. There are extra costs for the provider, especially for support services, for most out-of-state students in DL programmes. It does not make sense to charge distance learners the full out-of-state tuition and campus-based activities fees. But some questions are raised about charging in-state rates, subsidized by state taxpayers, for distance learners located in other states. As e-commerce advances, this issue of costs and fees for DL services will evolve further.

About two-thirds (66%) of DL programmes deliver courses to the home, with community colleges taking the lead in this modality. Half of the providers have made arrangements with other IHEs (50%) to deliver instruction and support services. This is reflected in the increase of inter-institutional agreements and consortia-building activity one finds around DL in US higher education today. Technology has made these collaborations more important than ever. Half of the DL providers (50%) have their own branch campuses or satellite sites where remote students receive instruction and services. It will be interesting to see if offering DL programmes leads providers to increase their own branch and satellite centres, or whether inter-institutional and consortia-type of arrangements will become more common. Some IHEs will try to specialize internally and collaborate with other providers (or outsource to other agents), while other IHEs will try to manage DL programmes within their own comprehensive infrastructure. We will return to this theme at the end of the paper.

WCET found that two in five institutions deliver instruction via DL to work sites (47%) and to public libraries and schools (43%) in their respective regions. The public IHEs lead in these delivery modes. The rise of DL has coincided with greater outreach by IHEs to business and industry. The need by industry for training has certainly grown, and the technology developments have made new modalities more cost-effective. It is said that the future university in the US will deliver a third of its instruction on campus, a third to the workplace, and a third in the home. We are a long way from this ratio of the three delivery formats, but all agree that home and workplace settings will grow as reception points for instruction as broadband technologies diffuse in the next several years.

Survey of support services for distant learners

With this general picture of DL activities in IHEs, the WCET study documents more specifically how universities structure their non-academic interactions between themselves and their students who study beyond the campus. These services include:

- Recruitment, promotion and orientation;
- Admissions and registration;
- Academic advising and programme planning;
- Financial planning and management;
- Library and bookstore services;
- Technical assistance to students;
- Career and personal counselling;
- Social support services;
- Degree and transcript audit;
- Services to special populations;
- Relationships with businesses and community sites.

The WCET study concludes that:

> In spite of the breadth and length of experience, most of the IHEs offering distance education courses and programmes seem to have concentrated on delivering already existing courses without exerting much effort to develop new support services for the student populations they are reaching electronically. Consequently, it is not at all unusual for a student to be able to access course materials electronically or even communicate electronically with the professor and other students, but to have to travel to the campus or a remote campus facility to take advantage of other student support services that are readily available to on-campus students (Dirr 1999, 16).

The WCET study cites several key findings that show the development of support services lagging behind instructional services in many DL programmes. For example:

- 27% (of DL programme providers) have yet to develop promotional materials to attract distant learners;
- More than half (55%) require distance learners to complete formal admission requirements before enrolling in a course;

- One in six (15%) requires distance learners to register for courses in person at fixed sites;

- 90% offer in-person academic advising but only on campus when that service is needed;

- Almost one-third (31%) provide no special access to library services for distance learners;

- One-third (37%) require distance learners to obtain their textbooks on their own;

- One-third (32%) provide no intervention strategies for struggling students who need academic assistance;

- Three-quarters (76%) have developed no social support networks to help distance learners overcome a sense of isolation in their studies.

Furthermore:

Fewer than half of all colleges and universities that offer distance education courses and programmes offer personal counseling services to distance learners (44%), take special measures to assure that students accepted in to their distance education courses and programmes have the technical skills required to use the delivery technologies (29%), and have developed a plan for the retention of distance learners (5%) (Dirr 1999, 16).

The conclusion reflects:

One might speculate on why IHEs have been slow to use available technologies to deliver student support services to distance learners as readily as they use those same technologies to deliver course instruction. At many institutions, distance education has been an 'add on' to the core instructional offerings, and it has grown slowly over several years. In many cases, the distance education offerings have existed without the support (or even knowledge, in some cases) of top administrators. However, delivery of student support services requires support from top administrators, and a change in the way many offices on campus do business. Student support services is not something that can easily be changed incrementally (Dirr 1999, 18–19).

Indeed, the study convinced WCET that the effort to help institutions re-direct and re-design their support services would have to be less 'as a captain redirects a large tanker, slowly but all at once. Instead, WCET might have to look on the support services at an institution more like a school of fish and help each service office try to redirect its efforts, while at the same time trying to keep the school of fish together' (Dirr 1999, 19)

Efforts on US campuses to re-engineer support services for distant learners have been guided by a set of common themes that emerged throughout the WCET study. They are:

- Student-centred customer service;
- Integration of services (a 'cross-functional' approach);
- Data system integration;
- Centralized student service buildings;
- Cross-functional staff training;
- Staff as knowledge navigators and problem-solvers;
- Direct access to information for student and faculty;
- Use of technology as enabler of routine transactions (Dirr 1999, 17).

WCET asked the providers to rate their own effectiveness (1=not effective and 10=extremely effective) in supporting students at a distance. They had hoped to identify exemplary practices that could be diffused within the region.

> The mean score ratings were modest, ranging from 6.1 for registration services to 3.6 for social support services. The services that the group as a whole thought they were doing best were: registration, programme planning, degree and graduation audit, and transcript evaluation. Social support services, career counselling, and counselling services were rated lowest (Dirr 1999, 12).

Web-based student support services

The Web has been the major focus of experimentation in service delivery. DL providers have been found by one study to be going through a progression of possibly four stages (Dirr 1999). Most institutions are probably at the first stage and beginning to move to the second.

> The first (stage) seems to be to provide basic institutional information and references online. This might be followed by (a stage of) electronic paperwork, such as online registration. A third level might consist of

placing databases of records online that make it possible for students to get up-to-the-minute reports of their status as well as to see the consequences of adjustments they might want to make to their academic plans. A fourth level might be a carefully integrated suite of online services with complete information, communication, interaction and transaction capabilities (Dirr 1999, 19).

This study did not find an institution at the fourth level. 'Many are comfortable with the progress they have made with the first two levels. Some few are at the third level.'

The Campus Computing Project conducts an annual survey of IT on US campuses. In recent surveys they found that IHEs are increasing online services available to general students, whether residential, commuter or at a distance. For example:

> More than two-thirds (69.5%) of the institutions in the 1999 survey provide online undergraduate applications on their Web sites, up from 54.4% in 1998. Three-fourths (77.3%) make the course catalogue available online, compared to 65.2% last year. Library-based course reserves readings are available on the Web at one-fourth of the institutions, up from 17.9% in 1998. <www.campuscomputing.net>

The problem has traditionally been posed as: how can we offer support services to distant students on par in quality, cost and convenience with students who have access to the campus Web-based applications developed to solve these problems and which are beginning to find broader utility throughout higher education systems. For example, all students have a greater expectation these days to be able to access their academic records online like they can access their financial records at the bank. As new Web applications for distance learners are used to solve problems for all students, they will attract the more resources needed to create systemic electronic support services that will be increasingly required by consumers of any DL programme.

In any case, questions about, 'How do we serve students at a distance?' are increasingly re-framed as: 'How do we serve all our students with student-centred, customer-oriented, technology-based strategies?' Thus distance or virtual learning programmes, still largely on the margins of most IHEs by measures of enrolments and revenues, are beginning to stimulate broader systemic changes in the way US higher education institutions manage and deliver services to their students.

Pedagogical and institutional issues for distance learning in the US

Debates about learning and teaching in universities

Recent growth in technology-mediated learning has stimulated further discussion in the US about student-centred, project-based and activity-oriented learning. Scholars advancing 'constructivist' theories of pedagogy point to the diverse ways in which students assemble and use knowledge from disparate sources of information, given their unique prior structures of perception. This is especially valid for adult learners.

Given the requirements for active learning in DL courses, the teacher's role tends to shift from the traditional 'sage on the stage' to the role of 'guide at the side.' Advocates of DL envision the teacher becoming a designer and facilitator of learning activities; a coach and mentor in the learning process; and a navigator for students to encounter and become skilled in new worlds of information. This shift in the role of the teacher may be a consequence of several forces: the explosion of knowledge and ease of access to it, the speed of technology change, the growing demand from the workplace less for specific content than for learning how to learn, and a growing gap between older teachers and younger students in the advancing techno-culture.

This sense of a change in teacher and student roles in a DL context is abetted by the many adults who are 'returning to learning', coming back to education looking for further qualifications. About half of university students in the US are now over the age of 25. Clearly their minds are not 'tabla rasa' to be filled by educators, but already dense with constructs and assumptions that need to be re-thought and re-ordered in view of the new economic, social and intellectual requirements of their lives.

The new key term in broad parlance is interactivity. Action, enactment and performance are essential to learning. Cognitive acquisition is only one dimension of learning, albeit the dimension most prized in our exam and reward systems. There is growing interest in multiple intelligences, including analytical thinking, creative intelligence and practical intelligence. Memorized knowledge for passing exams may be valued by education systems that manage those exams, but not very much beyond graduation.

US employers are increasingly pressing universities to teach more explicitly such skills as initiative, cooperation, working in groups (especially in multi-cultural and mixed gender settings), peer training, evaluation and ethical reasoning, problem-solving, decision-making, obtaining and using new information, planning, and lifelong learning skills. These skills may have emerged incidentally from learning the traditional curriculum in campus settings. But there is new emphasis placed on making these outcomes more explicit for learning systems. Heated debate continues about the feasibility of DL to advance these outcomes more cost-effectively than traditional campus-based programmes. This has created new demand for research and evaluation into the efficacy of various strategies and delivery modes of distance education for specific target student populations.

Issues in commercialization of distance education

A new wave of commercialization is sweeping over higher education in the US. The forces behind this trend are much larger than DL, but the debate over commercialization is often closely tied to it.

In the post-Cold War culture in the United States, many people assumed the turn of global events validated a broad range of 'market-is-king' thinking. Meanwhile, public institutions of all kinds are faced with growing public doubt and scrutiny about transparency and accountability. In fact, state and federal investments in technology and innovation have been quite important to the recent expansion of DL programmes. Many of these programmes are actually financed on a full fee-recovery basis by the continuing education units of public universities. Some of the funds generated by these units are transferred to the traditional campus sector to help keep them solvent rather than, in some cases, invested in the services required to assure quality for off-campus and DL programmes.

New private online institutions, such as the University of Phoenix, Kaplan Education Services and Sylvan Learning Systems, raise their capital on the NASDAQ stock exchange. Billions of new dollars have been attracted into the higher and continuing education sector with the advent of digital technology firms developing new business strategies and delivery tools that literally 'go around' the traditional providers directly to the student market. This new capital also enables start-up ventures to launch new organizations purpose-built for DL without the legacy systems of traditional institutions. Some major providers have grown fast through DL; others emerged on the scene and disappeared soon thereafter. Despite reversals in the fortunes of some 'dot-com' investors in 2000, it is likely that this sector will continue growing as a source of new capital and services for e-learning in association with established IHEs.

The University of Phoenix enrolments grew from 31,000 in 1992 to 68,000 by the beginning of 2000. Enrolments in the University of Maryland University College's (UMUC) online courses have doubled from 20,000 to 40,000 in the past three years. They expect continued robust growth in online enrolments, with faculty supply as the key constraint on future expansion.

Distance learning belongs to the volatile technology sector of the 'new economy.' Some major entrepreneurs such as Glenn Jones of the International University (formerly Mind Extension University) based in Denver have invested heavily in new online courseware and delivery services. Despite recent downturns in the NASDAQ and cooling of initial enthusiasm for dot.com IPOs, there remains a strong perception in the capital markets that there is money to be made long-term by well-positioned technology-based distributed learning companies. Early investors have already reaped large profits, although more recent enthusiasts for these stocks have been disappointed. One can track the markets in e-education through Eduventures at <www.eduventures.com>. Developments in DL in the US can also be monitored through the Virtual University Gazette <http://www.geteducated.com>, a free monthly online journal about distance education.

The start-up, for-profit educational service companies do not have to carry the heavy recurrent costs of traditional campuses, or wait for fractious faculty committees to approve new academic programmes or student policies. They also do not need to feed the 'iron rice bowls' of faculty tenure, but rather can staff up with many adjunct instructors on short-term, performance-based contracts. This trend haunts teaching staff of mainstream universities, and fuels their scepticism and anxiety about megatrends in higher education (not unlike the changes towards managed care in the health sector in the US), which they tend to associate directly with DL.

The commercialization of distance education can be seen in the pages of advertising in the *Chronicle of Higher Education*. For example, Real Education, Inc, now renamed e-College.com, claims to have enabled over 60 universities to go online. They offer their IHE clients to put 20 full courses online in just 60 days. They will create a complete 'online campus' for any institutional client by building websites for a whole range of operations:

> ...course catalogue, an academic calendar, inquiry and application forms, electronic registration, degree requirement tables, add/drop policies, online admissions, financial aid procedures, bursar office functions, administrative services, academic advising services, faculty directory, career counseling, bookstores and student unions.

Most universities do not have the internal skills and resources to undertake such comprehensive reforms in their bureaucratic operating systems. Even if they did, internal staff opposition would often prolong the process.

Similar services to DL providers are offered by Blackboard.com, Pangaea <www.pangaeanetwork.com> and Embanet <http://www.embanet.com>. Professional conferences of IHEs have large vendor shows where new online companies market their services to university administrators seeking to go digital. The Caliber Learning Network <http://www.caliberlearning.com>, a joint venture between MCI and Sylvan, has positioned itself to expand into teacher education and other professional development courses delivered nation-wide by satellite, videoconferencing and personal computer networks to students at homes, in businesses, in public libraries and in computer kiosks and cafés in public areas such as shopping malls.

Unbundling and outsourcing elements of the distance education process

Until recently, US universities were largely self-contained organizations. Faculty members developed their courses and assembled materials, taught their courses to students in classrooms on campus, and assessed their students' performance. These functions were 'bundled' together in one role. The university provided important services for enrolment, advising, financial aid, record-keeping and transcripting credits. They also provided essential instructional support through libraries, computer labs, and bookstores, as well as social services through student unions, dining halls and housing facilities.

In the new economic environment, some senior university administrators ask themselves: what are the 'core functions' that must be fulfilled directly by the university and which the university is best suited to deliver? On the other hand, what functions might be outsourced to other enterprises that can deliver the services in more cost effective ways?

Most outsourcing has been done in the business and administrative area. Food services and bookstores on campus are rarely operated directly by universities. As DL has emerged, more academic leaders are asking whether some instructional functions and support services might also be outsourced to specialized companies with new Web-based applications for academic systems. The increasing use of adjunct instructors is a kind of outsourcing.

Most regular teaching staff may know how to lecture in classrooms to some degree of effectiveness. But even good teachers in classrooms do not necessarily know how to design and produce effective learning tools and activities in an online environment. This requires teamwork among content specialists, curriculum designers and computer support staff. Course production for DL is no longer the private preserve of individual faculty members who convert their lecture materials into correspondence learning formats. In the future, more universities will lease online courseware and course management software, adapt it to their students, and have instructors serving as 'guides at the side' to their students, many of whom they will know mainly through email and teleconferencing.

Likewise, the assessment function may no longer belong exclusively to the individual faculty member. We can expect advances in computer-based evaluation systems. Distance learning has pushed the agenda of outcomes-based assessment of learning. Many teaching staff are rightly concerned about issues of authentic assessment. Clearly they stand to lose some traditional power relative to the student in a transition to outsourced evaluation. Some teachers may welcome taking off the black hat of the examiner and wearing only the white hat of the tutor and mentor. Some disciplines and forms of knowledge lend themselves more easily to external assessment than others. In any case, the teacher/mentor will continue to have input and insight into individual students' progress. But these insights, based on the direct contact they have with students, will be one aspect of a student's performance measurement.

The online environment will require that students use many self-assessment tools, which will require that they actively plan and reflect on their progress in learning. As more students and programmes accommodate self-paced learning in various ways, the traditional academic calendar will become less relevant. Students will proceed at their own speed, advancing as they pass pre-arranged assessment events. (Self-paced learning may come at the price of group projects and collaborative learning, which require students to move as cohorts through a body of academic material.) Faculty workloads have to be re-organized and compensation packages re-calibrated.

In the age of digital technologies, a university really has two fundamental assets. One is the knowledge embodied in its faculties, and the other is the authority to evaluate learning and award degrees and other credentials. Managing these assets will be of greatest importance. Other functions now conducted by universities may be critical in some way for good educational services, but they may not be as fundamental to the university. Provided the university has means of holding contractors accountable, more services can be outsourced to specialized, Web-competent agencies and 'dot.com' companies that will outperform the paper-based, personnel-intensive services of the traditional campus. This belongs to the logic, however ruthless, of the new knowledge economy of the future.

Partnerships and alliances among universities for distance learning

The Internet emerged in the 1980s in the research-based, faculty-friendly environment of the university. To teach, early users of the Internet simply transferred their courseware onto websites. At first this seemed quick and inexpensive, and seemed adequate to augment regularly taught courses on campus. However, as a greater percentage of the instruction had to occur online as an alternative to classroom contact, especially for off-campus students, this simplistic form of 'shovelware' (i.e. simply posting class notes on websites) clearly was not adequate. Solid instructional design was required. Creating good online courses required much time and cost and experimentation.

To use the power of the new digital technologies to their fullest, universities tend to partner with like-minded IHEs as well as commercial companies (such as described in the outsourcing section) that often have the skills and entrepreneurial orientation that universities did not have. Some alliances grew up among institutions to jointly offer degree or certificate programmes through DL in various formats. Many regional consortia have grown up around live, closed-circuit television networks. Several state community college systems (e.g., Colorado, Oregon, Maryland, Michigan, Texas, Illinois) have created an online college or campus to coordinate and rationalize the Internet-based course offerings of their members and to assure cross recognition of credits towards degrees. Governors State University, an upper division institution based in Chicago, collaborates with over 20 community colleges around the US in the ABELINC network to offer a '2+2' Associate and Bachelor's degree combination through DL courseware and joint provision of student services <http://www.govst.edu/bog>.

Other partnerships and alliances for DL are organized and sustained by 'third party' organizations. Most notable of these is the Going the Distance (GTD) Project of the Adult Learning Service of the PBS <http://www.pbs.org/adultlearning>. More than 180 colleges and universities offer degree courses through telecourses, which are being augmented with Web components. The PBS is now designing Web-based advising tools that will enable adult learners anywhere in the US to evaluate their readiness to learn at a distance, and then to select a programme from among a growing number of degree offerings in a complex national DL marketplace.

To design, develop and deliver a quality online instructional programme leading to a degree is a complex process. Most universities do not have the personnel or the technological resources to do this. Maybe more important is the administrative will and support from faculty to evolve or 'migrate' a substantial portion of their courses into online formats for more flexible delivery. Because this is so difficult and different from mainstream teaching, a new industry of 'third party' facilitators for distance education is arising such as some of those mentioned above (e.g., e-College and Blackboard.com).

Conclusion

This chapter has provided a broad overview of the state of DL programmes and services in the US at century's end. Two major studies provide the best available statistical summary of the volume and direction of this dynamic movement in higher education in the US. With the growing concern to build integrated online support services for distance learners, a new industry of specialized technology-based learning services has emerged with new capital, business models and technology strategies.

Keen debates have arisen in campus-based institutions about the shift towards distance delivery. These include pedagogical issues, questions over accountability and commercialization, unbundling and outsourcing of academic functions to specialized providers, and the trend towards wider consortium- and alliance-building to promote DL programmes and services among higher education institutions.

Postscript: international students in US distance learning programmes

The WCET study found that only 2% of all IHEs involved in DL have any students outside the US. The limited international presence in US DL programmes may simply reflect the limited proportion of international student presence in the overall national system. Only about 3% of students in US universities are on student or exchange visas. In any case, it appears that very few DL programmes have consciously sought to involve students from outside the US. It also suggests that the potential for exporting US academic services via new communication technologies has had only modest beginnings to date.

The low numbers of international participation in US DL programmes may relate to the still early stage of development in comprehensive DL support services. It also suggests that the groups in universities advancing an international agenda are not the same groups who are developing and administering DL programmes, many of whom are based in continuing education units. Another interpretation could be that the new student demand for flexible learning within the US, stimulated by the rapid diffusion of new telecommunications technologies, has meant that most IHEs are still gearing up to serve the burgeoning US domestic market. In this context, they do not have the time, resources or inclination to venture further into student markets abroad where technology diffusion may be slower and credit unit standards less negotiable in the US education context.

In any case, the maturation of online support services is likely to occur rapidly in the US in the next several years. As technology diffuses globally, barriers to adding international students to domestic DL programmes will come down. Greater international participation in DL courses will benefit all students as well as bring additional revenues to the providers. It is possible that countries with mature DL programmes that have smaller domestic markets, such as the UK, Australia and Canada, will be more motivated to include off-shore students in their DL programmes.

Ironically, the US's lead in consumer access to technology and its greater internal market demand for higher education may slow rather than accelerate the shift to a global perspective on the potential for distance education. But the education sector, like other service sectors, is being globalized through the diffusion of digital technologies and the penetration of e-commerce. This will eventually force education leaders in the US to incorporate trans-national thinking and planning into the development and delivery of new generations of DL programmes.

References

Dirr, P J (1999) *Putting Principles into Practice: Promoting Effective Support Services for Students in Distance Learning Programs (A Report on the Findings of a Survey)*, Western Cooperative for Educational Telecommunications, CO: Denver. Available at <http://www.wiche.edu/telecom/projects/studentservices/Survey%20Report.pdf> (24 Jan 2001)

Dolence, M and Norris, D (1995) *Transforming Higher Education*, Society for College and University Planning, Ann Arbor.

Green, K C (2000) *The 2000 Campus Computing Survey*, Campus Computing, CA: Encino. Available at <http://www.campuscomputing.net> (24 Jan 2001)

Julian, E and Anderson, C (2000) *The US Corporate eLearning Market Forecast, 1998-2003*, International Data Corporation, Bulletin 21323, MA: Framington. Available at <http://www.idc.com> (25 Jan 2001)

National Center for Education Statistics (1999) 'Distance education in higher education institutions', Washington, DC: US Department of Education. Available at <http://nces.ed.gov/pubs98/distance/index.html> (24 Jan 2001)

Primary Research Group (1999) 'The survey of distance learning programs in higher education 1999', February, <http://www.primaryresearch.com>

Rochester, J, Boggs, R and Lau, S (1999) 'Online Distance Learning in Higher Education, 1998–2002', Report W17827, January, <http://www.idc.com>

Note: Throughout this chapter, Universal Resource Locators (URLs), electronic addresses, have been included to permit the reader to pursue additional information on sites and topics referenced. These URLs are valid Internet addresses as of Jan 2001. Due to the nature of the World Wide Web, and the restructuring of homepages by webmasters, the addresses might change by the time the reader tries to access the referenced sites. In the event of an 'Error 404' or 'Invalid Location' message, we suggest deleting the last part of the URL in order to at least get to the homepage of the host organization site.

Authors' details

Australia

Colin Latchem was previously the Head of the Teaching Learning Group at Curtin University, Perth, Western Australia and is a past President of the Open and Distance Learning Association of Australia. He is now an international consultant in open learning and educational development.

Colin Latchem and Associates
11 Reeve Street
Swanbourne
Perth WA 6010
Australia
Email: clatchem@iinet.net.au
Fax: (61) 8 9384 7384

Bangladesh

Prof. Dr M Aminul Islam is the former Vice-Chancellor of the Bangladesh Open University.

'Rose Corner'
22/A Sonargaon Road
Hatirpool, Dhanmondi, Dhaka-1205
Bangladesh
Email: aminul@bangla.net
Fax: (880) 2 8615750

Hasibul Haque is an Assistant Professor of the School of Social Science, Humanities & Language at the Bangladesh Open University.

Bangladesh Open University
Gazipur-1705
Bangladesh
Email: hhaque@bou.bangla.net
Fax: (880) 2 9800822

Canada

Dr Colin Yerbury is the Dean of Continuing Studies, Simon Fraser University.

Simon Fraser University
8888 University Drive
Burnaby, BC
Canada V5A 1S6
Email: colin_yerbury@sfu.ca
Fax: (604) 291-3851

Dr Joan Collinge is the Director of the Centre for Distance Education, Continuing Studies, Simon Fraser University.

Simon Fraser University
8888 University Drive
Burnaby, BC
Canada V5A 1S6
Email: collinge@sfu.ca
Fax: (604) 291-4964

Patricia Graca is the North Growth Management Program Assistant for the Morris J Wosk Centre for Dialogue at Harbour Centre, Simon Fraser University.

515 West Hastings Street
Vancouver, BC
Canada V6B 5K3
Email: pgraca@sfu.ca
Fax: (604) 291-5098

China

Prof. Dr Ding Xing-fu is Librarian and Director of the Distance Education Institute at China Central Radio and TV University (CCRTVU) in Beijing.

160 Fuxingmen Nei St
Beijing, 100031
PR of China
Email: xingfu@crtvu.edu.cn
Fax: (86) (10) 6641 9025

Hong Kong

Prof. Olugbemiro Jegede is the Director of the Centre for Research in Distance & Adult Learning at the Open University of Hong Kong.

30 Good Shepherd St
Homantin, Kowloon
Hong Kong SAR
Email: jegede@ouhk.edu.hk
Fax: (852) 2715 9042

India

Prof. Asha S Kanwar is Professor of English at the Indira Gandhi National Open University. She has been Director, School of Humanities and is also a former Pro-Vice Chancellor of IGNOU, New Delhi.

826, Lavy Pinto Block
Asian Games Village
New Delhi 110049 India
Email: ashakanwar@hotmail.com
Fax: (91) 11 6859267

C R Pillai was formerly Director, Planning and Development Division, Indira Gandhi National Open University, New Delhi.

A-62/2, SFS Flats
Saket
New Delhi 110017
India.

Indonesia

Tian Belawati, PhD is Head of the Center for Indonesian Studies at the Indonesian Open Learning University.

Jl Cabe Raya
Pamulang, Tangerang 15418
Indonesia
Email: tian@ka.ut.ac.id
Fax: (21)7490147

Japan

Dr Wong Suk-ying is Associate Professor in the Department of Sociology at the Chinese University of Hong Kong.

The Chinese University of Hong Kong
Sino Building
Shatin, New Territories,
Hong Kong
Email: sukyingwong@cuhk.edu.hk
Fax: (852) 2603 5213

Aya Yoshida is Associate Professor at the National Institute of Multimedia Education, Japan.

National Institute of Multimedia Education
2-12 Wakaba, Mihama-ku
Chiba 261-0014 JAPAN
Email: aya@nime.ac.jp
Fax: (81) 43 298 3484

Korea

Dr Jung In-sung is Director of the Multimedia Education Institute and Associate Professor of the Department of Educational Technology at the Ewha Women's University in Korea.

#11-1 Daehyun-Dong, Seodaemun-Ku
Seoul 120-750
S Korea
Email: isjung@ewha.ac.kr
Fax: 82 2 3277 3208

Malaysia

Dr Gan Siowck-lee is Director of Studies at KDU (Damansara Utama College), Malaysia.

Kolej Damansara Utama
SS 22/41, Damansara Jaya
Petaling Jaya 47400
Selangor
Malaysia
Email: gansl@kdu.edu.my or
siowck@slgan.jaring.my
Fax: 6 03 77277096

Mongolia

Prof. Bernadette Robinson, Special Professor of Comparative Education, School of Continuing Education, University of Nottingham, UK

17 Church Lane, Costock,
Loughborough, Leics. LE12 6UZ.
UK
Email: B.Robinson@open.ac.uk
Tel/Fax: (44) 1509 852268

New Zealand

Prof. Tom Prebble is Principal Extramural and International at Massey University, New Zealand.

Massey University
Private Bag 11 222
Palmerston North
New Zealand
Email: T.K.Prebble@massey.ac.nz
Fax: 64 6 350 5654

Pakistan

Dr Mussaret Anwar Sheikh is the Director of Institute of Mass Education at the Allama Iqbal Open University, Islamabad, Pakistan.

Block 10,
Allama Iqbal Open University
Sector H-8, Islamabad
Pakistan
Email:massedu@aiou.edu.pk
Fax:(92) 0519257019

South Pacific

Ruby Va'a is an Instructional Designer in the University Extension section of the University of the South Pacific.

University of the South Pacific
Suva
Fiji
Email: vaa_r@usp.ac.fj
Fax: (679) 300482

Josephine Osborne is an Instructional Designer in University Extension, University of the South Pacific.

University of the South Pacific
Suva
Fiji
Email: osborne_je@usp.ac.fj
Fax: (679) 300482

Dr Andrew C Nyondo is a lecturer at the University of Technology in Lae, Papua New Guinea.

University of Technology
PMB, Lae 411
Papua New Guinea
Email: anyondo@cms.unitech.ac.pg
Fax: (675) 4757667

Sri Lanka

Prof. N R Arthenayake is the Senior Professor of Mechanical Engineering at the Open University of Sri Lanka. He was the Vice Chancellor of the Open University of Sri Lanka for six years from 1994 to 2000. At present he functions as the Secretary to the Ministry of Science and Technology, Sri Lanka.

The Open University of Sri Lanka
Nawala
Nugegoda 10250,
Sri Lanka.

Taiwan

Dr Caroline Sherritt is Director of Associate Faculty at The United States Open University.

The United States Open University
9125 East Lowry Place, Building 905, Suite 212
Aurora, CO 80230 USA
Email: c.a.sherritt@open.edu
Fax: (720) 859 1577

Dr Wang Cheng-yen is Associate Professor of the Graduate Institute of Adult Education at the National Kaohsiung Normal University of Taiwan.

National Kaohsiung Normal University
116 Hopin First Road
Kaohsiung
Taiwan
Email: chengyen@nknucc.nknu.edu.tw
Fax:(886) 7-7229273

Thailand

Dr Chaiyong Brahmawong is Senior Professor and Vice-President for Academic Affairs of Sukhothai Thammathirat Open University, Thailand.

9/9 Muang Thong Thani Road
Park Kred, Nontaburi,
Thailand 11120
Email: chaiyong@iname.com
Fax: (662) 503 3554

USA

Dr Glenn Shive is Director of the Hong Kong America Center, Hong Kong.

The Chinese University of Hong Kong
8F Tin Ka Ping Building
Shatin, New Territories
Hong Kong SAR
Fax: (852) 2603 5797

Dr Peter J Dirr is President of the Public Service Telecommunications Corporation and Director of the Professional Development Institute of Cable in the Classroom.

4900 Seminary Rd, Suite 1120
Alexandria, VA 22101 (USA)
Email: pdirr@nova.org
Fax: (703) 845-1409

Vietnam

Prof. Bernadette Robinson (*see Mongolia*)

Dr Le Van Than is Director of the Centre for Distance Education Development, Hanoi Open University.

Hanoi Open University
Hanoi, Vietnam.
Email: de.hou@fpt.vn

Tran Duc Vuong is Vice-Director of the Centre for Distance Education Development, Hanoi Open University.

Hanoi Open University
Hanoi, Vietnam
Email: de.hou@fpt.vn

Index